Children & SEX

The Parents Speak

Children & SEX

The Parents Speak

THE STUDY GROUP OF NEW YORK

Emily Trafford Berges, *and others*
Shelley Neiderbach
Barbara Rubin
Elaine First Sharpe
Rita Weinberg Tesler

FACTS ON FILE   NEW YORK

Children & SEX : *The Parents Speak*

Copyright © 1983 by Emily Trafford Berges, Shelley Neiderbach, Barbara Rubin, Elaine First Sharpe, and Rita Weinberg Tesler

Published by Facts On File, Inc.
460 Park Avenue South
New York, N.Y. 10016

Library of Congress Catalog in Publication Data
Main entry under title:

Children and sex

Bibliography: p.
Includes index.
1. Sex instruction for children.   2. Sex customs.
3. Parenting.   I. The Study Group of New York
HQ53.S49   1983   649'.65   82-7475
ISBN 0-87196-603-4   AACR2

Printed in the United States of America
10 9 8 7 6 5 4 3 2 1

For all the parents,
and for the children in our lives
Jonathan and Nicole
Danny, Michael, and Margaux
Clara Ildiko and Julia Eve
Alison and Richard
Judith, Joshua, and Rachel

Acknowledgments

With many thanks to: Robert Amussen, Julian Bach, Amy J. Browne, Rita Glassman, Susan Iwanowski, Harvey Jacobs, Corinne Kyle, Linda Lyons, Stephanie Marcus, Marcia Newfield, Kerry Regan, Winkie Regan, Donald Sharpe, Henrietta Susser, Aaron S. Tesler, John Thornton, Jack Victor.

Explanation of Codes

M = Mother
F = Father
g = girl
b = boy

Numbers indicate ages of children.

Sample listing: Mg11 = Mother of eleven-year-old girl

Introduction

This book, like so many books, began with conversations among friends. As confidants and colleagues at the same college, we often sat together and talked about our work and our pasts. We would remember our childhoods and frequently we would discuss our children. The year was 1979, The International Year of the Child. It was also the end of a decade that had produced a number of important books concerning adult male and female sexuality. We read them and discussed them and considered what they had to say.

In the midst of our conversations it occurred to us that no major study had ever examined children's sexuality from the exclusive perspective of those whose influence on it is the earliest and the most profound—the parents. What were the problems confronted by the people who were actually watching and dealing with the emerging sexuality of children on a day-to-day basis? What were the anxieties they faced, the insights they gleaned from the process? The more we talked and thought, the more we realized the need for such a work. There were five of us—all writers and researchers with extensive experience in studying social issues. We decided to conduct the study ourselves.

From the outset we wanted our work to be an open inquiry into the ways parents react in their daily lives towards their children's sexual growth. But more than this, our vision was to create a sourcebook in which parents could speak directly to parents. Most of the books of the last decade had been written from the perspective of the specialist. Parents' views appeared in these books only sporadically, given to confirm or to illustrate the point or prescription the expert was offering. The parents' statements were anything but outstanding, wedged as they were between the pronouncements of the author.

Our focus would be different. We were seeking the insights of those who were engaged in the adult–child dialectic every day of their lives, who had the awareness that comes from living up close. Stretching beyond our own lives and geography, we sought to interview parents in other cities and states to hear what they had to say. And, as much as possible, we wanted the study to be expressed in their own words. We would see whether there was a voice, a common wisdom; then share what we found.

There were related social issues to be explored as well. We were interested in discovering what attitudes toward sexuality and children had emerged, what had remained from the past, and what had been let go. In our lifetime we had witnessed a sexual awakening in American society. How had it affected young people as they became parents? What did it hold for the newest generation? Perhaps there were new trends that could be pinpointed, perhaps there were none. We would listen and find out.

We met weekly over a period of many months and vigorously sorted out our respective visions of the book. We agreed from the start that our study was to be descriptive rather than prescriptive; we saw ourselves as journalist-researchers exploring the range and variety of parents' behavior regarding their children's sexuality. Our intention was to report the findings, not to judge them. Any suggestions offered or positions taken in this book are those of the subjects, and we have been scrupulous in presenting a balance of opinions and recommendations from all perspectives.

The so-called "neutral" approach on our part is not to suggest an absence of any philosophical stance regarding our topic; those of us who are parents, and even those of us who are not, have our particular views on childrearing practices. But we have tried to direct them away from our research, to keep them where they belong—in our own homes and families. Our goal then has been to "get the stories," the parents' renderings, and to pass them on exactly as we heard them. In short, we felt it important to get a multitude of perspectives—intellectual, emotional, and spiritual—on a variety of issues and to present them without bias, without an imposed schema, and without censorship.

If this was our intention, then our questionnaire had to be of a certain kind. We aimed for a comprehensive, practical treatment of the matters that arise in daily living, from the most obvious to the most subtle. Naturally we would ask parents how they would respond to the universal question, "Where do babies come from?" But we also aimed to get at the secmingly infinite, sometimes matter-of-fact, sometimes whispered, nitty-gritty concerns of family life—walking around nude, showing affection and sexual interest, using the bathroom, storing sanitary napkins and contraceptive devices, using dirty words, and so on. We knew, too, that the questionnaire had to be flexible enough to allow parents not only to answer our very specific questions but to move in related directions of their own, to those corners of recollection and pockets of concern that open spontaneously if the interview environment is one of trust. Within these personal zones we hoped to find additional rich material, intimate and idiosyncratic, and we wanted to be sure to leave the interview door open to it.

Therefore, we first identified a group of core topics: reproduction, body awareness, pleasure, sexual language, sources of sex education inside and outside the family, media influences, and the issue of parental sexual privacy as it conflicts with children's ongoing needs for attention and care. Each of these broader topics inspired many more specific questions, and the responses to these became the essence of the ten chapters in this book. We offer here a few representative questions taken from these chapters.

What is the first question your child asked you about sex?

Do you walk around nude in front of your child?

What areas of your body do you not allow your child to touch?

Has your child ever discovered you making love with your spouse?

What do you do when you see your child masturbating?

What do you think your child knows about orgasm?

What sexual language is permitted in your household?

What do you do when your child is watching a TV show or commercial which has erotic content?

We decided to limit our study to children ranging in age from three through eleven. In selecting three as our youngest age we were in no way implying that this is the chronological starting point of children's sexuality. Anyone who has spent time with infants knows that sexuality begins at birth. Rather, we began with age three because this is the time when children have enough command of language to ask rudimentary questions and to understand elementary answers. In short, some semblance of discussion can be held with three-year-olds. However, sometimes parents reminisced about how children behaved when they were under three; in these cases we have not interrupted their recollections, and this accounts for the few references to one- and

two-year-olds. We chose to end at age eleven because twelve generally marks the onset of puberty, the beginning of a new era in sexual
expression. That is a book in itself.

To locate our subjects we approached professional contacts in cities across the country to recommend parents who would be willing to
be interviewed and taped. We sought parents of diverse philosophical
positions who could grapple with our questions and articulate their responses in a coherent and thoughtful way. We asked the assistance of
schools, community centers, businesses, religious organizations, and researchers in aligned fields. Our sample of 225 lived all over the country.
The largest group came from the suburbs, followed in number by those
from major cities. The smallest number was from rural America.

The parents in our study are primarily middle class. They repre-
sent a variety of professions and work roles: housewife, doctor, lab
technician, college professor, police officer, lawyer, secretary, real es-
tate agent, accountant, playwright, track coach, bookkeeper, dress
designer. They are married, divorced, separated, widowed, and never
married, and are drawn from various denominations of the Protestant,
Catholic and Jewish religions. Their ages range from twenty-one to
fifty-three; half are men and half are women. Of the children discussed,
approximately half are girls and half are boys.

The coding that appears in the margins of the text identifies the
sex of the parent speaking and the sex and age of the child referred to.
For example, the code *Fb10* tells the reader that a father of a boy who
is ten years old is being quoted; the code *Mg7* indicates that the material used comes from a mother of a girl aged seven. Occasionally two
or more children are mentioned in an anecdote. Although each parent
has been interviewed about one of his/her children only, we found that
some parents spontaneously talked about their other children as well;
references to more than one child are noted in the coding.

We assured the parents of their anonymity in order to encourage
as candid a response as possible. Therefore, all subjects and their children have been given fictitious names. All material has been kept in-
tact except for any personal information that might reveal the identity
of the subject.

Tape recorders in hand, each of us set out separately to interview
our subjects. An interview might take place almost anywhere—an
office, a restaurant, at poolside, in an airport. However, most of the
interviews took place in the parents' homes, where we were surrounded
by the ambience and personal objects of their daily lives. Sometimes
we met their mates or partners, and, much to our delight, the children
they were talking about. But the greatest part of our time was spent
privately with each other, parent and interviewer, each serious and committed to the exchange and particularly to the child behind it. We cannot overstate the importance of the interview, mirroring as it did in so

many ways the responses of the wider society to so universal and human a topic.

From the interviews emerged insights not only for us but for the parents as well: discoveries about themselves, their mates, or their children that they had been unaware of before. One mother realized that she had explained the mechanics of sexual intercourse to her eight-year-old son but had never linked it for him with the feelings or desires behind lovemaking. In another interview, a father confronted for the first time the connection between his own sexually repressed childhood and his unwillingness to talk at all about sex with his nine-year-old daughter. Over and over again, epiphanies were sparked by the material, by the recollections of parents, and by the actual occasion of such an exchange. Many subjects returned to their families with resolve to address some issues they hadn't before, or to reconsider a stance, or to rethink an idea.

Though participants differed in the way they interpreted their family needs and in the way they responded to various issues, in one respect they spoke with one voice: Parents *care* about the sexual development of their offspring and face a number of similar concerns in dealing with the process. No matter what their backgrounds, no matter what their philosophical bent, no matter what solutions or actions they chose in confronting the various situations that arose, they all wanted to "do right" by their children. Indeed, the vast majority were conscientious in their efforts to help foster healthy sexual attitudes and to create a positive home experience. Those with negative memories of their own upbringing were consciously attempting to make their children's growing-up years better than their own.

Yet despite the good intention to act on what they considered to be their adult, enlightened attitude toward sexuality and their children's sexual development, many parents discovered that it was no easy task to exorcise the ghosts of the past, those deeply ingrained lingering reflexes acquired during their own childhood. These parents thus found their own backgrounds to be a source of internal conflict and a deterrent to their functioning easily and without anxiety. Intending to behave in one way, they often would find themselves behaving more like their parents instead. Sexual attitudes of past generations would have a way of rising up from some subconscious level to contradict or in some cases even to sabotage the more open attitudes of the present.

It was also interesting for us to discover that parents who labeled themselves as conservative or liberal did not unfailingly keep to their own self-stereotype on all sexual matters. We often found that some of those who thought of themselves as liberal approached certain issues with a great deal of reserve, while the self-styled conservative approached the very same subjects with a great deal of ease. Moreover, there were those who began parenthood with one set of attitudes only to discover those attitudes shifting as the child grew older. Then, too, many open and expressive parents had children who preferred more privacy and formality, and vice versa. Stereotypical responses dissolved.

Though we were meticulous in interviewing as many fathers as mothers, there are more quotes in our study from mothers. We found that fathers often tended to be shadowy figures in the sex education of their children. Many fathers regretted this fact, explaining that they were not around the house often enough to deal with the process. The result was that mothers frequently were left to confront their quandaries alone.

In reporting our findings we offer not only the specific factual information but the contradictions and complexities in the parent–child encounter. The issues are presented in the raw, as it were. Many points of view are given. Each has something important to say about how parents are struggling to educate their children sexually.

1

The

Parents

Speak

There was a time when families did not talk about sex. Most of the parents interviewed for this study, people who grew up in the Fifties and Sixties, reported that they had received minimal sexual information at home, sometimes none at all. Often, because the subject was too uncomfortable or taboo-laden, their own parents had found it easier to assume, Freud notwithstanding, that children were not sexual beings. And children had gotten the message and obligingly avoided asking questions.

But the present generation of parents has entered a new world. In addition to all the information about sexual choices, birth control, pregnancy, and abortion which is accessible to children as well as adults, the attitude toward discussion of these topics has altered. Parents are now encouraged to talk to their children about sex, advised that even when they do not say anything they are constantly sending out subtle sexual signals in the ways they behave, in their attitudes toward nudity, in the rules they set for their children with regard to entering the bathroom or bedroom while they are there. They assume that their chil-

dren are absorbing information about sex and sexuality as they absorb
any other concept from their environment and are likely to raise frank
questions that require careful answers.

Some parents expressed discomfort with this kind of openness;
others enthusiastically welcomed the opportunity to be "candid" with
their children. But nearly everyone admitted that talking about sex
was not easy, had hidden pitfalls, evoked unexpected emotional reactions in both children and parents. There was sometimes little correla-
tion between the attitudes people believed they should have about
sex and the way they actually acted or felt in relation to sexual situations.
No stereotypes applied. Many parents who said they were liberal in
their attitudes toward sharing sexual information with their children
were startled by their "uptight" responses to certain subjects. They
told their children everything about the physiological aspects of intercourse and reproduction but avoided any mention of pleasure, or they
talked readily about sex in marriage but were unsettled by questions
about unmarried couples or homosexuality. At the same time, there
were parents who labeled themselves conservative who turned out to
be surprisingly easygoing about the same issues. Clearly parents brought
much more than just the straightforward facts to any discussion of sex.

Most parents said, for instance, that no matter how dedicated they
were to being honest, the reticence and secrecy they had learned from
their parents would often suddenly emerge to check their responses.
For some parents the bugaboo was language. Simple anatomical terms
which they had not known until they were in their teens were every-
Mg5   day vocabulary for their own children. "Sometimes I still say 'wash the
front,' " one mother confessed, and she corrects me, 'the *vagina!* ' "
Other parents, determined not to repeat the old stork or cabbage-leaf
stories, were disconcerted when they were called upon to give some
explanation of male/female intimacy. A mother described such an interchange with her five-year-old daughter. The child introduced the topic
by repeating what she had already learned about conception but startled
her mother with a follow-up question.

Mg5   I know the seed and the egg meet after loving, but I've been
       thinking, how could the seed get into the woman? Now I gave this a
       lot of thought." And she counted off, "There are just so many open-
       ings in the body. The eyes and the nose and the mouth and the
       ears, and the belly button—I'm not too sure how deep it goes—and
       then there's the . . ."—and then she hesitated and she just sort of
       skipped a beat, and I knew exactly what she was skipping. She was
       skipping the vagina area—". . . and then there's the tush. And that's
       about it. So how does it happen? How does it get in?" I didn't give
       her the right answer. I should have given it right away. I just for-
       got everything I knew was correct. When they ask you a technical

question, they're ready for the answer. Instead, I asked her, "How do you think the seed gets in?" And she said, "Through the mouth, through kissing. That's why kissing is so important. But I'm not too sure." So that's what she gave me two weeks to think about. She said, "I'll give you two weeks, because I know you know how. You did it once.

Though parents hoped they could be more casual with their children than their own parents had been with them, they were not sure it was altogether possible. "I'm anxious because I don't want to be anxious," a mother said.

Mb4

Generally parents felt that current attitudes toward sex were healthier than the ones they had grown up with. They thought that the relaxation of pressures around marriage and wedding-night performance was all to the good. But they were not always sure that by having their children aware of a variety of sexual choices—living together, single parenthood, open marriages—they were ensuring their happiness. And delighted as they were to see the old watchwords—"Nice girls don't go all the way," "Men only want one thing"—disappear, they felt something had been lost in the modern pursuit of self-satisfaction without commitment and physical gratification without love. They did accept the fact that this generation would have its first sexual experiences far earlier than they themselves had, certainly before marriage, but they worried that their children might have little concept of personal responsibility around those experiences, that they would be casual or callous about intimate relationships.

Finally, parents felt awkward with the fact that no matter how dispassionately they talked about sex, their children were bound to associate what they said with what they did in the bedroom. Most parents felt it was harmful for children to have too many details.

I think it's hard to picture their own parents—I'm sure you remember how you felt. I assumed my parents had done it three times: three children, three times. I think that's a traumatic thing for a kid and I'm not sure how to handle it.

Mg11

They were also concerned about being on stage, about having no intimate preserve in their own households. Some children in fact had asked for specifics about their lovemaking or wanted to observe them in bed. To these parents their children's curiosity seemed more like voyeurism.

Most parents had set extremely high standards for themselves in terms of frankness and comprehensiveness, but no one had formulated a policy that worked in all situations. *Their* parents hadn't told them enough; but now . . . had they gone too far? Were they telling too much, more than the children really needed or wanted to know? Did the children know everything already, simply from existing in the modern world, talking to friends, watching TV, reading the headlines? Where were the boundaries between their children's right to information and their own right to privacy? Some children did reward their parents with luminous examples of sexual health and self-confidence. Other children, though scrupulously well informed, appeared just as ill at ease about sexual topics as the offspring of previous generations. You couldn't win.

Nevertheless, for many parents the struggle was clearly a joyous, even a therapeutic one—a method of overcoming what had been painful or ambiguous in their relationships with their own parents, a special way of being close to their children. Some admitted that they might not fully come to terms with their complex reactions to sexual issues. But they discovered that addressing their troublesome feelings or adopting an "I'm-doing-the-best-I-can-but-I'm-not-perfect" attitude was an important step in talking honestly with their children about sex.

The six parents who are described in the following pages share the concerns, doubts, anxieties, and successes that were discussed in one way or another by all the parents whose voices are heard in this book.

Paula

Paula's interview was marked by bursts of robust, sometimes self-deprecating humor, tempered by thoughtful concern and a startling honesty. She is a working mother, an employment counselor, who shares much of the upbringing of her two children with her husband. But she took pride in the special relationship between her and her daughter, Jenny, eleven, when it came to discussing sex—an identification of woman with woman. Like other people of her generation—she is in her late thirties—Paula felt her sexual upbringing had been inadequate and wanted to provide her child with more information than her parents had provided her with. She believed that the open exchange she had with her own daughter had brought them closer together. Except on two subjects—"She cannot watch and she doesn't have to know how many times I do it"—Jenny could ask any question she wanted.

Mg11b8

Paula tried to reconstruct the various stages in this relationship. The earliest conversation took place when Jenny was three-and-a-half and Paula was pregnant with her son. "I wanted to open up communication with her. I knew people talked about 'pregnant' and I told her I was going to have a baby. We talked a bit about how you get a baby. I tried to explain the whole thing, or as much as I felt she was ready to accept. We didn't talk about storks." Later, more details—about birth control, labor, natural childbirth—were added. Generally Paula waited for the questions that revealed what Jenny wanted to know. She even made a brave attempt to describe intercourse right after that initial discussion, when Jenny repeatedly asked how the penis got in and what happened afterwards. "I told her the Daddy puts his penis into the mother when they make love and that the sperm is—it's hard to explain what the sperm is—and the sperm goes up and it—it *was* difficult to explain at three-and-a-half!" Paula did feel that sometimes she was a little overzealous in trying to explain too much too soon. "I think we rush this information in an attempt to be 'open' and they just aren't ready for it. There were discussions of homosexuality, abortion, giving the baby away. She didn't care about that. She wants to know whether she should play spin the bottle."

Paula talked candidly about the resistance—outer and inner—she had encountered in talking so honestly about sex with her child. From the beginning she felt it was important to use correct terminology, but when Jenny proudly showed off her new vocabulary to her grandparents and some neighbors, they were shocked. Even Paula herself was brought up short in one instance. "I fumbled for fifteen minutes once, trying to find the right words—'Oh my God, she's talking about the clitoris!' I didn't know about the clitoris until way later. It's scary sometimes. She knows more than I'm sure I did in my twenties. I know that part of what I am is my mother's voice. It's what I keep hearing."

Taking a stance in relation to current ideas about sexual freedom also required adjustment on Paula's part. When her daughter was young, she explained sex exclusively in the context of marriage. But now that Jenny is eleven Paula admits that this view of sexuality can only be a "fairy tale" to a child growing up today. She wanted to prepare her daughter for the subtle and complicated choices that exist within the rigidly defined boundaries of currently acceptable behavior. "I know Jenny will have intercourse way earlier than I did and that's scary," she said. "It was easier to believe that good girls didn't. I know that she's a good girl, and I know she will have intercourse. . . . I'm trying to make sure she realizes there's a responsibility, that sex shouldn't be indiscriminate. At the same time, I realize that times have changed. She has told me that she will not wait as long as I did because she has asked how old I was."

When asked at what age she expected Jennifer would have her first sexual experience, Paula replied, "I would like to say eighteen or seventeen. I'm afraid it may be sixteen. And I'm hoping it won't be younger, *fervently* hoping it won't be younger."

For Paula, as for many other mothers, the area in which choice could realistically be discussed had shifted from "Wait until you're married—or at least engaged," to (with a sigh) "When you do it, be sensible and use some protection." Sex in the teens might be inevitable, but "getting into trouble" was inexcusable. Paula was unequivocal about this. "We talk about it. We talk about the precautions one can take. She sees my diaphragm, she knows what it's used for. I think it's a big mistake to have a baby unless you're married. Being a mother is a difficult job. I don't see having it as a seventeen-year-old child!"

George

George is a man in his middle thirties. After working at a variety of jobs in construction, he recently returned to school and completed a degree in engineering. Though he grew up in a Southern California town, he now considers himself a New Englander, since he has lived in Boston for many years. Both George and his wife were raised in rigidly traditional households—he Catholic, she Jewish—but they no longer accept their parents' dictum that nice people should not talk about sex.

Fg7   George felt his parents' attitudes were typical of a negative tendency in this country to equate sexual freedom with crime, whereas often just the opposite was true. "I think sexual crimes and things of that nature—I'm just giving an opinion—are symptoms of a repressed sexuality, if you will, that explodes in other directions." He added with a slight grin, "I shouldn't even be saying this, but I recall a picture of President Nixon walking along the beach in a *suit and tie.* That tells you something about the hang-ups. I think a healthier acceptance of one's body makes for a healthier environment. It's a natural thing."

For this reason and because his own sexual education had been unsatisfactory, George was determined to be more open with his child. He had seen rewards, too, in his daughter's responsiveness and easygoing acceptance of sexuality in the world around her. For George, educating his child had become a personal victory over what was inhibiting in the culture and in his own past.

"I like the idea of mankind trying to learn more about himself, herself," he said. "I think no sexual topic should be taboo as far as my daughter is concerned. And that every sexual topic should be discussed in the proper perspective. Just to say such-and-such is grotesque or bad in a pure vacuum is not the way. My wife and I agreed that if we were asked a question we should answer it honestly and not try to hide and say, you know, 'Wait till you grow up.' I think that's a mistake. I think if we try to say, 'Well, the stork brought you, or the bogey man,'—I just don't like that. I didn't like it when my parents did it to me. We trust our daughter. We think she's a very bright child and she can handle these concepts. She's not embarrassed by the subject. I've never really seen her embarrassed. She's curious, like anyone else."

George also seemed undisturbed about the things his daughter is learning "from the street", and from her friends. It did not unsettle him that his daughter at seven was far more sophisticated than he had been at her age. There was even a touch of admiration in his voice when he spoke of the kind of issue that gave so many parents sleepless nights. "Kids growing up in the city—they're so much more aware. They're surrounded by all kinds of things. And that's a very raunchy bunch she runs around with, a very fast crowd of seven-year-olds," he adds with a laugh. "I think at this stage my daughter knows everything anyway. She could probably tell *me* a few things."

Marilyn

Marilyn grew up in an American city, but she and her husband spent several years in France. Her eldest son was born in Rouen. Currently, they live an an apartment in a New Jersey suburb, where Marilyn has set aside a bedroom for herself as a studio in which to make ceramics. Since her husband, who works for an airline, is away from home very often, Marilyn is the major source of sexual information for her two sons, André, ten, and Guy, eight.

Marilyn's outlook was, by her own description "essentially old-fashioned." When the boys were very young, she had been reticent about talking to them directly about sex, though she had never stopped them from listening in to grown-up conversations. She spoke of how André had, in effect, "entered the bedroom" by overhearing discussions between her and her husband or other adults about conception, pregnancy, childbirth. "He's been around when there were conversations about when I went to the hospital, what happened and how it snowed . . . I remember explaining to somebody that the midwife climbed up on the table and put her knee on my stomach and pushed him out, and he thought that was funny, a football game. And he may have been around when I've discussed experiences with other friends, and maybe my sister-in-law." Marilyn suspected, too, that both boys picked up all kinds of details from their friends. "I think they found condoms when we were walking to the beach and a friend who knew more than they did said, 'Oh, look at these,' so they must know something, but we haven't discussed it in our house."

When André entered school, at age six, Marilyn felt it was time to give him, and Guy as well, more organized and comprehensive information about sex. But she was never quite comfortable in the role of mentor. Like a number of other parents, she feared that by teaching the children how babies are made, she was giving up something of the privacy she cherished. "Discussing it in a biological way was okay. It was just an explanation, as if I were teaching biology or something. But then I thought that maybe there was a better way to explain it than I was doing and I bought them a book. And I remember reading it to the two of them. And they were giggling all the while and made me feel embarrassed when they discussed intercourse in the book. They were laughing, so I laughed, too. I felt embarrassed. I felt that shyness about exposing myself. It was the sort of association I was having with things that went on in the bedroom. You know, that they were finally into what was happening, that they were sort of innocent but now they were going to put all the twos and twos together."

Despite her shyness, however, Marilyn was conscientious about how she explained sex to her sons. She tried to be aware of the various sources of sex education in their environment—peers, magazines, TV—and use things that came up as springsboards for focused discussions. She was also adamant about conveying not only information but a sense of values. She clearly eschewed the easy sexual attitudes and liberties of the present. "We live in a society that has sex without love. For my way of thinking, the physical gratification without the emotional is not satisfying at all," she said firmly. *Knowing* about sex was not enough. "I think they know enough. They may have to get a lot more information about being responsible for their actions sexually. I think our whole culture fosters only the aspect of performance and not the emotional benefits one can receive in a relationship. I don't think you have to look at just the physical aspect of sex."

Henry

Henry is divorced from his wife but has remained actively involved in teaching his child, a girl of six, about sex. Part of his positive feeling about his role seemed to come from his interest in communication in general—he teaches social studies in an urban junior high school—and from his experiences in the Seventies at a college where speaking one's mind was encouraged. Paradoxically, however, like so many other parents interviewed, he traced his determination to talk freely to his daughter back to a more negative source, his growing up in a family and a community where children were told almost nothing about sex. "I remember so many crazy conceptions kids had because their parents weren't talking to them," he said angrily. "I'd rather she know. I don't want her thinking you get pregnant from toilet seats. Stupidity is dangerous. Ignorance is absolutely dangerous. I don't want her to have to unlearn bullshit."

His method with his own child, Nora, was to wait for her to ask for information—"She's in enough contact with sexuality in the environment that she brings up questions on her own"—then to reply as fully as possible. But he would be guided by her responses, ending the discussion or returning to the same points, according to what she signaled she was ready to hear. "When she's grasped as much of the conceptual details as she can handle, she'll even change the subject on you in the middle of a sentence." Did she usually understand what she was told? Henry was not sure. "What tends to happen is that she says 'Oh, okay,' and walks away. She processes it for a little while. She may come back with another question three weeks later."

Pamela had only recently begun to ask for very specific details about how babies are made. When she was younger, starting at age two, she was mainly interested in the anatomical differences between girls and boys. Henry recalled that it was seeing others—children in her playgroup, her parents—nude or partially nude that sparked the first questions. "One of the ways we toilet trained her was letting her see very succinctly what was happening when we went to the bathroom. I'm sure she asked about the difference between penis and vagina somewhere in there." Henry believed that the more completely and positively he conveyed facts about sex and sexuality, the more likely it was that Pamela would not end up with the distortions and fears he had seen in his own generation. Therefore, when she wanted to know what the penis and vagina were used for, he felt that, in addition to talking about urination and the function of the vagina in childbirth, he should acknowledge her unspoken, perhaps incompletely understood curiosity about how men and women come together. "I told her very early on that one of the things the penis and vagina are for is for making babies and that's done by putting *this* in *there* and doing *that*." He also was not as disconcerted as many parents are when their daughter wants to know why she cannot grow a penis. When Pamela asked the question, Henry took the opportunity to give her good feelings about her own body. "I explained to her that men get penises as developing babies in their mommies. Unfortunately men never get vaginas and women can never get a penis and that's terrific—you have to get your own. (So much for vagina envy.)"

At this point, Pamela is interested in what sex feels like. Because of its self-revelatory aspects, this was an especially difficult subject for most parents to discuss with their children. But Henry wanted his child to know that sex is associated with pleasure and had found a way to explain the act in terms comprehensible and unembarrassing to a six-year-old. "I told her when people choose to have babies there's affection between them. There's arousal. They take pleasure in each other. There's physical contact and it feels good. When people are loving each other very much the woman's vagina gets wet and warm and the man's penis gets bigger and the man will put his penis in the woman's vagina and they'll rub it around and have a great old time doing all that. Then I finished by telling her that babies come from the combination of the man's semen and the woman's egg and the baby grows, and so forth."

Though Henry knows that he is probably regarded as a "liberated" person, he wanted to make clear that he is not libertine. His own parents had communicated the idea that sex was not so much *dirty* as *private*. "You didn't talk about it. There was a certain amount of embarrassment at being caught showing affection." For this reason, he wanted his daughter to know that there is a tie between love and sex. Affectionate relationships are the crucial things, sexual relationships merely extensions along the continuum. "I don't want my child to be repressed—physically, sexually. I don't want her to be promiscuous, either," he said. "I want her to know sex is pleasurable and it's fun, but because of babies it's something that has to be handled responsibly. If the child's being responsible around her relationships, then she's going to be responsible around her sexuality. That's how I hold it." He added, still more seriously, "If you don't love yourself, you can't have a relationship. If you're very attracted to somebody and you really care about them, then you really take pleasure with them. This is one of the things that happens."

Peggy

Peggy lives on a street of modest brick houses in a working-class section of a midwestern industrial city. Her husband is a teamster and Peggy has recently taken a job as a bookkeeper, now that her three children are busy with school and afterschool activities.

She was aware that her inclination toward sexual conservatism runs deep—her family is devoutly Catholic and she was sent to parochial schools for all of her education. However, she reported that the attitudes she grew up with were being challenged every day as she went out into the business world and as her work brought her increasing confidence in her opinions. "I finally realized, well, I wouldn't want anything on my back if [the girls] should get pregnant, and it was best that I told them everything I knew." But following her own good sense instead of listening to the voices of her childhood involved an ongoing struggle. "I wanted to tell them and I didn't want to tell them. It was a battle I had to fight with myself."

Peggy was on her own in this process. For though she has a warm and loving relationship with her husband, she saw him as a hindrance—

she feels he is far more narrowminded and uncompromising that she—when it came to discussing sex with their children. "Once in a while he'll come out with something that stuns me, that I think is old-fashioned. It's not that I confront him about it. I just want to make sure—well, they can listen to their father, but I want to give them an alternate view."

Within their family, Peggy's children first learned something about sex from simple observation. "At the time they were growing up I had like five aunts and cousins and each one of us was pregnant at one time or another, and I think they always saw that, so I never really had to face any questions about it." When her eldest, Skipper, was five, however, she decided to provide him with more specific information. "I told him the woman makes eggs and the man makes sperm. And when the sperm and the egg meet they unite and form an embryo—I used that word—like a little seed. And it travels around inside the mother and connects itself to the uterus and grows for nine months and gets all sorts of apparatus and workings. I went into *that* detail but I didn't talk about penetration or the penis and the vagina or the love part and how it happens."

With the girls, Elizabeth, now thirteen, and Angela, now eleven, Peggy—clearly thinking back to her own past—wanted to be sure that they understood the changes that would occur in their bodies. She remembered how she had introduced the subject to Angela when she was nine. "I figured she was going to start menstruation soon, and I really didn't want her to be afraid. I realized she might not be ready for all this information. I remember telling her that whenever she wanted to stop listening, she could just get up and leave, and if she ever did have any questions, you know, to come back to me and I would try to get some answers for her."

Recently, particularly with the two older children, Peggy has had to deal with more than just the biological facts. Her children have wanted to know about such things as intimacy, arousal, intercourse. Though frank discussion of sexual issues was still difficult for her, she remained determined to provide unbiased information. This openness between her and the children was a gratifying step away from her own inhibitions. "The way you're brought up, it was the fear that if you told them too much, they would use it. I've gotten over that. I would like my children to know they have the right to their pleasure, each and every time, and that there are different kinds of pleasure, and I want them to have the fullest . . . though with Angela, I haven't hit on those yet."

Peggy also hoped to ease the inevitable pressure on everyone by exposing her children to as many points of view as she could, without demanding that they accept or reject anything she told them. "As soon as I hear about it I go home and I share it. But I do tell them, 'Look, if you can't handle it, that's fine.' I don't want them to get the wrong impression, either from church or from their friends or my husband or my mother. Like I said before, I want to make sure that they form their own opinions. I do want them to have the truth, but I don't want it only to be the truth as I see it."

Daniel

Daniel is the father of a five-year-old boy and a two-year-old girl. Born and raised in Michigan, he is presently a business executive at a large corporation in a city in Virginia. The family resides in the suburbs, where his children are growing up in an environment not unlike the one that Dan himself experienced as a boy.

He gave a rather poignant description of his own unsatisfactory sexual education and voiced regret that he had not as yet been able to come to grips with educating his son. He noted the uncanny way patterns of poor communication between father and son could repeat themselves generation after generation. "You're asking me questions I haven't thought about. It's significant that I haven't thought about them. I had no sex education to speak of. I think at one point my father gave me a book and said, 'Read it. If you have any questions, ask me.' I probably had questions, but I certainly wouldn't have asked them. The relationship wasn't that type. He wasn't around a lot. I wasn't close to my father and I would have liked to have been, but it didn't happen. I suspect there are a lot of questions my son has that he never addressed to me, but that doesn't mean he doesn't have them. There are issues I have never thought about. It's probably time to start."

Daniel was most comfortable leaving his children's sex education to his wife. When his son did come to him, he tried to treat his questions about sex like any other request for factual information. "I think we have told him that babies grow in mommies' stomachs. He's seen pregnant women, obviously, and he's had friends whose mothers had babies. He's likely to have learned something from his friends when the babies were born. We must have said that babies grow in the stomach and get bigger in the stomach. I didn't make a big deal of it." So far, Daniel's son has been content not to ask for more information.

"When his sister was born he would see her being changed and would talk about it. 'She has a vagina and I have a penis.' It was a fact. He just accepted it and that was the end of it." But Daniel was concerned about what he would do as his son grew more curious, wanted more detail. "I'm not being defensive—it's just never been an

Fb5g2

issue. When he gets ready for these questions I hope I have the answers for him."

Many parents, from different areas of the country and diverse backgrounds, told similar stories about their own experiences in teaching children about sex. Though the subject was often difficult for them and forced them to confront their prejudices and hang-ups, a surprising number, like George, had worked their way through to a comfortable, even affirmative, attitude toward sex, which they were able to pass on to their children. In most cases, they had no well-formulated idea of how and when they would begin. They made mistakes—introduced the discussion too early or long after their children had become quite knowledgeable about sex on their own, provided information which was skimpy or overly elaborate. Like Paula, Marilyn and Peggy, many suggested that while at first everything had been trial and error, the process had become considerably easier once they had lived through it with one child.

Sometimes the problem was the gap between what parents were ready to talk about and what children actually wanted to know. There were parents who felt they were a step behind their children, who could not yet fully accept that their children were secretly likely to have more curiosity and, perhaps, more information about sex than the parents wanted to admit. A mother of an eleven-year-old summed it up in this way: "You sort of roll along, day by day, year by year, and I really hadn't stopped to say 'What about his sexuality?' " Like Daniel, these parents felt they had to give more thought to the topics which could come up. Given the speeded-up timetable according to which children today gather information about sex, they wondered if they were as well prepared as they should be for the enormous variety of questions they might be asked.

2

Where

Do

Babies

Come

From?

Before they began to talk about sex to their children, parents had to make a number of difficult decisions. They had to decide, for instance, who would initiate discussion—they themselves or their children. If parents brought up the subject they ran the risk of rushing in with information the children might not be ready to hear. But waiting for questions had its drawbacks too, since children could not always put into words exactly what it was they needed to know.

Parents also had to decide who was going to take responsibility for giving out sexual information—the mother, the father, or both parents equally. Often one parent opted out of the process and the task then fell, by default, to the other. But the decision about who spoke to which child about what might depend on other factors: the temperament and inclination of the parent, the age and/or sex of the child, the nature of the topic, the context in which it was brought up.

A third question involved setting limits on sexual discussions—deciding how much to tell, when to speak openly, when to temporize or conceal. No one told children "everything," particularly at first. But this meant most parents had to know exactly how much information their children were capable of receiving at any given moment. Parents wanted to be able to recognize the right psychological moment, the precisely appropriate time, to introduce (or withhold) concepts such as intimacy and passion, pleasure and pain, if children were not to be "put off" or aroused in unhealthy ways.

Communicating honestly with children about sex turned out to be a very complex process, one which could not easily be explained, planned, or codified; one which developed subtly, often surprisingly, providing new insights at every step along the way.

Initiating Discussion

For many parents, the easiest way to talk about sex would have been the old way: sit down formally, explain everything all at once, *get it over with*. But almost everyone agreed it was far better to allow the child to initiate discussion when he needed information. As Marilyn put it, "You can't say 'This is my calendar for sex education and it's May, so I have to talk about abortion.' " But this "Wait until he is ready" philosophy required a careful balancing act on the parents' part. The atmosphere in the home had to be supportive, accepting, and attentive. The child needed to feel he would receive a constructive response if he brought up a delicate or embarrassing topic. Also, letting the child initiate did not mean waiting for the obvious, clearly stated, book-perfect question. The child might be too shy to ask directly or might not know enough to realize he should ask (a kind of "Catch-22"). Parents had to read the signals in his behavior which indicated he wanted to know something and seize those opportunities to work facts into the conversation. Parents worried about this method backfiring. There were those difficult gray areas where they could not tell just what the child was asking for, or whether it was best to plunge in with information and risk being intrusive, or to hold back and wait for a more propitious moment.

Polly takes pride in being something of an "oddity" in the small Vermont town where she lives; she considers herself more liberal than her neighbors, more open in discussing sex with her boys, seven and five. However, she was aware that though she had let them know there was nothing they could not ask, she did not always understand whether simple questions demanded simple or complex answers. "Where do babies come from?" might mean "Where do babies grow?" or "How are they made?" or "How are they delivered?" And even if the child expected only a five-word answer ("Babies grow inside the Mommy"), it might be best to elaborate further. Polly was not sure. "I might have really missed an opportunity there. So, do you, you know, just tell them? I'm not really certain of that." She faced the same quandary when she overheard her sons discussing what made little girls different from little boys. "I don't know if I should then come bouncing in and talking about it or how I should handle it."

Some parents found that the policy of waiting for children to ask did not work at all times, particularly when the child was reticent and unlikely to ask questions. As children grew older and needed to know about subjects like menstruation, erection, and wet dreams, parents sometimes felt obliged to step in to make sure they understood what was going to happen to their bodies. They also had to decide how to act in relation to information that children might be getting from the environment. A small number of parents believed that children would learn all they had to know from more worldy peers, adult books and magazines at home or the library, soap operas. But many were uncertain about what to do when a situation which clearly required discussion came up, but the child did not seem to want an explanation. The mother of a five-year-old described such an instance: "We saw a movie the other day—they were really going to 'do it' on TV. I said, 'Why don't we turn the channel?' He said, 'No, no.' He was really interested. They were huffing and puffing in bed. He'd never seen that before, but he never asked any questions."

Parents could not always know what worked best for them until after the fact. There were those who thought they were prepared for
Mb5   questions and then were startled into guilty evasions—"Babies are brought home from hospitals"—when children suddenly asked where babies come from. Others, either on their own or in response to children's curiosity, prepared dissertations on a topic, then looked back
Fb8   with regret at such examples of overkill. "My sense was that we over-explained. I don't think he fully understood it," Harold said ruefully. Many felt that if they had it to do over again, they would think more carefully about the kinds of things they would say, and how and when they would say them.

Who Takes Responsibility?

Parents thought it was best to share responsibility for the sexual education of their children. And families who had this arrangement emphasized the organic way in which it worked and the ease both parents and children felt around sexual discussions in general. As issues came up, a child could ask either parent, or both, raise questions at a family powwow or a more intimate *tête-à-tête*. Often, mothers and fathers were equally adept at providing scientific facts but felt that when it came to describing experiences—orgasm, menstruation, childbirth—it was best to leave "male" topics to fathers and "female" topics to mothers.

As a single father, Sam is the primary source of most of his daughter's sexual information. He laughed when he was asked how he intends to describe orgasm to her. "I don't know, since I'm not a female. Fg7 I don't know exactly what her orgasm is going to be like but I would be willing to describe it as probably being the most physically pleasurable act that she's going to experience in her life. I can describe breast development, her period, but I think it might have more credibility coming from a woman, but I don't think I would like to see any of those things come necessarily exclusively from a woman. The big problem is that I can't really describe what anything feels like and a question will come up as to how credible Daddy is."

It must be pointed out, however, that though parents said a sharing of responsibility was *ideally* what they wanted, most reported that it was *actually* the mother who found herself giving out sexual information. In some families the father did not participate at all. "If she Fg5 came and asked me how the baby got into Mommy's belly, right now, I would think, 'Mom—help!' " Mike said. Though normally a talkative person, he acknowledged that this was an area in which he was unexpectedly reticent. "I would not be fit for words at the time. I'd leave it to my wife." A number of other fathers felt the same way. Sometimes the mothers themselves recognized that they had to take over if their children were to learn anything at all. Leigh gave up a job in order to be a full-time homemaker after she was married, and she has devoted a great deal of her time to raising her children. When it came to telling them about sex, her husband handed over that task as well. "One day, my son came to ask me a question and I was prepar- Mb8 ing for a party, and I said, 'Ask your father,' and he said, 'I asked him. He told me to go to you.' " One mother put off talking to her son about sex in the hope that her husband would initiate discussion. But when it looked as though the child might have to go outside the home to get the information, she decided to step in. "If I waited for his father, Mb5 he'd probably be married."

In other families, the fathers tried to give varying degrees of assistance but their roles turned out to be vague and limited. Generally, at least in this area, the mother was perceived in rather old-fashioned terms. In Lew's first marriage (he has since been divorced and remarried), he re-created the stereotypical behavior he had observed in his own family when growing up in Oklahoma. His wife was the keeper of the house and the children; he went away "to the office" each morning in order to earn a living. "For the first three years of my son's life I Fb11 really wasn't involved in being responsible for him other than being the father that comes home and, you know, plays for an hour every night and does things on Saturday," he said. "Very traditional kind of a way, and his mother was really responsible for his real care and day-to-day things."

Even in families where both parents wanted to share equally in giving out sexual information, however, the father's obligations outside the home were likely to keep him from participating fully when it came to educating children about sex. George said, "My wife has probably spent more time with my daughter than I have. I've been going to school, late at night, and I just haven't been spending as much time with her as I should." Another reason suggested for the woman's greater suitability for this task was that she was, by nature, a perceptive, responsive personality, a warmer, more open human being. "We both find that her father is reticent about discussing sex," a mother said, speaking for her eleven-year-old daughter as well as herself. Daniel thought his wife was "very patient . . . in some ways more sensitive to what's going on with my son than I."

Fg7

Mg11

There were a few families in which fathers did take on the most active role in talking to the children about sex. Generally the children were boys, and the assumption was that the father would do a better job, "man to man." In some cases, however, fathers felt that their relationships with their daughters were close enough to allow for conversations even about intimate subjects. This group of fathers might send their children to their mothers for information on menstruation or childbirth but often did not mind dealing with such female-oriented issues themselves. Ray has a three-year-old girl, Andrew an eleven-year-old boy. Both of them were more comfortable discussing sex with their children than most of the other men in this study.

Fg3

I think I could talk about menstruation. She might relate better to her mother. But I think I would be able to empathize with her and to handle her. We're not talking about just the information, but even the information—information's easy. I would take a shot.

Fb11

Okay, we started out explaining how the baby changes, the fact that girls grow breasts and once a month they have a period. . . . Girls get breasts and they wear brassieres.

Mothers in a parallel position were more anxious about describing male sexual anatomy and related physical experience to children of either sex—not because they lacked *factual* knowledge but because they lacked *first-hand experience*.

Mb8b5

Never having had any brothers, I really feel inadequate to discuss some things with boys. I think the father should discuss, well, how they may *feel*, if they're getting toward their teenage years, and so forth.

I'm not so sure I understand about such phenomena as wet dreams and embarrassing times that erections take place. Mg7

But of course very few mothers had the option of sending the children to their fathers for explanations. No matter how uncomfortable they were with these topics, they felt they had to inform their children.

It is not surprising, therefore, that some mothers felt put upon and some fathers expressed uneasiness or guilt because the task of explaining sex to their children had fallen to the mother. Fathers who became aware that the limited nature of their participation was causing tension between them and their wives, or closing off discussion of sex with their children, hoped they could change. One father talked about how he had tacitly avoided sexual topics with his nine-year-old daughter. "She's going to get her information from her mother, to be Fg9 perfectly honest. I don't think that's fair, but if you ask, that's the answer," Peter said. "My father waited till I was twenty-two years old. He figured, 'This guy's slow. I better tell him something.'" Peter added thoughtfully, "I've left that responsibility to my daughter's mother. I'm aware now of a need for me to reevaluate that."

Setting Limits

Most parents admitted to difficulties in deciding whether to set limits on the information they gave to their children. So many factors were involved. The child might be too immature to understand what he was told. Or he might be overstimulated, aroused, by graphic details. The parent might be unsure of his facts or uncomfortable around an issue. And parents and children might feel awkward relating to each other about sex. Nevertheless, when parents were asked what topic they would intentionally omit in discussing sex, their rule of thumb seemed to be: If the child asks he should be answered. This father's comment was typical. "I wouldn't omit anything. I think there's a time Fg3 that everything is appropriate, but I don't think at any time everything is appropriate. I was given technique when I was ten years old! I think that was too early. It's just the time when the questions come."

"Telling," however, did not necessarily mean telling *all*. Many parents were aware of walking a fine line between two equally undesirable extremes: if you told *too little*, you might leave the child vulnerable to misconceptions, but if you told *too much*, you might frighten or confuse him. Parents therefore had to choose what not to say at different stages. For instance, most were willing to talk in a general way with fairly young children—aged three, four, or five—about the Daddy putting the seed in the Mommy and the meeting of sperm and egg. But many glossed over the mechanics of the male role in intercourse—arousal, erection, penetration, ejaculation—until the children were quite a bit older. Fathers might be a little more open with boys who were experiencing erections and knew about nocturnal emissions, but they felt shy letting girls know these private facts about themselves. Mothers, as has been mentioned, disliked explaining specific male experiences to their children. Other topics which parents preferred to avoid were those they considered esoteric or taboo—sadomasochism, sodomy, oral sex. Some were leery about entering into any discussion of homosexuality, even when their children had picked up street references to *queers* or *faggots* or *dykes*. Though parents wanted to be liberal and allow their children to choose any lifestyle they wished, they admitted that they would not be happy if the children turned out to be homosexual.

Many parents avoided talking about miscarriage, labor, cesarean section, or stillbirth because they did not want their children to associate sex with pain. But, surprisingly, a very large number also left out any reference to pleasure—physical desire, orgasm. Their difficulties were, in many cases, extensions of several general problems: a self-consciousness around personal sexual areas and a need to preserve privacy; conflicts between relatively rigid upbringings and the present, more permissive society; greater ease in dealing with factual, as opposed to emotional, issues. However, there were additional areas of worry specific to the topic of sex and pleasure.

Mg11   Quite a few parents were afraid that telling their children the act of intercourse was enjoyable would encourage them to experiment with sex at too early an age. A mother talked about this problem: "At the age of eleven I would not describe it in such exciting terms, because I know this kid in particular, and I know she'll be on someone's doorstep tomorrow to try it. I know that, especially the way she masturbates. I'm afraid about when she'll experiment."

Some parents knew logically that their children must have already learned about sexual pleasure from friends, TV, books, their own bodies. But they wanted to hold onto a more irrational, magical feeling: If I don't tell them, it won't be real. This desire to protect children from what they evidently could not be protected from seemed to reflect the parents' wish to preserve their children's "innocence" as long as possible. And it *was* difficult for parents to perceive their children as sexual beings—no matter how sophisticated they were, whether they had read Freud or not. Parents who had observed examples of sensuality in their young children described them with wonder.

Mg2   Karen's own sexual education—or, rather, "lack of education in that area"—had not prepared her for her daughter's frank enjoyment of stimulation when she was being bathed. "If I washed her in the vaginal area, she would tell me that it felt good. I can remember being surprised at how early sexuality was there, the 'nice feeling' and all. I do remember thinking that, 'My God, it starts at such an early age.' " In many ways, Karen was delighted by this uninhibited response.

Roy had a similar feeling when he took his daughter on a swing with him. "She didn't sit on my lap, she faced me, so she straddled me. She was hysterically laughing—she liked the way it felt when I pumped. I could see the beginnings. I have observed a lot of sensuality at the three-year-old level and it's incredible! It's like thirteen- or fourteen-year-olds going through the same thing, but it looks so *innocent* at three-years-old!" But others admitted to darker and more complex emotions: awe at the power of sensuality and an inability to reconcile themselves to its existence in such small bodies. And, as the children grew older and approached puberty, their emotions became stronger, more troublesome. `Fg3`

The entire topic was also obviously a "loaded" one for many parents because it brought to the surface deeply buried memories of their own first sensual discoveries, their parents' reactions to these discoveries, and the self-images that had been created for them around the whole issue of sexuality and pleasure. The mother of a seven-year-old boy, Clarice had grown up with the idea that sex was taboo, and she was concerned that, despite her awareness of her own problems and earnest efforts to overcome them, she had still not shaken those early feelings. This uneasiness was particularly focused on the area of physical pleasure. "I wonder why today I still haven't really made the connection between love and sexuality. Maybe it's just because he hasn't asked, but sometimes I wonder if it's there and he's asking and I don't want to pick it up. Because *I* wasn't comfortable with it, unconscious or conscious, or whatever." Even Paula had not quite overcome the inhibitions instilled in her by her parents when it came to discussing physical pleasure with Jenny. "I try to be as honest as I can. I think sex is a wonderful experience, but I think too much of my own upbringing will prevent me from making it sound like the experience of a lifetime." `Mb7` `Mg11`

In a few families there was virtually never any discussion of sex. Privacy was a concern. But parents were also afraid that to broach the subject was to open a Pandora's box and find themselves suddenly face-to-face with more complex issues than they were prepared to handle. They simply found it "too scary" to introduce information on their own or encourage questions from their children. "I'm a coward," Jean confessed. "I've been letting my husband handle it and he doesn't handle it. I wish I was different. I wish there was some magic answer." Like other parents with this difficulty, she went on to point out the difference between *theory* and *reality* in child-rearing. "My major in college was child psych and I wanted to be a nursery-school teacher, and `Mb8`

I always knew exactly what I was going to say. I knew how I would tell a girl about her period, and I knew if I had boys how I would tell them about sex. But being a mother, it's not easy. When you have time to sit down and think it out clearly, you know exactly what you are going to say. But with a child, you never know what the questions are going to be. You can be in the middle of cooking dinner and they'll say, 'What does it feel like to have sex?' And all of a sudden it throws you off balance and your first reaction sometimes is 'Oh, go ask your father,' which is absolutely the wrong thing to say. Timing is important. When they ask you that question it's right now and they want the answer right now. Two hours from now, after you have done the dishes and you are ready to sit down and talk about it, they are not interested in it anymore. They have other places to go and people to see."

Some parents in this group were aware that they were repeating patterns which had been established when they were growing up. *Their* parents had not spoken to them about sex; *they* did not know what to tell their children. Mothers, in particular, were not always sure how to overcome the misconceptions and negative feelings they had been given about female sexuality in order to talk freely to their daughters. It was difficult to describe objectively details about their bodies which had caused them so much ambivalence as children. Louise talked of the lasting scars that had resulted from the harsh messages she received at age twelve about becoming a woman.

Mg11   I just find it a difficult subject. My mother never talked to me about it. She gave me a book and I felt that it was horrible that she gave me a book. I remember when I had my period. . . . I had a sleepover the night before and I remember there was a lot of sexual play between me and my really good friend and the next day I had my period. I was the first one in my group to have my period. I couldn't believe that I . . . I had a very, very, very low self-esteem and I couldn't believe that I would have it before all my other friends who I looked up to. You know, I didn't deserve to have it first. And my mother became hysterical when I had it and said, "It's okay, it's okay. Don't get worried. Nothing's wrong, nothing's wrong," and meanwhile she was hysterical.

Cassandra also experienced tremendous confusion at the time of her first period.

Mg6   My mother didn't tell me about no menstrual period or anything until after the first day I had it. I thought I was bleeding to death. I started crying, went into hysterics, and then she tells me. All she tells me was, "You have to be careful because if you don't be careful, you'll wind up with a baby." She didn't tell me anything about birth control. She didn't tell me anything about this is the man and putting the penis in the vagina or anything. So I still didn't know this, and the first time I had intercourse I was pregnant. I didn't know this was the mistake that I made. I didn't have any information. I used to be in a crowd and be hanging out, like, and the fellas used to tease me because they knew I didn't know.

There were also parents who were waiting for the proper moment to bring up the subject. Cassandra's daughter, aged six, had been told that you have a baby after you finish school, get a good job, and find a husband, but nothing else. Like other parents of young girls, Cassandra believed that she would sit down with her daughter and give her the "facts of life" when she was about nine, close to the age when she might get her first period. Other parents, some with ten- and eleven-year-olds, were not sure when their children would no longer be "too young to understand." It's true they suspected that their children knew a lot more than they were letting on. But the parents were content to assume that if there were gaps, the children would approach them for the missing details. And so "waiting to tell" often became, in effect, "not telling at all."

The First Thing They Wanted to Know

What was the first thing children wanted to know? Often they did come up with the classic question, "Where do babies come from?" But they might begin with far simpler inquiries about their own genitals or the differences between boys and girls or the bulge in the tummy of the lady next door. It was not uncommon, in fact, for the initial question to be, essentially, a non-event, passing off quite unremarkably among the vast number of other demands for information from little children. As one mother put it, "When you're answering a lot of different questions—you know, 'What makes the grass grow?'—it was just another question and it was handled in the same way."   Mb5

Parents supplied diverse examples of the variety of ways in which children first revealed their curiosity. Often the triggering mechanism was the child's taking notice of a woman who was pregnant.

> Our babysitter was pregnant and our daughter noticed her stomach   Fg2
> getting bigger and bigger. I didn't want to say that's a watermelon or
> a pumpkin or that sort of thing. That was a baby and that's how you
> came from mommy.

> He'd seen somebody pregnant and asked me why she was so *fat*. I   Mb3
> said she was going to have a baby and then he asked, "Well, how
> does the baby get inside her?"

Children were also generally puzzled and intrigued by bodies—their own and those of playmates and siblings.

Mg2   She wanted to know why her brother looked one way and she looked another way. Or why Mother looked one way and Daddy looked another.

Mg2   She asked, "What's this?" when she pointed to her vagina.

Mb2•   He exclaimed, "Look, Mommy, it goes up and down!" He knew he had a penis that he could make go up and down. He could barely talk but he was amazed at that. I thought it was terrific.

Sometimes the questions would occur when children saw their parents nude or partially nude.

Mg2   I remember she used to be very amused by my hair in the genital area. She said something very funny, something about being fuzzy. She wanted to comb it.

Mb2   I remember his seeing me come out of the shower. He asked me where my penis was.

Fg2   She saw me in the bathroom going to the toilet and I think she asked me why I was standing up.

Or it might come like a thunderbolt out of the blue, apparently unrelated to the situation or context, to astonish, charm, or perplex the parents.

Mg4b3   My daughter was in the car. She said to me, "How are babies made?" It was at night and I'm not a good driver at night. I almost drove up on the sidewalk. *Oh, my God*—you know. And then my *son* answered, "That's easy, Lisa! The man puts his penis in the woman's vagina." He was three!

Mg5   I was absolutely, totally, unprepared. My daughter said to me one day, just sitting in the kitchen, "How does the seed get into the mother? Does it get in through the mouth or the belly button?" I said, "Through the belly button." Then I went into three days of absolute trauma because I'd lied. Within three days I told her the whole thing.

Sexual Anatomy

Not surprisingly, the task of teaching children about sexual anatomy was considerably eased in families containing both male and female children or in extended families containing male and female cousins.

As the infants and toddlers were bathed, changed, dressed, and undressed, their young relatives learned quickly and naturally about the
differences between girls' and boys' bodies. And these differences
seemed far less threatening to discuss for both adult and child when
the bodies in question were small.

> After her brother was born, they used to bathe together. He was
> born when she was fifteen months. But she asked. I'd say, "That's
> Joey's penis."   Mg1

> He has a cousin who's a girl and I said, "You remember you saw
> Sally being changed and you saw that she doesn't have a penis." He   Mb7
> said, "That's right," and he kind of went off and thought about it.

Parents were also more comfortable if the child they were speaking to was of the same sex. This was especially true of mothers who
took pride in the fact that they could be more direct with their daughters than their own mothers had been with them. Karen hoped her
daughter would feel "comfortable and very, very natural about sex" if   Mg2
she talked openly and easily about anatomy. "When she was learning
to speak, I remember hearing a program on the radio that said, you
know, we teach 'This is the arm,' and 'This is the leg,' but we manage somehow to avoid the genitals. I said, 'This is the vagina.' She
repeated it whenever she talked about parts of the body as a baby—
'the vagina,'—automatically." Rosaline treasured her role as prime
educator where her daughter was concerned; their discussions gave her
the opportunity to transmit some of her own delight in being female.
"I told her, 'I'm so pleased that you're a girl. Little girls are so beautiful.'   Mg3
Because it's a female child, I think it will be easier."

Fathers, though generally less involved in the sex education of
their children, were often able to talk reassuringly to sons about male
phenomena—penis size, nocturnal emissions. Tom has two small sons.
"They look," he said. "We all go and urinate at the same time. The   Fb6b4
two boys and me. And they look and they say, 'How come yours is
bigger than ours?' and I said, 'Because I'm five times your size.'" A
number of other parents, as well, reported that this kind of straightforward talk worked well with their little boys who had questions
about male anatomy. "I remember their discussion about erection," a   Mb5
mother said. "I heard his father say his is bigger because he's got a
bigger frame, and when he grows up he will get bigger, too, because
his whole body will grow. They were comparing sizes. There was a
discussion of testicles, too. It was a pretty easygoing kind of thing."
Older boys often asked about wet dreams. Sometimes they had picked
up bits of information from books or more sophisticated friends and
were not sure just what to expect of their bodies. One father was surprised that his ten-year-old recognized the term at all, but he tried to

Fb10 deal simply and directly with the boy's concerns in this area. "All he wanted to know was if it was very messy and if you had to change the sheets when it happened. I told him no, you just had to change your underwear or change your pajamas and go back to sleep again."

But any discussion of genitals became more difficult if the parent and child were of the opposite sex. Fathers tended to be disconcerted by their daughters' curiosity about their penises.

Fg3 Whenever she saw me naked in the shower or the bath, she would start playing around. She would ask, "What's that?" I would tell her, "It's my penis." It becomes rather annoying when everytime you take off your pants, the kid starts fooling around.

Fg7 She's seen me "hard," if you will, and she did make a comment that it was very big, but I didn't elaborate on that. I think it would have been difficult for me to explain. I feel that if I showed myself to be embarrassed, I would do more harm.

Mothers of boys had to deal with another issue. Often their sons were less interested in what was there than in what was not there. Polly is the lone female in a family of males. When her oldest son was seven, Mb7 he wanted to know, "If you don't have a penis, what do you have?" Polly confessed to being "stumped" by the question; she went on to describe the problems in explaining how she was "different" to her son.

I'm thinking to myself, when he says that, what does he *mean?* What does the question *mean?* Is it the penis as something you can see and show and handle, or is it the penis for urination, which is the most obvious thing for a child. (How can I stand up and do it, right?) Or is it the fact that he already knows that it's pleasant to touch? Is that what he's talking about. Should I say "clitoris" or should I say "vagina" or should I say "uterus?" There isn't any *thing* that's exactly the same. But that question means something and I can't quite get to what the question is. I'm not sure I've really hit on the thing that's bothering him.

Polly's statement reflects the general concern mothers had about understanding a subject emotionally. This was the reason many had given for their reluctance to discuss male sexuality with children of either sex. Fathers, however, usually bypassed the emotional "hidden agendas," the questions behind their children's questions, by sticking to the facts and conveying information in a blunt, pragmatic tone. How would a man describe arousal and erection to a child? This father's com-
Fg7 ment was typical. "I would explain the role of blood and capillaries and maybe not talk so much about emotions and stirrings."

Except in families who invented a private, affectionate vocabulary for parts of the body, almost all parents used the correct terms for penis, vagina, testicles, and so on with their children. Sometimes this policy created conflicts. Parents had to resist disapproval from relatives or neighbors, or overcome residual discomfort of their own. Several described incidents—humorous only in retrospect—in which their children innocently demonstrated their mastery of these anatomical terms to the world at large, while the parents stood red-faced in the background.

> Joey walked up to a man in a store and said, "Mister, do you have a penis?" I almost dropped dead! I thought I would die. He had learned a word and he was simply curious as to whether somebody else knew it. Well, the man did such a double take. And I blushed and looked away. He tried it with one other man and the other man was even worse.   Mb2

> Well, he knew the word *vagina*. And he would bump into people at the movie theater. "Oh, I'm sorry. I hope I didn't hurt your VAGINA." When he was four years old! It was rather an embarrassing moment in the movie theater.   Fb4

> We were at the elephant house and a little girl was pointing to a specific part of the elephant which was indeed large. And the little girl said, "Mother, what's that?" and the mother said, "That's the elephant's trunk." And the little girl said, "No, not that, *that*," and the mother said, "That's the elephant's tail." And the little girl said, "No, not that, THAT," and the mother said, "Oh, that's the elephant's leg." The little girl said, "No, not that, *THAT! THAT!*" And my daughter said, "That's the biggest penis I ever saw in my life!"   Mg5

But despite occasional embarrassment, these parents believed that by giving the parts of the body their proper names, they were letting their children know that sex is something natural, not shameful or funny or obscene.

Castration Fear/ "Penis Envy"

Few children, it is interesting to note, just accepted explanation of sexual anatomy and walked away. A surprisingly large number of people said their children were particularly concerned about the male organ— boys wanted to know why girls don't have one, girls wanted to know why boys do. One father said, "My youngest one thinks his cousin who's the same age is in a sorry state because she doesn't have a penis."

Parents found themselves called upon to allay a number of fears about the possession and/or possible loss of this organ. Very often, especially with boys, mere factual reassurance was not sufficient. Children's questions continued to be repeated long after the initial explanation had been given and apparently accepted. There really seemed to be no "solution" to this problem. Most parents eventually resigned themselves to repeating the correct information patiently, calmly, and as frequently as was necessary.

Boys tended to express a persistent lurking anxiety, a stubborn disbelief in the facts. They feared that some joke was being played upon them, even when repeatedly told that women did not possess penises, were not concealing penises, had not lost penises through mischance or punishment. This was true of a great number of boys, including those who seemed relaxed and undisturbed about other sexual material and generally comfortable about their bodies. Mothers described their experiences in handling this problem with exasperation, sympathy, and humor. The little boys seemed so puzzled, so vulnerable, so reluctant to accept even the testimony of their own two eyes.

Mb4   He insists that I have a penis and that all girls, of course, everybody, has penises. I'm not sure if he's teasing. I said girls are born without penises, and so it's not something that *happened* to them. I explained that to him. I even showed him a book, pictures of girls and boys and the differences. Even after that, he insisted that girls have penises. A few days ago, we went over it again and I think he finally accepted that . . . I must have *both!*

Mb7   He's been very concerned about the fact that I don't have a penis. To the point that sometimes he will insist that I do, that I'm hiding it. I don't know whether it bothers him in the sort of classic Freudian sense that he worries about "castrating" or it worries him, "Why is Mommy different?" He sees me without clothes on and he's asked me, just to make sure, thinking, Well, maybe I'm not seeing right, this couldn't *be.* And you explain over and over and yet it's still some kind of question in his mind that he doesn't understand.

Parents also reported that their little girls tended to be keenly interested in the differences between their fathers' and brothers' bodies and their own. But these little girls exhibited far less anxiety and more plain curiosity than did the little boys:

Mg5   When she was little, she saw her father, she saw her brother. She had friends who didn't have brothers and they would come over here hoping to get a look.

Mg7   She makes comments about the fact that her brother has the same thing that her daddy does, and it must be difficult to go to the bathroom that way. She finds it much easier sitting down. At least that's how she feels.

Maybe she was poking fun at her brother, but she had this little draw- Fb7g4
ing of a boy with a penis and then this line that went all over the
place. I said, "What's that?" and she said, "Oh, he's peeing." I
thought it was a beautiful drawing. In fact, I kept it. The way it just
went all around and spiraled and traveled all over. A ten gallon pee.
That certainly shows an interest!

One little girl at three did demonstrate anxieties about becoming
a boy, similar to those of little boys who feared becoming girls. Her
mother, Rosaline, a divorcée who had primary responsibility for the
child's upbringing, described the situation. "She seemed fearful of ap- Mg3
pearing on the outside like a boy, perhaps that her inside would change
to be a boy. She didn't like to wear pants. You know, normally little
girls like to be comfortable in pants. Not that she would say, 'Will I
grow a penis?' But she sure didn't want to wear pants, which I thought
was a secondary sign of this anxiety." Rosaline found that she was able
to deal with the problem by reassuring her daughter that she was un-
doubtedly feminine, though it took a long time for the message to sink
in. "I would say to her, 'Little girls grow up just like mommies, just
like me. You're going to have the same thing that Mommy has.' I had
to go over it many times, and still it took her until the age of six-
and-a-half to be comfortable wearing pants." Indeed, it was not only
Rosaline's positive manner but her daughter's awareness that she was
developing the outward signs of feminity—long hair, for instance—that
helped her to overcome her fear. "Now, at this age, she's looking al- Mg7
ready for breast development. She stands in front of the mirror, nude,
shaking her hips and twirling around, looking at the little nipples. A
lot of it is still focused on the bodily attributes of femininity."

"Can I See Yours?"

Children occasionally responded to anatomical discussions by requesting
to see the parent's own genitals. Almost everyone felt that satisfying
these requests would be highly inappropriate.

He wanted to see my vagina, and I wouldn't do that. I told him I Mb4
would show him a picture of it, because I feel that's not an appropriate thing to do. No way!

He's always looking up my skirt and I say, "If you have some ques- Mb7
tions and you're curious, I'll be very happy to answer them, but you
cannot do that."

Fg7   No. I would not let her touch me and I wouldn't point things out
           to her. (If she happens to see us in a state of undress, we just treat
           it as natural.)

As this last parent pointed out, the *situation* was all-important. If a child
happened to catch sight of a parent's genitals in "natural" circumstances—bathing, getting out of bed—that was quite acceptable to
many parents. But display specifically for educational purposes was not.

Intercourse, Conception, and Birth

Many parents said that the earliest discussion about having babies
occurred before their children were five. Sometimes a child was obviously curious about her identity or origin and would ask, "Where did I
come from?" Or she became aware that her small world seemed suddenly filled with babies—her own or friends' younger siblings, new
cousins. Often, in fact, these first questions came after she had been
told that her mother or a close relative or friend was expecting.
      In most families, explaining where babies come from turned out
to be an ongoing process that continued until children were teenagers.
Almost everyone agreed that at the beginning it was best to give out
only a few basic facts, enough to answer children's first questions, and
reserve more complex topics for later discussions. As the father of a
Fg3 three-year-old put it, "They can only process so much. I think there's
information they don't need." Parents worried that burdening children
with too many details too early could confuse or frighten them.
      The first time around, therefore, many parents began by talking
about conception—the meeting of egg and sperm, development of the
fetus, and sometimes delivery. The focus on biology allowed them to
teach children something about their internal anatomy and to avoid
issues like intercourse and pleasure, which were potentially uncomfortable to all parties involved.

Fb3   We told him that Mommy and Daddy had done something—I don't
           think we went into detail. The baby had been an egg and had been
           fertilized. I guess that wasn't the word used because it sounds too old
           for a three-year-old. And the baby was growing in the mother's stom-
           ach and would come out from where Mommy made a wee-wee—he
           had watched her so he had an idea what that was.

Mb3   I've just described it in a linear sense—that the Daddy does this and
           then the Mommy does that, and the sperm unites with the egg. I
           don't think I've every really used the word "conception." Just inad-
           vertently left it out.

Some parents found that emphasizing mechanics, rather than emotion, also worked when they were called upon to describe intercourse. For, generally, once children had gotten the initial facts—and often they asked to have the information repeated until they finally seemed to have absorbed it—their next question was about how the sperm got in.

> I used the analogy about when I get up in the morning—sometimes   Fb5
> my penis is hard. I said to him that sometimes your penis gets hard
> and then when you're older and you're capable of producing sperm,
> that sperm goes into the vagina.

> First it's thought of as an all-female activity. Later on they begin to   Mg6
> ask, "How does the seed get in?" or "What does the daddy do?" or
> "Why do you need a daddy?" At which point we explained about
> the penis and the testicles and the sperm cell coming in and meet-
> ing the egg.

Because very young children might be easily confused and might not be able to communicate what their fears and fantasies were, parents were especially scrupulous about preventing certain common misunderstandings. Children often mixed up elements of reproduction with other bodily processes. Several mothers reported that young children thought they had somehow been eaten before they were born. "Did you swallow me?" Linda's son wanted to know. "You swallowed   Mb4 me and I got into your belly." A father with a boy about the same age was concerned that his son might think he could become pregnant by eating too much, "that he might be frightened if he had a stomachache   Fb4 or thought his stomach was getting big."

Other parents believed that unless they made the process clear to their children—sometimes simply by explaining that the baby did not grow actually in the stomach but in a special place called the *uterus*— the children were likely to have strange images of how the baby lives inside the mother's body. When Lorna was pregnant with her second child, the family could cajole her into drinking her milk by saying, "So   Mb4 go ahead and do it. This one's for the baby." Lorna thought the little in-joke probably had misled her three-year-old son, who believed "it was literally for the baby. I mean, he thought the food fell on the baby and things like that."

There was also concern that children might confuse intercourse, conception and birth with urination, that they would think you "pee the baby out" or that ejaculation and urination are the same. Parents spoke of the importance of letting children know that these functions were unrelated.

> It's very important that the child learns soon that urination is not   Mb4
> related to sex. The child associates the penis with urination and then

the thought of inserting the penis and ejaculating sperm into the female becomes distasteful, because to them it's like urinating on another person. Likewise, it's very important to explain that the opening
for urination in the woman is not the opening the man enters—they
are very close, but they are different. My attempt to differentiate it
from other bodily functions.

Sex and Pleasure

There were people who had no trouble discussing the association of
pleasure and sex right from the beginning. This was particularly true
of those parents who felt easy, in general, introducing sexual topics
with their children. George, for instance, had described the relationship between love and making love in simple terms for his daughter
Fg3   when she was only three, just beginning to ask questions. "I said that
daddies put their penises between mommies' legs, which is called the
vagina, and they did this because it felt good and they love each other.
And, as a result of doing this, a seed was planted in mommy's belly
and a baby is formed. And that's how you came." Helen was one of
the few parents in this study who grew up in a home where she received full information about sex, and she intended to give her children the same positive attitude she had gotten from her own mother.
Thus, like George, she felt it was important for them to understand
early on that affection and sex were related. When her son wanted to
Mb3   know where babies came from, she told him "that a mother had a uterus
and a father had a penis and that when they were feeling very fond of
one another they would lie very close to one another and the penis
could be inserted into a special opening in the mother's body. If they
wanted a baby, the sperm from the husband's penis would fertilize
the egg and—SHAZAM!"
    But because the issue tapped so many different kinds of emotions,
it is not surprising that a large number of parents hoped to put it off
until the children were older. This was not always possible, however.
Children who understood that the penis had to deposit sperm in the
vagina if a baby was to be conceived often raised questions that made
it necessary to allude in some way to passion, desire, arousal. For
instance, they personalized the information, wondered how they would
perform. Some parents found they could reassure them by explaining
that where there was warmth, love, excitement, the man would have
an erection, and penetration would be easy. Parents, particularly those
who had girls, thought it was important, too, that children understand
that the pleasure is shared by both people.

Dorothy's daughter is rather mature-looking at ten and, though   Mg10
in many ways she is still a little girl, Dorothy is aware that the "older"
boys at school are attracted to her. "I guess at this age I wouldn't want
my daughter to have any really negative feelings about sex, such as I
wouldn't want her to hear any statistics like, you know, ninety percent
of women don't enjoy it or something like that. I would want her to
come into her sexuality with some very positive feelings. I wouldn't
want her to think her first encounter is going to be very painful or I
always thought the first time is never any good for anybody so I should
accept it. I don't want her to accept nothing on her first time. I want
her to go into it thinking it is going to be an enjoyable act and she
should receive pleasure from it. I don't want her to think that it's just
the man who is going to get all the pleasure."

Sometimes it was necessary to talk about pleasure because the child
thought that marriage, intercourse, and conception were automatically
related and once you were married, you would immediately have a
baby. For this reason, there were children who were confused when
they heard about single mothers or when they observed that their parents did not seem to be producing more children. Alice's seven-year-
old, who had heard her father say, "No more babies," would try to   Mg7
prevent her parents from kissing or hugging when she saw them in
bed. "No, no, no, Daddy! You said you don't want any more babies!"

Different Ages, Different Needs

Children approaching puberty generally wanted specifics about many
of the topics they had already heard discussed. For instance, whereas
children under eight years old were often satisfied with the notion that
the sperm got into the woman when the man put his penis in her
vagina, older children asked for fairly explicit details about erection,
lubrication, ejaculation. They also wanted to know more about birth
control, labor, delivery. The other area that concerned them was sexual pleasure. Some of this curiosity was related to information they
had picked up outside the home—from peers, or elder siblings who
were dating, or from books and the media. Clearly, they were beginning to associate romance and sex. Since Margot had never made any
topic off limits, her daughter, Erica, had heard the basic facts—everything she wanted to know—by the time she was eight. At ten, however,
Erica had begun asking questions again, this time related to passion.
"She asked me, 'Would you do that when you don't want to make a   Mg10
baby?' So now she has a concept that one has intercourse for pleasure

and not just reproducing." And Margot has continued to be as honest as possible. "She asked me about it and I told her that 'Yes, you do it for pleasure and it's fun and nice.' "

Did children grasp what they were being told? Most parents believed that much information simply went over their heads and that children absorbed only the facts that intrigued them or did not make them uncomfortable. For about two weeks after learning about how babies are made, one little girl drew pictures of sperm, "a cute, little wiggly thing, two eyes and a snake-like tail." But her mother was pretty certain that she had not yet taken in anything about lovemaking. Jim's daughter passed on that she had understood to an entire housing complex when she hollered out the window of her apartment to the man who mowed the lawn, "Hey, Al, you know what? My mommy's going to have a baby. My mommy's got a baby in her stomach and in a couple of more months it's going to come out." Though parents tended to think that it took a long time—years—for children to get the entire picture, they felt it was important to allow them to pick and choose what they were ready to deal with from the information they had received. The rest would fall into place at a later stage.

Mg7

Fg3

Observing Pregnancy

Observing pregnancies in the world around them—especially in their own mother, a relative, a close family friend or a teacher—could provide children with the most vivid and direct illustrations of where babies come from. They learned new facts through exposure to the day-to-day processes of pregnancy itself. And, when parents were willing to share their own reactions and to be sensive to children's special needs, relationships within the family could be strengthened. Another benefit was that children often became curious about themselves and wanted to know the circumstances of their birth. The resulting discussions were helpful not only in providing information about the birth process but in giving children a positive sense of their individuality, a new awareness of their place in the family's history.

Mg7

They want to know, and this is perhaps less sexual than about identity, that you were really there when they were born. Maybe there's that little fear of, "Was I adopted?" And she asked, "What time was I born and what did I look like?" And I was able to give her that information, that her eyes were open a little bit in the beginning and she was cold and that she seemed to be hungry right away, that Daddy was there too, and how he named her right away.

I said to him I thought it was the most terrific thing in the whole　　Mb7
world. "I was awake the whole time and I saw you being born." I
told him I saw his head come out first and his shoulders got turned
around and his feet came out, and Daddy was there. And I said,
"You were *this* big," and I took out a ruler. And he said, "I couldn't
have been that small." I said, "You *were!*" And then he went to the
album and we looked at it and he saw my stomach pregnant and saw
how little he was, and he said, "I guess it's true." Oh, and I told
him we had champagne, Daddy went dancing and I wanted to go
dancing but they wouldn't let me out of the hospital. And that's exactly the way it was, too. An Up thing.

Even in children to whom the reproductive process had been fully
explained, observing a pregnancy sometimes brought to the surface
gaps in understanding or anxieties that had been hidden previously.
Parents needed to keep sensitive antennae tuned to pick up their children's needs for reassurance and information:

He was concerned about his mother. She was "pregnant," and sud-　　Fb3
denly she was bigger and then she had to go to the hospital. And
that was traumatic because he had to be kept with a babysitter. So it
was very important that we explain exactly what happened. We sat
down and we talked about crowning and how the baby comes out,
umbilical cords, and so on. I think some of the questions arose from
certain fears, fears about himself and maybe a certain jealousy about
the baby, a certain happiness about the baby, a certain fear maybe
about something happening to Mommy, the hospital. . . . Curiosity,
excitement and fear.

My sister's pregnant so there's been some discussion of her having　　Mb4
the baby. He was aware of her growing stomach, et cetera. And he
said, "Well, how does the baby get out of the mother's tummy?"
And I was somewhat taken aback when he asked. All I said was,
"There's a special place the baby comes out of." And the second
time he asked, "How does the baby get out of the Mommy's tummy?" I have the same answer, and this time he said, "Where is this
special place?" In the last month or so I said, "It comes out of the
mother's vagina." He seemed a little surprised. I think he had some
question about how could the baby fit through the mother's vagina.
And I said that when the baby's ready to be born, the vagina stretches.
And that was the end of it. He hasn't asked any more.

In some families frequent pregnancies provided relaxed, almost
automatic ways for children to learn. Several parents acknowledged
that children growing up in such households cannot help overhearing
intimate talk among sisters, sisters-in-law, aunts, cousins, about various aspects of the process of birth. The general feeling among these

parents was that as long as the overheard material was not of a frightening nature, such experiences were natural and harmless, even helpful in demystifying the subject.

Fg6   One father had told his six-year-old "that she was a Leboyer-Lamaze delivery" in order to stress that childbirth could be "untraumatic and unpainful for everybody." A mother thought that her son was aware of the family's surprise when an aunt became pregnant immediately

Mb7   after giving birth to her first child. "I think perhaps he overheard the discussion. But it was not a negative kind of thing. It was like, 'Here we go again.' "

Children's reactions to pregnancy varied according to their ages and experiences. Some seemed not to notice, some accepted pregnancy as the natural order of things, some grew more aware of changes in the pregnant woman they observed.

Fg5   She told her little friends about it. She told her grandparents about it. When Francis was born, she came with us to the hospital. She came up to see her brother. She accepted everything pretty much in stride.

Fb10   He's conscious that a woman gets fatter when she's pregnant and in fact he realized his aunt was pregnant before we even told him anything. He said, "She's getting fat. I *thought* she was pregnant." Very straightforward.

At least one mother, who was pregnant at the time of her interview, intended to give her son the option of seeing his youngest sibling being born. Ellen has two children, a boy five and a girl one; she is expecting her third child. She described the "maternity center" where she was receiving prenatal care and where the baby would be born. According to the policies of the center, she was permitted to take her children with her on all visits, from routine monthly examinations right up to labor and delivery itself. As a result, her son, Carl, had been exposed to a great many more technical details about pregnancy than most children.

Mb5   He can go and watch me do my exercises, so he knows the breathing patterns and everything, about the cord and what the baby lives in—that type of thing—he knows all that. He's seen the placenta. He saw the one with his sister. He didn't see her birth but they film them at the center if you want them to and so we took him up there and let him see. He went with me last week. Carl had never seen me being examined, and the midwife said to Carl, "Why don't you come with us?" They do an internal. So he watched. On the way home he wanted to know why she checked me there and I told him that was the opening where the baby came out.

There were things Ellen preferred Carl not to see.

> There are some mothers who scream and holler, and this mother in
> one of the films, she kind of let go a little bit. She lost control, and I
> just don't think he has to see that. And the blood. That's the only
> thing I really don't know if I'm sure that I want him to have to see.

But, overall, she felt she would not exclude him from most other aspects of the delivery process.

Carl's reactions to what he had learned so far had been casual and matter-of-fact. "It really doesn't seem to affect him too much," Ellen said. "He feels the baby move. He knows how it's positioned in there and what it's doing, but, I guess because we are open, he doesn't seem to care one way or the other. Poor Carl has seen pregnancy so many times he's kind of wondering this time—he and my husband keep laughing—if I'll ever be thin again. 'I don't know, her stomach's awfully big.' " But though he had been so well informed, Carl still came up with his own version of the facts. Like other children his age, he had taken in something of what he had been told and dismissed the rest. Ellen recalled how he had described a film about the birth of a little girl at the center:

> He has seen the birth of a baby. He knows where it comes from.
> But apparently he forgot because he was telling a friend of ours that
> she came out of the *belly button!*

"Oh, Sick, Gross!"-Children's Reactions

Children reacted in a variety of ways to the explanations of conception and related phenomena. In many cases, they seemed to take the information quite calmly, to record and digest it without apparent difficulty. This was true not only of older children, who might have discussed the subject with peers before parents ever got around to it, but of younger ones as well. A mother described her five-year-old's response to their first talk about sex. "He looked at me and said, "Oh." Something like that. He accepted it. Perfectly matter-of-factly. Nonchalantly." Some children asked the same questions again, the way they might request the same story to be read over and over. Some listened for a while, then lost interest. A few appeared to have absolutely no reaction—"He just seemed to go on as if I hadn't said anything at all"—or reactions so bland or discrete they could not be assessed. One father described the frustrating response he got from his six-year-

old daughter after he had carefully introduced her to the facts of life.
Fg6   "Well, the kid's funny that way. She'll look at something very wide-eyes and nod her head sagely and say, 'Oh, okay, uh-huh,' and you don't know what the hell is going on in there."

A large number of children reacted more actively, sometimes negatively, with play behavior that imitated parts of the reproductive process, or revealed shock, disgust, or amusement. Parents recounted a variety of stories illustrating the range of these responses. Here is a sampling of the ways in which children dealt with the sexual information they had received.

Mg4   There was some play from the age of four about giving birth to bunnies and cats and with her toys. She'd put them in her tummy and come out with a little one from her leg.

Mb6   We went to a museum where they had a little sliced-in-half uterus with the fetus and the different months and so forth. And he seemed a little bit afraid, or disturbed, about it. That's the first time I ever recall that happening. If we look at it in a book, of course, it's not as graphic or something. But he didn't seem to want to look at it. I don't know if he was frightened or he just didn't understand it or just would rather look at the dinosaurs. But he didn't want to be there, really.

Fb7   After a while he said, "Oh, sick, gross," or something like that.

Mg8   When she expressed disgust at the way babies are made I told her that it was nice, that it was a nice experience, nothing disgusting. I said, "Look at all the people there are around. It can't be all that bad."

Mb8   He really laughed about that part that something came out of your penis and went into the woman and he said, "Is that the truth?" and I said, "Yes, that's the truth." He thought it was funny.

Mb11   When he was about five years old and had had all this information about where babies come from, there were like little gaps in his education that I suppose he needed filled in. And he said, "I understand where the babies come from and I understand that the man plants the seed in the woman's vagina and the egg and the sperm meet, but I don't understand how the sperm gets *into* the woman's body." So my husband says that the man puts his penis into the woman's vagina. And my son looked at him and said, "No, *really*, dad." He thought he was putting him on.

In this chapter parents described the numerous ways in which they and their children *talk* about sex. But a great many intimate facts are transmitted to children in nonverbal ways. Whether parents were open or reticent, no matter how much they chose to tell, children received sexual information simply by observing other family members. Parents were generally conscious of how important it was to say the right things if children were to have positive feelings about sex. They also became aware that in establishing policies around nudity, dressing and undressing, the use of private spaces in the household, showing affection, touching—even when these policies were for their own comfort—they could not help but affect their children's attitudes toward the body and toward the larger issues of sexuality related to it.

3

━━━━━━━━

Body

Talk

Until the first child came along, many couples had not given much thought to how they were handling the most intimate details of day-to-day living—dressing and undressing in front of each other, leaving the bathroom door open or closed. Generally, at sometime early in the relationship, they had found a style that was mutually comfortable and allowed each partner both the togetherness and privacy he or she wanted.

But children entered the family, in a sense, as outside observers. It was much harder to be nude at home without thinking anything of it when there was a small human being around who was growing increasingly interested in the differences between male and female bodies or comparing adult genitalia to his own. Also, children—especially very young ones—were not respecters of privacy and were likely to need attention or intrude on parents at moments that had previously been inviolable—when they were taking a bath, sitting on the toilet, changing a tampon. Parents often discovered that policies around nudity and bathroom behavior that had evolved unconsciously when they were only two people had to be adjusted consciously when they were three or more.

Nudity

The subject of nudity was especially complex, tied into almost every facet of family living. In a sense, styles of undress were what primarily differentiated one family from another, since very few people were as open about displaying their bodies on the outside as they were within their homes. Questions about nudity touched on many related emotions and attitudes, sometimes jostling against one another, which made it difficult for parents to fix firm policies to cover the variety of conditions that already existed as well as those that continually arose spontaneously in the home. Whether or not a parent personally approved of nudity, it was just about impossible to live in the same space with several people without seeing the others nude or being seen nude oneself. Parents had to decide how to handle the most ordinary daily situations which required putting on clothes or taking them off—getting into or out of bed, entering or leaving the bath, lounging around.

Often, they initially took an easygoing approach to such activities; this often worked as long as their children were fairly young but made them feel awkward as their children grew older. The rules—written or unwritten—also varied depending on the sex of the parent and the sex of the child. Furthermore, children themselves developed feelings about exposure, and parents tended to respect these in determining how much nudity should be allowed. Juggling the multiple needs for privacy and comfort in a family of three or four or five called for a great deal of sensitivity and ingenuity on the part of the parents.

There were other concerns, as well. How the family behaved in relation to nudity affected children's concepts of what was acceptable among people outside the family. And, as has been pointed out, in seeing unclothed bodies, children were absorbing all kinds of subliminal information about sex and sexuality. Almost everyone agreed that children should get the message that there is nothing shameful about human anatomy, and a number of parents were quite purposeful about going nude, in the hope that this would encourage their children to be at ease with their own bodies. But in this area—perhaps more than any other of the study—parents could not always act as they thought they should. Too much of their behavior was dependent on personal styles, inhibitions, feelings about appropriateness, and requirements for privacy so deeply ingrained that they could not be readily overcome. Parents had to find guidelines that were not only healthy for their children but comfortable for themselves.

Un/Covering The Body: Doing What's Comfortable

To a degree, whether parents were easy or cautious about allowing family members to see one another nude was influenced by their recollections of the policies their own parents had established. Perhaps predictably, a number of parents found themselves doing pretty much what *their* parents had done. This was especially true of people who had grown up in households that were fairly relaxed about nudity. Mark said that he always walked around nude when his son and daughter Fb10g7 were present. "My father did that," he said, "even though he came from a Missouri dirt farm. Nudity was natural." Roy was also raised in a family where nudity was regarded as "very natural." Even as adults, he and his sister and brother are still comfortable about appearing nude in front of one another. Roy had adopted the same style in his own household and attributes some of the family warmth and openness to Fg3 their positive attitudes toward going unclothed. "What it does—we have feelings come out, emotions that wouldn't ordinarily come out, because you're kind of 'stripped.' You may talk about family problems, spouse problems. With family around, it seems that nudity opens us up even more."

Similarly, there were parents who traced their more conservative feelings about nudity back to constraints in their upbringing. Ezra was Fb8 emphatic about not appearing nude before his son. "I never walked around naked. I was never into nudity as an adult. No." He could see the influence his parents and sisters had had on his point of view. "Here's the thing," he said. "I was brought up as one boy with four sisters. And I was really concerned about carving out my own space. So that may have something to do with it. But, anyway, nudity in our family was not encouraged." Kathy's feelings echoed Ezra's. Not only did she avoid going nude at home; she did not allow her daughter to Mg7 come out of the bath without any clothes on. "I don't go into a rage, but I tell her, 'You don't do that!' " Kathy was aware that she reacted to nudity "probably because of the way I was brought up and you can't change that," but she was not ashamed and did not regard herself as excessively inhibited. Modesty was important. "I will never forget—my husband told me once that his friend's sister would come down the stairs in her bra and slip. He would be sitting there because they were very friendly. This was just the way she walked around the house. My husband did not think anything of it, either. This was the way they lived. I lived a different way. I never thought that was right."

But of course not all parents necessarily repeated what their own parents had done. In fact, a surprisingly large group of those brought up in conservative households were much less reserved than Ezra and Kathy were about nudity with their children. Sometimes conservatively brought-up parents adopted the attitude of more easygoing spouses;

sometimes they reacted consciously to overcome what they felt had been artificial restraints during their childhoods. Larry said that because he and his wife wanted their children to be aware that there were two sexes and not to be embarrassed, they often went nude in the house. But he added another reason. "And I guess also because both our families—no one ever walked around that way. I really want them to have a much more open attitude because my parents didn't." Ellen, was not at all bothered by the fact that at home her son frequently saw her in a bra and pants. She felt she had come a long way from a family where "my mother still tells Dad to put on a robe when we're there." Leigh spoke good humoredly about the differences between her liberal attitudes toward nudity and the more conservative ones with which she had been raised. "I want to make one thing perfectly clear (call me Nixon)—My girls and I frequently walk around nude in front of each other. We have no shame whatsoever and I feel good about it, possibly because I'm trying to break down certain things as far as my mother was concerned. I didn't think there was any freedom whereby my mother and I could walk around or see each other nude."

In at least one instance a parent found he had been more influenced by the free and easy attitudes of his community toward the body than by the less tolerant guidelines of his strict Catholic family. In addition to talking openly to his daughter about sex, George hoped to transmit to her the positive feelings about the body he had gotten growing up in a beach environment. "I come from a tropical climate," he said. "I've always been into water sports. We lived on the beach and, my goodness, up to the time I was a young adult, there were always various stages of dressing and undressing among my group of friends. Even when I wear a bathing suit, it's usually a bikini. I think I'm more bodily conscious than most males." He paused, then added. "Not that I'm a member of a nudist sect or anything! But I don't make a big thing of nudity. I think it's a real hang-up in this country, to be honest with you."

As has been pointed out, most parents, even those whose household rule was "Cover up" or "Close the door," shared George's feeling that it was important not to make "a big thing" out of nudity if children were to feel okay about their bodies. But it was not always easy to respond casually when children "caught" them nude or wanted to see what their bodies looked like. Some people could not tune out the messages they had gotten from their own parents. Others, for complex and mysterious reasons buried in their psyches, were extremely uneasy about being naked, especially with children. Parents found themselves arranging and rearranging their standards and priorities for allowing nudity in a variety of idiosyncratic ways.

Sam is divorced. He described himself as very "open," easygoing about sex. Since his marriage broke up he has had a number of intimate relationships with women. Nevertheless, where his seven-year-old daughter, Laura, is concerned, he is quite protective. He said he had always intended to take a natural, matter-of-fact approach toward nudity with Laura, but he was surprised to discover that when she saw him come out of the shower, his natural reaction was to put his hands over his penis. "I'm not sure why I was covering up. I guess the reason is because I don't want her to say, 'What's that, Daddy?' I don't want her to make any big deal of it and attach any special importance to what is a penis and why is it so big and why is it so hairy and why is this and why is that. I guess I just didn't want her to think of it as a peculiarity yet. But my natural tendency is to cover up and therefore make it a curiosity and that's a contradiction." Sam was not sure where all this was coming from. "But my gut reaction when she confronted me naked was to cover myself up abruptly, which subtly communicates to her it's not good for her to see Daddy nude—or nudity. I don't believe that, but yet instinctively it happens. Like I said, I'm not sure why."

Fg7

Mb7

Clarice, also a divorcée with fairly liberal views about sexuality, felt the same "instinct" pushing her toward cautious old-fashioned standards. "I can't say, 'Oh, because I'm liberated I can liberate my son, too,' " she began. "For instance, I was at a house this weekend with my son, and a woman was walking around nude. And I felt uncomfortable about it. And yet, I was thinking, 'Well, why not?' And then my son said to me, 'Oh, Look! look!' And I was saying to myself, 'That's not really good.' But I told him, 'Oh, she's just walking around without any clothes on,' and once I said that, it was nothing. He said, 'Well, why don't *you* do it? And I said, I don't feel comfortable doing it, but other people do. I like to wear clothes.' " She experienced the same reaction when she and her son visited a home which had a hot tub in the backyard and the guests were invited to jump in. "My son got in naked with the men. The women got in with their bathing suits. And he wanted to know why we didn't take off our bathing suits. I really didn't have a good answer. I said, 'Well, I just feel more comfortable with my suit on, but it's okay if you take yours off.' I didn't want to take my bathing suit off in front of men that I didn't know. And I didn't think it was appropriate, as free as this world is, for my son to see his mother taking off her bathing suit in front of some strange men." But she had not fully resolved the issue in her own head, for she added this final comment. "And then I think that maybe that modesty seems ridiculous. But somehow there's an instinct that says it doesn't seem right. It's confusing. So I say, 'I just feel uncomfortable.' "

Many other factors, or combinations of factors, determined just how comfortable parents were with family nudity. There were people who preferred not to let children see them nude because they felt self-conscious about their weight, their under- or-over-development, or lines and marks on their bodies. Mothers who had undergone Caesarean sections did not always want to deal with questions about the scars. Too little heat indoors or unbearable summer weather outside might affect family policies about clothing. Families living in small apartments or houses with limited bathroom facilities, where complete privacy was impossible, grew used to seeing one another nude. Brent, who had grown up in a big house, believed it was easy never to see one's parents naked under those circumstances. "The bathroom door was always shut when my mother was taking a bath, and I remember great embarrassment once when I nearly walked in the bedroom when my mother was naked. She sort of scrambled back into bed." But things were quite different in his own home, a two-bedroom apartment in a big city, particularly after his son was born." You're much closer in an apartment. I was kind of pleased to notice that nudity was never thought about. We walked around with nothing on, got in the bath with him and stuff." Fb11

In some instances, family had established unwritten rules about nudity early on, and these continued to influence the way they behaved. Many families, for instance, had morning routines—going naked from bedroom to kitchen to start breakfast or to the bathroom to brush their teeth—which had become natural and embarrassed no one. On the other hand, if the family had been strict about nudity all along, no one was likely to feel at ease undressed at any time. Probably because of her conservative background, Peggy had never allowed nudity even when the children were very small. "I just didn't think they should, so we never did it. And they've never seen me. I don't think they ever have. Only in my underwear. Even if I'm just going through the house, I always make sure I have panties and bra on. Now they do that, too. For the girls a bra and panties and for the boy a pair of shorts." But Peggy had begun to question some of her policies. "I worry that they might get the wrong impression, that the human body isn't beautiful. I really want them to be very proud of themselves, proud of their bodies." But she thought it might be too late to change the style to which they had all grown accustomed. "We've lived with the privacy so long. I don't know . . . I like my body, sure. You see, that's part of it. I'm trying to fight a little bit of upbringing and I'm saying to myself, 'You like your body, yet you've never shown it to the children in any way. Why? And I don't have any reason." Mb11g7g4

"Anywhere It's Appropriate": Contexts for Nudity

A number of parents felt that that there was nothing wrong with nudity in certain contexts. Attitudes toward nudity in Andrew's home are fairly easygoing. But the message has always been there: Going with-

out clothes is okay in some situations; going without clothes just anywhere is not. "I'm very comfortable," he said. "I walk to the bathroom,
to the shower, I walk around my bedroom. If he walks in I wouldn't
rush around to get dressed. He could see me nude, it wouldn't bother
me. I wouldn't *walk around the house* nude." His son, Kevin, who is
eleven, was allowed the same freedom in his room or coming out of
the bath, "but not just leisurely walking around the house nude." Many
other parents made similar comments. Going nude was acceptable if
family members were in the bedroom or bathroom or in transit from
one to another but unappropriate in the public spaces in the house—
the kitchen, the living room, the playroom.

> If the kid happened to walk downstairs, getting dressed or undressed
> and said, "I need this or that," it wouldn't bother me, but I would
> probably say, "Janey, go up and get dressed, you shouldn't walk
> around the house like that." I wouldn't walk around the house my-
> self like that.

> I try not to overdo it, but if I just happen to have to run for a piece of
> underwear and she's in there, I'm *casual.* No "Oh, don't come in"
> or anything like that. But I don't go out of my way to do it. I mean.
> I'm just not generally the kind of person that walks around nude. So
> it has to be just to get a nightgown or before I put the towel on. I'm
> not like *cooking,* or anything.

Andrew brought up another point, one that was mentioned by
other parents, as well. What parents showed children about when and
where it was acceptable to be without clothing was part of making them
into social human beings. Andrew talked a little about the situations in
which Kevin might be nude with people outside the family. "With his
friends? Well, it depends where. Certainly in a locker room. Yes. Certainly anywhere where it's appropriate. But not in our house. I would
think not in his friend's house. I guess what I'm saying is that at this age
I no longer think it's appropriate for him to walk around nude in front of
his friends. And now, if there are other boys around or other girls, he
makes a point of going to his room or to the bathroom to change."

Though Ezra was more insistent about covering up than Andrew,
he did believe that nudity was as much a social as a sexual issue. If he
restricted the situations in which his son could be undressed, he was
also teaching him about propriety. "I wanted him to know that there
was a proper way to be attired among friends. Social, like he's a host.
If they walked around nude getting ready for bed it would be fine.
Okay? But if they walk around nude in the living room, watching
television, I think it would be unnecessary. I would frown on that. It's
improper. It's not socially functional. I'm really concerned with the
assets he ought to have in society. I want him to know how to behave
properly and be accepted by people."

Fb11

Fg3

Mg7

Fb11

Fb8

There were a number of steps in this socialization process. Children of either sex might go nude with their peers until they were five or six. At play groups, nursery schools, swimming classes, lockers, camps, pajama parties, they undressed in front of one another as a matter of course and nothing much was made of it. But a number of parents thought that by the time they were eight, children had to adapt to "tribal" standards, to learn to be more cautious about nudity with their friends, particularly those of the opposite sex. At that point, in some families, rules about nudity were instituted for situations like sleepovers or swim parties, where it was necessary to change clothes. Most parents found, however, that their children's own sense of comfort, privacy, and appropriateness made them automatically more modest with their friends as they grew older.

> Even now when her friends are over she just doesn't walk around naked. They see her naked in nursery school or sometimes when she's dressing or going in the bathroom. They see her seminaked. I think when she starts first grade I'll say something like "When your friends come over it's more polite, it's courtesy. You stay dressed, you don't take off all your clothes and run about. *They're* dressed." Mg4

> Sometimes she herself has become modest, saying, "Oh, a boy is here, I mustn't let him see my panties." So around the age of six, six-and-a-half, she's gotten a little modesty. With her girlfriends, they do get dressed and I'm not in the room to supervise. They change their whole outfits, so I think they probably strip all the way down. They seem to freely undress. But I find that acceptable. Mg6

> I don't think he ought to walk around nude in front of his friends anymore. I'm seeing that this preadolescent thing of latency is like a myth nowadays. They are very sexual at the age of seven or eight and I'm concerned about overexperimentation and overstimulation. Mb9

Parents might begin to limit their children's nudity in the presence of adults, family friends, and relatives, when they were considerably younger, from as early as the age of three. Toddlers were often allowed to run about nude or in diapers, or to invite guests to watch them splash in the tub or "go" on the potty. Generally, the feeling was that exposed genitalia or a bare bottom was adorable—and asexual—in a baby. But when the child was clearly a little person, could communicate readily with company, nudity seemed asocial and offensive. Sometimes parents were alerted to this because a visitor was uncomfortable when the child had nothing on. "I noticed an increasing reluctance on a man's part to come in, perhaps feeling a little embarrassed," a mother recalled about those times when her daughter still might appear nude among adults. "And that of course helped me to think that maybe it wasn't the most appropriate thing when she was Mg6 six." Other parents discussed similar situations in which a child's nudity was inappropriate:

Fg6

She's already learning you can walk around nude in the family spaces of the house and not in the public spaces of the house—I don't want her to have to deal with people's reactions. Some people are very flaky about that, embarrassed or offended. I'm sure there are times it's going to happen anyway—kid's in the bathroom, kid's changing. On the other hand, to come down for lunch with a houseful of people, some of whom are business acquaintances—it's highly inappropriate for the kid to come in wearing a ribbon.

Mg7

Since she's become let's say six and a half or seven, I have not permitted her to be nude in front of my male or female friends. A little bit more with the female friends is still all right, but not with the male friends. I say, "Oh, well, now we need a little more privacy as we're getting older, so it's best to dress now in the bathroom or the bedroom before we come out. So-and-so will be very pleased to see you in your nightgown."

Parents also restricted nudity in their children outside the home. Most of them said that at a pool or beach, for instance, they seldom allowed even young children to be undressed, except to change from wet to dry clothes. Often the children themselves were uncomfortable about displaying their bodies. But, again, the major reason given was the desire not to offend others and some sense that children must become aware that public nudity was unacceptable.

Paula described the response a group of vacationers had to children playing nude at the beach. "I remember once we went to the

Mg6b3

beach and there were some children who were about five or six who were nude and some of the people were very upset by it. They thought it was *disgusting!* A six-year-old boy and a little girl." Paula herself, well-traveled and fairly sophisticated, did not think the situation was at all disgusting—"Europeans do this more than Americans"—but she did not intend for her own children to undress at the beach for fear that they would provoke a similar reaction. Daniel felt the same way. He was not sure that letting his son swim nude would bother him personally. But he added, "At the beach, convention seems to limit that.

Fb5

Conventional cuss that I am, I think bathing suits serve a function."

Even parents who were very liberal about nudity in the home felt that they had to create different rules when children from less permissive homes came over or their own children played just outside the house. Neither Polly nor her children had ever thought much about being undressed around family members. But she described several instances where she had to change her standards in deference to less tolerant members of her community. Once or twice, when her boys were very little, maybe two or three, they had had little girls come over to play, and the children had seen each other nude. "It's gotten me in trouble a couple of times," Polly confessed. "I know some parents were very upset by that." She also recalled a time when her son Charlie was about three and had gone swimming in the backyard pool without a bathing suit. She had found the scene charming. "He looked so cute I ran out with my camera after him. There I am in the backyard, taking pictures of my kid, you know, front and back views." But the neighbors seemed shocked, and Polly did not intend to allow her permissive policies to provoke any more negative repercussions. "I don't want it to be a problem. I don't want to do anything in my house that's going to upset them when their children are here." <Mb7b5>

Another mother had a similar reaction when her two-and-a-half year old daughter ran naked into the hallway of their apartment building and met some teenagers. "They were very embarrassed by her being nude. I found it very striking that it was just one more thing for us in our family, but that there were other people who might be embarrassed by this kind of situation." George wanted to be sure that his daughter understood the different standards that existed outside of the family. At home he did encourage her to be comfortable with nudity and to be proud of her body, but she had to know that, in the larger world, nudity was sometimes appropriate, sometimes not. "If I were to go to a beach where nudity was acceptable, we'd be nude. We go to public beaches and we wear brief attire, what's acceptable at those beaches. There's a time and a place for everything." <Mg2½> <Fg7>

A Sense of Privacy: When to Cover Up

Sometimes parents began to cover up almost unconsciously, reacting not only to the signals indicating that their children were sexually aware but to the sense that as they became little people in the household, parents needed space for themselves. They wanted the same freedom from scrutiny they expected from adults. Gail and her husband live in a tiny apartment above the office-supply store they operate. So, by necessity, they have had to establish flexible policies around nudity with their daughter, Emma. Gail said they had already begun to stress the need for privacy and was sure that "at a certain age, I can't say when, there will come a point when we will feel less comfortable around her when we are naked, and she'll feel less comfortable because children pick up on these things also. It's part of their becoming a complete, whole, adult person." Gail believed her husband was already a little more restrained now that Emma was four. "I notice now in the <Mg4>

mornings he's usually dressed earlier than he used to be. I think it's a father toward his daughter, and it could be completely subconscious."

Two other mothers of daughters also spoke of preserving their separateness from their children. Florence had not fixed a particular time for her and her child to stop walking around undressed in front of each other. But when nudity began to make her feel uncomfortable,

Mg8   both she and her daughter became more careful about covering up. "I do not play with her when she's nude. When she was a baby and even a few years old I might, but not at eight. Again there is this sense of some privacy about one's body and her getting to be a big girl, so to speak, and one doesn't play the same kind of way. It came so gradually I don't know if I remember when it started to happen. If I walk into the room and she's in the process of getting dressed, I will give her a hug, then tell her to get dressed." Diane made a similar comment.

Mg4   "We've talked a lot about privacy. She used to be able to walk in and out, and I know not everybody does that. I'm not sure I would have done it in advance, if I'd thought about it, but it seemed natural. And now I feel it's natural, but as her sense of herself grows, I'm asserting more of my sense of self, so that she knows I'm a distinct person. Therefore there are certain things I'd like to keep to myself. They pick up what is private and what is public."

A number of parents reported that once they began to limit their own nudity in the household, they saw corresponding restraints on their children's part. Clarice decided to stop going nude in front of her son when he was five. She described the intricate dynamic that occurred between them. At seven, he let her know that he too wanted privacy. In addition, he suddenly seemed embarrassed by the possibility that he might catch a glimpse of her naked and had given her clues that he wanted her to be more aware of how she was dressed when he was

Mb7   around. Clarice believed she was getting a mixed message—"I don't want to see you but I do"—and she felt she had to be sensitive to her son's complex reaction both to her sexuality and to his own. "I must say up until about a year and a half ago I was careless about it. I was more lax than I think I should have been. I would never go into his room without a top on, but I would wear a bathrobe and if my bathrobe opened I wasn't closing it. Or if he came into my room when I had no clothes on I wouldn't run for the towel right away. Whereas now I will say, 'Please wait. I'm not dressed.' I'm very conscious of the issue now, but I think I should have been earlier."

In some families where there were both boys and girls beyond the age of four or five, parents felt it was necessary to restrict nudity in their children. At times, the children themselves seemed uncomfortable when they were nude with each other. They refused to bathe together, rushed to cover up when the opposite-sex sibling was around, made joking comments about each other's genitals. There was also some fear that nudity, especially in girls from the age of eight on, could be provocative not only to the opposite-sex sibling but to the opposite-sex parent.

In many cases, however, it was the children, not the parents, who took the initiative in becoming modest. By the age of six, many children, both boys and girls, began insisting on bathing, dressing, and undressing themselves, and started refusing to be changed in public. By nine, their sense of personal privacy was very strong. On one level, covering up seemed to be a response to signals from society or deep-rooted instincts about what was suitable or "right"; on another, it was clearly part of the separation-from-parents process through which all children go. "I think there's probably an age—they'll probably let you know. They'll get modest," Polly said. One of her sons had, on his own, stopped running around nude at age seven. "I don't know what you do if they don't," she added. "You say, 'Get modest!' " The mother of an eleven-year-old first noticed this shyness in her daughter and her friends when they returned from camp. "It was almost as if they ate the apple," she remarked.

Parents gave different examples of the shifts in attitudes that had occurred in their households. Some who had always had access to a bedroom or bathroom when the child was in there began to encounter closed doors and were told, "Don't come in, I'm dressing." Others said that little girls at about age five often no longer wanted to be seen without their tops on. When parents suddenly intruded on them, both boys and girls might grab for a towel or bend over to cover up.

Robert is the father of a four-year-old girl, Elyse. Since he is divorced from her mother and can see his daughter only at certain times during the week, he spends a great deal of time alone with her. They have developed a special relationship, an easy intimacy that includes walking around nude and taking baths together; Robert has even taken Elyse with him to the men's club where he belongs. He was therefore startled by how shy she became, seemingly overnight. "All of a sudden, this past weekend I tell her to take her clothes off because she has to put her bathrobe on to go to sleep, so she takes her clothes into the bathroom. I say, 'Where are you going?' She goes, 'Well, I don't want to. . . .' I say, 'What! Are you nuts? Give me a break! All of a sudden you're shy about your body?' She went in there, and then she had to take her clothes off for something else and she covered up." He noted another change as well. Elyse had always been aware of *his* body. "When she was two or three, she was fascinated when I went to the bathroom. She used to stand in there and look at it." But now she no longer seemed at ease with him when he was naked. Though Robert did not believe in covering up, he thought he might have to adjust his policy for Elyse's comfort. "I don't know. I may have to start."

Like Robert, many parents who favored a relaxed, "natural" approach to nudity altered their behavior to suit their children's instincts toward reserve in this area. Polly would have liked the option of appearing nude within her home but felt that her sons, aged seven and nine, were growing more shy, and she did not want to make them uncomfortable. "If they're uncomfortable, I begin to feel that way, too." Andrew reported similar changes in his household. "All of a sudden Kevin seemed more self-conscious. I would say at nine-and-a-half, ten. And my wife is getting more conscientious. He's getting to the age now where she shouldn't walk around nude in front of him."

Andrew also talked about the "accidents"—when Kevin walked in upon his parents nude. "If he does walk in there's no big scurry that something's wrong—'Get your clothes on!' " he said. "It's more on his side than in us saying anything on our side. And, somehow, in the last year, he's going to knock first." A mother spoke of how important it was to take the inevitable intrusions in stride, to treat them in a low-key manner. "Sometimes we all walk around nude. I mean my husband tries to control it more than the rest of us, being the lone male in a household of females. But I mean he doesn't scurry behind the door if the kids wander in while he is getting dressed or anything."

Clearly, the more naturally parents acted, the more comfortable everyone was, and the less likely children were to believe they had seen or done something shameful or outrageous.

The most important influences on parents' attitudes toward nudity were the sex and age of the child they were dealing with. Almost no one felt discomfort about being undressed around very young children. Parents gave examples of daily child-care activities in which they were likely to be nude—getting out of bed in the middle of the night to quiet a crying infant, breast-feeding, watching a toddler and using the bathroom at the same time. Roy had been at ease with being nude in front of his daughter since she was nearly newborn. "Do I go around nude in front of my child?" he said. "Absolutely. Very early on, very early on, three, four months old, I was getting up in the middle of the night and I was holding her—I don't sleep in pajamas—and it felt very nice to have this new little body pressing against my belly. And I took a look at that, whether or not that was okay, and I decided it was. Since then, it has been. I look at it every so often and I come up with the same decision."

Most parents, however, began to alter their behavior as the children grew older and no longer regarded parents as extensions of themselves but as *other*, sexual beings. It was difficult to pinpoint the moment at which the change occurred. Many parents believed the "sensitive" age was around five; others saw it as older, anywhere from six on up to nine. In some cases, they took their cues from their children's sudden awareness of the adult body: embarrassment at seeing parents nude, interest—sometimes joking interest—in genitalia and breasts.

> He makes comments. He once went to a Fire Island Beach where he   Fb8
> saw women with their breasts out. He was so excited that he ran up to
> them on the beach and pointed and pointed. I was so embarrassed.
> He really liked it. It was really unusual for him to see a naked woman.

> She's intrigued with nudity, there's no question about that. With   Fg10
> the swimming pool we have in the back, every once in a while I'll go
> back there and she and her girlfriend are running around swimming
> in the pool nude and, of course, they dash for the corner of my eye,
> like that. I think for the most part I'm probably the most immodest
> one in the family and even then I don't think my daughter has seen
> me nude in eight years, and she's ten.

Provocative Nudity

Over and over, parents expressed the fear that once children were aware
of sexuality, adult nudity might be provocative or stimulating to them.
As might be expected, the greatest anxiety was about appearing nude
in front of a child of the opposite sex. Generally speaking, the least
comfortable were mothers with sons. Marilyn no longer thought that
Guy should see her undressed when it was clear that he had grown
curious about her body. "I used to [go nude] more, but I don't any-   Mb7
more because he started to make me feel embarrassed by his comments.
When he would draw attention to the fact that I was nude, well, it
must be that he's ready for me to cover up. He was about seven. When
he was little, since he didn't react, then I didn't feel embarrassed, but
his reactions since have made me feel it's time to cover up." Fran,
whose son was four, had the same feeling—that there would come a
point when his interest in her body would make her feel that undressing in front of him was not quite right. "He comments about my   Mb4
vagina," she said. "He'll just say, 'That's your 'gina, that's your vagina.'
But it's at the back of my mind—when does this become the seductive mother?"

This was one of the areas where parents thought it useful to find
out what child psychologists had to say about the far-reaching effects
of parental nudity on children's emotional health rather than follow
their own inclinations. Until Janet's sons were five, she had been very
easy about nudity with each of them, holding them, taking them into
the shower with her. But she had begun covering up after reading several books that suggested a connection between reading problems in

Mb5   boys and the degree of sexual attachment to their mothers. "I heard of little boys who were so overstimulated by the openly sexual atmosphere in the home that they became troubled and could not learn. I thought that overt stimulation was not necessary for the children, so I stopped doing it when the boys were five years old." Janet was not altogether happy with the change in family style. "One area in which I've always been comfortable—I've always had the feeling that the body is a very normal, natural thing. I think that's the way it should be." But she wanted to do what was best for her sons in the long run. "I wish I could feel comfortable walking around nude in front of my children and not be afraid of imposing restrictions on their emotional development." Other parents—fathers as well as mothers—indicated that they were sensitive to the psychological issues of going nude before children of either sex, whether they had done anything about it as yet, or not.

Fb5   I feel no discomfort about appearing nude in front of my child. We always have. I've been told by a friend who's a Freudian analyst that it's not wise for me to do so. I've never dealt with it. I think we're probably beyond the age, according to this fellow. The shrink says even with me there's a problem. Maybe he's right. I don't know.

Mb10   I've noticed that he's usually the one who comes into the bedroom when I'm getting dressed. I'm very aware he's staring. He's curious. If I were sure of myself, and I'm not, I would say, "Stay and look all you want," but I'm not sure that's right and healthy for him, so I follow my husband's inclination, which is to say, "I'm getting dressed, could I have some privacy, please?" without making a big to-do over it. I mean, if it's just curiosity, maybe he should look; I'm really not sure. I don't want to go out of my way to keep him from getting his peeks, since I want him to see whatever it is he's looking for.

Mg11   My husband still walks around nude in front of her though I've begged him not to, because I recall reading that you shouldn't walk around in front of a child of the opposite sex after the age of ten. If the child was ten, it might stimulate certain feelings or thoughts in the child and it can possibly cause the child to feel guilty—"Gee, I shouldn't be thinking about Daddy in those terms."

    One woman wanted to be sure that she did not appear as provoca-
Mb4   tive to her own son as her husband's mother had been to him. "My husband's not the right person to give me the answer," she said, "because he had a very seductive mother. She still, to this day, will come out of the bathroom with a towel in front of her, when he is there. He just accepted it as the way she is, and figured that was why he had to go into therapy for eleven years."

    As can be seen, like mothers with boys, fathers had concerns about being nude with girls. Ken would have liked to be as comfortable undressed around his daughter as he was with his son. But even when he was moving from the bathroom to the bedroom, he was sure to cover himself with at least a towel, so that she would not see his penis. "With my daughter I do cover myself now. I walk around in underwear. She knows that I have a penis and it gets hard and soft. She says, "Look how big it is!""

Fg8b4

But whereas mothers generally went nude in front of their daughters without thinking about it very much, fathers were sometimes cautious around their sons, aware that they might be frightened or diminished by the sight of adult male genitalia.

It's a theoretical thing. Theoretically it's not good, from everything I know about a child, to see their parents' bodies, because it's sexually provocative. Like my little boy, the other day he saw his father, which he usually doesn't, and he said *[deep, audible breath]*, "You're so BIG." And he begins to compare, if he's so little, my God. . . .

Mb4

I am aware of my son looking at my body occasionally. He is very modest and never wants to be seen without his clothes on. He gets embarrassed because, you know, at the beach or in a public shower or something, I just go in [nude] and the other people all around are all trying to take a shower wearing their swim suits.

Fb11

Breastfeeding

There were several instances in which nudity or partial nudity seemed no problem at all. Women who were breast-feeding generally nursed openly, not only in front of their own children but sometimes before others, as well. In public, a mother might hold the baby under her blouse as she sat in a bus or on a park bench. At home, she might expose her breasts quite freely. Though Peggy reported that her son "got very sick in the alley and threw up" after he first saw a woman breast-feeding, most parents found that their children were fascinated, and they took the opportunity to teach them something more about female anatomy. Until one little girl was told about breast-feeding, she had not been able to figure out the purpose of breasts. She had said to her mother, "Gee, you can't even see your toes. You can't even see your vagina." It was precisely this attitude that a mother hoped to counteract by allowing her six-year-old daughter to watch her nurse a younger sibling. "I wanted her to know that your breasts are not there just to sit up there. They're for use and it's a good purpose." She continued wryly, "But if you don't want to nurse, then they are for men's fun and games, for women maybe to prop their blouses up. I don't know."

Mb6

Mg7

Mg6

Mg7 Most children personalized the information they received in some way. They all were curious about whether they had been nursed as infants, and mothers often had to explain why a person might choose one feeding method over another. Alice's daughter, Eleanor, saw someone nursing her baby in the ladies' room of a department store and asked, "Why doesn't she use the bottle?" Alice gave her several possible reasons. "Well, sometimes people don't want to use bottles because they cost money, they have to carry them, and the milk goes sour. This way it's always ready. Maybe the mommy likes the baby sucking her titties." With all those advantages, had Elly been nursed as an infant? "No," Alice told her, "I started you on a bottle, so your daddy could help your mommy feed you, and I just thought it would be easier for me and easier for your daddy."

Mg4 There were children who liked to watch the milk squirt from the nipple, or who were curious about how it was different from milk in a container. Children also had questions about where the milk came from and why it was not always there. A four-year-old wanted to suck just as she had when she was a baby. "When you were older, you were able to eat and drink other food." her mother said. "My body stopped producing the milk. So, first of all, it's ridiculous. It's only meant for babies; it's to give them strength. But you have to eat solid food and the breasts are not ready, for that big a child cannot nurse on its mother." Some parents talked about the production of milk as one of the changes that takes place in a mommy's body when she's pregnant. One six-year-old who had heard all about how having a baby stimulates the flow of breast milk applied the knowledge in a special way when her aunt and

Mg6 uncle adopted a baby. "She has to drink from a bottle," she announced to all her little friends. "She's adopted."

Underwear

Fb11 People also had few reservations about the partial nudity associated with going about in underwear. For some, underwear was the comfortable, at-home costume when the family was together. That was especially true of fathers, who did not necessarily see the difference between undershorts and walking shorts. "It's a joke in my house that I walk around in my underwear and my wife runs around pulling down all the blinds as I walk from room to room," a father said. "Literally, I've been down in the den when guests are coming to the house and she's got to run and say, 'Get his bathrobe.' My son walks around also in his underwear. No problem." Parents often reported that children did not even seem aware that underwear was actually a state of undress.

Ethel said that when they were getting ready for the day, her family was comfortable when "they have their bottoms on, and I have maybe panties or stockings with no bra or something like that." Rosaline believed her daughter noticed underwear only because it was a handicap in the race the two of them had each morning to get dressed. "She knows I have to put on a bra and that takes longer than what she has to put on. She seems to be glad that I have this other garment that she does not have. She always wins the race." Mg14b12b10 Mg7

Though a number of mothers wore just a bra and panties in the house, sometimes in order not to soil or crease the clothes they intended to wear when they went out, a few felt restrained in front of their sons. In general, they were more conscious about their appearance than their husbands, and they feared that underwear could be as provocative as nudity.

> When I'm slim enough *[laughs]*. It's a matter of vanity, almost. But I guess at a certain point I think that walking around in underwear, if it's really sexy underwear, can be even more provocative in a way to him than walking around nude. I pretty much wear a robe. I sit in my nightgown, but in general that's as far as it goes. Mb9

> The type of undergarments I wear aren't cotton, triple-woven, heavy-duty underpants, Carter's Spankypants. They're as seductive or more than the nude body. And the same thing with the bras when I wear a bra. That seems to be more acceptable than nudity because they've seen me in a bathing suit, which is almost the same. But no, he isn't totally comfortable. In the last year or so he's become much more conscious. Mb11

Bathroom Behavior: The Need for Peace and Quiet

A surprising number of households had an official "open door" policy that permitted children to walk freely in and out of the bathroom no matter what the parent was doing—showering, bathing, urinating, defecating. This was particularly true when children were young, constantly needing attention and fearful of being alone. Lesley has a four-year-old son who is now at that "clinging" stage. "If he wants to come in I don't let him scream on the outside of the door. Children always follow you, especially at this age. They don't leave you alone. He has fears. I say that I'd rather be alone. Depending on how frightened he is of the monsters, he will either leave or not." Mb4

With older children, many parents did try to shift to a "closed door" policy, but in practice it seldom worked. Sometimes the pressures of day-to-day family living—everyone trying to get out of the house at the same time in the morning—made it necessary for parents Mb5 and children to share the bathroom. "If my son has to get his teeth brushed or go to school and someone is sitting on the toilet, that's the way it is," one mother said. Generally, too, especially in homes which had only one bathroom, children had come to regard it as a public area— "Grand Central Station," one mother called it—a storage room for a variety of personal items, a home for the cat, a place to chat. Even as they grow older they seemed to fail to recognize those moments when parents might want to be inaccessible and they asked to be let in, sometimes because they wanted to use the toilet or sink themselves, sometimes because they had a question that needed answering "right now."

Mg3　　　　Off limits. That's my policy, but it never works. I mean, she's in the other room and she's banging on the door, "Mommy, I have to come in, I have to come in." So it's easier to let her in than listening to her banging on the door.

Mg11b8　　The door's always closed, but it's not locked, and although I say, "This is private!" there's usually a face that comes in. They think that I'm a captured person, which I am, and I have to listen. I say I want peace, but there they are. They can't wait.

A number of parents would have liked to stop children from walking in on them when they were in the bathroom. In a few cases they were shy about being seen, particularly by a child of the opposite sex. But, overall, their concerns in this area had little to do with nudity or sexuality. The reason almost everyone gave was, again, privacy—a simple need for peace and quiet, and a place to be alone—rather than any shame connected with the body and its functions. One mother, beleaguered by multiple responsibilities, described her bathroom as her Mb10 sanctuary. "I'm trying to develop my career, and at one point I was working two jobs, all the hectic things that are going around. And I needed the space and the bathroom is the only place you can go to lock yourself in, you know? And I think that, more than anything else, kept me from [letting my kids come in the bathroom with me]. Basically, I need this time to myself, just to sit and relax and collect myself."

Parents did try to maintain this solitude in different ways. They locked the door, insisted that children knock first, or told them outright to go away. Once in a while, when children had begun to exhibit signs of modesty themselves, they appealed to *their* sense of privacy— "You like the door shut when you're in there; so does Daddy." These methods met with varying degrees of success. Though children might respect the parents' wishes, sometimes their own demands were too urgent or they were so accustomed to free access to the bathroom that they came in anyway.

What usually occurs is if I am in the bathroom and the door is open, I'll close the door and not make a big deal of it. If she persists, I will say that I want to be alone or my wife will deal with it. In fact, I've heard her say, "Daddy would like to be alone in the bathroom." It's a sense of privacy, not that it is wrong or ugly.

Fg3

I close the door but it doesn't make any difference. I don't lock it unless I have other kids in the house—I'd have *them* in there too. I mean, closing the door is *nothing*. You might as well take the door off its hinges.

Mb7

Bathing, Urinating, Defecating

To some extent, how adamant the parent was about enforcing bath-room policy depended on what he or she was doing in the bathroom—bathing, urinating, or defecating. Most parents were not at all uneasy about having children of any age enter the bathroom while they were in the tub or shower. Nudity in these instances did not seem to be a problem. Parents were willing to give up their privacy as long as the child did not interfere with the other comforts associated with bathing.

She can come in when I'm showering—open door policy. It has to be. Otherwise the bathroom is a swamp.

Fg6

They do come in. They better close that door when I'm showering because if that hot air goes out I could kill.

Mg11b8

Not unexpectedly, privacy was a far greater issue when children wanted to enter the bathroom while the parent was on the toilet. As with nudity, parents did not want children to regard bodily functions as evil or dirty, but their own comfort was important. Many people, even fathers of girls, said they did not mind urinating but felt awkward defecating in front of children. If they had stomach cramps, they did not like to be disturbed, and they were embarrassed by the unpleasant odors. But "going to the bathroom" was also a code term in many house-holds for "Do Not Disturb," and sometimes defecating just meant get-ting time for oneself.

I definitely want some privacy. I think more so when I'm defecating than when I'm urinating. So I say, "Susan, you can't come in now." She sees I go into the bathroom with a book or magazine and then I probably don't want to be disturbed.

Fg3

If my son comes in while I'm urinating I certainly think nothing of it. Defecating is something else. I think that's very private. I guess I look terrible when I'm grunting and crunched up.

Fb11

It was, of course, often impossible to sit on the toilet, tend to a child, and preserve one's privacy at the same time. But one mother
Mb4   offered at least a partial solution to the problem: "I never go into the bathroom without a big, long robe because I'm sure I'm going to have company after a while."

Tampons/Menstruation

Mothers were especially uncomfortable about having children intrude upon them when they were changing a tampon. For many it was. a
Mb9   more personal activity than urinating or defecating. "When you're menstruating, you're taking care of *yourself*," one mother said em-
Mb11b9 phatically. Marilyn spoke of how embarrassed she would be using a tampon if her two sons were watching. "I don't think my husband's around, either, when I'm putting on a Tampax. I just think it's a private moment for a person and I don't care to share it with anyone." In fact, a number of women who did not otherwise shut the door when they were in the bathroom locked it when they were menstruating. Some were more strict about the knock-first rule at those times, telling children peremptorily to please wait until they were finished. In addition to privacy, there were other concerns around the issue. Mothers were afraid that children would be alarmed by the sight of blood. Such instances had occurred in a few households. Often, when the child had walked in on the mother changing a tampon, he or she was
Mb3   afraid something was wrong and had to be reassured that "Mommy was not hurt." The mother of a three-year-old had this experience. "My son came in once while I was taking out a tampon and he saw all the blood and he became upset. He thought something was wrong with me and I was bleeding, and I did say to him that it's something that happens to women once a month and I'm not cut and nothing's wrong. But I hope that it wasn't traumatic for him. Children that age are not tremendously logical nor do they remember things exactly the way you tell them. After the explanation, he seemed calmer."

Menstruation was also a topic that most parents left out of early sexual discussions with their children. Since it was possible to explain conception and birth without referring to menstruation, and children did not know enough to ask, parents did not generally introduce it. Many felt that the specifics were too complex and possibly frightening for young children to handle, and they postponed talking about the subject until their boys were about ten or eleven and their girls were about eight or nine, approaching menstruation themselves.

Some women were reluctant to explain the mechanics of insertion of tampons, expecially to little boys. They felt that any description of how a tampon is used would provide their children with a more graphic picture of female anatomy than they were comfortable drawing. For this reason it was often easiest to store sanitary products at the backs of closets, where children were unlikely to discover them and ask embarrassing questions. But children, of course, often employed that uncanny radar which ferreted out just what their mothers do not want them to see. Sometimes explanations were demanded much sooner than mothers expected because children had found the tampons or pads. Quite a few felt the best way to deal with the situation was to say that these were things that women use and pray that their children would ask no further questions. Frequently this response was sufficient, though there were children who on their own came up with ingenious interpretations of how these strange objects are used. One mother found her five-year-old son trying to figure out which "crevice" in his own body a tampon fitted into. Sandy's son, at three or four, was certain that tampons were cigarettes. "He once came out of the bathroom with one in his mouth." Mb3

The whole topic had still other extraordinarily strong—often negative—emotional associations for women. Many of them thought of menstruation as a liability in their lives. It meant cramps, weepiness, nervousness, interrupting normal routines. "I mean, it's something I go through, but I don't find it a joyful experience," one mother said. "I'm not happy once a month, when it comes, except that it means I know I'm not pregnant." Mg11

For some women, like Cassandra and Louise, the onset of menstruation had been a terrible experience. Their mothers had told them nothing, and when they got their first periods they were made to believe that somehow it was shameful or dirty. Though their own views had become far more enlightened, it was hard to shake those early feelings. These mothers hoped the experience would be better for their own daughters, but several of them found that no matter how well prepared girls were, the traumas of the last generation seemed to persist in this one. Karen noted that her eleven-year-old daughter didn't "seem to be in a particular hurry for her first period. Her friend, who had just gotten it, had "spent the whole night in the bathroom, sobbing hysterically, 'What do I need this for?' " Karen believed the reaction was unhealthy, a vestigial sense that menstruation was "the curse." But she wondered if the reluctance she saw in her daughter and her friend about beginning menstruation was also a desire to hold onto childhood a little longer. "The kid wants to be a kid." Peggy's older daughter, Elizabeth, at ten, was the first girl in her class to get her period. "That was one of the hardest times I ever had," Peggy said. "She was very ashamed of having gotten her period and it was a case of hiding—I almost freaked out myself—if blood got on her panties, she wouldn't Mg11

Mb15g13g11

wash them out, she'd put them in the hamper with the rest of the wash. It was just, anything concerned about it she wanted to hide." Like Karen, Peggy thought the adjustment to this new phase of growing up took time, but she did notice that things improved when other girls in the class began to menstruate and they all could chat, commiserate, share the experience. Communicating woman-to-woman was important for girls at this stage. Peggy believed that her younger daughter, Andrea, also one of the first among her friends to menstruate, had an easier time because she could talk with her older sister.

Just about everyone agreed that the best way to explain menstruation, no matter the age and sex of the child, was to emphasize its positive connection with health and potential pregnancy. Even if children did not "get" all the details, it was important for them to realize that blood does not mean loss and destruction but nourishment and fertility. Girls also needed reassurance that the experience was normal—something that all women share.

Mb5　　　I found it very complex for him. I tried to explain it—that this is what catches the lining, that keeps the baby, the lining of the womb that feeds the baby, and [when] there's no baby the body doesn't need the lining. It makes a new one each time, so it's nice and fresh, and the body's throwing this one away because it wasn't used. In fact, those are almost my exact words.

Mg10g6　　It seems like whenever I'm changing a Kotex or Tampax they come into the bathroom right at that moment. I've never locked the bathroom door whenever I was in there doing anything, so they would look and say, 'What are you sticking that into?' and 'Yuk, why does it have blood all over it?' So I explained that when the woman is not pregnant and the egg has not been fertilized, the body has been kind of like collecting and getting ready to be pregnant, and when it's not, each month you get this discharge and the blood comes off the tissues.

Several parents also wanted children to be aware that the period Mg11b10　could be accompanied by emotional irritability. "I tend to be very high-strung when I'm menstruating," Karen said, "so I tell them that I'm menstruating so that they know that if I'm crazy that may be the reason for it." Children were then expected to be more sensitive to their mothers, sisters, cousins, and friends at those times of the month. Andrew and Peggy made a point of letting their sons know that sometimes girls were uncomfortable during menstrual periods:

Fb11　　　We explained that when a girl reached a certain age the egg starts coming down all by itself and once a month they have a period, meaning the egg wasn't fertilized by a sperm and has to go somewhere, so it gets ejected by the body and that's the period. And girls don't feel well at that point in time. At the beginning it's harder for them and you have to understand. They usually don't go swimming, you know, and you have to understand there are differences between boys and girls.

I remember I made a point of going and talking to him again once the girls had both started menstruation, telling him—you know, sometimes in the month we're up, sometimes we're down. I think what brought it on was that they were arguing—one of the girls didn't feel too good and all she wanted to do was sleep and they were going back and forth. And I told him, your sister, she's having her period, and you have to be a little nicer. It wouldn't hurt for you to to do this—and, you know, not that I make a big thing out of it, because I try to make the girls feel as if, you know, life goes on.

Mb15g13g11

Body Odors

Parents were also asked to talk about body odors—about their general attitudes toward the odors themselves and towards discussing them within the family. Only a few parents reported that they ever discussed genital or menstrual odors. As a rule, most parents merely indicated briefly, even curtly, that such odors were not spoken of at all. On the other hand, most households took a matter-of-fact approach to breath, foot, and underarm odors, those which perhaps have been demystified to the greatest degree by popular comedy and by television and print advertising. Almost all parents reported being equally comfortable discussing flatulence and bathroom odors with their children; flatulence in particular was evidently a rich source of family humor, even in relatively "conservative" homes.

Here are some representative comments on the body odors which were frequently discussed.

Breath Odors
He didn't know what bad breath was and I explained to him that your mouth can smell bad. He didn't want to brush his teeth and at one point I really was shocked to notice that he had bad breath. God, I thought, what will the teacher think?

Mb4

Oh yeah, we've discussed that. It smells like cheese is growing in there. We've discussed that not in terms of sexuality per se but in terms of cleanliness or hygiene.

Fg6

Underarm Odors
When she washes she makes sure she washes herself. Her father showed her how to do the whole big thing so she likes to wash herself the way Daddy does. And I bought her a little make-up toy

Mg3

thing— they have all these things—and she knows she likes to powder underneath the arms so she'll smell nice.

Fg6

She asked me why I use deodorant and she doesn't. I'm not too hot
on physiology but I probably said it was a side effect of having hair
under your armpit that traps perspiration and then you get fungus.
She doesn't have to worry about that because she doesn't have hair
under her arms yet.

Mg11b8

My daughter sees I use underarm deodorant and her father does too.
But so far, we talk about cleaning their bodies, so they won't smell.
My son tells me that he can't stand this kid in school because he
smells. We talk about washing. We don't mention anything specifically except that people who are dirty smell.

Foot Odors

Fg3

We always carry on about that. She says "Smell my feet!" and I say,
"No, not your stinky feet!"

Mg7

She likes her feet odors. I mean, she'll take off her socks and smell
her socks *[laughs]*. She says, "Boy, it really *smells!*"

Mb8

Yes, you could die. I mean we do it with sneakers. My son wears a
pair of socks until they stand by themselves and walk, and we have
to pull them off his feet. So we do talk about the terrible odor.

Bathroom Odors: Urine and Feces

Mg7

If a few drops of urine have come on her panties she might say, "Oh,
I'll have to get rid of these panties." And I say, "Well we can just
wash them out." That happens very rarely anyway. She's very fas-
tidious. We do talk about bowel-movement odors. She'll say "Oh,
Mommy, that smells," in reference to my own bowel movement.
about her own she hasn't made a reference *[laughs]*.

Mb10g11

Sometimes they have little accidents. Much of it had to do with
shyness not wanting to ask in school to go to the bathroom so at
three o'clock they come tearing through the door but don't make it.
So I'll say, "Go and change your underwear because it'll smell. With
bowel movements there's no problem with my daughter. She's clean.
There's never a trace of anything on her panties whereas her brother
is different. We talk a lot with him because it's all over everything. I
hold up his underwear—"How would you like to wash these?" It
smells, yeah. Oh my God. We're not subtle *[much laughter]*. In fact I
went in yesterday and I almost keeled over.

Flatulence Odor

Mb7b4

The kids get really gassy, depending on what they ate. My husband
usually says "Who did that?" And Georgie always says it's Frankie
and Frankie says it's me or Georgie. He thinks it's funny.

Both of us have at times passed gas. "Oh, Mommy, you made a   Mg7
fart!" She doesn't readily admit that she does it herself, which hap-
pens occasionally. But when the cat does it, we *all* comment. She
says, "You made a smelly fart, Mittens. Oh, Mittens smells, get her
away from me!" It's a joke but like with a little disdain. But I think
if we can accept it or kid around about it with the cat then we can
accept it more with ourselves.

Whatever the kid joke is—"You did it, you did it!" But basically kid   Fb8
stuff and we tend to ignore it as much as possible when it happens at
the table. We'll tell him to cut it out or go elsewhere. It's just annoying. We tell him you can go up to your room and do that up in
your room. Say all those silly things up in your room but down here
it's annoying and you're bothering us and so on.

Flatulence is always good. That's a good one. "Who did it?" Right?   Mg11b8
But we talk about it. We light matches, we try not to put too much
fluorocarbons into the air, so we try for matches. There is a smell.

We joke about that. And it happens. My husband jokes, "Here comes   Mg11
an SBD—"Silent But Deadly!" *[laughter]*. This is the way educated
people talk.

I call her sometimes the anesthetist, also known as a gas passer.   Fg11

4

Touch/

Don't

Touch

Almost all parents in the study were enthusiastic and positive about the value of touching—as a special form of communication; a way of expressing love, warmth, and trust; a method of reassuring children and helping to shape healthy, confident personalities.

It was clear, however, that many more complex sets of attitudes and standards coexisted with this overall sense of approval. How much touching of certain parts of the body was appropriate between parent and child? How could one set limits—on one's own behavior as well as that of one's children—without inhibiting that flow of trust and affection that was deemed so valuable and important? Where did feelings of sensuous warmth, pleasure, and beneficial intimacy cross some invisible barrier and become erotic and potentially destructive? How did affectionate touching differ from or blend with the types of impersonally necessary physical contact that are involved in so many daily routines of parenting? In what ways did policies around touching have to be altered as the child grew older?

Parents were also concerned about the kinds of touching that went on between their children and outsiders. Obviously, limitations had to be set on physical contact during play that could become dangerous or hurtful. Sometimes, too, the touching children engaged in with their friends was exploratory, a way of satisfying sexual curiosity. Parents did not always know whether to intrude when they became aware of this behavior or accept it as a normal part of growing up. And though no one had any doubts about putting an immediate stop to any kind of sexual touching between their children and older children or adults, it was unlikely that such contact would take place when a parent was present. Therefore, children somehow had to be taught to distinguish on their own between friendly relating and inappropriate approaches from others, warned away from strangers, and admonished to report incidents that made them uneasy. Much as parents wanted their children to be comfortable with touching, it was necessary to help them recognize its negative aspects, as well.

Attitudes Toward Touching

"I'm Not A Kissy Mommy"

A small group of parents, predominantly mothers, characterized themselves as "non-touchers." These parents were conflicted. They were uncomfortable touching their children but admitted feelings of guilt or inadequacy on this score.

Rachel was one such mother. She stated firmly that she did not take pleasure in various types of touching behavior—the types that most other parents seemed to find gratifying aspects of parenting. And according to Rachel, her husband shared her style of behavior. "We are not a touching family," she said. "We are pretty circumspect people." Gestures of physical affection among all of Rachel's family members—between husband and wife and between parents and children—were limited to situations when such gestures were socially unavoidable. "With other people where this public kissing is expected, my husband and I participate," she said, and added, "I am sure that when my children visit grandparents they would give the expected kiss or hug, but within the family circle there is hardly anything."

Rachel made it clear that she was not entirely happy with her family's extremely reserved style. She confessed to some doubts, some regrets, even guilt, as she observed her children growing up in an atmosphere that was lacking in overt spontaneous demonstrations of physical affection. "Although in some ways I am comfortable with the way my family operates, in some ways I feel guilty about it. We aren't demonstrative. I think, as a result, the kids just seem to sense it. Although Brad is still very affectionate, my other children are really not.

I think with the older children, particularly my daughter—she *feels* more than me. She has almost expressed it verbally from time to time, that she would like us to be more obviously affectionate. I think she has experienced that kind of hugging, kissing atmosphere in a group she is active with in school. She loves it and it is almost as if she is starved for affection. In that regard I think we have made a mistake. Even though it doesn't bother *us*, we probably should not have fostered this kind of non-touching atmosphere on the children."

Gina echoed Rachel's regret and guilt when she described her feelings of uncertainty where spontaneous, warm physical contact with her children was concerned. She was able to recall those moments of uncomplicated pleasure she took in cuddling her son when he was little—"he was just all lovely skin, he was just something to be loved and adored"—but she had begun to pull back once he was past toddlerhood. Now that her son was approaching puberty, Gina realized she had set even greater limitations on the types of touching allowed between them. "It's interesting," she said, "I'm getting the gist in my own mind, it's sort of crystallizing. As long as it [touching] could be medicinal or in some way helpful—because of either a crisis or an emergency—it's okay. But when it comes to just perhaps enjoying the stroking—I mean, it could be a close thing. I'm seeing it now. Perhaps it might be some sexuality involved that I haven't realized before."

Her situation was, perhaps, exacerbated by the fact that she did not perceive this constraint as a general part of her whole family's lifestyle, but rather as an aberration she alone exhibited. She saw her reserve as a deficiency, almost a character flaw. "My husband is more physical, more demonstrative, than I am," she said. "How much kissing goes on between me and the children? I would say not very much. I kiss all of them good-bye in the morning and all of them goodnight. That's the kissing I do. If I'm particularly pleased or happy with something that's happened I'll kiss them, but I'm not a kissy mommy." She stopped for a moment, and then continued in a soft, somewhat embarrassed tone. "I've always seen myself as having a problem physically. I've thought myself rather undemonstrative physically, particularly with my boys, and that bothers me. I guess I put more blame on me—I'm still the adult and still set the pace and I don't do anything about changing it. I see a sort of contradiction in myself. I see myself as being fairly liberal and open with my children. I'm not big on 'no's' and what they can't do. And yet I find myself to be somewhat rigid, physically rigid."

"I Let Him Know How Delicious He Is"

As has been noted elsewhere, parents generally believed that their early experiences with sexuality in the home determined the degree of comfort they brought to their intimate relationships as adults. Non-touchers were concerned that their children might be harmed or stunted by not being exposed to the same amounts of beneficial contact that they believed other children were receiving as a matter of course. One group of parents who had been raised in non-touching households, where displays of physical affection had been frowned upon, were consciously attempting to avoid this rigidity with their children.

When it came to *talking* about sex with her child, Fran had many of the fears and inhibitions instilled in her by a rigid sexual upbringing. But she felt easy about *touching* her small son's body and spoke quite frankly about the pleasure she derived from their little exchanges of affection. "I love to kiss the back of his neck," she said. "I think it's a   Mb4
great place. It's soft and it's nice." Like many parents, Fran also admitted to feelings of nostalgia and regret that as her son grew older—he is four now—he needed less help from her and began to set his own limits on the kinds of physical contact he would accept. "I used to kiss him on the stomach more. I said, 'You used to let me kiss you on the stomach.' He used to *ask* me to kiss him there. Well, now he's limited it to where he wants me to kiss him. He has told me, 'You are allowed to kiss my nose and my cheeks and that's all.' I said, 'Come on, I can kiss any part of your body, you're my little boy.' And he says, 'But Mommy, it's my body.' And what can I say?" She shrugged and smiled rather sadly. "He has a sense of *his* body now. He should have that integrity." She added, "I certainly am not going to stop kissing his neck, but to some extent I can't argue with that."

Judy grew up in a family similar to Fran's. She said, "I was raised   Mb5
in a household where no one saw anybody in anything less than full regalia. If my father saw me in a bra and half-slip, it was a scandal!—so that I would really so much like to be free and natural and comfortable about touching." Judy's touching behavior with her five-year-old son was remarkably more relaxed than the one she had grown up with. Her face softened at one point, as she mentioned the kind of special moment with her son that she cherished. "I've been turned on by holding him," she said rather shyly. "He'll sit on my lap, he'll be half-asleep, I'll be reading to him, or he'll be upset about something. I'll read to him and he'll lie next to me and I'll put my arm around him. It's very warm."

However, like many other topics discussed in this study, the way people behaved around the issue of touching was idiosyncratic, the product of a variety of influences. Many of the parents who displayed relaxed and open attitudes toward physical contact, not unexpectedly, came from families where such attitudes were the norm. Richard, for instance, described his parents' low-key response when they discovered him as a child experimentally touching a little friend's genitals. He felt that this approach had been a healthy one and had helped him develop good attitudes toward his own body and sexuality, as well as his children's. "I got the impression from my parents that that wasn't a   Fg8b4 *horrible, terrible* thing to do. One friend's mother went berserk, went crazy! I got the impression that *that* was an abnormal reaction. My parents did not convey the message to me that I was evil, rotten, would disintegrate in hell for what I did. I never felt guilty about it." Touching had become an important way of communicating love to his son, four, and his daughter, eight. "You absolutely need that physical contact," he said, with a smile. "I would urge every parent to get down on the floor and bite and touch and roll around with that child! Let *all* people that you love or that you like—physically, let them know.

Mg17b13b6

But the reserve both Rachel and her husband, Tony, showed about touching with their children represented still other reactions. Whereas Rachel's family had allowed little affectionate interchange— "We didn't kiss or hug except on state occasions like when someone was going on a long trip"—Tony came from the opposite kind of family. Rachel said, "Tony's mother is a clinging, overly affectionate type who, as soon as she sees him, pounces on him—he was an only child—and smothers him with affection. He hated it, or so he professes, so he was very glad to find someone willing not to."

Fg1

The majority of parents for whom touching in all its forms—hugging, holding, picking up, fondling—was vital agreed that loving physical contact helped to ensure the development of secure responsive individuals. This point of view was expressed by Martin, a first-time father at thirty-six. Now a carpenter and cabinetmaker in a West Coast city, he spent a year and a half as an adviser in Vietnam in the mid-Sixties, and traced some of his attitudes toward touching back to that experience. "The thing I began to notice about Vietnamese kids was that you never saw one crying," he said. "I mean, just as soon as any kid started to cry, somebody picked him up. Sometimes it was his mother, but it could even be just an older kid, a brother or sister. You know, a five-year-old would pick up a three-year-old, a three-year-old would pick up a one-year-old. And the kids showed it, whatever else you wanted to say. Kids I saw, they smiled a lot, they seemed happy. It was a good lesson. Now I pick up own daughter every chance I get. My wife does, too. It's our policy. The minute she cries, somebody picks her up and holds her. We want her to have that secure feeling. Especially when she's too little to explain things to. That's all she knows right now—how it *feels*."

Mb3

Carla, an ardent feminist, unionist and civil-rights activist, is another product of the Sixties. She spoke powerfully, and with infectious humor and delight of the way she has used physical contact to give her three-year-old son an overall glow of security and self-confidence. "I let him know how delicious he is, as much as possible, all the time," she said. "I nuzzle him and tell him he's gorgeous and fondle him all over, all over. I felt—especially when I was dealing with a little baby— that you communicate attitudes through your body and through your

face and your reactions, not only through words. And it's very important for a kid to have a real sense of how delicious his body is." Carla
was able to discuss frankly, as well, the kinds of situations in which
many parents may find it difficult to maintain *loving* physical contact—
those necessary, not always pleasant "service" tasks of parenting—
wiping after toileting, changing diapers, and so on. "I've seen parents,
for example, when they're cleaning off their kid's genitals after they've
defecated or something and they can't help themselves. They go
'Uuuuueeegh!' And that can't help but communicate itself to the kid.
I have made a real effort to smile and play and *not* go 'Eeugh!' or hold
·my nose, just so the kid doesn't have a sense that that's a dirty area or
that that part of the body isn't as delicious as the rest of the kid." Many
other parents, from a diversity of backgrounds, corroborated Carla's
and Martin's ideas.

> Out of all three of my children, Keith was the baby, the one that
> was more fondled. Somebody was *always* picking him up. And as he
> grew, it seemed like that rubbed off on him. He has always been a
> *very* affectionate child.

Mb3

> I try to make an effort to hug her and to touch her as much as possible.
> She can be shy and withdrawn often, especially in crowds, and when
> I see those moments when she sort of—she's sort of off out there in
> space—I hug her. And there are times I will hold her hand as we
> walk and talk or something like that.

Fg9

Since Alice's husband has returned to school, she has become the
family breadwinner, the manager of a small catering business. That
means that her daughter, Cara, seven-and-a-half, has to be left with a
babysitter several times a week. Alice believed, however, that Cara
was not at all upset by the situation because she was so sure of her
parents' affection. "Touching for Cara is for affection, for loving, for
feeling wanted and needed and protected. COMFORT." This comment seemed to sum up the way the majority of the parents in this
study viewed touching as it related to their children's development.
Touching was a vital factor in good relationships between parent and
child. Children who were touched warmly and often were children who
felt safe, and confident that their parents loved them.

Mg7

Many parents described with equal warmth and eloquence the
benefits *they* derived from close physical contact with their children.
The experiences they cherished tended to be sensuous rather than
sensual, and involved feelings of increased intimacy and emotional well-
being that often suprised them in the midst of the most mundane of
daily parenting routines. Bedtime and bathtime rituals—helping a small
child into nightclothes, snuggling together while the parent read a story
or toweled the child's clean pink skin—were mentioned by many par-

ents as times when they felt especially close to their children, able to take uncomplicated animal pleasure in the physical contact that was shared.

Fg8b4

One father spoke of the simple physical delight he took in touching his children. "I love it, playing with Noah," he said enthusiastically. "He's soft, cute, full of down all over his body. He's going to be a very hairy person. He's already got hair all over him." He laughed at this point and explained, "he takes after his mother's side of the family. My side is not particularly hairy. *I'm* not particulary hairy, and so he's a very soft thing to touch. And my daughter, I still bathe her. I still wrestle with her when she's nude. I do a lot of biting of tushies. There are no sexual overtones. It's just warm feeling. Warmth. Totally."

Mg8g5

Mary was raised in a traditional, close-knit Polish Catholic home. Her conservative background made it uncomfortable for her to discuss many sexual topics. Nevertheless, she talked easily and enthusiastically about the pleasure she felt when her daughter touched her. "I mean, my daughter herself does a lot touching. Just because she's five years old and that's her *way* of communicating, her touching takes the full gamut," she added with a laugh, "from socking somebody to really hugging them and kissing them. It's part of her life. But there's a lot of warmth. And much more is said in the feelings that transpire between us than I think is in talking." "It's mainly affectionate touching," she continued. "Like if she's watching TV and I'm reading the newspaper and laying on the bed, I rub her back. This sometimes happens after school." But she added softly, making an awkward but expressive little gesture with one hand, "She is very, like, *squeezable*, and chunky, so you will just—kind of chunky hands that are. . . ." Her voice trailed off in embarrassment for a moment or two, but then she continued, "And *she* really likes to be hugged and cuddled, too. And there's a kind of closeness before she goes to bed. It's just very nice for a parent."

"I Don't Want To Be Turned on by My Own Kid"

Parents were asked if they had encountered situations in which their pleasurable touching experiences with children had gone beyond the merely sensuous to become sexually stimulating. Mothers and fathers tended to respond quite differently to inquiries on this rather sensitive and personal subject.

Mothers, as a rule, were much more comfortable confronting the sensual aspects of physical contact with their children than were fathers. They did not seem threatened or disturbed by the idea that it might be possible to be aroused or stimulated by such contact, and usually gave frank well-considered answers to questions on this aspect of their behavior. Judy, for instance, when asked if she had ever been aroused as well as emotionally gratified by close physical contact with her son, replied without hesitation. "I've been aware of that," she said. "I wouldn't be surprised. I've been aware of sexual feelings. It wouldn't take much to push over the line." But she added, "Maybe some of these feelings *are* sexual, but it's hard for me to separate the tremendous loving warm feelings I have now. I look at him and cry. I took at him and my heart swells and some of that may be sexual. It's hard to separate." Judy, like other mothers, seemed to feel at ease with the ambiguity of her feelings, to the point that some degree of sensual response was simply taken as natural. "I guess I think of him partially as a child and partially as such a loving extension that I don't think of discomfort in those [sexual–sensual] terms. I'm not uncomfortable with anything in a physical way." Mb5

Life has not always been easy for Ethel, a black woman who has held down a job, returned to school, and raised three children all on her own. But her situation has also helped create a special closeness between her and her family, and she admitted readily and cheerfully to a certain sexual quality in her feelings for her sons, now twelve and ten. "Well, I'll tell you," she began with a deep chuckle, "My son, I'm always teasing, the middle son. He has a big penis. And I say, 'When you get to be fourteen. . . .' She laughed again. "I guess I think, 'Okay, if this was somebody that I could really get involved with. . . . Boy, what I could do!' You just sort of fantasize about all different kinds of things, and then you bring yourself back down and you say, 'Okay, now put yourself back in the mother's shoes.' You think about that. I mean, hey, maybe I'm abnormal, but I do. My son, he'll get a little smile on his face and he says, 'Oh Mom, you're too much!' They laugh it off, really," Ethel did not, in fact, seem to think she *was* abnormal," and was apparently unconcerned about putting any sort of label on her feelings. She, like Judy, accepted them in all their complexity, seemed comfortable with them and with herself. And her children, as she described them, reflected her own tolerant, unapologetic attitude toward sexuality. Mg14b12b10

Margot prides herself on an advanced, flexible approach to parenting, on her close "comradely" relationship with her ten-year-old daughter. She thought very carefully before she began to answer questions about the line between sensuous touching and erotic touching with regard to her daughter. "I felt aroused when she used to nurse," she began. "I loved that. I'm not aware of feeling aroused when she touches me now, but it is possible but I just block it." She clarified this point a moment later; it was evident that she was searching her mind carefully, trying to offer as accurate a picture as she could. "I'm very in touch with what I think is appropriate and what I don't, so I'm good at blocking feelings that I don't consider appropriate. I could see being aroused by her touching me. I find her a very sensual kid. And Mg10 that may be why it's uncomfortable for me if she's too sexual. But she can *talk* to me about anything. And I am very physical with her. I don't cut it off. As long as it doesn't get into that barrier that I set up in my mind, that I'm provocative with her." She paused again. "Or maybe it's that I don't want to be turned on by my own kid. I don't know. It's both."

Fathers, on the whole, could not talk easily about the sensuality that might exist in their relationships with their daughters. For example, unlike mothers, no father indicated that he was aroused by a child of the same sex. A few fathers thought it was inevitable that they would sometimes be turned on when they saw their daughters nude, played
Fg9   with them, bathed them, changed their diapers. "A natural thing. You know, it's not anything that I feel ashamed about. I don't see it as an incestuous thing." At least one father, Robert, a single parent who was exceptionally close to his daughter, admitted that he thought of her as "a very sexy kid." The attraction had begun when she was about one-and-a-half and had gown stronger as she became more and more a lit-
Fg6   tle girl. "It's hard to describe what sexy is. I sometimes tell her she's sexy. I don't know what she thinks it means. She gets embarrassed. I treat her like my girlfriend. I think somewhat she's a substitute for having a permanent girlfriend who I'm in love with or something like that. Because I'm definitely in love with my daughter, and half the time she's my daughter and half the time she's my girlfriend." Robert was aware that his attitude might be regarded as incestuous, and had discussed it with his therapist. But he also thought it would be unnatural for him to suppress this warmth and intimacy or curb his demonstrativeness, though he did have strong feelings about inappropriate physical contact. "I wouldn't play with her vagina, but I put my hand on her behind because it felt good and she might think it feels good. But I would never fondle her anywhere."

Most fathers, however, did not seem at all comfortable about contemplating these feelings in themselves. Their policy generally was to avoid the whole issue of eroticism in their interactions with their children by making sure that the children, particularly girls, understood just which kinds of touching were unacceptable and which were not. Richard was candid in discussing many aspects of sexuality, including his own sensuous pleasure in touching his children. When he was asked whether he was ever aroused by the physical contact with them, he spoke of the need to make parts of his body off limits, as a way of dealing with his daughter's erotic inclinations. This daughter, Robin,
Fg8b4   is now eight. "She will make covert attempts to touch me, sort of like pretend she's rubbing up against me. They both get into bed with me on Saturday mornings. It's a tradition. They both get into bed and we lay there and watch television together and she will make attempts to

touch me. She'll just brush up against me. You can kind of tell, you know. I usually won't say anything unless it's so overt—she'll like sort of poke and I'll say, 'Robin, stop that.' That's all."

Oliver, who has a daughter the same age as Richard's, reported a similar attitude toward eroticism in his relationship with her. He characterized himself as a liberal person with relaxed attitudes towards sexual behavior in general. "I want my children to learn about sexual matters," he said, "and I don't want them to be embarrassed about their body or to be unaware of what a man's body looks like. But if it turns overtly sexual in an active way, then it strikes me that that's inappropriate for their development. They shouldn't be manifesting those feelings, if they have them, in quite that way. I think if my daughters wanted to fondle my penis for a period of time to see what happened, I think I would call that overtly sexual. Curiosity is one thing, and I don't want to discourage that. I guess in a way I'm teaching them that they should focus it not on me but in some other way." Fg9g5g3

One father, Irv, spoke quite unashamedly of his delight at being touched by his seven-year-old daughter. "Sure, it's sensual, he said, with a rich, rumbling laugh, "You feel these little tiny hands, you know, these little sensual hands on you." But he also added as a qualification, "It's not something that I think of in a sexual way, as you would in an adult or someone else. You know, she'll tickle your neck or scratch your back or something like that. It's nice, it doesn't arouse you." And Irv, too, spoke of the limits he felt it necessary to place on his daughter's contact with his body. "I wouldn't let her touch me genitally. I don't think it's appropriate. She hasn't ever tried." Fg7

Some mothers of boys had similar concerns about the need to restrict their sons' contact with their bodies as the boys matured. But they felt that the limits had to be set on their *own* behavior, not their children's. Ruth's son had always liked to crawl into bed with her, to cuddle. But at the age of ten, he had begun to rub against her in an innocent but erotic way, and she felt this was unhealthy for both mother and son. She had decided to put a stop to this intimacy without making him feel guilty or ashamed. "It's not just to keep warm [in bed], she said. "I'll be aware of his . . . he'll have an erection. When these things happen, that's when I get out of bed. I say, 'I have to do things, Mommy has to get up.' He's not aware of why I'm getting up; I don't think he's aware of what's happening to him, and if he is, it's just a nice feeling to him. I don't make a big deal about it." Mb10

Another mother was aware of the contrast between her touching behavior with sons and her daughter. "I used to bring my daughter in the tub with me, when she was a baby, up until easily a year or two of age," she said. "We used to bathe together and she would touch me and it was very natural and there was never any feeling about it. I just Mb14b11b8g5 never allowed myself that freedom, that sexual freedom, with my boys. I touch her much more than I do the boys. I touch her and would not have the awkward feelings of touching her as I would with them."

Mb5 Though Judy still allowed her five-year-old son to touch her quite freely, she thought she might feel more awkward as he grew older. Actually, it was her husband who raised the question of whether this kind of physical contact was "appropriate." Judy put it this way: " 'Can I hug you?'—my son always asks that question when I have no clothes on. What he's really saying, I find, many times, is 'Can I touch your breasts?' And I used to say 'Yes.' Until about a month or two ago I had absolutely no problem. Conversations with my husband have forced me to focus on the fact that it may not be good for him and I'm beginning to be concerned." As with the issue of provocative nudity between mother and son, this was an area where parents felt it important to find out what professionals in the field had to say, rather than trust their own instincts about touching behavior. Judy, like other mothers facing the same dilemma, intended to do some reading to see how realistic her concerns were before altering her style.

"I Just Move Her Hand. They Don't Touch Daddies"

Parents described the diverse ways in which they dealt with inappropriate touching between their children and themselves. Mothers more so than fathers, favored "talking it out," allowing the child to discuss his reactions or intentions in order to clarify what was going on. When asked what she would do if her eleven-year-old son tried to touch her breasts or pubic area, Gina replied that she would "open it up and say, 'Why did you do that?' " She hoped to get a response she could enlarge upon, "explain to him a little etiquette and how *I* felt about it." But, like Ruth, she did not want to alarm or embarrass her son, who might be unconscious of his own motivations. "I don't want to say, 'No, you don't do that, that's not allowed!' I want to know what provoked it."

Fg6 Some parents pulled away or pulled their children away. Others changed the activity, diverted the child's attention to something else. Jerry described situations in which his daughter had tried to play with his penis. She would pull at the towel he wrapped around himself when he came out of the shower. "Or she'll sit on my lap and she'll touch and nothing is said. Then she'll touch a second time. The first time we are aware it was accidental, but the second time it's like, 'Oh, I got away with it,' then she'll touch it again. And I just move her hand. They don't touch daddies." While Wanda and her ten-year-old daughter dressed to go out, she did allow her daughter to feel her breasts, particularly since she recognized that little girls are likely to be curious about how they will develop. But when the touching was prolonged and Wanda began to feel uncomfortable, she would say to her daughter, "Okay, finish getting dressed." Mg10

Many parents simply told their children to stop. Often the best method was a direct order, delivered without anger. Gail recalled how her daughter had tried to get in on the action while she and her husband were "just horsing around" in their small kitchen. "My husband Mg4 patted me and all of a sudden I felt two hands on my bottom and it was my daughter. I said, 'What are you doing?' and she said, 'Daddy did it.' He wasn't making a grab for me, he just patted me, but she knew it was something different. And I said, 'Well fine, let's all stop patting one another.'" Sandy believed her son could be very seductive. "He's probably rubbed himself up against me in a way that was arous- Mb11 ing me. I would say that he probably has, because he's a very physical person. If I have ever felt this, I have told him it's not appropriate to do that to your mother."

For some children, touching their mothers' breasts seemed to have less to do with eroticism than with a throwback to babyhood, an association with the sensuousness, warmth, and security they had experienced when they were nursing. Mothers who were aware of their children's feelings were sympathetic but tried to make them understand that growing up meant separation; mother and child had become two distinct individuals. "I breast-fed her till she was a year old and she always Mg8 slept in my arms with her hand on my breast," Veronica said. "Automatically, when she is on my lap now, her hand is always there until I say stop it. I say, 'Stop that. That's not nice.' She likes to play with my nipples. I play it as a joke, really."

Penelope's daughter, Tracy, at five had actually pulled down her mother's bikini top at the beach and wanted "to drink." Penelope told her, "I really think you're too big for that. There is nothing here to Mg5 drink, and anyway you have a full set of teeth and you might hurt me. It's a delicate part of my body." Though she suspected there was something sexual about the request, she also felt the enormous pull of the infant still inside her little girl. "And yet, while she was getting herself into this—it must have all been in the space of three seconds—she was curling her feet and going into the exact position she did when I nursed her. Then it flashed through my mind, 'that memory is there.' That's what I remember from that experience. That memory was truly there. And I could almost understand primitive women nursing their children till they become very big, and the need for it." One evening two weeks later, Tracy wanted another drink. This time Penelope suggested she ask one of her grandmas, who have much bigger bosoms. When Tracy dismissed the idea—"Oh, no, yucky, I want it from you" —Penelope replied, "Well, gates are closed, there's no new baby, there's no milk, so if you want milk you have to go to the fridge." This combination of empathy, humor, and firmness worked extremely well in letting the child know the boundaries that existed between her and her mother without dismissing the complex impulses and needs that had motivated the request. Penelope reported that Tracy was very content after the discussion "and then she went to sleep."

"A Parent Can Do Just So Much"

Interestingly enough, all parents—the majority of "touchers," the minority of "non-touchers," those comfortable with being touched even erotically, those who felt the need to set limits—came to the same conclusion about what they believed to be the ultimate consequences of their parental policies around touching. No matter what you did, no matter how much or how little you hugged, kissed, fondled, and petted your child, and allowed him to touch you in return, there were no guarantees. Children would grow up and away into the world and behave in ways parents could not control. The environment itself, in all its complexity, might alter their standards and needs. Their own unique natures might also determine for them different standards from those of their parents. Children's experiences, some which they would never confess to an adult, might change them irrevocably and, again, in ways beyond the parents' control.

Margot, clearly someone at ease with all forms of touching, said at the close of her interview, "I don't think it helps to say to someone 'You really *ought* to touch your child and it's good for them and it makes them feel wanted and loved and good about themselves.' Because I've seen mothers who think, 'I ought to do X,' do it, and not be comfortable with it and it doesn't come across as real. The other thing, too, is maybe there are other ways of demonstrating love to a child besides touching and they can be just as valid. I don't have any proof that a child can't grow up and feel just as good about themselves without the touching."

Ethel, too, said, "A parent can do just so much, and then there's that outside environment and there are friends around you whose thoughts are not along the same line as yours are, and there's that conflict there. You never know what may push him one way or push him the other way. Let him grow along and see what happens."

Rachel, a "non-toucher," concluded, echoing Ethel and Margot, "It is better to be what is true to your own self, and your kids will have to learn to adapt to it and you hope that it all comes out right. But it is better than trying to squeeze yourself in a direction that you are not comfortable going. I have pretty much tried to go with that. I hope the results are going to be good."

Where To Draw The Line

Despite the fact that parents reported having positive feelings about the overall value of physical contact, they also clearly believed that there would always be situations in which touching behavior would have to be limited. As has been pointed out, they placed boundaries on the erotic nature of contacts they and their children shared. They also felt it necessary to prohibit certain kinds of touching between a child and her peers, and to warn the child of possible inappropriate approaches from older children or adults.

There were other considerations, as well. What was the best way to control children's physical curiosity without inhibiting them or damaging their self-esteem? Did parents have a responsibility to curb their own touching—in public or in private—in order to instill in their children those concepts of social decorum that would guide and protect them as they matured? The dilemmas became more complex as their children grew older and more sophisticated about the touching behavior they saw all around them and more aware of their own sexuality and that of their parents and peers.

Parents' responses to these questions were often of necessity spontaneous, existential, and incomplete. Policies tended to develop gradually and organically, dictated by the requirements of different individual and family styles. Most parents were ready to admit that they were treading a narrow, ambiguous line between what they perceived to be two kinds of potential harm to their children: from exposure to excessive or inappropriate touching behavior and from excessive or inappropriate parental reaction to that behavior. In the main these parents wanted to be relaxed and low-key, yet not complacent or negligent in dealing with incidents that might leave lasting imprints on children's personalities.

Parents Touching Parents

There was no agreement among parents on how much affection they would allow their children to observe between them. Many parents kept a clear distinction in their minds between what they considered merely affectionate touching, which children could be permitted to see, and what they considered overt sexual touching, which ought not to be indulged in when children were present. But the definition of sexual touching varied considerably from family to family. Whereas hugging rather than kissing was acceptable in certain families, just the opposite was true in others. And while some parents believed all kinds of fondling were acceptable in front of their children, another group felt hugging and kissing were permissible only if they avoided touching particular parts of each other's bodies—kissing on the lips, caressing breasts or behinds.

Generally, parents did not perceive too much difference between the way they displayed affection in private in their children's presence and the way they displayed affection in public when with their children. Demonstrative people tended to be a little more moderate outside the home, their affection taking the form of less obvious or prolonged caresses, hugs, and kisses. Many parents also felt quite easy about having their children see them with their arms around each other or holding hands when they walked down the street. Except in cases where the context was unsuitable for parents to engage in affectionate touching, entertaining professional acquaintances at home, attending church—people let their own comfort with touching generally determine the amount of affection they allowed their children to see.

Mb7   I don't think we do too much of it, kissing or hugging. We do some, but not very much. I'm not exactly sure why we don't. I think that a lot of the fondling is between the parents while the kids are away.

Mg8   A kiss or a hug or a tickling or a pat-on-the-behind kind of thing or sitting on the lap. Sometimes I will sit and watch TV and Eddy will say, "Oh, I'm so tired," and he'll come and sit down on my lap, that kind of thing. I think that pretty much covers it. Sometimes we'll walk with our arms around each other, like strolling through the park or something. He will sometimes kind of massage my back while I'm dressing. And my daughter will observe that.

Mb10   My son would see us kissing and hugging affectionately. Not too long ago we were sitting in the kitchen and hugging and kissing and my son came in. He used to take me to the train station in the morning. We would kiss each other when we got into the car. And holding hands, maybe caressing each other a little bit, playing around sometimes. He pinches me on my breasts. My son's seen that, never really making anything out of it.

Often parents let their feelings define what was sexual touching and what was not. There was no conscious decision to curb their behavior, but they did not allow themselves to cross the line from affectionate touching into something more erotic, more "heavy," more "turned on," unless they were alone. Several parents were able to give specific examples of the types of physical contact they considered "too sexual" for their children to observe.

Well, it depends on what one defines as sexual. I will kiss him on the lips. I might sit on his lap and joke with him. I will hug him, but I will not touch his genitals. And he won't touch any of my sexual parts. He won't touch my breasts in front of her. If he does, it's a slip. Mg10

Well, perhaps giving me a deep and prolonged kiss, that to me would indicate something more than a superficial sort of greeting, something that would mean more, perhaps to carry on later as a sexual encounter. I think if it happened I might push my husband away or stop it rather than continue it. Mb11

According to their parents, many children observed affectionate displays between them with pleasure and amusement. For some of these children, the parents' physical closeness seemed to be a source of reassurance, a signal that all was well, though sometimes they felt the need to know they would not be left out. Many parents described group cuddles in which the children joined in the action by piling on top of them when they were kissing or hugging each other.

We do family hugs. When she sees us holding each other or hugging or kissing, she comes whipping into the room, shouting, "Pick me up! Family hug! Family hug!" And we have to pick her up, hug her, kiss her. She loves it. We like it. It's fun. Mg3

For other children of various ages and various stages of sexual understanding, their parents' behavior was particularly interesting or a little disconcerting. They would air complex reactions by engaging in little teasing rituals—laughing and running away, making jokes—to blow off steam or let Mommy and Daddy know that they comprehended the private implications of the affection they observed.

One time I went to kiss my wife and my son sticks out his tongue and she [my wife] says "What are you doing that for?" And he says, "Well that's how Daddy kisses you." So he observes *everything!* Fb4

Sometimes she comments on the fact that we're kissing or touching and thinks it's cute or interesting or funny. "I see you kissing Mommy—I see what you're doing!" Fg7

I was on my way to work, and when I got in the car he had kissed me, and my son was standing there. He just came over and knocked on the window—"I see you!"—that kind of thing. Mb10

It was also not uncommon for children to react negatively to parental displays of physical affection. One boy, eleven, was embarrassed when his parents kissed or hugged in public. Milly's five-year-old son was very attached to his father, and became jealous when his parents spent time together or called each other affectionate names. He would try to irritate his mother by saying, "Well, I guess you're just making Mb5 love," or interrupt them when they seemed too close. "He tries to avoid it, to get our minds off this," she explained. "If he sees that look in our eyes, he'll say, 'Let's take a walk' or 'Let's go to the park,' or something like that. He breaks in. He wants to be included."

Many children, little girls especially, became extremely possessive of their opposite sex parent. Two mothers spoke of how their daughters tried to compete with them for their fathers' affection in very much the same way that Milly's son tried to compete with her. They would move in on their parents when they were talking or touching and divert attention from what was going on to themselves. Cassandra's daughter, Tiffany, would hug her father and kiss his neck. "This is my Daddy," she would proclaim. "It had gotten to the point where she wouldn't want him to put his arm around me," Cassandra said. "She would come right between us. She wanted him to hug *her*." Gail described a similar situation. "Sometimes Emma will deliberately disrupt a conversation by dropping a fork into a dish or something, just to distract me. Then she'll say, 'Know what we did today, Daddy?' " Both of these mothers indicated the importance of not being drawn into an encounter with their children. Instead each, in her own way, reacted with tolerance, sensitivity, and empathy for these feelings of being left out that she sensed in her daughter. Cassandra resolved the issue by limiting the kinds of affection she would let Tiffany observe. "So I just told him, if she doesn't see us do it, it would just die down, which it did." Gail and her husband found that verbal reassurance— "Mommy and Daddy love each other. We love *you*. We're a family"— was helpful to Emma, as was special time reserved just for father and daughter. "We make it a point now of having her talk about her day with him alone."

Parents Touching Children

How did parents feel about touching the sexually sensitive areas of their children's bodies? A very small number placed themselves at extremes in their behavior. Several said they would touch *any* area of a child's body, unconditionally. Far fewer parents described *all* sexual parts of their children's bodies as categorically and absolutely off limits, not to be touched under any circumstances, and this attitude was expressed for the most part by fathers who left child care essentially to their wives. One example was Ted. "There are areas of her body that I don't touch," he explained. "The pubic areas and breast areas. I pick her up and play with her and tickle her and so forth. But I don't touch those areas. I just don't feel that's appropriate posture. I'd feel the same way if my daughter were a boy, that those are the areas that would be inappropriate for me to touch."

The majority of parents, however, found that their attitudes toward physical contact with their children changed at various stages in their children's development. Often, their overall reactions had less to do with the sexual nature of a touching experience than with such other considerations as the age and/or sex of the child, the context, the child's need for privacy, his maturity or independence. Policies tended to emerge gradually out of instinctive caution and mutual respect rather than from specific sexually oriented distress, except in the case of opposite-sex children approaching puberty. Mothers of boys and fathers of girls reported being more self-conscious and more circumspect in approaching such contacts. Fathers, in particular, were extremely reluctant to touch their daughters' vaginas for any reason. Sam said he was not even sure he would check his daughter if she had an infection. "How am I going to know? I don't look down there to know. I guess she'll say it hurts and I'll call a doctor and we'll go to the doctor." Fg7

Some parents set limits on their contact with the sexual areas of their children's bodies because of the children's need for privacy. The reason the parents gave here were similar in many cases to those they would later give for phasing out certain "servicing" tasks of parenting. Sometimes the child himself forced the issue, by demanding to perform sensitive tasks by himself or by protecting parts of his body. "[By six] he didn't want me to wash anything near his penis, not even his thighs," Rachel said. Mike's daughter also became modest at about age five. "When I gave her a bath, she said, 'No, I wash myself, Daddy,' when I got down by there." Sometimes the parents initiated change as a way of encouraging mature attitudes and a sense of bodily integrity in the child. Margot spoke with some regret of the way in which she had begun to alter her touching behavior with her daughter. "I'm always tempted to give her rump a kiss or give her a little nibble—I sort of avoid that now. I think it's infantalizing at this point." Mb6 Fg5 Mg10

Quite a few parents set standards based on the purpose for any physical contact with sexual areas. Such touching was acceptable for "servicing"—checking on a rash or sore place, administering medication, toileting—but was otherwise avoided.

> I wouldn't put my fingers in her vagina. If she has an infection there, well, of course. If there is a reason for it, just like a reason for looking at any other part of her body, then it's fine. If there is no reason for it, then there is no reason for it. Fg3

> If she said, "I have a bruise here," or "Could you help me with this? then that's something different. At this point occasionally she'll have a slight discharge and ask me about it. It's not a problem. She'll come to me and she'll just show me and ask me about it. Mg11

Bathing

Bathing children is, of course, one of the most elemental of parenting tasks. It occurs almost daily and involves close physical contact with the child's body. In addition, the task may have warm, sensuous, deeply pleasurable associations for the parent as well as the child. On the other hand, bathing can also be one of the most drearily practical of parental duties, a time-consuming incursion into the daily routine. Children must be kept clean, often in spite of themselves. Like dishes, they have to be washed, and washed, and washed again—day after day, year after year. Some children are recalcitrant, prefer to be grubby, resist learning to care for themselves. Others become, or yearn to be, independent about their personal hygiene early. Most parents were able to state a time at which they no longer needed to bathe a child. But they offered a wide range of cut-off ages based on a variety of criteria.

A few parents believed there was a definite age at which a child ought to be able to bathe alone. They withdrew their participation at that age in order to encourage the child to become independent. Lesley saw bathing oneself as a way of learning responsibility, an impor-

Mb7 tant step toward self-sufficiency. "At this age he is perfectly capable of doing it himself and really should. It's more laziness than anything else that he doesn't. There is a certain amount of self-care, just as at three-and-a-half to four you have to learn to dress yourself. At this age you really should be bathing yourself."

A more typical approach was to allow the child to begin bathing herself at whatever age she seemed to display the necessary competence and self-confidence. Parents in this group set very flexible cut-off ages and allowed for a "two-steps-forward-one-step-back" process of development on the child's part, and also for differences in the abilities and temperaments of individual children. There was no single mo-

Mg11 ment when they stopped bathing their children. "It's gradual. I don't really know what to tell you about when it happened," Maeve said about the topic. "I would say it's in the last three or four years that she can go in and wash herself and come out looking clean." But like other parents, this mother relied on her own perception of the child's need as the major guideline for whether she would step in or not. "Even now there are times when I say, 'Get into the shower and I want to make sure you wash *here* and *there*,' and I'll be able to check."

Still another group of parents was willing to let the child determine the standards. As soon as children showed a need for independence and requested to bathe alone, those parents would permit them to do so. Most parents who took this approach were proud of their children's eagerness to "do it myself." Even if at times there were lapses in concentration, a bit of backsliding—an unwashed neck, too much splashing and silliness—parents wanted to encourage the child to develop freely and gain a healthy sense of her own maturing abilities. Such parents were also willing to accede to a child's request for help, upon occasion, regardless of the child's age, as this mother remarked: "When he told me he didn't want me to be in there anymore, I was not going to be there anymore."   Mb5

In some cases, the cut-off age was determined by a sexually oriented discomfort on either the parent's or the child's part. Though a substantial number of parents did not consider washing the sexually sensitive areas—genitals, buttocks, breasts—of their younger children's bodies an issue, a few did sense that this kind of touching might become inappropriate or embarrassing when children reached a certain age. This was especially true of parents of opposite-sex children approaching puberty. More often, it was the child who gave out signals that he needed privacy. When the child became modest or began to show signs of being overly stimulated, or when he simply requested that he be allowed to wash those areas himself, the parents would alter their behavior accordingly.

> He would get all giggly (he is very ticklish) and say, "Don't do it!" So it became easier to say, "You do it." I don't know if he stopped me because it was ticklish or because he thought it was a little sexual.   Mb6

> About a month ago, I guess, he was in the bathtub and I came in and I asked him if he had washed all the areas. I said "Give me the washcloth and let me wash under there and make sure it doesn't smell." He said, "Oh Ma, I'll wash there."   Mb10

> The older one got too old when he was about nine. And when he got too old, then the younger ones decided that it was probably not right for Mommy to help them take a bath so they used to take a bath by themselves. They told me not to come in, but when they all used to fool around in the bathtub I used to threaten I would come in, and they didn't like that very much at all. They could not let a lady see them.   Mb11b14

There were parents who said they continued to participate in bathing their children regardless of the child's age or competence. Some said it was safer to do so and intended to withdraw only when they were sure the children could protect themselves from bathtub accidents. Others, a very few, felt that bathing even older children was necessary if they wanted to keep tabs on their general cleanliness. For the most part, however, parents in this group continued to bathe their children simply because both they and the children found the experience such a warm, gratifying one—a chance to indulge in private little rituals of affection that remained important even when the children were well past the "baby" stage. Bathtime was a time of special emotional and physical closeness, which many parents were reluctant to relinquish.

Mg8   I'll wash her hair and then I generally walk out and I let her complete her bathing and play with the water for a while. And she'll tell
me when she is ready and then I'll often come in and kind of wrap
her around in the towel and give her a great big hug and rub her
down a little bit, and it's also time to exchange affection with the
towel around her as I kind of rub her down. And that's still a kind of
baby thing we both still enjoy. I imagine as she gets older she will no
longer want that either.

Mb12b10   I go into the bathroom when they're taking a bath—my oldest son is
twelve years old and I still do him the same way too. I don't actually
bathe them per se. I'll mess around in the water and I'll say, "Let
me wash you over here"—I'll sort of fondle, maybe play with them
a little bit. Or I'll take the washcloth and I'll—"No, you didn't get a
spot there"—kind of thing.

Mb13b11   Sure, I clean his ears, so I mean I touch his ears, sure, sure, and I
touch his head or I kiss him or I hug. They love to have their back
scratched or rubbed so I do that.

In their responses to the question of whether or not they bathed
with their children, parents talked about some of the same issues they
had raised in relation to questions about bathing children in general.
Almost everyone reported that until the children were two or three,
bathing together with them seemed completely appropriate. Being
right there in the tub, in fact, was often the easiest way to get a very
dirty child clean or comfort him if the water was frightening. A number of parents, especially mothers, continued to feel comfortable sharing a shower or bath even with older children—ten and eleven—not
necessarily as a consistent part of the family routine, but on various
occasions. The most common reason they gave was *pleasure:* both
parent and child enjoyed feelings of increased emotional as well as
physical intimacy; of playfulness and relaxation; of warmer, closer communication than was possible during the more hectic times in the
family's day.

Mg7b3   We've done it several times. She'll wash my back, I'll wash her back.
She'll make sure I have the soap out of my hair and I'll do the same
for her. We have a community—we've had my son in there too. I
think it's kind of a fun time. We do it maybe once in two weeks or
on the weekend when I have time.

Fg5   As a family, some nights just out of convenience we'll all take a
shower together or take baths, although it's kind of cramped for three
people in a bathtub. She and her mother often take long, kind of
languorous, luxurious baths and they'll play in the bathroom for half
an hour or so.

Sometimes we take a bath together. One time recently we sat in the Mg10
tub for about twenty minutes and just talked. That's a time when
she'll be very open, when she'll tell me everything that's going on
with her friends. And a lot of that has to do with their thoughts about
sex. What did I think of this, did I think it would be all right—that
kind of thing.

But some parents absolutely ruled out bathing with their children as
they grew older. Of these parents, a few gave such nonsexual reasons
for their disapproval as safety concerns (two or more people in a tub at
the same time was dangerous), the child's fear of the shower, or their
own desire for privacy. For Richard, the bathtub could be both a place
to work and relax after work. When he took baths, he needed to be
alone. "I mark papers in the bathtub. Sometimes when I have a lot of Fb4
papers, it's the only thing that calms me. The papers get wrinkled and
prune-like, but it's the price the students have to pay for having me
mark their papers. So I do take baths [with my son] but not very often."
The majority of parents who ruled out bathing together, however, did
so specifically for sexual reasons: they feared such intimacy might have
a disturbing or provocative effect, particularly on opposite-sex children.

We used to. At around two we decided that was old enough and we Mb3
stopped. I guess we were afraid it was too provocative for him. Or
my husband was afraid of that. We tried to stop before they would
sort of notice that there was anything different between Mommy and
Daddy, I guess. Or ask questions, which they never did.

Up to about five and that was about the time I stopped. I had the Mb5
feeling that this overt stimulation might have been counterproduc-
tive and could have resulted in their having problems and their being
unable to deal with it in a learning situation.

We used to take showers together. But that stopped. She knows that's Fg8
not something I would do. I'd say "No, take a shower by yourself." I
don't think we should take showers together, because I think men
and women, uh, fathers and daughters, should not take showers together after a certain age. Fathers and sons it's okay.

Sickroom Procedures

Parents were about equally divided in their attitudes toward giving
enemas. For one group, giving an enema to a child did not present
any problem, regardless of the child's age. Members of the other group
responded to questions on enemas with vehement expressions of dis-

approval and distaste, and in some cases reported similar strong aversion on the part of their children. However, both sets of parents seemed to find this an awkward subject for discussion, and few wished to elaborate on their answers.

Parents were more willing to discuss their policies about using rectal thermometers than about giving enemas. This procedure apparently involved less personal abhorrence and embarrassment and was easier to approach in a matter-of-fact, unself-conscious manner. Parents spoke freely and were more apt to illuminate their answers with specific material. Even though they did occasionally mention a certain amount of distaste for the procedure, these negative feelings were far less vehement than those expressed toward enemas. A large group of parents in fact reported that they had no difficulty whatsoever in using the rectal method, regardless of the child's age. And though there was some disagreement about which method of temperature-taking was more accurate, parents who felt that the oral reading was less reliable continued to use rectal thermometers even with children eleven and older, especially when they ran high fevers.

As with other issues, the decision to switch from the rectal method to the "more adult" oral method was generally determined by the

Mg8 child's competence. "I like to encourage the big girl in Suzie," Florence said, "and I think that using an oral thermometer is just one more way of doing it." If the child could follow instructions and manage not to chew up the thermometer, parents felt comfortable using the oral method.

Often the child's need for independence, privacy, or mature treatment affected the parents' attitudes toward inserting a rectal thermometer. Some children reacted so strongly to the rectal method—were so clearly mortified or so physically resistant—that many parents simply gave up.

Mb3   It bothers him, so it's a nuisance. He just doesn't like his temperature taken. It's just one of those "don't-interfere-with-my-body" things.

Mg6b3   Once it happened she told me she didn't like it, but I told her I didn't have any other way of doing it so that would have to be that. Usually they tend to get shy at four years old. Right now when my son goes to the doctor to get checked he doesn't like that and he's three. He'll put his hands to cover his eyes like he's so ashamed.

If the reluctant child was not yet able to use the oral method, the parents would simply not take his temperature, except when the illness looked like something more than a run-of-the-mill cold or flu. When Alice's daughter was sick and she absolutely had to have a temperature reading, Alice found an alternative to both the oral and rectal

Mg7   methods. "The doctor showed me a way of doing it under the arms so

I wouldn't have to do the rectal, since she finds it so unpleasant and she tenses up, which makes it worse."

Toileting

Parents' attitudes toward toileting ranged from mild distaste to strong revulsion. Generally, first-time parents and parents of children under a year, who were still eating a limited range of food in small portions, felt matter-of-fact about the procedure; it was part of the routine they were expected to carry out. But as the child got closer to nursery-school age, or in situations where she was the second or third baby in the family, parents—especially mothers—were increasingly unhappy about the task. They were weary of waking up at night to take a small child to the bathroom, and wanted assurance that the child could break this intimate tie with the adult. Some said they might stop supervising their children even before they were completely ready to take care of themselves. "I don't like to wipe other people's asses. That's why," Oliver said bluntly when asked to explain why he had hurried the training of his younger daughter.

Nevertheless, as a group, these parents were extremely conscientious about keeping their children clean. By far, the most important factor in their decision to continue or discontinue participating in toileting procedures was, again, the child's competence. When they felt the child was able to wipe herself in a satisfactory fashion, the parents relinquished the task. Others said they would withdraw from physical participation in the toileting process when they felt the time had come for the child to take on this responsibility. These parents wanted to encourage the child to be independent, to learn how to care for herself without assistance, and were prepared to deal with the inevitable "mistakes." Actually the age at which these parents wanted their children to begin to take care of themselves—three or four—coincided with the age at which most children seemed to attain competence, although some children as old as seven or eight were still having problems with this area of personal hygiene and continued to need parental supervision.

Certain children were by nature very modest or very independent, eager from a very early age to be allowed to take on all personal hygiene tasks for themselves. Parents of such children usually respected these wishes, although several added the proviso that in cases of evident distress—diarrhea, illness, fatigue—they would temporarily resume the tasks. And most parents did make a point of checking newly trained children after they had finished in the bathroom to see that they had "done the job right."

Mg3   I stopped probably about three-and-a-half to four, when I was sure
          that she really was doing a good job of it. She wanted to do it. She
          was very independent and she wanted to do everything by herself
          and she would say, "No, I do it!" She decided she wanted to do
          everything by herself, but there were times that she didn't feel well
          or things like that that I made sure that everything was done.

Mg3   Oh, no, I wouldn't do it for her. Though she doesn't do such a
          great job. I certainly didn't wipe for her if she urinated, but I might
          just check around. At what age? I would say about three. I think in
          terms of independence for the child, then I say, "Oh my goodness,
          she could do this herself, I don't need to do it any more."

          Despite the fact that toileting, like bathing and sickroom proce-
dures, requires parents to come into close physical contact with sexually sensitive areas of a child's body, almost nobody gave this as a
reason for setting a cut-off age for helping the child in the bathroom.
Mb7b4   Lesley, who continued to wipe her seven-year-old son after bowel
movements because his sensitive skin became extremely itchy and he
was miserable when he could not get himself thoroughly clean, felt ill
at ease with the process. Her sense was that at his age, her contact
with his anal area was "a little more stimulating," quasi-erotic, and
she was hoping he would be competent enough to take care of himself soon.

The Moment to Stop

As a general rule, parents seemed to feel increasing reluctance to touch
the sexual areas of a child's body for any reason as a child grew older.
For most parents, such changes in policy occurred gradually over a
period of years; rarely did one mention a sudden "revelation" or overnight alteration in routine. Instead, a point would come in the relationship after which certain kinds of contact simply "felt" inappropriate and
Mg7   began to be phased out. "You kind of pull back," Veronica explained.
"There's no need at that point to specifically touch a particular area,
so you just—it's not that you automatically stop—it just kind of phases
out that you don't touch. It starts seven or eight, this pulling back." In
several cases, that "point" at which contact was withdrawn was clearly
related to the sex as well as the age of the child in question. Fathers
of daughters and mothers of sons were uncomfortable with the maturing bodies and expanded sexual awareness of prepubescent youngsters.
          Occasionally, a child's response to routine parental contact—either
"servicing" or simply demonstrating affection—alerted parents to a
growing sexual awareness on the child's part; such incidents of over-

excited behavior often led parents to reassess their policies and adjust their behavior accordingly. And sometimes the opposite situation occurred: parents found that their own reactions to certain kinds of physical contact caused discomfort and required them to change their habits or to create policies where none had been needed before.

> He used to ask me to kiss him on the penis. That made me uncomfortable. But I did it. I remember saying to my husband, "What do I do now?" And he said, "If you feel uncomfortable doing it, you shouldn't do it. If you feel that it's okay, try to do it, because you don't want him to feel there's anything wrong with that part of his body." Mb3

> I would not intentionally touch her genital area because I think she would think—what are you intentionally touching? The age when you touch them is when you're diapering them or when you're bathing them when they're two or three. Fg7

> The other day I kissed her and apparently kissed her on the breast and she pointed that out and giggled hysterically. She said, "Oh, you kissed my breast!" She knows that is a sexual act. Mg10

> Any areas of his body that I don't touch? *[laughs]* Below the waist! I guess that's not really fair. I can remember tweaking his penis once when he was in the bathtub and he was little. But of course he was very young then. Now I just might pat his rear end, but I don't think I would stroke it or anything. Mb11

Children Touching Parents

A number of parents were uncomfortable when their children initiated physical contact with sexual areas of their bodies—breasts, pubic hair, genitals (or even, in certain cases, lips, faces, ears, necks, hair). But only occasionally did they relate their discomfort specifically to the sexual nature of the areas being touched or to any lurking sexual content in the child's caress. More often, parents described such gestures as unacceptable because annoying or painful, or because intrusive in generalized, nonsexual way—breaches of decorum or private "space." Others mentioned the age and/or sex of the child and the context of the gesture as important determining factors.

As was the case with nudity, many parents seemed to be setting limits on physical contact as a way of socializing the child, letting him know what types of affection, curiosity, teasing, or play were acceptable even between loving and related people within the intimacy of the family circle. These parents emphasized privacy, the integrity of each individual's body, and the individual's right to draw lines that others must respect in order for intimacy to work.

For some parents, mainly mothers, the age of the child would determine the kind of response they would make to inappropriate physical contact. Certain forms of touching were considered acceptable from smaller children, but were met with increasing disapproval as the children grew up. These parents felt children should be discouraged when their touching behavior seemed "babyish" or designed to provoke negative attention:

Mg3   A slap on the behind. She has done that to me occasionally, copying her father. I don't make a big issue out of it really. I'm not terribly comfortable with it simply because I don't think that's necessarily the way a child plays with a parent. That becomes the issue. It's not particularly sexual.

Mg10   One time recently she was playing around with the idea of sucking on my breasts like when she was a baby. I'll allow her to talk about it but I won't allow her to do it. I will tell her that I feel it's inappropriate because she's not a baby any more. She has an intense curiosity and she also likes to say things that are a little shocking. That's the ten-year-old—"I like to be a little shocking." She likes to see what will get a reaction from me. I think she knew that that was something I wasn't going to let her do.

Mb11   If my son touched my pubic area or breasts I'd say, "What are you doing that for, kid? What's your problem?" I'm sure I would say, "Don't do that." I would say, "You don't do that to a mother." Right, yes. Explain to him a little etiquette.

Some fathers set limits on physical contact based on the sex as well as the age of the child. Though Roy played with his daughter when he was nude, he was very firm about not allowing her to touch

Fg3   his penis. "I've said, 'You can't play with my penis.' Once that's stated, she doesn't play with it. She'll just poke around a little bit. She's more comfortable after guidelines are put there. 'No, you're not supposed to touch me.' I'm saying to her, this is special and you cannot touch it. It's more private than other parts. This is my private part and there's no touching allowed. And that's it. I don't really go into further explanations." Aaron took the same calm but no-nonsense approach with his three-year-old daughter. If she tried to touch his penis, he would

Fg3   say, "I would rather you don't do it."

In most cases, the rules fathers set for boys were different in emotional and social content from those they set for girls. Richard was not upset when his son touched his genitals while he was sitting on his lap or when they were roughhousing together. But he was distinctly uncomfortable with similar contacts from his daughter. "I don't make an issue, but I do set limits with my daughter. She'll giggle but she won't say anything. With my son it's man-to-man things. I feel more comfortable with him." Allen did feel it was necessary to restrict his son's touching behavior, not because it made him uneasy, but because he wanted to socialize him toward future contacts with other men. Here was an opportunity for an early lesson in the rules of "male bonding": "If he reached out and touched my pubic area, I think at this point, at his age now, I would say, 'That's really not something guys do.' "

Very few parents, however, made the sexual areas of their bodies absolutely off limits to their children. Their policies were flexible, dependent often on whether the child's manner seemed innocent and merely curious or blatantly sexual. A number of children, for instance, wanted to touch their mother's breasts, but often the contact seemed more playful than sexual. Elias described how his eight-year-old son liked to grab at his wife's breasts and run away. "My wife doesn't care," he said, "I feel he does it just as a joke." Florence's daughter would press on her breasts and "go 'bong, bong, bong.' " Agnes's daughter also liked to poke at her breasts, but she suspected that there was a strong element of curiosity in her play, "I'll say, 'What's the matter, Melissa? Someday you are going to have ninnies, too."

Just when did the child's behavior cross the line and become provocative or suggest he was overstimulated? Most parents had no firm answer to this question; they allowed the "feel" of each particular situation to be their guide. Margot talked about this issue at some length. "I have strong divisions about what's appropriate and what isn't appropriate, what's sexually provocative and what isn't. It's largely instinct." She was aware that her daughter's interest in her breasts might spring from a number of impulses. "Erica could at times touch my breast and it wouldn't bother me. I experience it more as a testing of what'll happen—Is this appropriate?—You know, there's a testing of limits. She has an intense curiosity. She'll joke about that mine are big and she wants to have big breasts like mine. At other times I would feel it's coming from some sexual place and it would be." Margot had other indications that once in a while there was something more blatant than simple curiosity in her daughter's touch. "She's a teasing kind of kid. She will intimate that she wants to play a little sexual game with me, act out some sexual thing that she's seen on television, for instance. You know, it could be just a passionate kiss." In such a case, her own sense of embarrassment and discomfort became the yardstick by which she determined when it was time to put a stop to Erica's behavior. "I don't especially like that. I find that too sexual between parent and child."

Many other parents shared this point of view. There were situations in which they allowed children plenty of leeway for contact with their bodies—when the child seemed genuinely curious, or when he was going through a stressful period, perhaps after the birth of a new sibling or at the onset of sexual development. But when they sensed that the child was initiating physical contact out of a more sexually-oriented interest in the adult body, they pulled back.

Fg3   She likes to bat my penis. She thinks it's very interesting. It's the only one in the family. I tell her it's not a toy to play with if she seems to want to continue, but normal curiosity I don't try to discourage.

Mg3   Sometimes she'll touch my pubic hair and I'm a little embarrassed. I just laugh and tell her that when she gets big she'll have pubic hair, too, and she says, "It's soft and it's beautiful." I say, "Thank you," and that's the end of it.

Mb7b3   It started with my belly button. Janey would see Joshie pushing my belly button and then he decided the titties were much more exciting, so he pushed the titties. Carol thought that was very cute, that if Joshie can do it, "I can do it, too." She's at the stage when she's still jealous, so you've got to be a little more understanding.

As with other issues, however, these parents also emphasized the importance of keeping their reactions to any inappropriate contact relaxed and neutral. They hoped to conceal their embarrassment as much as possible so as not to alarm their children.

The questions in this study were focused on modes of physical contact which related to sexuality rather than to anger, aggression, punishment, pain. However, many informants wanted a chance to discuss the latter, most particularly in order to make a clear distinction—with a value judgment implied—between their attitudes toward aggressive as opposed to sexual behavior. A number of parents wanted to go on record to say that while they did *not* place restrictions on the sexual forms of touching, they had *very* firm rules about physical contact which involved hostility, aggression, intimidation, insensitivity to pain of others, and actual physical danger to either participant.

These rules obviously applied to the child's contact with the parent. When a child's touch became too aggressive or painful, when it began to get on the nerves, parents reacted quickly, with the same type of warning or irritated exclamation that might be used if the child came in rough contact with any other sensitive area of the body—toe or elbow—or if the child were making an objectionable noise or becoming reckless in play.

Fg3   I would tell her it's my penis and not to play with it because it becomes rather annoying. I don't know that she knows that there's anything sexual to it. To her, it's just the way you're built.

Mb3   My son still has a habit. He's three years old. I can have my back turned and he eases his hand under my arm to pat me on my breasts, you know, to get my attention. It's annoying but I don't let him know it's annoying. I just look at him and say, "What is it?" I have girlfriends that come and the first place he pats them is their chests.

Touching breasts, that's okay, unless she pulls too hard. Lately I say, "There's a human being here. It's skin. Take it easy!"   Mg3

But in a more general sense, parents felt it necessary to let their children know that hurtful touching was prohibited not only at home but, perhaps more importantly, on the outside as well. As this father made clear: "The limitations are she can't kick. She can't physically abuse another child. And if another child pinched my child, pushed my child, hit my child, slapped my child, I would not allow that to go on. That's a whole different kind of behavior, a whole different kind of problem. It is touching, sure. Getting run over by a car is touching too, but I mean we're not too keen on that as well. We censor out touching behavior that is hurtful and not touching behavior that is affectionate."   Fg3g8

Children Touching Children

What sorts of limits, if any, did parents place on their children's contact with the sexual parts of each other's bodies? Many parents with children of all different ages, could not say with certainty that there had been inappropriate touching between their children and peers, though they were willing to admit that they might simply be unaware of such contact. But a substantial number of parents had given some consideration to what they would do in this situation, and two sets of attitudes toward the issue emerged during the interviews.

One group was relaxed or "cool" about such contact, did not set many limits, emphasized the need for trusting the child and allowing for natural curiosity. A second group either placed definite restrictions on contacts between children before-the-fact *or* placed those limits spontaneously in reaction to particular incidents of inappropriate contact.

Parents who did not set limits on touching between children and their friends of *the opposite sex* often said they felt setting such limits was not practical or wise. They were resigned to the fact that they could not always be present to monitor children's activities and that children who wanted to explore one another would somehow find the means to do so, no matter what parents had told them. Ultimately, they pointed out, one must trust the child's own sense of what kinds of contact are safe, healthy, appropriate. These parents possessed generally tolerant attitudes towards mild physical experiments among children and assumed them to be normal events in the maturation process.

They didn't want children to be ashamed of their bodies or of their natural curiosity, didn't want to transform that natural curiosity into unhealthy obsession by deeming parts of the body "forbidden." This type of pragmatic, accepting overall approach was prevalent among both fathers and mothers, and among parents of boys and girls alike.

Mb3   I played doctor when I was five or six years old. What could be bad?

Mg7   I just think that when you make a big taboo with children who are young—"Don't do this, don't do that, don't touch this, don't touch that!"—that you only make them more curious. Because it's a "don't" they become more and more curious. They've got to grow up. They're going to get big and they're going to know. Whether you tell them or not, they're going to find out, and I don't always think that's wrong.

Fg8   If I came home and she was in bed with a little boy and they were touching each other I wouldn't say anything. Everybody goes through that, I would assume. I would ask her if she was supposed to be the doctor or the nurse because *that's* important, sex stereotypes. I'd say make sure she was the doctor next time.

Mb10   My older son told me that my little son, the ten-year-old, was out pinching one of the little girls. He wanted to see if she had any breasts. The little girls said, "See, they're not out yet." So I said, "Well, did she object?" And my older son said, "She must not, she didn't tell him to stop." So I says, "Well . . . as long as she doesn't say anything, I don't think you got anything to do with it," and I left it at that.

Parents who did set limits on touching behavior between children of the opposite sex found it was best to discuss these limitations with their children. Generally, they emphasized traditional attitudes towards sexual behavior, stressing self-protection and social decorum. Boys were told not to risk gestures which might be misunderstood—"That's not nice." Girls were told not to allow themselves to be "used." As soon as Leigh noticed her daughter's body beginning to mature, she sat down

Mg11   with her and spoke candidly about her concerns. "I let her know that you have to be careful with your own body because boys, males, will try to take advantage of you and you have to respect yourself."

In some cases, parents were direct, arbitrary, judgmental in voicing their objections to a child's touching behavior. Ethel spoke halfhumorously, half-seriously of how she had warned her ten-year-old son

Mb10   about inappropriate play with girls. "I have set limits to the point of asking that you don't do anything to anybody else that they don't want you to do. "Get-you-hand-chopped-off-if-they-don't-want-you-to-do-it kind of thing. *Beware!*" Most parents, however, were very conscious of moderating their reactions, even if they come upon their children *in flagrante* and strongly disapproved. They did not want to overreact and promote disproportionate guilt and shame in the children. Calm, straightforward discussion of the behavior was recommended, as was distraction—moving the children to a more supervised area of play or suggesting an alternative activity.

> It happened with a little boy about her age. I just brought them into the kitchen for juice. I said, "It's time to do something else." Mg3

> There was an instance in the backyard, three little girls and three little boys and they all had their pants down. The son's mother caught them. She was so angry she called me out the window and said, "They had their pants down! I tried to beat the shit out of mine. I don't know what you're going to do with yours!" I thought a lot of it was natural exploration and that they shouldn't be punished. I didn't punish my daughter, I just told her, "I didn't appreciate what you did outside, because it looks like it comes from the house. Don't do it again." Mg6

Overall, fewer parents reported setting specific limits on physical contact between same sex children than had done so for children of their opposite sex friends. Here again, many parents tended to be relaxed, tolerant of what they considered natural curiosity, or they were simply resigned to be unable to control their children's behavior at all times and in all ways. There were parents who discussed frankly the issue of homosexuality as it might be reflected in same-sex touching experiments. Some recalled mildly homosexual experiments from their own childhoods, and the tolerance they were willing to accord their children seemed to spring from serene and accepting attitudes toward their own sexuality. Gina described one such experience.

> I do know that my son had a homosexual encounter. He was sleeping over at a friend's house and I believe it was he who inserted his penis into his friend's rear end. I just figure it was a natural experience. It was bound to happen and I just never discussed it. I saw it in my own mind as a completely innocent act. I can remember in my formative years having a homosexual encounter with a close friend and I know that I'm heterosexual so I guess part of that is knowing that it isn't a matter of casting the die, so to speak. They have a close friend and sometimes a sexual relationship evolves out of that and I don't see it as necessarily threatening. Mb11

When parents did set limits on same-sex touching, however, the issue of homosexuality, though infrequently mentioned, seemed to be implicitly present in their thoughts. Ethel admittd she had never been as open with her son about the possibility of sexual exploration be- Mb10

tween boys and boys as she had been about the same exploration between boys and girls. "I haven't been comfortable in dealing with that,"
she said candidly. "I don't say anything one way or another, but I think
mentally I feel sort of inhibited about mentioning that." Other parents,
even those who were clearly conscious of not wanting to promote guilt
or shame, found that they were a little harsher about putting a stop to
sexual activity when it occurred between children of the same sex rather
than of the opposite sex. The first reaction—almost a reflex,—was,
"This is not how girls (or boys) behave together."

Fg3   She was with her cousin, who is six years old, and they were in this
        playful routine that we didn't like. We said, basically, "We don't
        like that. We don't do that," and that it was not a game. This policy
        did work. I think it was the tone of voice. We were rougher with her
        at that point.

Mg11   Yes, I would put a stop to it in a diplomatic, non-guilt-ridden way
        because I don't think I can go in there like a sledgehammer and say
        "No!" Possibly, though, a *little* bit of guilt. You know, "It's not a
        nice thing to do." That's what I mean by guilt.

        And, too, several parents mentioned health and safety as their
sole criteria in establishing standards for children's physical contact with
other children of either sex. For these parents, physical experimentation itself was not necessarily an issue. A certain amount of such touching behavior was considered normal, "nothing to get excited about."
But when it crossed a line beyond which it might become injurious to
the child, very firm, but generally quite matter-of-fact rules had to be
set. Some parents described instances in which they found children
trying to put thermometers into each other. Irv wanted his daughter to
Fg7   understand the dangers involved. "We didn't approach it in the sexual
manner," he explained, recalling the incident. "I won't deny her her
privacy, but we've told her, 'I don't want anything being inserted in
anybody.' They could have their privacy if she promises that *that* won't
happen." Lesley's son and another little boy had "used a Magic Marker
Mb4   on each other." She recounted the incident. "When my husband gave
Gordie a bath that night he found that his anus was black. They had
colored each other's anus! Gordie just said, 'We were coloring each
other's behinds.' I said we didn't think that Magic Marker was that
healthy to be on his anus. We said it wasn't very healthy to do that,
and please, they shouldn't do it again."

        It should be pointed out, perhaps, that there were a few parents
who said that they did not make any distinctions on the basis of sex
in setting standards for their children's touching behavior with their
friends. And, occasionally, the age of the child involved was mentioned
as more important than their sex. Oliver, for instance, said that though

he might be able to accept a certain amount of physical exploration as normal between two very young children, he viewed it as less suitable when children were older or when a gap existed between the ages of the two participants.

Others Touching Children

Parents were asked what they would do if an adult touched their children in a way they considered too intimate or sexual. Though, fortunately, only two people reported that their children had been involved in such incidents, the subject evoked highly emotional reactions in all of the parents interviewed. Ted, who is a social worker for a city agency in Des Moines, talked of his passionate revulsion at the thought of a child being victimized sexually by someone older. "I'm not a very good   Fg6
subject when it comes to that, and I roll it into the parameters of child abuse. In my job I was involved with situations similar to that and it became very difficult to attempt to restrain myself from actually wanting to smack this guy right in the mouth for what he did." Other parents described the firm rules they set down with their children—and repeated over and over—warning them not to talk to strangers, not to accept candy or gifts or go anywhere with anyone they did not know. Sharon said, "We try to keep this whole idea of strangers and you don't   Mb4
even go around the block, you just don't do it, you don't go anywhere unless I know where you're going and there's a reason. We do tell him you could fall and get hurt, first of all, but also someone could steal you, there are robbers who take children." She did not think this was the healthiest message to give a four-year-old, but she also believed that distrust of outsiders was the best protective measure she could instill in him: "You hate to have to put that kind of fear into a child. He knows all these things are there, but then he forgets, he's very cocky. He's that kind of naive little boy yet."

Sometimes the inappropriate contact came not from a stranger but from someone the parents thought they could trust. Cassandra stressed the fact that parents should urge a child to let them know if she felt a relative or family friend was making her uncomfortable " 'cause I have   Mg6
quite a few friends that have children from their father 'cause they were afraid to tell their mother and I never want to see myself in that type of situation."

In both cases where an adult had made some kind of sexual advances to a child, the person was known to the parents. Sandy's daughter, thirteen, was a visitor at a home where her friend's father was behaving strangely. "Looking at her breasts and at her legs . . . follow-

ing her around." Her mother was furious and created an on-the-spot policy forbidding her ever to go there again. Sandy was also very insistent that both her daughter and her son, nine, avoid any adult who made
Mg13b9   them feel in the least bit uncomfortable. "I've alerted them. Absolutely. I told them that there are people who have very big problems and who are crazy and you have to be careful, and you don't ever get yourself into a situation where you can't get out. I always told the kids that if something doesn't feel right, go with that feeling. Even if it's the slightest twinge, the slightest little whatever it is, listen to it because more often than not it's correct. They should follow their instincts."

The most horrifying story, however, came from a mother who was particularly adamant about remaining anonymous because of the delicacy of the situation. Her ten-year-old daughter had been molested by a delivery man who brought groceries regularly to their home and
Mg10   was well liked by the family. "He put his penis into her mouth. I really don't want to go into it. That's basically what happened," she began with great difficulty. The parents in this case had taken legal action to have the man prosecuted (though it seemed unlikely that anything would come of it), but their major effort was to minimize the emotional trauma of their little girl. Professional counseling had been effective in helping the child deal with her reactions to the incident, but her parents also took an active role in giving her feelings of self-worth. "What I was more concerned about was that she know she was a good girl. She did nothing wrong. *He* did something wrong." The mother regretted that she had not been at home at the time. "But sometimes parents can't always be there. This is how life is, sometimes," she said bitterly. "I just try to impress on her that I still love her. 'You're still the same Wendy.' . . . I was heartbroken that something like this happened to her, but it did, so where was I going to go from there? I was going to give her as much support and love as I could and the scars are still there. I just hope that eventually they won't be there."

Like Sharon and Sandy, the mother tried to make clear to her daughter that there are people who are sick emotionally and can be harmful. But she hoped that by reassuring her that not everyone behaves this way, she could rebuild rather than destroy her trust, so badly undermined in an encounter with someone she had once been fond of. "And I tried to show her that there are people in the world that are not very nice, that they may even be evil, but that doesn't mean that you are. *It is not a reflection on you. It's a reflection on them.* It's too bad there are things like this in our society, but you have to deal with it." One other concern was the effect this experience might have on the girl's attitudes toward sex, in general, as she grew older. The message her parents wanted to convey was "that not all men are that way." And, after a year, she seemed to be responding to their affection and reassurances. Though the memories continued to surface from time to time, she was less and less frightened, comfortable with male friends of the family. "She ran to hug and kiss a friend of ours, so she knows it's not all men. It was this one person in an isolated instance."

More often, parents had to handle incidents in which it was an older child who engaged in inappropriate contact with a child. Most parents felt that the ideal way to react in such cases was with direct intervention. Janet described how she put an immediate stop to this kind of behavior when she walked in on a fifteen-year-old, a friend of her son's, "kidding around" with her daughters, ages thirteen and eleven, trying to hold them on his lap. "I just felt that was a bit too much," she said. "I don't remember how I did so, but I let them know I didn't want any more of their shenanigans. I just put my foot down. I didn't give them reasons, just 'CUT IT OUT!' " Mg13g11

Most parents whose children had encountered such situations, however, were unable to act so decisively because, unlike Janet, they were seldom right there on the spot. Generally, the incidents occurred outside the house and the children, sensitive to their furtive or embarrassing nature, were reluctant to inform their parents until well after the fact. Usually, by the time the parent heard the whole story, it was too late to confront the offender. What remained possible then was only for the parent to discuss the incident with the child in a neutral but supportive fashion, offering reassurance where possible and attempting to bolster damaged self-esteem. Occasionally parents did try to get in contact with the parents of an offending child, but many expressed a generalized anxiety about the whole issue that prevented them from taking any kind of dramatic action. (This anxiety also seemed to make it difficult for a few parents to carry on extended discussions of the incidents with their victimized children.) Sometimes the parent of the offending child was known to be extremely severe or unreasonable, was even considered the possible source of the offending child's problems. In cases like that, the parent of a victimized child might not wish to be responsible for exacerbating these problems for an already troubled youngster. Most incidents of this kind, however, seemed to have occurred when parents were not close at hand, with children who did not have normal social access to the family's circle.

> We have a next-door neighbor, a boy, who is about four or five years Mg7
> older than she. This must have been when he was about twelve and
> that would have made her about seven. He said to her something
> about let me see your vagina and she felt it was inappropriate and
> walked away and told me about it and nothing was ever done. I felt
> it was an isolated incident and I know the family and I just kind of
> closed my eyes to the whole thing and told my daughter she did the
> right thing by not complying.

Mg9   A friend's son, he was in high school and he spent a bit of time here.
I liked him. I liked his mother and he liked it here. I think he tried
to kiss my daughter and he was just too affectionate. It was a situation where his mother and father were split and I think he needed
affection. My daughter couldn't stand him. I thought he was cute.
He kept going after her—"Come on, Sue, come on." She was really incredibly turned off. She was nine and the boy was in high
school. It's a big difference. It's not a healthy situation.

Mg10   It happened at camp last summer. She said, "I never told you about
it at the time because I forgot," but a seventeen-year-old waiter who
she had been talking to stopped her as she was walking down back
to her bunk and sat there with her on his lap for a long time, talking
to her. I said to her, "What was he doing?" She said, "Well, he was
really weird, he was playing with my hand and he was talking to
me." And I said, "Did you feel uncomfortable?" she said, "Yes. He
was weird." I said, "Well, did he do anything to make you feel
uncomfortable?" And she said, "No." And that was the end of it.

When they discussed their standards for touching or not touching,
particularly in the home, parents talked about behavior which was not
meant to be erotic, though, as has been seen, there were times when
physical contact between parents and children might violate an unex-
pressed set of rules. What began as playfulness, warm affection, or
innocent curiosity on the child's part might become something more
sensual, a cover for complex feelings underneath. It was of course also
true that children could be overt, though not completely conscious,
about seeking sexual pleasure, touching themselves in a variety of sensuous ways or masturbating outright. This kind of purposeful touching
raised questions quite different from the ones which have been covered in previous chapters. Since it was an isolated, personal activity,
which did not impinge on anyone else in the family, parents could
ignore it more readily than other kinds of touching. The decision of
whether to set limits on children who enjoyed touching themselves
had to be based on the parents' sense of how harmful self-stimulation
was, physically and socially. But the subject also involved more emotionally charged issues. Ultimately, people had to come to terms with
their attitudes in general toward sex as pleasure for pleasure's sake.

5

The

Pleasure

Principle

Children's earliest pleasurable experiences of the world come to them from touching and being touched. They reach out with fingertips, feet, faces, tongues to explore their environment and themselves; they are held, kissed, nuzzled, and rocked by others. And even as they grow, that sensuousness remains. Again and again, parents described how, long after babyhood, children continued to enjoy the special sensations of a great many activities which were in themselves quite unremarkable—holding objects, soaking in a tub, crawling under the bedcover, thumb-sucking. Clearly, they derived their pleasure in part from the association of these activities with security and being loved. But parents believed there was also something more elusive, more self-absorbed, about this behavior. Children touched things, other people, and their own bodies because, on the most elemental level, *it felt good*.

Parents' reactions when they observed such primitive gratification varied depending on how "innocent" they thought the enjoyment was. Few raised serious objections when children were attached to a special toy or asked to be stroked—or stroked themselves—on the cheek, trunk, arms, and legs. But, on the whole, parents were ambivalent about the fact that children also took pleasure in touching their own genitals. Though parents could not always be certain at what point sensuous play became sensual play, many felt uneasy about confronting these signs of blatant eroticism in their children. There were those who retained guilt-ridden memories of their own furtive experimentation with masturbation. In many cases, though, the discomfort was around the larger issue of sexual pleasure—desire, arousal, orgasm—which parents found too personal or too abstract to include in general discussions about sex with their children. Sometimes, in fact, when children masturbated, parents were reluctant to intrude on what they saw as an intensely private act.

There were other concerns, however, which made it impossible for parents to overlook their children's involvement with sensual pleasure all of the time. Some feared that masturbation, if it was excessive, could be harmful physically or emotionally. Just about all agreed that they would not want a child to be embarassed by other people's reactions if he touched himself in public. And many were anxious because the child's awareness of the connection between self-stimulation and intense pleasure, especially as he approached puberty, was clearly the prelude to sexual relationships—with others. As they talked about these subjects, parents found themselves reacting to and sorting out many feelings they had never fully acknowledged before.

"Cuddlies" and Other Pleasurable Things

Many parents reported that their children seemed to derive sensual pleasure from dolls and stuffed animals, especially the ones they habitually took to bed with them. They liked the simple physical feel of the toys, and they enjoyed cuddling, holding, or stroking them, particularly those which had appealing surfaces. Sometimes they took delight in objects that were smooth and hard—plastic or rubber figures they could bite, lick, or caress—but generally they responded best to soft, fuzzy, and furry things. Simon's little girl, for instance, had special favorites among her dolls. "Of course, the soft ones, the huggy ones." Alex's daughter had a similar preference. "I think, like most children, my daughter enjoys the softness of a stuffed animal, her teddy bear, or a particular doll. I notice that the ones she picks up a lot are the cloth dolls rather than the plastic ones because I think the cloth is much softer and the dresses are older and softer." Alex, a sculptor married to a silversmith, believed that both parents' special awareness of texture had been passed on to their daughter. "As artists, my wife and I are

Fg4

always pointing out the softness and the roughness of things, the tactile quality, so she's particularly aware of it. It does all tie in."

Most parents, however, noticed that their children began to enjoy tactile contact with their toys, especially the cuddly ones, quite spontaneously and naturally when they were very young. Doretta's son took pleasure in his collection of teddy bears—"Misha, the Russian bear; Pooh Bear"—when he was just an infant. "An example of his sensuality around his bears: I don't remember how old he was—he was just crawling. I used to blow into his belly button and he crawled over to the teddy bear and blew on its belly button, rubbed its tummy and looked into its eyes to see if it would laugh." She added, "It didn't laugh and he was very puzzled by that, but it didn't change his involvement. He's a very sensual kid." Lorna described her four-year-old son's sensuous responses to a variety of toys. "If you mean by sensual, smelling and light touching and things like that, yeah, there are a lot of his toys that I would say he gets pleasure from—the Pooh Bear, the fuzzy, cuddly things, even the scratch-and-sniff books. He cuddles them, hugs them, kisses them." The father of another four-year-old said his son's "Fuzzy Bear" was "his favorite of everything. He touches himself with it and smells it and seems to like it very much." Mb6

Some older children had maintained these affectionate, sensuous relationships with their "bed toys" even when other remnants of early childhood behavior had been put aside. The mother of an eight-year-old boy said, "He loves to cuddle furry toys and animals and he still sleeps with them. He has a little dog that has like a Santa Claus cap on and he'll fall asleep with it. He doesn't fall asleep without having his little furry animal. I think he is really a sensual child." Annette related that her eleven-year-old daughter "is always holding a stuffed animal and it always goes to bed with her at night. She kind of cuddles it to her breast or maybe right by her head." The mother of a ten-year-old girl said, "She sleeps with one to three stuffed animals." Mb8 Mg11 Mg10

Sometimes the special object was a blanket, an afghan, or some other bed covering. The child slept under it, wore it, stroked it lovingly. Harold's five-year-old daughter always had her blanket with her around the house. "She rubs it across her nose and her face, carries it upstairs with her." Cheryl's son, at nine, had a similar attachment to his baby blanket. "My son has had his blanket since he was a year old. It has lots of holes in it. It used to have flowers on it but it no longer has flowers on it. It's been worn as a poncho, it's been used as a Batman cape. He has a lot of pleasure out of smelling it, touching it, and perhaps it has become more sensual to him as he has gotten older." For some children, the blanket was a comfort at bedtime. Stephanie's son would touch his blanket and entwine it in his fingers when he went to sleep. Another child occasionally used her blanket as a substitute for a Fg5 Mb9

(marginal codes: Mb6, Mb4, Fb4, Mb8, Mg11, Mg10, Fg5, Mb9)

Mg10 parent's soothing hand, an aid to sleep. "She'll move her leg against the sheet," her mother observed, "like taking the place of someone stroking her. She's a very active child and I guess that's her way of relaxing, sort of unwinding."

Fg5 Sometimes it was not the soft, wooly centers but the borders of their blankets—"a really soft, silky kind of thing," Steve called it—
Mb11 that appealed to children. Stacey recalled that her son "did enjoy, as a really little guy, until maybe three or four years old, any blanket that had a satin binding on it. He liked to stroke that and rub it between his fingers. He had a pet name for it. It was 'the part.' I guess some-where along the way someone said to him. 'That's the part of the blan-
Fg5 ket you like." A father told this anecdote: "One time her grandmother got angry with her using this dirty blanket, so she cut off the hem, so it's portable. My daughter just went around with the ragged hem."

Several parents shared humorous or touching stories to illustrate the deep, persistent attachment children often retained for their "blan-kies" as they grew up. Steve mentioned having to buy an identical new blanket after his daughter's original favorite had finally disinte-
Fg5 grated and been thrown away. "Actually this is a replacement blanket. The first one went out, so we substituted another one. We had to go out and find the exact one." The mother of a rather mature and sophis-
Mb11 ticated eleven-year-old said, "It's true, if he's tired and he's not feel-ing well, he tends to cuddle up with a blanket and will stroke the binding or even put it in his mouth and suck on it a little bit." And Harold, who felt that his daughter's attachment to her blanket rein-forced her thumb-sucking, especially when she was tired, reported with
Fg5 mock exasperation, "We have a rule that she can play with it when she is going to bed, but she can't play with it when she is watching TV. If we take the blanket away she will be a little more active. We have this vision that someday she will get married and instead of a train she will have this blanket!"

Clothes, too, could be sources of sensual pleasure for some chil-
Mb6 dren. One mother, a clothing designer, told this story. "My son is aware of tactile differences. At one of the shows I was in I traded a piece [of my work] for a beautiful hand-crocheted sweater for him that had a very raised soft hair, and his first reaction to it was a sensual tactile one. He
Fb11 said, 'Oh, how soft!' even before he touched it. He pets it like a pussy cat." Brent, however, felt his son was "more visually oriented than tac-tilely oriented" in his sensuous preferences. "There are objects that visually attract him sensually," he said. "The normal sort of boyhood things like football uniforms or hats, particularly. It's a big thing now, his hats. He's making a hat collection. He seems to have a flair for dressing."

Children in families owning pets often derived sensual pleasure from stroking and cuddling the animals. One mother said, "We have cats and he is constantly, constantly stroking the cat. The kids are always stroking the cats and so am I. I'm a fuzz person." Then she added, "I remember being in Macy's and being two foot two and stroking the bottoms of fur coats. I would say that it was sensuous." Doretta remarked that her son "pets, he caresses, kittens *and* people." Leonard's daughter "loves to pet the dog. She does a lot of stroking, cuddling, with the dog. This would be sensual pleasure; she uses her senses, at least on the tactile level." He also pointed out how these sensual experiences were closely connected to overall feelings of warmth, love, and security. "She is really into the dog as being part of the family. She loves the dog and the dog really loves her." _{Mb14b11} _{Mb6} _{Fg7}

Children were capable of deriving sensuous pleasure from a wide variety of other objects. Their preferences were related to any number of factors—their experiences or associations, the influence of a parent who transmitted his own sensory delight in an experience to the child, the child's idiosyncratic responses to some sensation over others.

> She has what she calls her "fuzzy" which is the inside of a glove that I had many years ago that she likes to carry around with her. It's just a piece of fur. She touches it, holds it. _{Fg5}

> Feathers, pieces of grass—you know what foxtail grass looks like. Flower petals. We have a flower garden, so that kind of thing is very accessible. But especially feathers. Mostly on cheeks and necks and ears. _{Mb6}

> He loves to touch my husband's beard. _{Mb8}

> She likes to touch flowers. She likes to touch flowers with her nose right in them. She likes scents, she likes perfume *[laughs]*. She got this from me. I like anything sensual. I put body lotion on from head to toe. I keep fresh flowers in the house. I keep scented candles in the house. I have pink light bulbs in all the lights. I like an overall effect. _{Mg10}

Several parents believed their children's strong sensuous reactions to things, particularly bed toys and blankets, were more likely to indicate their need for security than sensual pleasure. Alex said, "Often when I put Marissa to bed, I realize this is a very pleasurable experience for her to have. Not only the security of having the father putting her into bed but also the security of having her own afghan right near her." Robert's daughter looked for her blanket whenever she was upset. Several parents believed their children's attachment to stuffed animals took them back to the warm feelings of being cuddled and loved when they were infants. Cynthia, whose ten-year-old son still sleeps with his "Bear-and-diaper," said "I think it's more of the baby security type. It's comfort, from way back, for whatever it meant to him when he was a little baby." _{Fg9} _{Mb10}

Nongenital Touching

Fg4

Mb8

Mb4

Mg11

Most parents seemed to think, however, that children's pleasure in being touched—stroked, cuddled, rubbed, caressed—all over their bodies, even the nongenital areas, was largely sensual. This held true for children of all ages, from the smallest toddlers to boys and girls just approaching puberty. Simon talked enthusiastically about his four-year-old daughter's responsiveness to being touched. "She's almost catlike in the pleasure she gets in being held, and she gets held quite a bit. I mean, physically we hug her a lot, touch her and are playful with her. I think there are a lot of pleasurable moments for her." Stephanie's eight-year-old liked to be cuddled. "He knows that there is a good feeling produced by physical stroking, touching, nerve endings. He likes me to pet him on the head like a pussycat or the doggy that he has in bed with him. I think he knows that there's pleasure from stroking." She added, "I don't think he realized that it's sexual. I don't think he understands that." Lorna's four-year-old was extremely sensuous. "He seems to enjoy touching his whole body. 'Boy, am I gorgeous!' Things like that. Touching his chest and tummy, in particular, when he's getting dried after his bath. And he enjoys his bath, laying back in the warm water and feeling it around his shoulders. He's just taking swimming lessons so he's just getting used to that feeling. But the warm water and playing in the dust and things like that too. All those things kind of give him pleasure. But most of all I would say his tummy and chest. And he loves back rubs!" Annette made a similar comment about her older child. "She likes to be kissed. More than even the kissing, she likes the touching, hugging, holding. She likes that. She likes to be touched on parts of her body. She likes her back to be rubbed, her arm to be touched. She'll often say, 'Stroke me, stroke my back!' "

Many children let their parents know which areas of their bodies gave them special sensuous pleasure. Sometimes one of the rather mundane requirements of hygiene—being washed for instance—became a source of pleasure. Often, there was a little ritual—being touched in a favorite place in a particular way at a specific time of day—which they asked to have repeated over and over.

Fg4

[She has eczema so] we look after her skin a lot. Her skin gets a lot of attention. Sometimes I wonder in what way that's going to be part of her sense of herself. I think she gets a certain amount of pleasure but it's also a certain amount of relief.

Mg10

She likes me to stroke her back and she's crazy about tickling. I brush her hair and I rub her neck. She rubs mine. We're overall body people.

He loves to have his ears cleaned, since he was a little guy. He would   Mb11
lay there and say, 'Oooh, that's nice, oooh,' and it was really a sensuous kind of response.

Children also enjoyed touching the nongenital areas of their own
bodies. Little girls, especially, loved to stroke and caress their own
hair. One father reported that his little girl played with her hair a lot.
"She was always conscious of her hair. She's proud ot it. And when-   Fg4
ever I mention cutting her hair, she goes crazy." Another father, whose
daughter is nine, made a similar observation. "For a little girl, she   Fg9
spends an enormous lot of time arranging her hair, coming up with
very unusual hairdos. I thought this came much later on, when they
were adolescents. I think it's a combination of aesthetic and sensual."
But Annette, whose daughter was "endlessly playing with her hair,"   Mg11
thought this habit was not so much sensual as it was a " 'pretty' thing.
It has to do with her looks."

Girls also apparently derived sensuous pleasure simply from the
act of dressing and undressing. Some of them clearly also enjoyed observing their clothed or unclothed bodies in the mirror and striking
"sexy" poses like those they had seen in magazines, posters, or calen-
dars. This was particularly true of girls who were eight or nine years
old, just on the verge of puberty.

She doesn't get pleasure so much from touching. She loves to walk   Mg8
around the house naked and look at herself in the mirror. She likes
to dress up. I tease her some day she's going to be an exhibitionist
because she does that all the time. She loves to stand in front of the
mirror and pose, one hand on her hip and one on her head, like Betty
Grable, and wiggles her heinie. You can catch her in some of the
weirdest poses sometimes.

She changes clothes constantly. We have relatives who are rather well   Fg9
off, and they have wonderful clothes and they donate them to us.
We get a lot of beautiful hand-me-downs, like, terrific clothes for her,
so she has got a great big wardrobe and she loves to try on all these
different things, color arrangements. And I think she is very aware
of her body.

Some children were quite sensitive to kinesthetic pleasure and
enjoyed all kinds of motions.

There is something he likes to do that gives him great pleasure, and   Fb4
that's when he's tired and goes to bed, he rocks himself to sleep.
Side to side. He knows just how to do it, too. He gets his arm a
certain way and he gets his bear a certain way and he just starts rocking back and forth.

She and I dance together. We move together. She likes things you   Mg10
can be active with, that she can feel and move with.

One group of children possessed certain "nervous" habits—nail-biting, thumb-sucking, nose-picking—that seemed to contain some sensual gratification as well.

Mb4   He picks his nose. That's the only thing that he does to his body regularly that gives him that pleasure. We can't seem to stop him.

Fb5   He picks at his fingernails. Just when he's tired and thinking about something or watching something in a trance, you know, he's picking at them. It probably does give him pleasure, because we can't seem to stop him.

Mb8   He's a touching kind of child. He'll touch his toes. He bites his fingernails. He puts his hands in his mouth.

These habits were evidently sources of concern for many parents, and for some of the children too, as they grew older. Annette said her daughter, now eleven, knows it's time to stop sucking her thumb. "Nobody has ever encouraged her to stop but she herself wants to. I decided not to say anything about it. She comes to me and says, 'It's embarrassing to me. I'm old enough not to, but, guess what, I still do!' and I'll say things like, 'When you are ready, you'll stop,' and that it's okay." Harold found it comforting to recall that his older child, Zack, had finally grown out of his finger-sucking habit. "In spite of all our worry, he seems to have gotten out of it, so we feel my daughter will get out of it, too." He described one of the ways he and his wife were trying to discourage the habit, without actually forbidding it. "If Naomi is sitting watching TV or playing with kids or whatever, like we will say, 'Oh, you're sucking your thumb, that must mean it's time for you to go to bed,' so she'll stop." Harold like other parents, had noticed that children seemed to have greater need for sensual gratification—especially in its more unconscious forms—when they were fatigued or out of sorts. Doretta took a positive and supportive view of her son's various forms of nongenital self-pleasuring. "I think it's lovely," she said. "I say to him, 'How nice you're hugging yourself, giving yourself a hug today. Sometimes there aren't other people around, and you do it when you need to do it. It's *nice* that you can do it for yourself.' "

A few children derived sensuous pleasure from touching other people—family members, friends, visitors to their homes. At least two mothers were very delighted with their children's sensuality and their ability to integrate it into socially acceptable behavior. Sandy talked about her eleven-year-old son. "He's very affectionate. He's not embarrassed by things like that at all. I keep saying to him, 'What am I going to do when you get older and you won't want to sit on my lap?' 'Oh, I'm always going to sit on your lap.' It's a very open channel with him." She mentioned that his teacher had described him as "unusual," a boy who could put his arm around someone else without pretending

Mg11

Fb8g5

Mb6

Mb11

to wrestle in order to do it. But he also could recognize when friends did not want to be touched. "I think he can sense," Sandy said proudly. "Kids have antennae that probably are a lot stronger than ours." Stacey, also the mother of an eleven-year-old, described her son's behavior in similar terms. "He'll cuddle when he's in the mood," she said. "He'll come right up and cuddle with people he likes. He's very selective about that, but if it's someone he really feels close to, he'll stand close and will even tolerate being patted on the head. And he likes to scratch backs. He thinks of himself as being quite good at it and he is. Just recently a friend has a stiff neck and I volunteered to massage the neck. I wasn't getting anywhere and my son said, 'Step aside—I'll do it!' He did and it was good. It was pointed out that he did a much better job than I, and he did. He is really good at that and he enjoys it. If you define sensual in that he gets pleasure from his body and others, I think he's very comfortable with his body. He's comfortable with body contact, but at his discretion. He's not constantly looking for it." Mb11

In some cases, particularly when the children were boys and outsiders were involved, this kind of sensuous touching created awkward or uncomfortable moments. Stephanie's eight-year-old son was in love with his older brother's girlfriend, even though she was almost twenty. "He'll see Ted holding her or hugging her and Tony'll want to do the same thing. His hand will rub against her breast and that's uncomfortable for me. She just laughs. She's a very kind of outgoing girl and she knows, really, what's going on, but I'm sure it makes her slightly uncomfortable, too." Mb8

Not all such incidents were resolved so tactfully or good-naturedly, however. When Doretta's son, at age four, had touched an adult male friend in a sensual but innocent way, the man's response was unexpectedly violent. "My son got dumped on the floor and thereupon I ended up throwing the good friend out of the house." Though she had let her son know that simple sensual contact was quite acceptable to her, she realized that other people found it problematical or upsetting. She went on to discuss her fears for her son in a society that sets what she feels are unrealistically stoic and restrained standards for male behavior. "I'm very guarded and protective of him. He's a boy. My feeling is I would like him to keep his sense around feelings and not squish it down, like these mutilated men that walk around all the time. My experience is, it's a lot of work, that most people, even liberal ones—I put that in quotes—they won't say the words, but they will want to say, 'Well, he's a *boy*, he's not supposed to be that affectionate, sensual, et cetera, et cetera. I want to keep him out of the sex-role stereotype category and maintain his interest and pleasure in pleasure." Mb4

"Cheryl believed that no matter what she taught her son, he would somehow learn from the environment that a boy has to hide his sensuality as he grows up. She talked of how, until recently, he had always

Mb11   loved stroking her hair. "I don't think he would let himself be caught doing that now," she said. "I chalk that off to maturity, not in a terribly positive sense. The older you get, you have a recognition of external judgment."

Genital Touching

Generally, parents took great satisfaction in observing their children's enjoyment of the various parts of their bodies—except when it came to genital touching. Though they spoke of tolerant views and policies around masturbation, the majority found it a complicated, embarrassing, anxiety-producing topic and had not officially discussed it with their children. And since children were less likely to bring up questions about masturbation than about intercourse, reproduction, or birth, parents hoped to avoid the topic altogether, unless there were specific incidents which required comment—a child masturbating in public, for instance.

For some parents, the reluctance to speak about masturbation was clearly related to the sex of the child in question. Mothers of boys and fathers of girls did not think they knew enough about how self-stimulation felt to the opposite sex to talk about it with their children. But the issue of privacy loomed particularly large in parents' decisions to omit this topic from sexual discussions. Any reference to the practice

Fb4   might be regarded as reproachful, guilt-inducing, even prying. "I can't picture myself sitting him down and saying, 'Now, Son, do you masturbate and, if so, why?' " Monte said. Drew was ambivalent about

Fb10   introducing the subject with his ten-year-old. "On one hand, I want to make him assured that it's a natural thing but he shouldn't feel guilty about it, although he's not a kid that carries around a lot of guilt. On the other hand, the old problem of the 'Let's talk about masturbation for the next half-hour' kind of conversation I don't think is very effective." Fathers were not alone in experiencing discomfort around the issue. Cheryl, ordinarily quite forthright in speaking with her sons, re-

Mb11   marked, "There has been absolutely no discussion about masturbation, period! I have no reasons to bring it up. I'm probably very willing to let the thing go by. Avoidance. If there is no problem, why rock the boat?"

Nevertheless, almost all parents acknowledged that their children derived pleasure from patting or stroking their genital areas, sometimes covertly—suddenly getting all giggly in the bath—sometimes quite openly and innocently. Parents were not always certain where to draw the line between casual touching and masturbation. Lorna, for instance, described in some detail the way her son delighted in playing with his penis, but she made it quite clear that she doesn't consider this real

masturbation. "He pulls [his penis] way out and stretches it and says   Mb4
'Look!' and I think, 'Jesus, doesn't that hurt?' But he says it tickles.
He'll smush it all down and say 'Look at it disappear!' and it pops out
again. So it is touching and stuff, though it certainly is not what I would
think of as refined, adult masturbation." Cynthia made a similar comment about her son's fondness for touching his genitals. "When he   Mb6
was about six years old, he touched himself a lot. He was always worried about arranging his penis in his shorts. It seemed it was a typical
thing to see the kids with their hands in their pockets on the soccer
field, but I don't think he masturbates." She added, "My husband
said it might not be pleasure, but just anxiety about school starting. It
doesn't happen now."

Sharon could not say for sure where the line should be drawn
between informal stimulation and actual masturbation. "Well, I don't   Mb4
know if my son is in effect masturbating or just, you know, he puts
his hands in his pants. If he's sitting in his pajamas he'll put his hands
in his pants. He's not moving in any way, but just sitting there holding, next to his belly, pretty close to that area, just there. The hands
are there." Annette, too, was uncertain. In her family, casual touching of the body, including genital areas, was acceptable for all—
parents and children alike—so it was often hard to say whether her
eleven-year-old daughter was masturbating or merely touching her body
in a familiar family style. "I have seen her hands in her pants, but   Mg11b4
everybody's hand is in their pants. She could be on occasion touching
herself, but it's so casual. My son has his hands in his pants. My husband has his hands in his pants. So it's very hard. I've never seen her
going up and down a pole or gone into her room and she was in there
with her hands in her pants in the covers. That I've not seen." The
father of a five-year-old girl said, rather dubiously, "She may hold   Fg5
herself, but I don't think she masturbated to the point of orgasm or
anywhere near it. I really don't."

Masturbation

A larger number of parents, however, observed a variety of forms of
purposeful touching in their children that were clearly masturbation.
Doretta said of her son, "Oh, yes, he masturbates. He walks around   Mb6
with his little hand on his penis for hours. It started when he was a
baby, I would say every night, going to sleep holding his penis. And
almost any time he was uncomfortable, sleepy, upset, he would go
and hold his penis. If he had a bad cold he'd go around holding his
penis. For comfort. That's just beginning to change at this point. He's

obviously experimented with it one way or another." Tovah reported
that her daughter was equally relaxed and open about giving herself
Mg10   pleasure. "She feels very comfortable with her body. She can be sitting in the living room watching television and stroking her legs almost up to the vaginal area. I think mainly she does it in bed. It relaxes
her to sleep. Almost every night when she falls asleep I find the quilt
between her legs. And she also does a certain amount of dramatic movement even when she's asleep, which I relate to a certain level of orgasm,
so I definitely feel that she masturbates." One mother related that her
son had confided in her how much he enjoyed masturbating. "He has
Mb5   this friend," she said. "He likes her very much. He says, 'She gives
me such a funny feeling and I have to come home and masturbate.'
And I says, 'Where did you get that from?' They pick up so many
things. He says, 'Well, it's just a feeling I have and it just feels great!' "

Parents supplied many other examples of the ways in which their
Fg9   children masturbated. "She certainly plays with her vagina," Oliver
remarked. "I know that because I see her doing it. I see her opening
her legs and playing with herself in the tub, or sometimes when she is
lying in bed reading." Agnes described the "evidence" she had that
Mg13g12g7   her daughters masturbated. "I walk in the room and see them on top
of the pillow or on top of the doll with their covers under them, you
know, all crunched under them. Paul observed of his five-year-old son,
Fb5   "He has a sense that his penis is pleasurable, that I know. He plays
with himself and he sleeps with both hands inside his pajamas, and
I've seen him play with himself. I've said to him, 'That feels good,
doesn't it?' and he says, 'Yeah.' "

Some children were quite inventive about masturbating. Leonard,
Fg7   whose daughter is seven, remarked with some amusement, "She loves
to slide the banister, or rocking back and forth in a chair, or a rocking
horse. She does all of that. I didn't figure it out until now." Clarice's
Mb7   son, also seven, "would rub up and down couches and sofas, against
chairs, against beds." A few children even enlisted their parents' aid.
Penelope described how her daughter demanded, "Wash me here,
Mg5   wash me there," when she was in the bath. "More in the vaginal area
than anywhere else. Sometimes she'll even say, 'I need powder for my
vagina because I think I'm getting an irritation,' and then she's serious.
But then when I'm powdering her, she says, 'Rub it in! Rub it in! Pat
it on!' and she's laughing, and I do!"

A number of parents noticed this autoeroticism in their children
Fg6   almost from the very beginning. "At approximately an hour and a half
of age, my daughter discovered her vagina and discovered it was fun
and so on," Henry reported. "Then she discovered that rolling around
on her bottle felt very good. She'd roll and push her bottle against her
vagina and clitoris and have a great old time. This is at a very young
age, probably two. She uses her fingers sometimes, now." Several par-

ents recalled the obvious pleasure their babies took in touching themselves while being cleaned and diapered. "As an infant, she was—they   Mg5
all are—very erotic," Penelope said. A father described how on the
changing table, his daughter—"she was maybe fifteen months old"—   Fg1
used to clamp the Vaseline jar between her legs in such a way that
it rubbed against her vagina. "And then she'd get a big smile on her
face. I'd say to my wife, 'Is she doing what I think she's doing?' And
she'd say, 'Sure enough!' "

Where parents had not actually observed their children masturbating, they had other signals that the children were indeed "doing it"
in their secluded, private moments. Several mothers had noticed a certain tension in the air when they happened to walk in on their sons
unexpectedly. "I don't really see him," Ellen said. "I'm sure he does   Mb5
it in the bathtub—he's playing with himself. Sometimes I walked in
without knocking and it's like, 'Oh, you scared me!' You know, that
type of thing, and I know he's been doing something." Stacey remarked
"I notice now there's a greater tendency for his bedroom door to be   Mb11
closed. I always knock and always wait to be invited in. There have
been a couple of occasions when the door wasn't really closed and in
the knocking the door pushed open a little bit and he was kind of quick
to get his bedclothes organized. I have not *seen* him masturbate." There
were other signals with little girls:

> That was the source of one of her rashes. It was clear she was getting   Fg6
> the rash from using dirty fingers.

> On one occasion she got an infection in her vagina because she had   Fg7
> dirty fingernails. That's happened a number of times. So that is indi-
> rect evidence [that she masturbates].

> I think [she masturbates]. Occasionally I have smelt it on her fingers,   Mg8
> but I have never caught her doing it.

A very few parents doubted that their children masturbated at all.
Some of them felt that until puberty, children were simply not mature
enough sexually to know about masturbation. As one father put it, "For   Fb10
my ten-year-old, I don't think he has those urges or desires, yet I could
be wrong. I just don't think he's capable." But some of these parents
admitted that they might be kidding themselves, refusing to "see"
what they didn't want to acknowledge and deal with. Cheryl was quite
candid about her possible "blind spot." "No, I don't think my child   Mb11
masturbates. I haven't made any observations, but I also have a way of
blocking stuff, I know. Some things are right under my nose and I'll
tell people there is no such thing and I really feel that I'm honest about
it. So it may indeed be going on but I am not aware of it consciously. I'd
be hesitant to say that my kids are the exception. I just don't see it."

"It's Actually Natural"

Most parents, even those who were not entirely happy about children touching themselves, tried not to interfere when they saw their children masturbating. Some of them thought masturbation was an acceptable way to relieve tension. Others believed that though it gave children pleasure, the sensation was not clearly sexual. Children were still, in a sense, innocent, and did not fully comprehend the significance of what they were doing. They played with themselves because it felt good—

Mg10   "just like she enjoys someone stroking her arm or rubbing her leg," Sally said—and parents were reluctant to make much ado about it. Most, too, were willing to concede that masturbation was probably inevitable, one of the normal, natural, and unavoidable aspects of grow-

Mb8   ing up. Stephanie commented, "It's something my son will go through, I'm sure. I can't say I object to it or I favor it or anything. It's just a natural kind of thing I think he will be doing." Other parents shared her attitude, resigned but tolerant. "It is actually natural," Harold said.

Fg5   "We are letting our daughter know that we are not thrilled about it, but not making a big case about it. We're accepting it." Though Constance preferred that her daughter not do it, she did not consider mas-

Mg8   turbation wrong. "That's what she likes to do, so it's okay with us. If she doesn't have to do it, fine. Because I didn't want to encourage it, either. We left it at that."

    Parents gave additional reasons for their relatively laissez-faire attitudes toward masturbation. For a few, the child's right to autonomy— control of his own body—was important. Clarice admitted that her first reactions when she discovered her son masturbating were negative, but that once the initial shock had passed, she was able to gain some

Mb7   perspective on the child's delight in his body. "I used to say, 'Jesus, what's happening with this kid, maybe he's a pervert!' I do remember having those thoughts and then I just cooled it and I let him experiment. Because after all, I would think it's a pretty interesting apparatus, myself."

    Other parents recalled their own experiences discovering their bodies. They had masturbated (some still did, occasionally) and had not been harmed in the least. They were ready to accord their chil-

Mg4   dren the same freedom. "I figure it's normal," Agnes said, and added, "I mean, who didn't? I did it when I was little, too." A father confided,

Fg7   "When I was a kid I was a big masturbator, enormous, and I didn't have any guilt feelings either. My daughter is a really turned-on sensual kid. I think it's wonderful. I was very much like that as a kid."

Fg6   Henry spoke frankly as a single parent. "From time to time I don't have a lover, and when I don't, I go back to masturbation. What's good for the goose is good for the gander. I have no feeling that it's evil, nasty, mind boggling, mind damaging."

There was also a sizable group of parents who saw masturbation as a positive—not merely inevitable—part of human development, a good thing in itself, a joyous and enriching experience. "I think it's great that he's learning," Dennis said about his son's autoerotic experiments. Lorna affirmed, "I think it's a fine thing to do, because you explore your bodies and your feelings and stuff." Doretta put it simply. "Pleasuring oneself, period. It's fine!" She recalled, with some tenderness, the way in which her son, at age three, innocently attempted to share his "pleasuring" with her. "I remember him coming over to me and rubbing his penis against me with a shy little smile. The first time I was really startled. I would not have guessed that a child that age would have been that precocious. I did a double take." But she added this comment about her subsequent reaction to the experience and others like it which followed. "It was nice," she said warmly. "I felt that it was nice that he would want on his own to develop a feeling of sharing sensual-sexual experience in that kind of way. There was just something lovely about it . . . that self-discovery, the wanting to share it." Fb5 / Mb2 / Mb3

Like Doretta, several other parents in the study took delight in observing children learning how to give their bodies pleasure. "It's loads of fun to see a little kid exploring himself," Carla said enthusiastically. "Sometimes he's got this erection and it's adorable. It's about an inch and a half long and there's this three-year-old with this 'enormous' erection!" And Helen told how she and her husband had shared the excitement of watching their son explore his body. "In the bathtub his penis gets really big. He rubs it a little and then it gets big. My husband and I joke about it. My son kind of enjoys it. He'll kind of like say, 'Look there, Superhero' or something. He takes a little pride in it, not because he sees it as a sexual organ, but he sees it changing and growing and he gets a kick out of it. He accepts it as a fact of life. It's one of the wonderful things about him." One father took an extremely practical view of the issue. He thought learning how to masturbate could be useful for a child, to help her deal with the tensions and disappointments of adult life. "There will be times in her life, probably she will need it as a device to get over a very bad love affair. There are many times in a person's life that it would be better to masturbate than get involved." Mb3 / Mb9 / Fg6

Despite these positive views, however, many parents did believe there was a point at which children could become too preoccupied with masturbation and that they had to be alert to the problems such activity might suggest. Some feared that masturbating too much could isolate children from other social and intellectual pursuits. "It can be something that the kid focuses on and slows up the development of other relationships with other people," Sean said. "So I wouldn't want to see my daughter develop that habit to a higher degree." Other parents believed that constant masturbation might be hiding deeper emo- Fg5 tional tensions that children were not talking about. Stephanie said,

Mb8
"If he spent all of his hours in his room masturbating, I think there would be something that would have to be worked on. Because that's

Fg9
not a normal kind of thing." Alex made a similar statement. "The only thing I would caution my daughter against is excessive masturbation. I think, for instance, if a child were to masturbate maybe five times a day, that maybe that would be like a crutch rather than trying to resolve some problems." A single father recalled the particular worries

Fb8
that had cropped up at the time of his divorce. "My wife and I were concerned about masturbation and playing with himself, whether it would become an acting-out diversion during the whole divorce. There were all kinds of nervous release—tension kinds of things—that go on. So we were concerned about that."

Some parents decided to draw the line at some point when they observed excessive masturbation in their children, though they were not always certain just how much masturbation was excessive or to what degree their own discomfort around the subject determined their policies. Fran described how she set limits on her son's genital play in

Mb4
the bathtub. "He likes to stretch [his penis] and see how long he can make it. He thinks that's hysterical. I don't say anything the first time, but if he really gets enthusiastic, I'll say, 'Forget it, wash something else.' He keeps doing it once or twice, and if he thinks it is funny, I'll say, 'Ha, ha,' but after a minute or two, I don't encourage him to continue." Jerry talked about the conflicts he encountered in his own mind around masturbation where his daughter was concerned. The issue had become a source of periodic disagreement between him and

Fg6
his ex-wife. "My daughter plays with herself a lot, actually. I brought it up to her mother a couple of times, only because I felt a couple of times it was just too much, that something might be wrong. It's always her vagina. She's always squeezing. First you think she has to go to the bathroom and then you figure, well, now she's exploring. Then you say it's just too much. How long do you explore? Maybe she has an itch, maybe she has a rash, maybe she has an infection, let's check it out. Her mother's answer is 'Nothing's wrong. She's just touching. She just explores a lot.' " Jerry was aware, though, that his attitude toward his daughter tended to be overcareful and "uptight." "I think I've been too protective too quick. My thing is a 'What's wrong?' attitude, as opposed to accepting the fact that she's just exploring." He admitted, too, that he perceived distinctions between his attitude toward his daughter and toward his son regarding masturbation that might not be entirely valid. "I think if my son was doing it, I would think it was cute. I think that I would feel a little uncomfortable—this is interesting—I would definitely feel a little uncomfortable with *her* doing it, playing with herself."

A number of other parents, especially fathers, admitted to the same kind of "double-think." Masturbation was natural in little boys but not

in little girls. Brian, who has a son as well as three daughters, was ap- Fg15g14b10g6
palled by the idea of his youngest child, a girl, masturbating. "If I
saw my daughter masturbating, God, I don't know. I would probably
scream, 'Go talk to your mother!' I don't know exactly what I would
do." And at least one father had always considered that before the age
of eight or nine, the practice was exclusive to males. "Little boys play Fg6
with themselves. Little girls certainly can't masturbate."

Several mothers noted that it often *seemed* as though girls did not
masturbate whereas boys did, but they believed what actually happened was that boys were obvious and public about it while girls were
not. As a mother of both a son and a daughter, and as a former teacher,
Sally had given some thought to this issue. Though she was not sure
exactly what personal or social pressures accounted for girls' reserve
about touching themselves in front of others, she did suggest that boys
responded to adults' good-natured tolerance of their masturbation
behavior. "My son occasionally masturbates. I've seen his little friends Mb12g10
when they were younger, maybe four or five or six, but I have also
seen it in some older boys in the seventh grade, eighth grade. Right in
school. I mean, they are doing work for me and their hands go down
and it's almost like a release of nerves. They are working, and this is
pleasure. They have gone to a frustration level; they are making themselves content by fondling themselves. But I haven't seen it with the
girls. Where they do it, I don't know, because I've not seen it in public.
I just haven't seen them ride anything or rub their bodies. They just
don't do it. I don't understand it. But with boys I have [seen it]."

Doretta offered quite another explanation for the same phenomenon. She believed that society was actually hard on children of either
sex who masturbate publicly. "There's a constant problem around people asking, 'Why don't you punish them? Why don't you hit them?
How can you allow them to?' et cetera, et cetera. It's an issue that
presses people's buttons." She went on to point out how little girls
benefited from having a "hidden" organ, the clitoris. Unlike boys, they
could stroke themselves without detection. "There has been a constant Mg6
with all the little boys in the playgroup, it's not just my son. There's
real upset at seeing children masturbate. Now, little girls learn very
early to do it in a way that's discreet. I've seen them rub the nipple of
the bottle between their legs, all discovery. No one has shown them. An
adult will stand there and not know what they were doing. The little
boys' parts don't work that way. It's a bizarre screening that goes on."

"It's Not a Normal Thing"

Parents who possessed negative or unaccepting attitudes toward masturbation were in a distinct minority. In fact, only two parents in the
study fell into this category. Both of them ascribed their views on mas-

turbation to religious teachings. Vesta had once taken a "liberal" attitude toward all kinds of genital touching, but her views were altered

Mg11   dramatically after her conversion to "born again" Christianity. "Now,
as a Christian, I see that it's not a normal thing, because your body is
not only something for pleasure. It belongs to God, and when you're
married you enjoy that part with your husband." Sean, a Catholic, had

Fg5g3   a similar point of view. "I am against it on moral grounds. I'm against
it because I just don't think it's the proper approach to developing
sexuality and I don't think it's a good habit to develop. I think I feel
this way because of my own background and my Church, which tended
to give the impression that sex of any type outside of strictly the marriage act was totally wrong and I feel somewhat that way myself, even
today." Both of these parents, however, were reluctant to take a "hard
line" with their children around the issue in spite of their own convic-
tions. Vesta believed that her daughter's decision to masturbate or not
had to come from within herself. "I can't say to my daughter, 'Masturbation is a sin, don't do it.' She will decide for herself if she likes to
do it or if she doesn't like to do it. I can only guide her by my life."
Sean was resigned to the fact that because some experimentation was
inevitable, his daughters were likely to masturbate in private. "I would
not want to put them in a position where if they felt that if they were
going to do it they had to make a big secret out of it and feel guilty
about it, because with the kid growing up there is going to be a certain
amount of that happening. I want my daughter to develop her own
morality," he concluded.

    Other parents reacted against what they perceived as unhealthy
attitudes toward masturbation instilled in them by their religious training. All of these parents vividly described the fears and guilts around
masturbation they had endured as children, although a few wryly added

Mg4   that they had masturbated anyway. "I went to Catholic school," Agnes began, "and I can remember one time when they handed out a
paper on masturbation, saying how bad it was and everything. That
didn't stop you. What the hell, how could something so good be so
bad?" A moment later she admitted, "I felt guilty, though. I guess I
felt guilty, yeah." Alex spoke at length about the excruciating conflicts

Fg9   around masturbation he had experienced during adolescence. "I went
to a very tough high school. The pressure there was so competitive
that it would just get to me and I found that masturbation was a terrific
way to release it," he said. "And because of the Catholic upbringing
there wasn't any room for the normal heterosexual kinds of involvement with girls, so I shied away from that and I didn't want to get into
a homosexual relationship, so masturbation was the perfect [outlet],
although with a tremendous amount of guilt. Oh, tremendous guilt.
Yeah, in fact that guilt has remained with me to this day." Although
Alex is still a practicing Catholic, and takes his children to Mass every
Sunday, he feels that both he and the Church have changed for the

better since he was that beleaguered, guilt-ridden, but highly sensual, child. "I'm beginning to modify my views, especially in relation to my children," he concluded. "I took it all too seriously. I believed all of it when I shouldn't have." Veronica was brought up in the Greek Orthodox tradition. Like Alex and Agnes, she still retained some of the conflicts and free-floating anxieties produced by her family's interpretation of religious doctrine. She had not, in fact, dared to masturbate as a child or even known what "masturbation" was. It was one of the many activities she was taught to regard as "forbidden" in her strict, religious upbringing. "Now, like I said, there is a lot of things that I'm   Mg8 overcoming through my background. Growing up, [masturbation] was something that was never done and it was never talked about. If I was caught doing it, I probably would have gotten beaten. But it never came up when I was a child, because I just didn't do those things. I would be punished. You know, just cursing at an elderly person—'God is going to punish you and you are going to lose your hand if you raise your hand to your mother'—and things like that." Because of such experiences, these parents were among those who made it a point to present a neutral, non-judgmental view of masturbation to their children. They didn't want the children to suffer the same guilts, fears, and inhibitions that they had.

"I Saw No Reason to Stop Her"

None of the parents told their children the traditional punitive stories that had been popular when they themselves were young—"If you touch yourself down there you'll go blind, you'll get acne, you'll get warts, your growth will be stunted." In fact, their policy was to underplay their reactions when they saw children masturbating and, if possible, not to interfere at all. Clarice preferred this approach, though she pointed out that her attitude was considerably more relaxed than that of her husband. "His father and I would be reading a book to my   Mb4 son and he would have his penis out and be rubbing it and his father was more uncomfortable than I was. I remember once or twice his father would say, 'What are you doing, Larry?' I never drew attention to it. I just let him play with himself."

Some parents were so astonished or moved by children's obvious pleasure in touching themselves that they allowed the activity to continue undisturbed. Wanda said she had been quite taken by this experience with a small boy who was visiting her home. "I walked into the   Mg10 room where they were watching TV and my daughter's friend—he was five—looked up at me with a just wonderful gapped-tooth smile and said, 'I have a boner.' I was really worried about the rug," she continued with a rueful smile. "I said, 'Well, Gee, Bobby, sometimes that happens if you have to go to the bathroom. Wouldn't you like to go potty?' and he looked at me, thought a bit and said, 'No, it feels too good.' And so I really learned something." Penelope described an incident in which her own daughter and the daughter of a friend were Mg5   riding a Brahma bull statue at the local library. "My child said to my girlfriend's child, 'If you ride real fast, it feels really good when it rubs your vagina.' They continued riding until my daughter got a very delirious expression on her face." Both women took such delight in the girls' uninhibited enjoyment of their sensations that they decided to say nothing. "I said, 'Let's just see what develops. Let's see how far this can go.' And then the head librarian came in and said, 'You're not supposed to sit on the bull.' But at least she didn't give her any ideas that she was doing a wrong thing by rubbing the bull. I saw no reason to stop her."

"It's Something You Do In Private, If You Want to"

Most parents, however, wanted their children to know that, though masturbation was completely acceptable in private, it should not be done in public. Oliver talked of how, in setting this kind of limit, he expected to develop in his daughter some understanding of the "personal nature" of sex. "I would tell her that you don't masturbate in public. Things with the genitals are not for public display. They are for in the house and they are for private." Parents also felt that teaching children when and where masturbation was acceptable was a way of protecting them from censure in the outside world, another step in Fb8   the socialization process. "We were concerned vis-à-vis how people would perceive it," Ezra explained, "I would like him to have a tension release that is the least dysfunctional to his acceptance in society. And a child sitting in class and rubbing his balls is less functional than somebody who twitches occasionally."

The majority of parents affirmed these points. They did not intrude on children if they were alone but stopped them, in as gentle a way as possible, if they touched themselves when others were present. Several parents described the practical, nonpunitive approaches they took when they observed children masturbating in front of family, Fg8   friends, or outsiders. Richard said, "My daughter masturbated for a long time, much to the consternation of my mother-in-law. It's a big deal [to her]. Both my wife and I agreed my daughter had to be aware she couldn't do it in public, and there were times when we wouldn't want her to do it in our presence. In fact, that became the policy, that if she wanted to do that she had to go to her room. That's not something she could do on the couch while watching television with us around." Fg8   Maeve had been faced with a similar situation. "I noticed at times she might even do it with a baby-sitter or something, and I felt that wasn't appropriate. She would, when she was very tired, for example, or when she was feeling lonely. I know she had done it once [when] her grand-parents were visiting and she was very tired, for example, or when she was feeling lonely and feeling left out at the moment. I spoke to her about it. I told her in essence that is something one does in private. For instance, one goes to the bathroom in private. One takes a shower in private. One attends to personal grooming in private, and this is just one more thing that one did privately. I didn't want to put a taboo on it and yet I didn't feel it was appropriate. She pretty much seemed to accept this." Lorna had handled the problem this way: "If he's doing it in the bathroom and I'm just in there for something, I don't tell him he shouldn't do it. But if he's doing it out, like in the store or something, I say, 'No, wait till you get home or we're with other kids.' I would say to him that people do that when they are alone, when they have privacy. In front of family members, I would say about the same thing. I mean, I wouldn't rush over and pick him up and carry him from the room or spank him or anything, because I think at his age, at four, he's just beginning to learn what's appropriate with people and what isn't." One mother found it helpful to compare masturbation to nongenital touching habits that, while harmless and pleasurable, were not "nice" to do in polite society. "I would say that is some-thing like, you know, picking your nose. Everyone enjoys picking their nose, but you do not pick your nose in public. I mean, let's face it, there are some things that you just do in the privacy of your own home or bedroom. To say it is wrong to do, no. I would say there is a time and a place for everything."

　　Two parents recounted amusing anecdotes that illustrated the need for such "In private yes—in public no" rules. Drew described his exasperation and embarrassment at a community baseball game well-attended by family, friends, and acquaintances, as he watched his son, the center fielder, absentmindedly fondling his genitals. "The first time, I said, 'Okay, so he's got an itch, so scratch it for a minute. But not the whole inning!' I'm sure other people saw it, too. My wife nudged me and I went over to the dugout in between innings and said, 'Please pay attention to the game and don't touch yourself.' He was a little embarrassed, but he didn't do it any more. Again, it was unconscious. He was probably involved in the game." Fran told this story, hilarious now, though she had been mortified at the time the incident occurred. "He had his hand in his pants and when he got an erection he talked about it in the loudest voice on the bus—about his penis getting big—and I was not pleased. What do I do? Do I say, 'Please be quiet!' and make the child feel really nervous and self-conscious, or do I allow it to go on? I'm very puzzled about the right thing. People did laugh. I know that I felt embarrassed about it. I just had to get off at the next stop before anybody saw me." Fran was can-did about the kinds of conflicts many parents faced, even if they did not disapprove of masturbation and had opted for "not in public" practical standards. "I'm faced with how do you explain, how long do you tolerate the child's playing with himself, how do you differentiate between appropriate and inappropriate times, and how do you explain why it's inappropriate without making him feel self-conscious about his body? I don't have the answer."

Some parents took pains to warn their children that although the family accepted masturbation as natural and harmless, some people did not. Cynthia said her son had walked around with his hands in his pants constantly when he was around six and, while she and her husband were "cool" about this habit and expected Justin to grow out of it, they had been concerned about negative reactions from other children, or their parents, or even passing strangers. "We alluded to the fact that people might think it's strange if you touch yourself in public and it is something you do in private if you want to. His reaction was, 'My penis is uncomfortable. I got to rearrange it.' So we said, 'Rearrange it and leave it already!' " She added, "I mean, if he wanted to be totally absorbed in his own pleasure, well, he should do that privately. If he wants to touch himself in front of my husband and me, that's okay."

Another mother made a similar remark. "I have asked him to please keep his hands out of his pants when we're eating dinner. I have touched on the subject that maybe it's not a good idea to have his hands in his pants when he's not at home because it makes other people feel uncomfortable and it's a little inappropriate." She added, noting, as Cynthia had, the persistence of such habits, particularly in little boys, "He keeps on doing it anyway, in the elevator, in the bus." In Lesley's family the same kind of distinction had been made, and had met with the same kind of resistance on the part of her child. "In terms of the outside world we feel kind of funny for him to be sitting there pulling on his penis. I mean, people would look at him a little weirdly, so we try to stop him. He says he can't help it—I'm itchy!' So we've tried to cure the itches rather than saying too much about it. It's hard to deal with. I think there is some kind of public reaction to masturbation."

Henry had told his daughter that strangers, or mere acquaintances, might be less tolerant of genital touching than certain trusted family intimates. "I let her know that there's almost nothing she could do that would bother good friends; however that's not true of other people's houses. There are some people who would be upset or uncomfortable or not understand what she's doing, and it would be a real good choice to do it at home. She asked me, 'Is it *okay?*' and I said, 'Sure it's okay, but at home, where it's appropriate.' So generally at home she can do whatever she likes, provided she doesn't do it with the dog." Doretta, who lived in an urban working-class neighborhood with slightly more conservative attitudes than her own, spoke of the problems she faced

when two sets of standards about masturbation clashed, and the child
stood to suffer. "My problem around him and masturbation has been   Mb6
the area in which we live. My concern is handling reaction out of the
house if one of the children does something experimentally in a setting where they may be hurt by the reaction—the repressed kind of
things that bodies are dirty and the genitals are filthy. My son has heard
that on the street and I attempted to explain, 'Well, that's a person
that thinks their body isn't okay.' That kind of thing came up, very
grossly. I think he knows it's not okay to touch his genitals outside. I
notice he doesn't do it. I think he's picked up the attitudinal differences around the children."

A number of parents used distraction—"Let's find something else
[to do] now"—to deal with the incidents involving genital touching
at inappropriate times. Sally said, "If my daughter was in a shopping   Mg10
mall and had her hands in her pants, I'd have to see what I would do
at that moment. I think I would just change the situation, give her
something else to do—push the shopping cart. Both hands are on the
handle and she can't do anything." Quite often, however, it was the
children themselves who, like Doretta's son, began to monitor their
own behavior, either because experiences outside the home or their
discriminatory "instincts" had alerted them to the general social disapproval of masturbation. Though attitudes toward all kinds of sexual
behavior were relaxed in Ellen's family, she had never had to tell her
five-year-old son that it's not "nice" to masturbate in public. "He's   Mb5
never done it in public. He does have a friend who's always playing
with himself and my son said things to me like, 'That doesn't look
very nice, does it?' I say, 'What do you think about it?' He says, 'No,   Mg10
it doesn't look very nice.' So he knows. He just kind of likes to have
his privacy."

"Anything You Do With Yourself Isn't Bad as Long as You Don't Hurt Yourself"

In addition to educating children about the private nature of masturbation, parents offered several other reasons for discussing the subject
with them. Some parents were worried about safety and cleanliness.
They told children that stimulating the genitals with fingers, or even
with objects, was essentially "okay" as long as sensible precautions
were taken. Leonard advised his daughter, "If you're going to do that,   Fg7
wash your hands. Don't touch yourself with dirty hands." Veronica
said, "I would tell my daughter not so much that she can't do it. I   Mg8
would tell her she could hurt herself—where she's inserting the thing
up, she can hurt herself that way or she can get germs, cause an infection, transfer that to her mouth and whatever." When Irv's daughter
would insert her finger in her vagina, he said to her, "You shouldn't   Fb7

keep playing with yourself, you'll scratch yourself." He was not altogether sure, however, how much of his reaction was a real concern with
hygiene and how much was discomfort with his daughter's sensuality.

There were also parents who wanted to protect their children from
feelings of shame or fear they might develop about touching themselves. This was particularly true when the children had older relatives,
teachers, or friends who were likely to pass on "old wives' tales" about
the subject or when there was a strong cultural or religious prejudice
against masturbation in the community or the family background. Peggy
Mb11   fell into this category. "I said they might hear from the kids that it's
bad," she said. "And I said actually anything you do with yourself isn't
bad as long as you don't hurt yourself and don't overdo it." Alex
Fg9   remarked, "I think a child might be getting it from the peers that this
is something you are not supposed to do and there could be an element
of guilt not even imposed by the parents or the Church. I would tell
my daughter she was going to hear negative reports against it but we
felt it was okay and that as she got older we would hope that other
things would take its place."

Other parents wanted to reassure children that in stimulating
themselves they were not damaging their genitals in any way. Sandy
made it clear that she and her husband talked about masturbation with
their son when he was still quite young in order to inform him about
Mb11   how his body worked. "We told him about it, so that if it should happen he shouldn't be horrified at what he's doing and what is coming
out of his penis." A single mother with a very young son ended up
discussing masturbation (though being shy by nature she might have
preferred to ignore it) for much the same reason—because he had
Mb3   seemed so puzzled and so frightened by his erections. "He said, 'I
don't want it to get bigger.' It worried me when he said that. Why
does he think that's bad? Why should he feel uncomfortable about it?
So I said, 'It's really not bad, it's very normal. It gets bigger because
you're holding it. If you don't want that to happen, stop holding on to
it. Take your hand away for a few minutes and it will get smaller.' "
She added that speaking so reassuringly, which had been somewhat
difficult for her, had apparently helped her son to accept his body and
its phenomena without anxiety. "He hasn't said that in a while. In fact
he's more fascinated by it now. Now he thinks it's great that it gets
bigger. Now he's pleased!" Another mother achieved much the same
effect by discussing masturbation in a very open and personal way,
using her own pleasurable memories to help generate good feelings in
Mb4   the child. "I've told him about masturbation experiences of my own
on the level that, 'Yes, Mommy does that,' and as it first came out,
'Mommy used to do that when she was a little girl.' And he was more
taken with the idea that Mommy *was* a little girl. And then the question came up in another form. I think he asked me did I ever touch

my vagina. I remember the use of the word *vagina*. So he asked me, and he said, 'Oh, yes, that was very nice, wasn't it?' "

Orgasm

A topic closely related to masturbation, and to pleasure in general, of course, was orgasm. And here, too, most parents had difficulty initiating discussion. A few parents were pretty certain their children had picked up information either directly or intuitively from outsiders, but they indicated, rather apologetically, that they themselves had never brought up the subject. A mother recalled, "I intended to discuss it Mb6 with him, once. That was because he's made an observation around a little peer, a female who had just finished masturbating. And something must have happened. My guess is that she had had a little orgasm. He knew something special was going on. But my feeling is that yes, he knows what it is." The majority of parents, however, did not think their children had any understanding of what orgasm was. "It may be my lack of awareness rather than hers, but I don't think Fg9 my daughter knows what it means."

The reasons most parents gave for not discussing orgasm were quite similar to those given for not discussing masturbation. Primarily, parents were not entirely comfortable with the subject itself. But they found, too, that orgasm, like masturbation, was a topic that had no natural "triggers" to provoke questions or allow for smooth, timely explanations. (It was therefore possible that even children who had actually masturbated to orgasm already might not know what to call what had happened to them or even that a term for it existed.) Stephanie admitted that she had said "nothing at all" about orgasms to her Mb8 son. "The question never arose and at his age I don't know if he would ever question. I don't think the information he has right now would lead to him questioning orgasm." Oliver remarked, "I've said nothing. These things seem to evolve over time. We don't have any timetable set up. If she asks questions we'll tell her when it seems appropriate." Even Stacey, whose son has received information on all manner of sexual issues from a very early age, confided, "No, I don't think we've Mb11 discussed orgasm. Everything that I've told him about has come about as a result of a conversation or something else that's happened. I don't just sort of in the middle of nowhere say, 'Let me tell you about orgasm.' I haven't done that."

Quite a few of the parents who had not discussed orgasm with their children had been stymied not so much by scruples, embarrassment, or lack of opportunity as by the elusive and personal nature of orgasm itself. How could you put into words accurately, to a child—to any other person for that matter—such a complex, peculiar, utterly unique set of physical and emotional responses? As one typical father pointed out, though he definitely believed it was important that his daughter learn what orgasm was, he certainly did not expect explaining it to be an easy or a comfortable task. "I would tell her that it is a feeling of extreme pleasure that everybody feels differently," he began. "It's awfully hard to tell her exactly. It expresses itself differently in every human being and it is something you cannot explain. But I will tell her about it," he insisted. A mother expressed an irony not lost on many parents. "It's clearly an area we would have to leave till he had a better vocabulary," she said. "The vocabulary simply wasn't there and that's where it broke down. And yet I'm really sure he knows what it is, that he himself has experienced it."

Several parents had thought to solve the problem by consulting "expert" sources. Marilyn used a children's book which treated the topic in a relaxed and amusing way. "They said it was like having to sneeze and having this little tickle and how it has to come out and how it was a pleasurable sensation." But Lorna, who had seen the same kind of description in several books, reacted strongly to the understated, unemotional quality of the explanation. "I've seen books on how to tell your kids about sex where orgasm is described as a special tickle," she said. Then she continued with some vehemence, "Well to me it's *not* a special tickle. I'd tell him that there was such a thing as orgasm and that it was a very special feeling and a very nice and terrific feeling, but I certainly wouldn't describe it as a *tickle*." Lorna also felt it was a perfectly valid approach to tell the child that orgasm simply could not be satisfactorily explained, that "it's something you simply have to wait until you are an adult or until you are older to experience. I don't think there is anything wrong with telling a child that. And I don't think there is anything wrong with the child thinking it's a grown-up activity and thinking that he too can look forward to it some day." Several parents had opted for rather simple explanations, emphasizing general pleasure and physical release—"just sort of saying that it would be the height of excitement, a climax," as Helen put it, with a giggle. Or, in another mother's words, "It's a pleasurable feeling and when you make love with a person you love, it's a nice feeling to have an orgasm." Cheryl, too, had used this warm, positive, nonspecific approach. "I've told my son very little about orgasm except that it is a pleasurable thing, a pleasurable sensation, a release of tension after sexually stimulating a sexual organ, female or male, and that was probably it."

A few parents added a bit more technical detail. "I would tell my daughter the truth," Janet said, "That when you make love, the anatomical thing is that all the blood in your body—not all the blood, but a great deal of the blood—goes to those particular areas, to the vaginal

Fg5

Mb6

Mb9

Mb4

Mb9

Mg7

Mb9

Mg11

area, and that it builds up and that it reaches a climax and it's just a
fantastic feeling!" The mother of an eight-year-old boy related, "I   Mb8
would probably start by saying it's a release of feelings, that a man and
woman come to a very high point in their relationship in sexual intercourse and that they both have a release, and that's called orgasm. I
would mention the fact that the sperm at that point is deposited into
the vagina. I would say also that the male orgasm is more visible than
female orgasm."

Passion and Desire

Many parents had been unable to discuss with their children another
important pleasure-related issue—sexual passion, the overwhelming,
often irrational physical desire for another human being. They shied
away from this whole area of discussion, just as they had avoided any
reference to pleasure when giving out information about intercourse,
conception and birth.

Even the few who tackled this subject did so rather cautiously,
but with conscientious intent. These parents wanted to prepare children for the demands of their bodies and prevent them from making
tragic mistakes—"going too far" too early, becoming sexually involved
before they really understood what was happening to them. Alex's
daughter is nine and he was concerned about this. "I don't think she   Fg9
knows that passionate kissing may be a prelude to other sexual activities and that's what I would have to explain," he said. "I'd say something to the effect of—kissing, because it is a sign of affection, is very
nice and it makes you feel good. But if it's prolonged or passionate, it
could lead to other things—for instance, intercourse. They haven't been
informed of what the consequences are and it's a totally new thing for
them. They just get carried away. That's bound to have some strong
mental and physical reverberations and implications that could take a
long time to heal." Brent shared this concern. "I think I've tried to   Fb11
sort of indicate how people might move from just physical contact to
more physical contact, toward sexual activity. I've tried to explain that,
but how much can you explain it? What else can I say? He knows what
it's all about." Another father said, along much the same lines, "Even-   Fg5
tually it's going to lead to intercourse somewhere along the line, in
some context, and my daughter has to be aware of where it's going to
lead her so that she can draw up guidelines for herself."

Often parents found that children's own attitudes toward sexual
passion could act as a deterrent to such discussions. Younger children
in particular tended to be bored, amused, or mystified by the whole

idea of wanting to touch another person's body for pleasure and could not be reached by any approach until they grew into some actual experi-

Mb8   ence of the phenomenon. Lily remarked with some exasperation, "I tried to explain to my son about passion and desire. He's smart, but he really didn't understand it. Two people very much in love, that as a concept they want to go to bed together or make a baby together or live together. If he sees people kissing passionately, it's 'kissing bugs!' He finds that funny. He laughs and turns it off, just walks away from

Mb11 it." Another mother said that her son was "still at the point that he feels that the love stuff is boring. He's still there and I'm waiting for a

Mb10 change right about now." According to Cynthia, her son "has seen people hugging and kissing, showing passion and desire, but I think it's a mystery to him." She added, with a wry smile, "If he does know, he jokes about it. He doesn't like girls, but his father tells him, 'Some day you're going to feel differently about them and you're going to think about them a lot.' But right now he doesn't like them."

As Dennis pointed out, it was often difficult to help a child make the leap between the kinds of love he might understand through relationships with parents and siblings, with friends or pets, and the urgent

Fb5   physical stirrings of carnal love. "At night I'll kiss my son good night and I'll say 'I really love you a lot,' and he says 'I love you too,'" Dennis observed. "I think he knows what love means. To him it means not wanting to be apart from you. About between man and woman, no, he doesn't have any sense of that. Most of his playmates are girls

Fg5   and they just play like boys." "We've talked to my daughter about love," Oliver said, but added with some bewilderment, "passion, I

Fg7   don't know." Leonard admitted with a sigh, "That's a heavy question." He was resigned however, to allowing his daughter "to discover it for herself at the appropriate age."

Some parents noted with amusement that their children under-

Fg5   stood passion completely, on one nonsexual level or another. "Maybe pizza," Harold remarked with a chuckle, defining his daughter's concept of the highest physical pleasure. More seriously, he said, "I haven't told her about passion as it relates to sex, no. Nothing I would consider sexual, only craving about food, how each of us may like a certain food, we would love to eat that all the time, or we would go anywhere to get that food, or 'I could eat this all day long.' Or her brother's passion for athletics. Outside of that, no. So she understands passion in that sense." Another father made a similar comment about

Fg5   his five-year-old son. "As far as passion goes, like if he wants something really bad, he'll go all out for it and plead and beg. Like we were once out shopping and he wanted a toy or something. He really wants it *bad*. It's passion of sorts, I guess. Passion in relation to sex and love or kissing or that kind of thing, no."

Many parents preferred to rely on their own behavior to convey positive concepts relating to physical passion and desire to their children. They believed this method of dealing with the topic was ultimately more effective than explicit verbal approaches. Leonard put it this way: "I think the only real way to do it is sort of demonstrate it, Fg7 not talk about it. I mean that if I'm affectionate to her and I allow her to be affectionate to me and we enjoy that part of it, that's more than talking about it. It's sort of letting her experience it, because she is an affectionate and sweet person. I get uncomfortable about intellectualizing sex because I really don't know what I'm communicating. It sounds very abstract and remote and not really connected to experience." Sally said, "My daughter sees her father hugging me, she sees Mg10 him kissing me, she sees us holding hands and it's normal. She sees us in this type of relationship and I think she just sees it as another expression of love. I have to say I think she's innocent enough yet that she does not see it as a form of just sexual pleasure. I don't think she is that sophisticated yet, to realize that people do it, other than mommies and daddies."

Stephanie had not made a conscious point of conveying information about passion, but she realized, when she stopped to think about it, that her son must be aware of his parents' deep physical affection for one another, simply from the way they behaved together—sharing private jokes, laughing and touching a great deal. "I've never given Mb8 him reason to have any feelings about pleasure related to sex, but he might have picked things up." Tovah said, "I've talked to my daughter Mg10 about pleasure, but I'm not a person who uses what I consider legalese. I like touching, cuddling, hugging, these kinds of things. Everything to do with sensuality is touching and that's to me necessary to life. And this is how I explain it to her: that there is pleasure in the body, there's communication, and it's an essential part of loving—male-female loving, not to be mixed up with or used in place of other kinds of loving."

In talking about sexual passion, several mothers repeated a point made in Chapter One by Paula, Marilyn and Henry and echoed by other parents throughout the survey. They wanted their children to grow up to be sexually responsible adults—compassionate in their treatment of future lovers, ready to seek spiritual as well as physical gratification from their relationships. "You shouldn't touch anybody because Mb6 you feel like it. Anything *doesn't* go!" one mother had told her son. "I Mb11 would like him to know that just a *physical* intimacy doesn't give you a taste of the whole," another mother said. Sally summed up these feelings: "Okay, it feels good, but a lot of things feel good," she pointed Mg10 out. "A warm bath feels good, too. That doesn't mean you're making a lasting relationship. There has to be more. I think my daughter and I definitely would discuss the fact that there is more to sex than just the sheer act of sex. To me sex has to have a relationship with it. I think you should make more or less a commitment. You're not doing it just for the half hour that you are in bed and then that's it and there's no feelings before or after the act. I think you are doing it more than just for a physical purpose and that is something that would have to be discussed." She added that she believed this approach to sex was something that could not be conveyed simply by discussion or admonishment. "I would hope that she would get some of that feeling just by watching her father and me. There is more to our relationship than just the hours that are spent in our bedroom. I think they would have to watch the whole process." Tovah remarked that she thought "passion is simply dealt with as a wanting to touch and be close to someone. Simply no big deal was made out of that. It can be nice and it can be lovely." However, she noted that in discussing passion and pleasure with her daughter, even in so positive a way, she had included concepts of self-respect and responsibility. "It really was a very fast conversation about the fact that she would have feelings of increasing strength, of wanting to touch and be touched and to be close to a male person. And we talked about a combination of pleasure in that and a certain amount of responsibility. I want her to be a whole person. I don't want anyone pressuring her in any direction. I'm not involved with what the world wants, I'm involved with what my child wants." Tovah also confessed that, as a single mother, a widow, she was concerned that her daughter might try to make up for the lack of a male parent by seeking out sexual relationships prematurely or indiscriminately. "I don't want her to arrive at an early-teen age and see other people having sex and decide that this is a way to make up for that which she doesn't have. I'm very clear on that. There is pleasure to be had, but it's not a replacement for other things."

6

![black bar]

Behind

Closed

Doors

Despite the fact that parents in this survey repeatedly stressed their need for privacy in sexual matters the parental bedroom in many homes was not a particularly private place. It had assumed the roles of TV room, library, gym (with the bed as a trampoline), a place for group discussions and cuddles. In some families not only the bedroom but the bed itself had become the social center.

> We watch TV in our bed at night. We play "Cookie," a new game   Mb5
> he got. He brings all his toys in, or he's reading or drawing. He knows
> it's our room and he has certain access to it. It's familial, rather than
> "this is the place where Mommy and Daddy do something that I
> don't know about."

In general, children were not allowed to sleep with their parents, but up until the age of three, and even older, they were often accustomed to coming in at will because they were hungry or thirsty, had to go to the bathroom, or wanted reassurance or affection. Most parents felt the needs of their children, particularly young children, came before their own need for privacy.

For these reasons the majority of parents agreed that the quality of their sex lives had changed drastically with the arrival of their children. They found themselves constantly attempting, sometimes without success, to achieve some sort of compromise between finding freedom from distraction in order to enjoy each other fully and being available to their children. The issue was complicated by the fact that parents felt it was healthy for children to know that Mommy and Daddy liked each other and slept side by side. They did not want children to assume that they were banished from the bedroom because a dark and awful event was taking place in there. While there were parents who did not like to embrace or cuddle in bed when children were around, a large group allowed their children to observe them together in bed under most circumstances other than actual intercourse, especially if they were covered by bedclothes or wearing underwear or pajamas.

Mb6   If we were just kissing or hugging in bed I would not scream, "Get out!" if he walked in. He can see us cuddling, reading, watching TV in bed.

Mg7   She has probably caught us in bed holding each other or hugging each other. My husband would say, "I'm kissing Mommy," and I would say, "It's time for you to be in bed." She'd say, "Oh, could I have a kiss, too?" One of us would get out of bed and give her a kiss too and she'd go back to sleep.

Mg8   My daughter has walked into our bedroom and had seen me lying with Sam's arm around me. You know, with the blankets up and so on. Just relaxing very closely beside each other.

Fb8   Often he comes in and sneaks a peek, just to see what was going on. I mean in the morning he would want to pee and he would get up just to see what was going on. And I would be almost conscious of that and not lock the door so that he would be reassured there were two people sleeping in the bed. There was nothing frightening or strange.

Some parents, primarily those whose household policies on nudity were flexible, said they were comfortable, as well, when children saw them naked in bed together. A few said it was even acceptable to them if a child happened to observe the father with an erection.

Fg3   My girlfriend recalled the story where I got up and I had a hard-on, and my daughter's eyes kind of popped open wide. She didn't question it, no. She saw it, though. She saw me.

Fg7   I think she's seen us in bed with the covers over us or something like that. She's seen us both get out of bed nude.

Mb16g14g11   When my husband sleeps, very frequently he'll be erect and sometimes he'll sleep without covers so he'll just be sticking up through the opening of his pajamas. My children will come in sometimes and actually the blanket will be raised in that area, and they'll sort of point to it and laugh. It looks funny, like a flag all the way on a pole or whatever.

But though parents thought it was not necessarily harmful for children to perceive them as sexual beings, they did think it could be harmful for children to be exposed to the sight (or sound) of intercourse itself. There was, however, no simple way to announce that the bedroom was off limits at certain times. And family life being what it is, very few parents believed their children had no awareness at all of what happened between them in bed.

Sorting out the multiple priorities—responding to children's needs, teaching them about love and affection as well as sex, protecting one's own privacy—became a process of finding realistic solutions to perennially recurring dilemmas. It was important to determine, for instance, how to handle potentially traumatic—but occasionally unavoidable—incidents, such as children walking in on the parents during intercourse or erotic play. Other decisions had to be made as well: choosing when and where to make love to ensure that children would not enter the room, setting limits on children's presence in the bedroom at other than sexual moments, making appropriate sleeping arrangements in the home or on vacation trips. These were typical of the day-to-day practical problems parents confronted in attempting to achieve satisfactory compromises between their own sexual needs and their children's emotional welfare.

Intercourse: A Private Act

Most parents were very firm about one point: they hoped at all cost to avoid having their children see them making love. "I have great fears [about her walking in while I'm making love]," Sam said. "I picked that up somewhere and always these stories about How I Became a Nymphomaniac—'I popped in one day accidentally and saw my mother and father doing it and ever since that time. . . .' Those type of stories have left an impact on me so that I'm overly concerned, I suspect." Aaron's response to the same issue was almost a reflex. "Would it be harmful for my daughter to see me having sex? Yeah," he said without hesitation, but then stopped and thought for a few moments. Eventually he went on to qualify that first categorical statement. "I don't know whether I'm thinking about the idea of it being *harmful,* or whether it's just not the right thing for her to come into contact with at any stage in relation to her parents. She might be wondering what it was

Fg7

Fg3

all about. It might seem to be an aggressive situation that she might not like. It might lead to a sense of embarrassment for us, the parents, and by creating that sense of embarrassment might lead later on to her feeling that there is something wrong with us." Aaron emphasized that awareness of sex should come to a child gradually and naturally, rather than by abrupt exposure. "By allowing her to come into contact with lovemaking on her own, when the time comes," he pointed out, "you're not creating a situation that might be psychologically damaging."

Fb4   Richard, whose son is about the same age as Aaron's daughter, echoed this idea. "Sure, yes," he said, "I don't think that he should watch me make love. I think that's distressing. I don't think he knows what's going on. I think he has to wait until his feelings about this activity are better formed." For Richard, observing sexual intercourse itself was not the only potentially damaging aspect of the experience for the child. Like Aaron, he felt that a subtler issue was also involved: the appropriateness of the child seeing his father in this different and rather startling role. "It's a combination—of me being a parent and his not understanding the activity," Richard said finally. Other parents

Mb7b4 made similar observations. "I think sexual intercourse is not good for the child to see," Lesley said immediately. "It can be frightening, so that would be one reason. He doesn't understand it." However, Lesley also made it clear that she would feel uncomfortable about the fact that the child was observing her, the parent, engaged in activities she thought it completely inappropriate to share. "For our own privacy, also," she added. "We believe that it's not good for them, that it's stimulating."

Carla, who prided herself on a generally easygoing attitude toward subjects like nudity, touching, language, and erotic play between children, felt very strongly that her son should not see any sexual activity between her husband and herself. She believed that such exposure involved both potential harm to her child and a violation of her own

Mb3   ideas of privacy. "I'm not comfortable with the idea of Dylan's seeing us making love," she said emphatically. "I don't think that real little kids can realize from grunts and things that people do that it's a pleasant thing that's happening. I think kids might have trouble understanding that." She added, "I've heard stories about kids misunderstanding and thinking that something *terrible* was going on." Carla acknowledged that there was some discrepancy between her lack of self-consciousness around other sexual issues and her need to keep so personal an activity from her son. As she put it, "I'm not so hip and groovy and relaxed about it all that I can fuck in the middle of Grand Central Station. The only thing he hasn't seen is us making love. I don't think that it's—I can't imagine that would be a terribly good thing."

Many other parents of children of all ages—from toddlers on up to prepubescent boys and girls — said they would not want children disturbed, confused, or frightened by exposure to parents' explicit sexual activities before they were able to cope with this aspect of life and their parents' place in it.

> At this stage I think she could be confused or upset. For example, some sexual activity appears to be violent. That might frighten a child. I think right now she couldn't handle it.   Mg3

> I often think that children hear or see things that they really are not able to interpret and then form misconceptions that can be damaging or frightening. I think sex *can* be frightening in some ways.   Mb6

> She's not ready to see it. She doesn't understand a lot of things about male-female relationships and sexuality. I can see that it bothers her if she sees something on TV that's a little different from what she's used to in her life. I mean, her expression always is, 'It's GROSS!' I think seeing too much sexual play goes against her reality right now and might be a little hard for her.   Mg11

For another group of parents, instilling principles of sexual privacy was the overriding concern. What these parents believed could be damaging to a child was not the observed act of intercourse itself, but the breach of some very elemental code of sexual decorum. They felt it was not right for anyone to observe this profound and deeply private experience. Sensing he had broke some basic human or "tribal" law could be very stressful for the child and might also negatively affect his own future behavior around sexual intimacy.

Irv, like Carla, a parent who is generally quite open about sex, stressed the importance of maintaining absolute privacy during intercourse as a matter of principle. He believed that not to do so could eventually be detrimental to his child's developing attitudes towards sex. "Yes, I think seeing too much can be harmful to my child," he said slowly. "I don't think it's appropriate for a child to see you having intercourse. I think it raises the question in their mind at a certain point later, retroactively, thinking that, well, when should *they?* I still think sex is a private act that shouldn't involve a third party. That third party, even if it's your child, is still a third party."   Fg7

Henry also placed a high value on sexual privacy for both his own sake and his daughter's; he wanted to provide her with an example of healthy reserve about when and where sex should take place. He said, "I would not make love to my mate on the kitchen table with the kids running around. My basic attitude is that sexuality is more pleasurable and fun and also more appropriate in privacy, and that would include privacy from my child. One of the things I want her to learn about sex is responsibility, privacy, and so forth. You don't do it in front of stray neighbors."   Fg6

Parents also spoke of privacy as something that was valuable in itself because it enhanced their own pleasure in sex. One father put it this way: "I think sex is an important area of life. It's brought me a lot   Fg8b4

of pleasure and I want it to bring them a lot of pleasure. I want them
to be comfortable with all of the instincts within them. I don't want
them to feel bad about themselves for anything. I want my children to
know I'm a sexual person. But I don't want them to know the details
of my sexual life. It's not something I want to share with the rest of
the world. It's private and special." Several mothers emphasized the
fact that sex is an exclusive involvement with another person. Ethel
said, "I enjoy the feeling of being free, just with my partner, without
the audience of the child. Yes, I choose not to have him see me. For
my own privacy." Doretta made a similar point. Lovemaking was the
one time when her own needs were more important than her children's
demands for her attention. "I prefer my sexual privacy, and I am not
an exhibitionist in the sense that if I'm relating to someone sexually I
want to relate to *them*. I mean, I couldn't be sexually intimate and full
with a person with the kids running around wanting to know where
their shoelaces were—that's what happens with kids. They're not
observing, saying, 'Look at this show!' I think that's a myth. It's
usually other things going on. They tend more to see that guy's got
Mommy or has got her attention or whatever, and 'I don't like that.
I'm first.' "

Mb10

Mb6

Though parents felt that children should not witness intercourse
itself, they did not necessarily feel it would be harmful for children to
know when sex had taken place or was taking place. Some even believed this kind of awareness could be beneficial. They wanted children to understand that their parents cared for each other deeply and
physically, and to accept that physicality as a natural part of a loving
relationship. Roy alluded with some amusement to the several times
his three-year-old daughter had entered the bedroom shortly after
intercourse. "At times, in the morning, she comes up and sleeps with
us and we're both naked. I think it must be pretty clear to her that
there's something else beside sleeping going on. I don't try to hide
anything." Another father took the same kind of amused and tolerant
attitude. Even though observing sexual intercourse itself was totally
inappropriate for a child, being exposed to an atmosphere of loving
sexuality might be quite healthy. "I guess it would be harmful and
sick if we said, 'You got to stay and watch us making love,' but if they
come in and catch us, my wife and I would just start laughing. It would
be funny. We'd say, 'Oh, that's just how mommies and daddies kiss
and hold each other all the time.' "

Fg3

Fb8g6

A few people recalled hearing their own parents making love and
spoke of the fear and embarrassment they had felt at their unexpected
involvement in this intimate aspect of family life. In some cases they
were unwilling eavesdroppers on disturbing private encounters between
their mothers and fathers; in others they sensed they had trespassed
onto forbidden terrain. Yet these people shared the feeling of most
other parents in this study—that overhearing parents making love need

not be disturbing to children if they are also aware that sex is a healthy, joyful activity between two people who love each other.

Rachel, for instance, remembered her complex emotional response when her parents' disagreements in bed were audible in her own room. "What I am doing is flashing back to my own childhood," she said. "I know there were things going on in the bedroom which seemed intimidating. That was something I knew as a child. I found it to be a problem. It always seemed to me that we heard too much in my house. I was aware of the fact that sometimes my father wanted to do something and my mother would say, 'No.' I was always sympathetic to my father. I always thought my mother was either cold or unfair. I know that I was aware that they argued about the fact that she was saying no to him. In my own childish way I was very sympathetic toward him. 'What a shame!' That was what I felt. As I grew older my sympathy became much more with my mother." As an adult however, Rachel is not afraid that her children will suffer the same kind of stress if they know that she and her husband are having intercourse. "It is not that they always know," she said, "but, on the other hand, I don't have a way of hiding it. It's a problem if you are worried about their knowing, and I am not worried. I would be concerned if they thought we *never* made love." Mb6

Janet's memories reflected an intense and profound embarrassment that did not seem to have carried through to her dealings with her children, either. "I remember myself as a child at the age of ten to thirteen, living in a straight-through row house. I was in the back bedroom, and my parents were in the front room. And I remember hearing my mother giggle in the middle of the night and being embarrassed to tears at hearing the bed shake, and being just devastated and holding my ears and putting the covers over my head and being humiliated. My son's room is right across the hall from our room, so he's close enough to hear things. I know he has heard noises because I will hear a reaction the morning after. 'I heard you and Daddy last night.' I'll smile and say, 'You're right, you did.' " Janet is delighted that her son is comfortable enough to talk to her. "I never would have said to *my* parents, 'I know what you did last night.' I just couldn't deal with saying it," she said, shaking her head in amazement, but clearly not disturbed by her son's frankness or by his awareness of her sex life. Mb11

Dealing with Intrusions

Parents were asked what they would do if a child did walk in on them while they were making love. Many believed that the manner in which they handled the incident was of far greater significance than the incident itself. If the parents overreacted, revealed distress, anger, or shame, children would receive negative signals about both their own and their parents' sexuality. On the other hand, if calm, matter-of-fact explanations were offered,—explanations that stressed the warm and loving aspects of sex—children would be less likely to be damaged by what they had observed. As Ethel put it, "I don't think sex is harmful in any manner. I think not understanding it is harmful. But not if you can sit down and deal with it—say an incident, something like walking in and you're actually having oral sex. I think a follow-up explanation is important. You don't just drop it. I try to teach them to be very open anyway, and that sex is not bad. I don't want them to think sex is bad. I want them to understand that you enjoy it with the person that you want to be with."

Several other mothers—especially some with three or more children nearing or past puberty—had reassuring practical advice on this issue. As one said, "It depends on how the parent deals with what the child sees. I think that if the parents describe it as making love, as being a very beautiful moment of sharing that the parents enjoy together because they care about each other, and it's moments such as this that produced him or her—then I think it can be something beneficial: 'This shows how much Daddy and I care about each other.' Or it can be covered up as something that,—'Oh my God, it's horrible. You shouldn't have seen it!' Then it can be harmful: 'We're embarrassed that we do things like this.' And then the child ends up with a very negative feeling—'Oh my God, what *are* they doing?' " Another mother said simply, "My advice is that if parents get caught in a sexual activity, talk to the child and explain that it's nothing wrong."

These observations were borne out by the experiences of parents whose children had, in fact, walked in on (or overheard) intercourse: Those who had been able to react calmly and moderately to the child's intrusion seemed to have been the most successful in avoiding emotional repercussions. Many styles of behavior were reported by parents that apparently "worked." Some parents gave warm but truthful explanations of what they were doing, some simply (even rather peremptorily) asked children to leave the room, some made up preposterous excuses to cover their activities. But the *tone* seemed to be all important. Mild annoyance, for instance, could be a completely appropriate response to a child's interruption of sex, just as it would be to other interruptions of adult behavior—talking on the phone, doing the bills, going to the bathroom—and therefore might not be taken amiss. But anger that the child sensed as disproportionate, unreasonable, or rejecting could cause problems. And it seemed that telling the absolute truth about what the parents were doing was not so important as the willingness to explain, even if both child and parent knew the explanation to be ridiculous. The fact of communication itself overrode its content.

Also helpful, according to the accounts of a number of parents, were prevention strategies of many sorts—from choosing to make love at times when children were unlikely to interrupt to providing children with enough advance information on the nature of the sex act to shield them from traumatic discoveries. Follow-up discussions, shortly after an incident occurred or the next day while it was still fresh in the child's mind, also helped avoid confusion or anxiety, and gave the parent a chance to provide further reassurance.

Mothers: "I Would Tell Her We Were Exercising"

In general, mothers seemed more adept than fathers at handling incidents in which children interrupted bedroom activities. Janet, for instance, was quite relaxed and matter-of-fact. What had worked for her under such circumstances was determination not to appear flustered or upset, and at the same time to make clear to the children the connection between the physical actions they had observed and the loving relationship between herself and her husband. "We have been mak-   Mb11
ing love when the kids walked in," she said. "And we'll smile. We don't move away from each other abruptly, either. And then later on I'll say to them, 'That's right, we have made love because we do care about each other. We do love each other.' "

Two other mothers, Gail and Abby, were easygoing about being discovered in the midst of sex because they had developed ingenious cover stories to explain away their activities to intruding children. For Gail, the explanation was based on family physical fitness routines which her four-year-old daughter understood and enjoyed. "My daugh-   Mg4
ter would say, 'Mommy, what is that noise?' and I would tell her 'We are exercising.' Because she is used to seeing us exercising. She's exercised with us. Every type of fad exercise and yoga. And if she hears heavy breathing or other sounds during sex, that would be a logical explanation. She's used to hearing grunts and groans because we are terrible at exercising," she added with a laugh. "If she saw us in the little strange positions, don't forget, there's a lot of yoga things that have very strange positions."

For Abby, the logic or credibility of the excuse she gave was apparently less important than the fact that she gave it. "My son hears   Mb6
noises from our room. He says, 'I hear you talking. I hear noises.' My husband then says, 'I am talking in my sleep. We will be out later.' My son laughs. I think he realizes that the reason is ridiculous. But he accepts it. He does not give you a hard time. Obviously we are not coming out, so he eventually gives up." Abby also made some comments that pointed up the importance of "prevention"—explaining to children beforehand about sex itself, about its intimate nature and the need for occasional seclusion, so they would be prepared to take such incidents in stride. "I have discussed with him the fact that Mommy and Daddy need a private time, time to be alone together. He knows something is going on."

There were some qualifications to these relaxed approaches, however. The age of the child could make a difference in the way the parent handled an incident. Gail's daughter, at four, was satisfied with
Mg4   the "exercise" story, but Gail knew this would not always be true. "When she gets older we'll have to deal with it differently, depending on how much she knows at the time. If she understands about sex, then we'll just say, 'Look, you interrupted us,' and that's it. We wouldn't lie if she said, 'Oh, is that what intercourse is?' or 'Is that lovemaking?' My daughter has a way of asking very direct questions. And I'll just say, 'Yes.' " Gail also pointed out another "prevention" factor—the most obvious of all—discretion, making arrangements for sex that would preclude or lessen the chances of children walking in or overhearing. Ultimately, Gail said, "We'll just be discreet. I'd rather avoid the problem than have to deal with the problem."

Other qualifications had to do with the type of sexual activity the child observed. One mother, Alice, did not believe it would be damaging for her seven-year-old daughter to observe intercourse as long as
Mg7   the sexual practices were "nice"—normal and healthy. "I don't think she would find that disturbing. I don't think someone beating on someone else to be pleasurable—to tell a child this is lovemaking I don't think is right."

Some mothers felt they could deal fairly comfortably with an intrusion as long as they were not discovered in an unusual position. Several said they would be most upset if children "caught" them at oral sex, either because the children might not understand what was going on or because they themselves did not like to reveal that they engaged in a less traditional form of erotic play. Janet spoke of her deep and
Mg17b13b11   irrational reluctance to discuss oral-genital sex with her children. "My children have never walked in when my husband and I were performing oral sex on each other uncovered. That might prove *very* embarrassing. I think I'd have much more difficulty dealing with that than just the act of having intercourse. Even though they know the terminology for it and they know the street language for it. They talk about it to each other. They giggle about it in front of me, which is an indication that they don't want to hide that they know about it. Still, I would have more difficulty explaining that to them. I don't know why. And it's not because I don't enjoy it, because I love it. I absolutely can't figure out why."

Fathers: "I Said, 'Get Out of Here!' "

Fathers generally tended to deal more peremptorily with intrusions on sex. Henry indicated that he felt he had been too abrupt with his daughter on one occasion. He had not been able to maintain a neutral tone of voice when she interrupted a daytime sexual encounter, and she apparently took his anger very much to heart. Her reactions—jealousy, resentment, hurt—caused considerable problems for a time. "She walked into the room. She was about four. I was not happy about her walking into the room. I had asked her to play downstairs and I'd always told her to knock before she comes into the bedroom. She said, 'What are you doing?' and I said, 'We're making love.' And she said, 'What's that?' and I said, 'Pamela, GET OUT OF HERE!' Afterwards, oh, she screamed and cried and bitched and moaned. She was in a clingy state for a couple of days. She felt excluded from the affection she saw going on." Interestingly enough, Henry was a parent who had reported being completely relaxed and candid in talking with his daughter about sex, and he saw himself as having liberal and enlightened views on the subject. And although he was eventually able to discuss the incident with his daughter, he remained remorseful, surprised and chastened by the "hidden" attitudes he had revealed. Later he commented, 'A dear friend surprised me recently be telling me I'm a prude, which doesn't quite fit with my self-image. I've come up with feelings of discomfort around sex a couple of times, predominantly in the area of my daughter seeing me making love. I'll have to reexamine that." Fg4

Even fathers who did not seem distressed or "thrown" by the unexpected appearance of a child in the midst of intercourse, said they would use a direct, no-nonsense approach, simply asking the child to leave the room. Richard, for instance, said, "I'd tell them to go back to bed. That simple. In the middle of lovemaking, I'd say, 'Robin, get back into bed. Noah, get back into bed.' That's it. If they said, 'Daddy, what are you doing?' I'd say, 'Mommy and I are doing private things. Go back to bed.' " Fg8b4

Another father used the same type of firm but calm method of treating the situation. "Once or twice my daughter's comes in the room. We were making love and she walked in. She never saw us naked—we were under the covers—but she saw us. I'd say, 'come on, it's too early. Go back to bed.' And she'd say, 'okay.' She knew she wasn't allowed in our room in the morning anyway. I'd say, 'Hey, too early! You don't come in here this early.' " But this father did point out that he would be disturbed if his daughter walked in not because of what she might have seen, but because of his own lack of foresight. "I'd be angry at *myself*, that I let it happen," he admitted. "I'd feel like I was stupid, leaving the door open, leaving the possible exposure there and having her walk in." Fg7

Andrew described what happened when his eleven-year-old son walked into the bedroom at the "wrong time." "We'd ask him quietly to come back in five minutes. I think he understands. There seems to be no self-conscious thing. He comes back later on. We find we're able to handle it very calmly. It does spoil the mood," he added with a laugh. "But in the last year he's started knocking on the door." Fb11

Here are other comments from parents who dealt successfully with the potentially traumatic experience of being discovered by their children during intercourse. As is evident from these accounts, the more matter-of-fact the parents' reaction the easier it was to handle the situation. In some cases children left the room unaware that they had interrupted anything intimate. Where parents felt that further explanation was called for, they let the children know, in some way, that the activity was pleasurable. Finally, a sense of humor was an asset in demystifying and defusing such moments for both parents and children.

Fg3   I know that my daughter's walked up those steps to my bedroom and I've been having intercourse and I've said, "Listen, I'll be down in a second." She knew. She's very aware that there was something going on there physically between two people. Sometimes she comes up and we stop. We don't necessarily cover ourselves up, because she's seen us naked. But we stop.

Mg7   She said, "What are you and Mommy doing?" and my husband said, "I'm making Mommy nice." And she said, "Will you make me nice too?" And I think that George said, "Sure." So she came in and he stroked her back and gave her a big hug and kiss. And she said, "Is this how babies are made?" And I think George said, "No, we're not making another little brother now." And she didn't follow it up, so we didn't follow it up.

Fg10   She wanted to know if her mother was okay. I think she was half asleep. I didn't respond because her mother quick said, "Everything's fine, just go back to bed and shut the door." She never brought the subject up again so we didn't either. We assured her that her mother was fine, and why don't you just go back to sleep.

Mb10   Well, it happened once. He actually came in *[laughs]*. I don't know if he really knew that we were love-making because we often lay on top of each other just in playing. So when he came in, I simply rolled over and said, "Okay, what do you want, what's the problem?" He had a stomach ache or something. That was about the only time, and I think he really didn't know that we were making love. He paid no attention to it.

Sexual Fulfillment vs. Parental Responsibility

As has been noted, the majority of parents in this study were conscious of trying to find a balance—admittedly somewhat precarious—between their own needs for sexual privacy and their children's needs for attention or care. With children below the age of five, however, there was just about no choice. The children's needs always came first. Getting up in the middle of the night to feed an infant or check on a strange noise from a toddler's room did not allow for frequent or relaxed sexual activity. Though the problems grew more complex as the children became older—as they became more likely to walk in on parents or understand what was going on in their bedroom—parents reported that their sex lives improved since they no longer had to be so acutely on the alert for sounds (or silences) that could mean a child was in danger. They gradually became more at ease about knowing when a child's demands needed immediate response and when they could be put off until later. The point was summed up by the mother of a three-year-old boy. "I guess there aren't any circumstances when my privacy is more important than my child's needs. There's no situation I can think of where I just let him keep calling until I am finished. I can't imagine that—it wouldn't be enjoyable, it wouldn't be relaxing, even if I could say, 'Go away, see you later, go back to sleep.' When he's a bigger kid, but not at this point." Mb3

There was a very small group of parents who felt that no matter the child's age, his demands should always take precedence over their need for privacy. One parent with this attitude was Brian, the father of a six-year-old girl and three older children, a boy ten and girls fourteen and fifteen. Brian, a firefighter in a small Indiana city, was in many ways a very traditional parent—by his own admission conservative in his attitudes toward political, religious, and sexual issues and totally committed to ensuring his children's welfare in every possible situation. "I can hardly feature a situation where I would push her away and say, 'I need my own time,' " he said earnestly. "I just can't hardly feature that. I can't feature anything that would be more important to me than her or the rest of my children so that I would say 'Stop, cease, desist, I need my own time.' I suspect that I would probably go to their needs as opposed to my own." Fg15g14b10g6

Another parent, Mary, expressed the same point of view, though her feeling stemmed from the fact that sex was not an important part of her life. "I'll probably still say that my daughter's need to be close would override my sense of privacy," she said. "I think if I felt that she was intruding on our lives I would set limits with her. I would close the door and make rules. But I've never really felt that she's been intrusive on our lives or our sense of privacy. I think both Greg and I are really conservative about our sexuality. It's not really that important a part of our whole marriage." Mg5

But Mary was unique. Almost all the other parents in the study regardless of whether they felt they balanced children's needs with their own or felt children always came first, talked about the frustrations of trying to be both a good parent and a fulfilled sexual person.

Accepting Frustration: "My Wife Runs Out and I Go Limp"

People of all backgrounds, with children of all ages, described—with eloquence, with humor, with resignation or resentment—the great variety of distractions, interruptions, inhibitions, thwarted orgasms, broken moments of romance that they and their spouses had experienced since becoming parents. For, in practice, it was the quality of the sex life rather than the quality of the parenting that tended to suffer the most when balance between the two could not be achieved. One mother
Mb3 of a three-year-old said, for instance, "What happens when you become the parent of a very young child is that you never fuck, that's all there is to it. My kid goes to bed about eleven o'clock at night and we never have any time to ourselves, ever, ever, ever. It's ridiculous. So we have a ridiculous sex life now." But the difficulties did not always fade away as children grew older, according to the mother of an eleven-
Mb11 year-old boy. She said, "If I hear a child cough just as I feel ready to achieve an orgasm, I will not. It will just disappear immediately and I will never be able to and I resent that very much." One father re-
Fb4 ferred with wry amusement to the parallel male experience. "Just when we're getting started, there's a call from the child," he said with a laugh. "My wife runs out and I go limp. It's like the telephone ringing." On the whole, however, mothers tended to be more voluble and more candid in discussing their feelings about these difficulties.

Mb6   Several times when we were actually engaged in making love he has
         come to the door and said something like, "Isn't it time for breakfast?"
         or "Aren't you ever going to come out?" Privacy is hard to come by.
         It's a tremendous problem.

Mg8   When I hear her saying, "Mommy" in the middle of the night, an
         intimate moment, that's been about it.

Mb11   We were making love—it was probably a weekend morning—and
         there was a knock on the door because of a fight. The children were
         fighting. And I was furious. They had no right to disturb us for some-
         thing that was insignificant and trivial. I was quite annoyed with it.
         They were told to stay out.

For the most part, parents tried to deal with these dilemmas by learning to distinguish one interruption from another. If the child had a real and pressing problem it would override the parents' momentary desire for sexual expression. If the demand was trivial or merely attention-getting it could safely be ignored. Underlying most parents' attitudes was a basic assumption that their wish for sexual privacy was neither frivolous nor self-indulgent: a healthy and complete sexual relationship helped foster the kind of warm loving atmosphere out of which good parenting could spring.

Achieving Priorities: "We Know When She's Just Being Ornery"

Gail described the way she worked out this balance between herself as a sexual being and herself as a concerned, responsible parent. Her own privacy did come first at certain times, she felt, and she wanted her daughter to learn to respect those times. But there were also situations in which the child came first, absolutely and unquestionably. Flexibility was an important part of Gail's approach, though; she emphasized realistic scheduling and keeping her parental antennae alert. "When Mg4 we are having sex, when we are in bed, certain times when we just have a need to be alone together because one of us is feeling down or something like that—at those times we expect Emma to understand. We try, though, to keep times like that till she is sound asleep. If we're in bed and we are talking or kissing or hugging, whatever, lovemaking, and she suddenly says, 'Come! I need you!'—well, if it's something that she's really upset about, okay. We know when she's just being ornery. Sometimes she'll come up with a zillion excuses for water in the night," Gail added, with an exasperated expression. "But if it's a bad dream, I usually go to her. If it's something really severe, I'll bring her into bed with us for about five minutes. You know, then we just stop [making love]. Everything stops if Emma is really upset about something."

Irv spoke in a similar way of setting priorities. He, too, wanted his child to learn to respect the parents' private times, and emphasized the importance of developing instincts for genuine as opposed to frivolous demands. "I think there are certain times when your child should Fg7 realize that you want to be left alone," he said. "You have to develop a feel for when your child truly needs you, or when he's just bored. If the child truly needs to be close, that's different. Then you're not denying him your time appropriately but," he shrugged with disapproval, "just not wanting to have the child there. But there has to be a time when your child realizes that everybody, including you, needs their privacy. And if the child doesn't need you for anything specific—if they need you to get them a cookie or something, you'd say, 'Look, I'm busy and I want to be alone.' I think that's appropriate. If you have a feeling that they're truly scared, if they really need you, that's fine. If they're doing it to be manipulative, then deny it to them without guilt. I can," he concluded firmly.

Like most of the fathers interviewed, Richard saw himself as tough in dealing with intrusions on his sexual privacy. But he too stressed the importance of evaluating each situation and gauging the quality of the child's need in its own particular context. "It depends on the circumstances," he said. "I would have to assess how distressed he is, how much he needs me. But generally, when I'm interested in sexual activity, when I am making love, I won't go to him unless I determine that his need for me is so strong that it warrants me giving that up. I *will not*, and that's adamant and hard-assed. I'm very suspicious. I come from Missouri at those times. He has to show me!"

But it was not always easy to decide what to do, when to "deny them without guilt," at what point to become "hard-assed." Janet acknowledged the difficulty in being able to tell the difference between a genuine demand and the "manipulativeness" or "orneriness" to which other parents referred. "The question is very open-ended," she said. "If my child is ill, my privacy of course is not as important as my child's needs. If my child wants to be held because of something that is fleeting, or if I know that it's just a manipulative kind of thing, I'll say, 'I'm sorry, I'm busy.' But I can't really pinpoint the specifics—when I would give up, for my kid, what is important to me in terms of privacy. It's very difficult to determine."

By and large, though, parents tended to echo each other strikingly when they spoke of their policies regarding sexual privacy and the need to strive for a compromise that was fair to both the parent and child:

Fg8b4

Fg3

I guess the one situation when our privacy comes first would be when my wife and I are making love, but I presume when the child requires to be close that it's something important, and at that particular time we would stop. I think we would stop and try to solve the problem rather than just saying, "Go away, we're busy," or whatever.

Mg3

Making love with my husband is one time when privacy is important. [If I were interrupted], if she had a nightmare—it doesn't happen very often—but I'd go in to see how she is, to see what's wrong, try to wake her up, put her back to sleep. I would resent it and I would mind, but I would do it.

Mg8

If she calls for me in the middle of the night, if it's an intimate time, if I don't go to her I certainly answer her. I would rather go there than have her come to me. I'll call out the door or something, but I acknowledge that she has called because I would not particularly want her to show up in our bedroom. If she's feeling sick, or if she has a terrible nightmare or something, then I might go to her. In other words, if I feel it is a serious enough request, then I would leave an intimate moment to go to her. Other than that I tell her to go back to sleep.

A small minority of parents were relatively uninhibited, able to continue making love serenely even if children were around and, perhaps, listening to their activities. However, the situations they described were not those in which children's needs—for attention or care—came into conflict with the parents' sexual privacy. In theses cases the children were merely there next door—"little pitchers with big ears"—but the parents had learned simply to tune them out.

> If they're in their rooms or even if they're walking back and forth   Mb10
> outside of my room, that doesn't bother me. I don't think it makes
> me uptight. I remember once specifically saying, "I wonder if we
> have an audience" kind of thing, but we never stopped *[laughs]*.

Emphasizing Give and Take: "There Are Times When You Just Want To Be Quiet and Alone"

One positive approach to the issue that many parents found useful was to focus on the reciprocal nature of privacy, to emphasize the give-and-take nature of their request for time to be alone together. A socialization process was often at work here, too, as children observed the kind of informal, unwritten "contracts" that made relationships viable and productive. If a child learned to respect, specifically, the closed door of his parents' bedroom, and if the parents equally respected the "closed doors" in a child's life, the child was learning an important lesson he could apply to other situations. And, too, he was given practical demonstration of the values of autonomy, selfhood and identity: everybody needs and deserves time to be alone.

In discussions with her daughter, Gail said she tried to emphasize the parallel between her own and her daughter's right to privacy, and also to suggest that privacy could be intellectual and emotional as well as physical. "I'd say to her, 'Just like you have private thoughts in your   Mg4
own mind, you wouldn't want somebody always to ask you, "Emma, what are you thinking?" There are times when you want to just be quiet and alone. Well, sex is an alone thing between two people and that's something I think you should respect—my privacy.' " Gail also felt that the calm, reasonable tone she brought to such discussions added to their effectiveness, as did the use of examples to which her child could easily relate. "I wouldn't act angry toward her, because

kids are curious and they want to know, but at the same time, I'd say, 'Well, when you get older, you won't want me to be asking you about your sexual feelings. That's something that you will have alone. It's something very alone and private and that's what's wonderful about it. That's your special feeling.' And I hope she'll understand it. Even now, I don't snoop if Emma has her private little treasure box. I don't snoop through it and pick apart every piece and say, 'What's this?' and 'Why do you have these rocks in your drawer?' I don't pick apart every little trinket she has. There is privacy and I'll expect her to respect mine. I think that just goes along with caring for somebody—respecting one another."

Several other parents echoed Gail's strong feelings about fairness and mutual respect, and the importance of maintaining privacy on both sides of the parent-child relationship:

Mg6 My children have this thing where they want privacy, they want nobody else to come in their room, and I would explain my privacy to them like that. Each one has this certain thing—"I want to be by myself, close the door!" So I would tell them the same thing: "Look, I want to be by myself. I don't want you to come in my room."

Fg8b4 Sex is a very important part of my life. I hope it's an important part of my children's lives. I hope they enjoy it as much as I enjoy it. I will accord them the same respect for their activities as I want them to accord me.

Mb11 I feel that just as I close my door and there's a privacy I expect, if they choose to close their bedroom door I would never think of walking in. I will always knock.

Bedroom Etiquette

The ways parents regulated bedroom activities provided additional clues to their attitudes toward sexual privacy. Most of the parents in this study were circumspect in their sexual behavior; they preferred to wait until children were asleep to make love and were not entirely comfortable unless the bedroom door was closed or locked. A few even used special secluded areas of their homes to ensure privacy. Another slightly smaller group of parents said they were able to make love comfortably with the door to the bedroom open at night or at other times of the day while children were awake elsewhere in the house. A surprisingly large number, including some who were otherwise very cautious, reported that under special circumstances they would make love while their children were asleep in the same room. The majority of parents believe that, in spite of all precautions, children were inevitably going to be aware of their parents' sexual activities from time to time. A majority also reported that they would allow children into bed with them under special conditions—a storm, a nightmare—but not to sleep. These parents would also permit children to observe or share such bedroom activities as cuddling, reading, playing, watching television.

Do They Really Think Their Parents Do It?

When asked if they thought their children really understood what was going on in the bedroom, however, most parents evinced doubt. They felt that even children who possessed all the relevant facts about intercourse had not yet "put it all together." Yes, these children knew the man put his penis into the woman's vagina and that's the way babies were made, but such knowledge was technical, abstract, and in a way unreal; they would not be able to connect these processes with what they sensed taking place behind the closed doors of their parents' bedroom (or even with the various casual forms of physical affection between parents they observed outside the bedroom). Parents of younger children were more confident that this gap between factual and anecdotal knowledge of sex existed; parents of older children often merely hoped.

> She's not aware of those things yet. She just assumes we go to sleep. You know, Mommy and Daddy go to bed and when the lights are out, everybody goes to sleep. She doesn't really associate that that's for something special and secret.   Mg4

> Of course, kids grow up a lot quicker, and I'm sure that things aren't like they used to be. I expect that probably with the acceleration of maturity, I may be naive in thinking that they are not aware.   Fg6

> Up here in his head he knows that a mommy and daddy come together and make a baby, but I don't think he connects it at all with whatever he thinks we are doing in the bedroom. He really is not curious about it. I think he is much too young.   Mg7

> I don't think he fully understands the whole process. He understands the petting, the kissing, and the fondling, and the playing with parts of the body. But actually saying, "Okay, they're going in and making love"—I'm not sure that he really understands what that's about.   Mb10

Some children, it's true, seemed amazingly precocious when it came to figuring out just what their parents were doing in bed. In at least two cases where children walked in unexpectedly on their parents during intercourse, it was the children rather than the adults who handled the situation with aplomb. Janet was startled to discover that despite the fact she and her husband were well covered with sheets and blankets when their eleven-year-old son came into their bedroom one morning, he immediately understood that he had interrupted some sexual activity. His straightforward, good-humored response dissipated the initial tension of the moment. "His reaction was, 'Oh, my God, they're being frisky,'" she recalled, with a grin. "My reaction is very casual then. And my husband will laugh." Milly has a boy of five and a girl eight. "They have walked in on us by mistake," she said. "I remember one evening, my eight-year-old came in and asked for something from the refrigerator. I think they wanted ice cream. They just came right in without knocking and there they found my husband and I." Her son was disconcerted—"his eyes just like blew out of his head" —and she had to explain lovemaking (and the need for privacy) to him later. But her daughter "knew exactly what was going on," took control of the situation, and spoke reassuringly to her embarrassed parents. "So she says, 'Well, I'm sorry, excuse me. Continue with your marriage.'"

Even if children did not understand specifically that their parents were making love, they seemed to have an instinct that something exciting, mysterious, and secret was occurring in the bedroom. In spite of all precautions parents might take to ensure privacy, the exigencies of family living often served to create certain "signals"—a closed door that was usually open, for instance—which children were quick to pick up. When parents had sexual relations, they were aware of a presence in the house, alert little beings curious to check on what they were doing.

Mb6

We switched sides of the bed. This sounds ridiculous, but when we were first married we used to sleep on certain sides of the bed. When we moved we rearranged the bed and for reasons that are totally beyond me now we switched sides for sleeping, but we go back when we are having any sexual activity. One morning my son walked in and said, "You're on the wrong side of the bed."

Mb10

I have shutters in my house where people can reach my room from the next room, and I say, "If you see those shutters down, don't disturb me!"

Mg11

They will notice when my husband gets out of bed that he doesn't have any pajama bottoms on or they'll see the pajama bottoms on the floor, and they might make some little comments about it, laughing, "Well, look at that!"

Mg17b13b8

He has got a pretty good signal to begin with. They used to laugh because the dog sleeps in my room. Of course the dog is put outside when we decide we want to make love. They know when the dog is outside the door something is going on. One of them would say, "Look at that end of the hall—the dog is out!"

Practical strategies

Special Times and Places

Parents described the strategies they used in order to ensure the kind of private and tranquil environment, free of the possibility of sudden interruptions, that they felt was necessary for intimacy. Some tried to get as far away as possible from their children in order to have sex. They had a bedroom at the other end of the house or on a different floor from where the children slept, or they went to a different floor especially to make love. One mother, a single parent, took her children to a neighbor's house when she expected her lover. "I sent them to my neighbor's house," She recalled. "I said, 'Would you watch them for me for a while?' And she said, 'For what?' And I looked at her and said, 'For what do you think?' And she started laughing. She said, 'Yeah, just send them over.' "

By far the largest number of parents said they usually waited until their children were asleep to make love. This was an obvious and simple solution for parents with children of all ages, but especially very young ones, who went to bed relatively early. Some parents even set special bedtimes to ensure that children would indeed be in bed, and asleep, by the time the parents were ready for sexual intimacy.

However, this was not a solution that worked for everyone, as the mother of a very young child rather wryly pointed out. Although she and her husband did prefer to wait until the child was asleep to make love, this meant, de facto, not making love at all. Some children were "night owls" by nature and did not actually fall asleep until so late in the evening that the parents were too exhausted to do much else but sleep themselves. "My kid goes to sleep very late," she said with a resigned sigh. "Like one o'clock in the morning. We're crawling into bed and it's no use." Another mother, commenting on the same problem, said with some vehemence, "It is inconvenient to hide making love: How can I hide it unless I wake up at three a.m., and who wants to do that?"

In some households, letting children watch television was an alternative to waiting for them to fall asleep. Parents would "take their chances" and attempt to make love while children were so engrossed in a favorite television show that they were unlikely to interrupt or overhear anything. But other parents felt strongly about not engaging in sexual activity while children were awake and busy around the house. Though they did not disapprove in principle, they were concerned about their own ability to enjoy such a precarious moment of intimacy. Most of them felt the distractions would be too great and the satisfactions too minimal for the risk to be worthwhile.

Mb3   There's no way I would try to make love when the kid is awake and around the house because it's just not going to be possible to enjoy it.

Mg8   We are not comfortable in making love if we know that she is in her bedroom reading, for example, or awake and playing where any moment she may walk in. That rules out making love during the day if she's at home.

Fg6   There's a time and a place for everything and so consequently when she and the rest of the children are about the house I guess that it's just not the proper time.

Bedroom Doors: Open? Closed? Locked?

About half of the parents in the study said they kept bedroom doors open while making love and the other half said they kept the doors closed. To some extent, the issue was tied to personal style and temperament. If the family lifestyle was easygoing and no area was off limits to children, parents often didn't bother to close the bedroom
Mb11   door when they made love. "It's very difficult to get up after the process has begun—to stop and close the door—so we'll just be a little more quiet," said one mother in a household where doors are never closed. On the other hand, those who were naturally cautious found closing the door an obvious necessity.

Sometimes the age of the child was an important factor in determining policies on this issue. Doors were generally kept open more often by parents of very young children, who still needed large amounts
Mb3   of parental attention or supervision. "Can't close the door on him and say, 'See you in a half hour.' He's too little. Just can't do that with three-year-olds," was one mother's typical comment. As children grew older and both more responsible and more sexually aware, parents found it possible and sometimes necessary to close the bedroom door and to insist that the child knock before entering.

The question of whether or not to lock that closed bedroom door elicited somewhat more vehement responses. Parents who were opposed to locking the bedroom door had strong principles when it came to adhering to these policies. They believed locking themselves away from their children could cause deep-seated feelings of rejection and frustration, and wanted children to be secure in the knowledge that their parents were always available to them.

> You mean like locking doors and stuff like that? No. I have a feeling that the people who owned the house before us were into that situation because they put a lock on their bedroom door. I think it was done for that purpose but we don't do that.   Fg3

> I don't think parents should lock the door, 'cause I think a child should know that if he has a problem or something he can always come in. The only time we lock our bedroom door is when we're getting dressed to go out and they keep running in and out to see what we're doing, and only because of the time element.   Fb4

Parents who locked their doors might do so in order to protect their children from unpleasant, possibly traumatic surprises. But often the reason was pragmatic: their privacy came first. Margot talked about how much more satisfying her sexual experiences were once she and her husband had moved into a new bedroom, one which did have a lock on its door. "I must say," she admitted, "I enjoy sex when the door can be locked. I don't like to be interrupted and I don't like to have to worry about whether or not I'm going to be interrupted."   Mg10

Here again, the age of the child often determined the way parents behaved. Several parents of younger children, who were not at present locking the door, indicated that they expected to have to change this policy as children grew older and more sexually aware:

> He's only four and the other one is six. Maybe when they're eight or nine and they really know what's happening, we'll lock the door then— and wonder if they're listening!   Fb6b4

> We haven't had occasion to develop a bedroom policy yet. I guess when they are older, then we'll put a lock on the door.   Mg8g6

Sleeping Accommodations and Sex

The most common sleeping arrangement among families in this study was for parents to have a separate bedroom from their children. There was one exception to this otherwise hard-and-fast rule, a couple who lived in a one-bedroom apartment and shared that one bedroom with their seven-year-old daughter. Both parents were matter-of-fact about this facet of their family life. Alice said that although she and her husband might choose to have intimate conversations in the living room

Mg7 they were not uncomfortable about making love when their daughter was sleeping and did not feel she was affected adversely when she happened to wake up and overhear them. "We all sleep in the same room and she has caught us in the middle, as it were, because we're not always quiet as mice." But neither parent was particularly concerned or embarrassed. They believed intercourse was a natural, healthy activity that could not harm a child who had been brought up to feel the same way.

While this arrangement was a rather dramatic departure from those that existed in most of the parents' homes, it was by no means unusual when families slept away from home. Many parents reported that there were circumstances—visiting relatives or friends, staying overnight in expensive motel rooms, camping out—when they shared a single room with their children. And a substantial number of those parents said they would indeed consider making love, enthusiastically if cautiously, while their children slept nearby.

Fg7g2 Would I make love when the kids are right in the room? If it was under the covers and she was sleeping. I guess that wouldn't be bad.

Fb9b8b4 We went cross country last summer. We camped and on real hot days or when we felt we needed it, we'd grab a motel room. We'd all stay together in the same room. It was a bit confining, but we even found a way to make love with all the kids in bed. It seemed to work out all right. They slept; they didn't notice anything.

Mb11 We'll make love with them asleep in the same room. Very quietly with a minimal amount of noise, and hope that there's a decent mattress in the motel. But we've done it and we've gotten away with it.

A few parents who said they had made love while sharing a room with a child were less enthusiastic, and spoke rather acidly of the diminished quality of these sexual experiences. Becky commented on Mg3 one such experiment, "The one time she was in a room with us it was very annoying because she tosses and turns and makes noise all night and so you feel inhibited. You worry that she's going to wake up and you can't make any noise and you can't do this and you can't do that." Mb11 Janet said much the same thing. "One can get very quiet, which is not as much fun as being able to make noise, to scream, as I can in the middle of the afternoon if nobody's home."

Several parents felt they would not want to take the risk of having sex in the same room with their children. They worried that children would listen curiously or be deeply distressed by their parents' Fg3 activities. As one father put it, "My wife will usually feel that we shouldn't make any noise lest our daughter wake up and have questions, embarrassment, or whatever. So usually we avoid making love

in situations that might cause complications, if we're in the same room."
Lesley adamantly agreed. "Cuddle or make love when the children   Mb7b4
are sleeping in the same room? That's out of the question!"

A very small group of parents said that on certain special occasions —at home or on vacation—the parents and the children would
all sleep in the same bed together. For one couple this had been a
warmly gratifying experience over a period of time, though it had been
limited to the first six months after the birth of their son. "Yes, he   Mb3
slept in our bed for the first couple of months. Oh, sure, that's the
delicious part of having a kid—when he was born, he *lived* in our bed!"
A mother of several children said that once in a while—for fun, for
comfort, for closeness—the whole family would sleep together in one
bed, although ordinarily each child used a separate room and bed. "At   Mg12g6g4b3
home sometimes we sleep together. In the same bed, yes. I guess we
all get the feeling we just want to be together, so we all pile up in the
bed and fall asleep together." She added that on one or two such occasions she had actually made love while her youngest child slept on the
bed. "I have had sex with him in the bed when he was asleep. I've
done that, taking a chance that he would wake up."

A number of families, in fact, maintained a fairly loose and tolerant policy with regard to allowing children to sleep in the parents' bed.
"There was a time," one woman said, "when my middle child wan-   Mb11
dered from one bed to another in the middle of the night and he very
often slept with us. He would get in the middle and it didn't bother
me. Another body—it's just more warmth." Another mother described
similar warm family sleep-and-cuddle sessions. "All of them, they all   Mb8g6b4g3
come in. Now what my son would do is, if my husband and I are
sleeping, he would go to the foot and crawl in the middle of us. That
means we have to move over and make room for him. And then my
baby she'll cuddle up under him and the oldest one will cuddle up
under me. Then you still have the fourth one looking around to see,
'Where can *I* fit at?' " She traced this custom back to her own childhood and spoke with amusement and pleasure of behaving much the
same way when she, as an adult, visited her own mother—eventually
all three generations would end up curled around each other in one
large bed. "When they go to their grandmother's house, we all sleep
in one bed together, everybody, including my husband. If I sleep at
the bottom, two is at the bottom with me and two is at the top with
him. That way it will be evened out. It's a king-size bed. I don't think
children really ever grow out of sleeping with their mother or father
'cause even right now when I go over to my mother's house I crawl
right up in her bed and go to sleep and my babies come right behind
me. And my mother says, 'Well, what are you all going to do? Put me
out of my own bed?' But it's like that."

Two other parents said they would allow children in bed with them at almost any time during sleep or waking hours, except when they were actually engaged in sexual intercourse:

Mb10   Often he has said that 'I just want to be in here,' so sometimes I will let him come in and stay with us, lay in bed till he goes to sleep, and then I'll get him up and put him in his own bed.

If I'm not in the process of lovemaking, then I will allow him to come in—just about anything besides actually making love.

Most parents preferred, however, to set some kinds of limits on the times when children were allowed into the parents' bed. Many were particularly adamant about not permitting a child to sleep in their bed, but offered different reasons for maintaining this rule. Sometimes a definite principle of social behavior was involved. Parents wanted a child to learn that he had his own bed and belonged there to sleep, just as the parents belonged in their bed. They felt a child should be expected to uphold this basic tenet of family decorum from a very early age.

Fb4   I allow them into bed with me when I'm awake at all times. I do not like them to sleep with me. I think children have a tendency to want to sleep with their parents and it's something they have to learn fairly early they can't do. I say,"You have your own bed," and they never question.

Fg7   I wanted her to get used to the phenomenon of sleeping in her own bed, alone. I didn't want her to scream in the middle of the night because she's afraid of ghosts and goblins and use it as an excuse to come in. I wanted her to get used to being alone and sleeping alone. She's got to see herself as an autonomous animal, not a function of her parent.

In some cases, age was the determining factor. Very young children might be permitted greater access to the parents' bed, but as they grew older they would be encouraged (or would choose themselves) to become more independent.

Fb4b2   When they were very young—two, three, or four—we'd let them come in and spend the night, but there was usually a lot of competition for the middle spot for the whole night, so it had to rotate around.

Mb5   There was a time when we were letting him do it out of sheer desire to get some sleep, I think. But we have a rule now.

Mb8   He would come in if he wanted to sleep with us. He used to come in almost every night. We think it's cute. But now he comes in very rarely.

For other parents, simple comfort was the main issue. They wanted children to sleep in their own beds because children were not considerate bedmates. They kicked or flailed about in their sleep, or they hogged the bedclothes, and it was for those reasons rather than because of more complex principles of decorum or privacy that the parents didn't want their children in bed with them.

> He's been in bed with the two of us plenty of times. Usually he doesn't sleep with us the whole night. I may take him back to his crib because it's very uncomfortable to have him flailing around. I wake up like a pretzel.   Mb3

> Basically it's not okay for her to get in bed with us because I'm not comfortable. She tends to want to lay sideways in bed, so I have to crawl out over her to get up in the morning and that's a major production. I don't particularly think it's good for the kid. I don't think it's good for the parents.   Fg5

> I don't like the idea of her sleeping with me all the time. I think that's partly because I like to sprawl out in my own bed and she kicks a lot.   Mg11

There were several types of instances in which the majority of parents were willing to allow children into their beds or to relax the normal rules—when children were in evident distress, ill or frightened, when they had had a bad dream; when they simply needed to be close.

> When we are sleeping and all, when I'm naked and Fred's naked, if she has a nightmare, if it's really something severe, I would bring her into bed just for a few minutes until she's calm, and then back to her bed I bring her, show her everything's fine.   Mg4

> Sometimes in the middle of the night she wakes up screaming. I put her in the bed with me. If they had a bad dream or if they're sick, definitely. 'Cause I want to keep an eye on them.   Mb8g6b4g3

> When they're sick. They've never really seen any sort of tragedy or death, but I think under those circumstances it would be all right, too.   Fb8

> Sometimes she's afraid—"I don't want to sleep alone tonight"—and that's okay. A thunderstorm is okay. Sometimes she doesn't feel real well and that's okay. And sometimes she just doesn't want to be alone, and I'll let her sleep with me at that time.   Mg11

Early in the morning was a time, too, when many parents were willing to take children into their beds, either for sleeping or for cuddling. For children the bed's main attraction was its association with family affection, security, and togetherness.

Mg3   I invite her to my bed sometimes in the morning when it's very early
       and I'm alone in bed, and I just refuse to get up. She comes in with
       me and goes to sleep.

Mb7   His routine is that if he gets up before us, and if he feels like he
       wants to cuddle, he can.

Mg8   Well, first of all I have to be awake. She's not allowed to come in to
       wake me up. But if I'm awake and it's in the morning and it's kind
       of a school holiday or we are having kind of a lazy day, they can
       come into bed with me for a little while and kind of cuddle and relax
       together. Occasionally I used to read them a book in bed, all three
       of us.

7

**** *Words*

Because language is so flexible and meanings of words take on different colorations in different situations it is not always easy for parents to establish firm policies around the use of sexual language. Indeed, not all parents agreed on what constituted sexual language and what did not. For all of those interviewed, words related to sex play—*make love, fuck, blow job, suck*—were clearly sexual, as were words describing the genitals—*penis, dick, cock, peter, vagina, pussy.* Many, but not all, parents also included other anatomical terms for buttocks, breasts, and pubic hair, as well as words describing excretion, in this category. Generally, parents did not see sexual language per se as dirty unless the dictionary terms were replaced by slang. Not surprisingly, *making love* or *having intercourse* were often acceptable terms for children to use, but *fuck* was prohibited in virtually all families. Similarly, *defecate* (a word actually little used by participants in this study) or *have a BM* were okay, but *shit* was not.

But the more parents discussed dirty language the more apparent it became that what determined what was dirty was not necessarily either meaning or level of language but a myriad of factors—the situation in which the word was used, the age of the speaker, the intent of the speaker, the sensibilities of the hearer. For instance, parents supplied a wonderful variety of affectionate family terms for buttocks—*tushy, ass, butt, behind, buns, heinie, rump, toopie, fanny*. But a number objected to the use of these terms as too intimate or inappropriate outside the home. It was also not uncommon for both parents and young children to use words like *doody, poopoo*, and *peepee* quite easily for toileting. For children at about four, however, these words became dirty jokes among their peers—they began calling friends *pee-nose* or *doody head*—and parents then had to decide whether to teach them the more formal terms.

Even parents who said initially that they could tolerate all kinds of sexual language realized that in effect they rarely allowed themselves and their children complete freedom of speech. They found that they were quite distressed if their children said *fuck* or *cunt* in front of grandparents or straitlaced neighbors. Or that while such language was permissible for the parents and their friends, it really did not sound nice at all coming out of a small child's mouth. Or that while men could use certain words to put down a group of rowdy strangers on the street, they would not dream of saying the same things in the bosoms of their families. A number of other mysterious—almost subliminal—considerations were involved; matters of image and personal taste (or phobia) often contributed to the complicated process of deciding whether a term was permissible, who could use it, and when. In other words, for most of the parents, double, triple, even quadruple, standards prevailed where sexual language was concerned. Many sets of rules overlapped one another and might be modified in subtle ways as a social or personal dynamic shifted. Parents were faced with the extraordinarily difficult task of trying to explain these complex linguistic rituals, customs, and taboos to their children.

Because sexual language, like all language, presents so many ambiguous or "gray" areas, most parents tried to take a rational, cool-headed approach to disciplining children who broke family language codes. Rather than use harsh measures, parents tried instead to teach their children how to judge for themselves when a particular word or phrase was "okay," and when it was "crude," discourteous, hurtful. They hoped fervently that children would eventually develop for themselves knowledge that would allow them to behave with ease and appropriateness at all levels of social, professional, and family life.

Dirty Words

As was pointed out in Chapter Two, parents in this study were conscientious about teaching their children the "correct" or "dictionary" terms for sexual acts and anatomy. "We use purely the standard dictionary terms," one mother said firmly. "*Intercourse* would be *making love*. It would not be *balling* or *getting a piece of the action* or a *piece* of anything. *Breasts* would be breasts, the *vagina* wouldn't be a *cunt*."

For a large number of parents, teaching the proper terms meant teaching children the proper attitudes toward their bodies, toward the opposite sex, toward sexuality in general. Because they did not want their children to see sex as dirty or sexual terms as put-downs, they limited the use of slang in the home. Penelope had strong feelings about this. "If you mean parts of the body, we use the dictionary terminology, the formal words. To me, the term *tit* is sexual language, more than *breasts*, which is an anatomical word. *Tits* is a street word. It's a bit offensive and it's slang. It's not slang if you're referring to a mouse or an animal that has teats, but it's like a bastardized word and I don't want to use that kind of English." Jerry made this comment: "When I talk about hard-core language I mean using street terminology, like *fuck*. And parts of the body that are used as street words—as opposed to *vagina*—we try to avoid that completely. *Intercourse* as opposed to *fucking*, certainly." Another mother said, "We don't want the children to get the wrong impression of love and sex. We don't want them to get the 'dirty' impression. We want them to get the very normal, natural, clean impression. We don't want to make fun of sexual parts or sexual language. Sex becomes kind of dirty then, when you joke about it." Mg5 Fg6 Mg7b5

For some parents, this negative view of slang terms was extended to what one mother called "baby words" as well. Jim had firm ideas on this point. "We have never baby-talked to the kids and I think baby-talking is about the same level as the use of a dirty word." Another parent said, with equal vehemence, "I don't like pet names. If he's going to talk about his body part, he should talk about it the right way." Penelope also preferred a formal term to the friendly diminutives her husband occasionally used and noted that her daughter now makes a distinction herself. "If her father says 'itty-bitty-titties,' she uses that term, but when she's speaking to me about something serious, she uses the term *breasts*." Fg10 Mb4 Mg5

Some children resented the "no-slang" restrictions their parents placed on sexual language. Older children especially tended to grumble about having to use "corny" dictionary terms when "all the other kids" were using the more fashionable and racy four-letter words. "They don't think it's fair, since everyone else is using those words. Every now and then they just sneak and use them when they think I'm not listening," said Millie, the mother of five children ranging in age from three to eleven. She added crisply, "They get lectured if they're caught." Sandy had encountered increasing resistance to these standards from her fifteen-year-old daughter, while her eleven-year-old son "follows our lead more because he's not at the age where he's rebelling yet, so he refers to *penis, breast, vagina*. The teenager uses other words. Now she Mg11g8g5b5g3 Mg15b11 uses words which for me were vulgar when I was growing up—*dick*, *cunt*, *tits*. They were street words when I was growing up. She thinks it's 'faggy' and 'nebby' to use words like *penis* and *vagina* and diction-ary words. That's what she thinks. What can I do?"

The use of street terminology was also seen as a way in which children related negatively—to provoke anger or call attention to them-selves—to their parents. Some parents regarded slang as disrespectful. A mother said, "They think it's real cute to tell me it's their *weiner* and their *dick* and I'll say, "I told you, I just don't want to hear those words, that's it. If you want to talk about it, all right, it's your *penis*." Others were more tolerant. They believed that children often "tried on" sex-ual language as a method of demonstrating that they were growing up, becoming sexually aware, "learning about life." Trude described over-hearing her small daughter and some friends trying out certain sexual terms; she was totally disarmed by the healthy, even Rabelaisian, qual-ity the youngsters brought to these old words. "There are one or two best friends where most of their delight is taken in saying the 'dirtiest' words they can think of. They just do it and laugh and laugh and then it passes. I eavesdrop as much as I can without making my presence known. I enjoy the conversations that go on. It shows me the social growth that's taking place," she pointed out.

Some parents handled such incidents by responding in a suppor-tive, matter-of-fact and totally unshockable way. Humor—a bit of friendly serious kidding—could help defuse the child's need for atten-tion. One mother told of a joke her eleven-year-old son had written out and left for her to find and read. "It was all there, all the crude street language, and I think he was as pleased as could be that he could show an adult that he knew all that. I think that was a piece of saying, 'Hey, look, look where I am in my knowledge!' I approved. I kidded him. I've done that on other occasions—'Oh boy, Mr. Macho is beginning!' "

Mild dismissal of the child's language—deeming it not particu-larly amusing, but not particularly shocking either—could also be a use-ful response. One mother described the way she reacted when her eleven-year-old daughter "tested" her with newly acquired sexual language. "She has come home and told me, to get my reaction. And I say, 'Oh, Katie, you've heard that one,' and my kind of just skipping over it sort of gives her the reassurance that it's okay and then it's dropped immediately." The mother of a smaller child used a similar low-key approach when her daughter brought home several scatologi-cal and anatomical terms popular among her peers. "She said, 'That's like a *poopoo* head.' I said, 'Oh, okay.' She said, 'Oh, *tushy*,' and 'I can say it!' and so I said, 'Say it.' It wasn't so exciting when she realized it wasn't something that was forbidden." When one man's son told a story with the punch line "Fuckerfaster!" in the car on a family drive, no one displayed shock. Instead, the boy was gently deflated by a com-

mon agreement among his listeners that the joke was a dud, regardless
of the racy language it included. "I told her that was the first joke I   Fg12b8
ever heard," the father said. "And my wife said, 'Gee, that's a dull
joke and it's not very funny.' And even my daughter admitted that
she remembered that as *her* first joke in elementary school. You know,
it's a terrible joke. But the reason it's appealing to kids is they get to
use that word." One mother described a "Chinese water torture"   Mg8
method of dealing with dirty jokes and other inappropriate uses of sexual language: "We'll say, 'Do you know what that means?' and if they
don't we usually send them to the dictionary. When he does know
what it means, we usually ask him why he thinks it's funny. We will
just say 'Do you know why?' 'I don't find that amusing, why did you?'
'What—where is the punch line?' And we play it so much that the kid
just wants to go away. By that time the whole joke is gone."

A few parents reported that in their household, when sexual language was used in a warm and intimate or a purely humorous way it
could be rendered harmless, almost neutral in meaning. A father whose
family was generally rather cautious about using certain expressions—
"four-letter" words as well as slang references to sexual anatomy—
nevertheless spoke of friendly sexual bantering sessions that were quite
acceptable. "Talking about kidding," he said with a smile, "a big joke   Fg10
at the table when my son was growing up was, 'Come on, eat your
food—don't you want to have hair on your chest?' And of course we
tried to use the same line on the girls, but none of the girls wanted
hair on their chest. So the line became, 'Eat your vegetables—they'll
give you big boobs.' It was a sort of lighthearted approach to it. But I
don't think we are really into dirty language itself."

In some families "dirty" words had taken on a magical aura: to
use them was to risk the lightning bolt. But only if the words were
spoken. If they were whispered, spelled, or written down, they somehow lost their power. "My daughter learns to spell words that are 'no-   Mg5
no's," Penelope said. "She spells them all. And I'm so geared into
academics [Penelope's husband is an economist] that if you *spell* it, it's
okay and if you *write* it, it's okay. She could not come home and say,
'Fuck you!' But she will spell it, with delight, to get a rise. And she'll
say, 'I know we can't *say* certain words, such as. . . .'—and she'll spell
it backwards. I can't think that quickly! It is acceptable that way. She
knows it." Other parents made similar comments about how terms
could be defused by not saying them aloud.

> It's not part of his speaking vocabulary. Things like *asshole,* he'll   Mb4
> spell it out, whisper it to me quietly. He already decided this is not
> such a good word. He won't say *fuck* because he learned somewhere
> that this is the worst word you're going to say. Those words he'll
> spell or whisper.

Mg7b3 He'll just say *"That* word." Or he'll say, "I know I shouldn't tell you, Mommy. Shall I whisper it?" *Shit* and *fuck*. He doesn't want to say it and he thinks I shouldn't hear it.

Inappropriate Language: Relating to Others

Often the meaning of a word or its traditional level of social acceptability had nothing to do with the parents' standards for sexual language. Many parents acknowledged that they allowed some words and banned others for purely subjective reasons. A word that was not particularly shocking to one person made another "shudder," or "see red," or "go bananas." Summing up her feelings on this issue, one mother said, Mg9g7 "It's really weird. There are just certain words I object to. And that's Mg10 just a very personal thing with me." And a father said, "There really aren't any criteria. What's 'dirty' to you may not be 'dirty' to someone else. It's really the boundaries you set up for yourself."

Of course, children, even those too young to comprehend fully the meaning of the words in question, could be adept at knowing which ones struck that peculiar chord in their parents' minds. Jerry, for instance, admitted that his particular bugaboo was the word *fart*, but his comments illustrate the kind of "magical" power all language—most especially sexual language—can exert over emotional behavior. "I dislike the word *fart* more than any other word man can conceive of, for Fg6 some reason. I don't know why," he said, shaking his head. "I think my daughter is aware of that. She uses it to annoy me sometimes. She's very clever in the way she does it to get a rise. I guess I should drop her pants and let her have it one time, but I think I back off because I know it's a personal issue—that word as opposed to really a terrible word. Whereas if she used the word *fuck* the same way I would definitely spank her."

Other parents also noted the way children seemed to develop a sixth sense for the words that "bugged" the parents most:

MMg6 She has a *vagina* fetish. She uses that word. It seems to be her favorite. I think she gets reactions from people when she uses it, older people, older meaning my mother and father. They'll look and she gets that attention. She's aware of it. She milks it, she goes for it.

Mg8 I can't stand when people say *fuck* and the other one is *frigging*. My daughter used *fuck* a few times when she was little. She didn't know what it meant, she just knew it got a reaction, and she was going to use it.

For some parents inappropriate use of sexual language was undesirable because of what such lapses indicated about one's social status—education, family background, level of taste and intelligence. Two fathers who felt this way had gone into business after college and were aware of how image contributes to success. Both characterized themselves as conservative in their attitudes toward a variety of issues, including child-rearing. Just as a child had to be taught good grooming and manners in order to "put his best foot forward" outside the home, it was important that he learn proper language, as well. One father made the following comment about why he preferred that his child limit her use of sexual language. "If you are not taught properly to use the English language, then these are crutches that you use. If you don't have an adequate vocabulary, it's easy to use a 'dirty' word. I feel that the use of these words only reinforces the idea that you don't have command of the language. There are better words." He added, "Let me put it this way. There is a stigma attached to it. There is a stigma attached to using dirty words just for the sake of dirty words. There is no stigma attached to the word itself." Fg10

The second father viewed sexual language in the context of a whole philosophy for civilized living. "I'm a person that believes in certain principles. I'm a conservative in the sense that I have certain values that I think are important, that I pass on to my kid. *Damn* and *hell* are okay, but any of the other words I will not accept. I just don't think it's proper. That's my opinion. My son and I talk a lot," he continued. "We go riding in the car and walking and stuff. We talk about how important it was for a person to strive to be a gentleman. I tried to define what I thought a gentleman was. We used examples of people we know and decided whether or not they were gentlemen." He recalled an incident where he had found himself chastising his son for using a popular vulgarism while watching television with his friends " 'Look at the boobs!' That's what they said. I said, 'I think it's disgusting to use that kind of language in public, and usually it's a very low person who doesn't have a very good command of the English language that has to express themselves in that way.' I explained that to all the boys the other night." Fb10

A third parent who had this point of view was Caridad. For her, language was an indication of how well educated one was. She equated inappropriate language with shoddy grammar—both anathema to her, with the latter probably the graver sin. "I've got this thing about grammar," she began. "There are a lot of children on the block who use *ain't*. It's a terrible word. My children go absolutely bonkers when they hear it." She added, half-humorously, that she was beginning to realize her children might have gotten the idea that *ain't* and other incorrect terms possess hidden 'dirty' meanings. "Here's something funny. Mb7b4

I think I've conveyed the wrong meaning of the word *ain't*. I want to tell them that it is improper English, not necessarily a naughty word!"

Social Settings

Within the family multiple standards for using language were relatively easy to explain and to enforce. But when children went out into the world, either alone or with their parents, they encountered situations that could be far more ambiguous. As with nudity and touching behavior, explaining the appropriate use of sexual language involved a rather complex process of socialization. It was sometimes difficult for children to gauge the kind of language that was permissible in a given situation, and it could be just as difficult for the parents to give them hard and fast guidelines on the subtle linguistic and psychological principles that were involved.

First of all, children had to learn to read the signals of whatever situation they were in and to avoid embarrassing faux pas. Diane described how she allowed her four-year-old to discover for herself what
Mg4   language was acceptable, and when. "My inclination may have been to stop her, and then I thought, she really has to learn how to approach people, how to socialize with them. You know, if she learns when she uses certain words that the people she wants to impress are not very happy about it, then she'll learn a lot faster how to talk to people than
Fb10   if we say, 'No, don't talk that way!' " Mark had begun by telling his son, "You ought to use the kind of language which will not offend the people you are talking to. You have to first sense where people are coming from." He was proud that, at ten, his son had developed the ability to adjust his conduct accordingly. "He knows he can talk around my brother openly and freely. On the other hand, we have some friends—I can think of a particular couple—who would be offended." Sandy also spoke admiringly of her eleven-year-old son's ability to as-
Mb11   sess people's attitudes towards sexual language. "He's learned it, God knows how," she said. "He's learned it from me, from what I've told him. He's also learned it from dealing with people. You know, you don't have to say a dirty word in front of a person to find out that they are tight-assed. A tight-assed person will react to lots of other things in a tight-assed fashion than just a word. He's very perceptive when it comes to reading a person and finding out where they're at."

Sometimes children had to learn not only what social situations were suitable for more relaxed sexual language, but also what particular kinds of sexual language applied in each context. Certain words
Mg15b11 were more "loaded" and potentially shocking than others, and "slips"

made with them were more dire. "I think our kids learned that fairly
early," one mother remarked. "Somewhere along the line of conversa- Mb11
tion you can say, 'This is a person you do not say *shit* in front of.' "
Another mother said, "My daughter knows *farting* is a kind of a bad Mg7
word. She knows you're not supposed to say it in front of other people.
And, as one father noted, certain good old-fashioned Anglo-Saxon four-
letter words were still not acceptable, even in relatively sophisticated
circles—especially coming from children. "I don't want my kids using Fb10
the word *fuck*, because I think it offends a lot of people. Even though
we live in an open community, a verbal community, I think that some
people are offended by that word and I just don't want my kids offending people."

In some households, it was understood that casual sexual language
which was "okay" among family members was not to be used *at all* in
social situations. In Cynthia's family, for instance, language standards
were flexible and tolerant, but her son realized that such might not be
the case everywhere. "We get into the habit of using words like *shit*. It Mb10
slips out. He knows it's something you say in the privacy of the home
and if you say it to someone else you get in trouble." A father, whose
son was about the same age as Cynthia's, described a similar policy. "I Fb11
consider sexual language inappropriate in front of adults who are not
really close friends, but in front of the family I don't consider it that
bad. I may pretend I'm mad, but I really don't consider it that serious
an offense. The children know that it does upset their parents if they
use it in front of other adults, and they don't do it very often." The
mother of a small boy said, "Well, if he said *shit* in public, with other Mb4
children or something, I certainly would move in and say, 'Don't say
that. Talking to people, it's not nice.' " The father of several older Fb15g13b9
children said, "That's one thing we really do crack down on. They're
really not permitted to use bad language outside the family. He does
not say anything really bad in front of anybody who isn't a friend. He's
sensitive to that.'"

In some cases the "not outside the family" rule could be narrowed
down to more specific social areas—"not in front of the neighbors,"
"not in front of your friends," "not in a public place." Sandy lived in a
working-class neighborhood with standards somewhat less tolerant than
her own. She liked her neighbors and respected their different sensibilities when it came to sexual language, and she did not want her son
to "gross out" the friends the family had made on their block. "If we Mb11
had a yard that was really secluded I probably wouldn't mind, but we
are in very close proximity to our neighbors. I would be afraid someone would overhear it."

Penelope described the way language behavior that was rowdy
and obstreperous but acceptable among parents and children in a family car was adjusted when the group went out to eat. "There could be Mg5

two mothers in the car after school, four children in the car, nobody holds back. They all get a big rise out of it. If we go to a restaurant, I see that the same moms and myself will say, 'Now, girls and boys, we are in public now, other people might take offense.' " She was amused to note how the other mothers' reactions matched her own. "We all seem to say the same things: 'Be more quiet or we won't go inside!' "

A number of parents had "double" feelings about restricting the way their children spoke in front of others. They realized that some language rules were confusing, designed to curb and inhibit behavior they might find delightful in a more private context. Jerry, for instance, was torn between admiration of his daughter's spontaneous scatological wit and acute social embarrassment when she decided to show it off in public. "We go out to a Chinese restaurant and we order platters. And my daughter starts with *poopoo* platters and works her way up to *farts*." He couldn't help laughing as he recounted this. "I was annoyed. I was embarrassed for her. In a Chinese restaurant she's doing Chinese jokes and 'poopoo' platter jokes. I was annoyed—what would these people think? But she was really being funny. I would have loved it if it was in our living room or somewhere. I would have been hysterical. It's the funniest routine I've ever heard. But the fact that it was in a Chinese restaurant—it gets a little embarrassing. I was a little upset with her that night."

As Jerry's comments make clear, parents often experienced complex personal anxieties about their children's use of sexual language. Many worried about the way children's occasional lapses would reflect on them, both as parents and as social beings. "It's embarrassing to me," one mother said. "I don't want my children to say words that people don't like to hear from adults sometimes and from children especially. People will think I like this in my children." They were also concerned about the way certain relaxed, intimate habits of family speech might be understood or distorted when transmitted to other parents. "Sometimes what he will do is, for instance, when he has a friend over to dinner—he tries to be very cool and he will use language which I might not mind if he didn't have a friend over, but I don't know how that friend's family's situation is," one mother confided. Some parents alluded to a related problem. If a visiting playmate picked up a "bad" word in their home and then used it in front of his mother or father, that child's parents might not allow the friendship to continue. "I don't want him to say these things, and the friends that I think he should have wouldn't want to hear them," a mother said. "The parents wouldn't," she corrected herself. "The kids I'm sure would love to hear it."

Several parents voiced a concern that the children themselves might be socially ostracized or, at least, badly misunderstood, if they used the wrong kind of language in the wrong kind of place. "I realize she has to be protected," a mother said of her daughter. "I do not find certain language offensive when it's used the way we use it in the house, but there are other parents going to come into play and I don't want her to be thought of as 'that child with the foul mouth.' " Polly, like Sandy a liberal parent living in a more conservative community, remarked, "If my son runs up and down the street saying this, people are going to say, 'Don't play with that kid!' or something like that."   Mb7 Cynthia, too, faced problems related to the cultural differences between her family and some of her neighbors. Certain words and expressions which had no negative connotations for Cynthia, a Midwestern Protestant by birth, or to her husband, an urban Jew, could be highly provocative "fighting words" when used on their integrated block. She told a story that vividly illustrated the kind of cross-cultural language misunderstanding that could take place among children of different racial backgrounds. "I remember the kids were starting to say,   Mb10 'Your mamma. . . .' and another little kid came and told me my son was saying it, too. He didn't understand. We told him he shouldn't go around saying that because he might get punched out!"

For many parents, language restrictions were based not so much on the meanings of the words in question, but on overall principals of decorum. Certain tones of voice, certain styles of body language, certain types of verbal expression were undesirable as breaches of subtle, unwritten laws governing private "space" in public situations. "It's not   Mb7b4 even sexual words, dirty words, even behavior," one mother struggled to explain. "It's something in there that just has to get out once in a while, aggressiveness in not using proper manners. I don't like it." Another mother put it this way, "If she goes on and on and acts like a   Mg5 clown, gets loud and raucous, what's coming out of her mouth isn't half as important as the fact that she's loud, disturbing other people." And Sandy, describing an incident in which she asked her son to leave a restaurant for "getting carried away" and telling "nutty" dirty jokes   Mb11 with a friend, emphasized this principle. "It was a behavioral thing rather than the use of the language, because nobody heard what they were being giddy about."

Emotional Settings

The general emotional ambience surrounding any use of sexual language often helped determine whether parents considered it acceptable or not. If the tone was negative—insulting, aggressive, suggestive— parents might be quicker to impose discipline. But even a term normally considered "crude" might pass if it was thrown off in a spirit of

playfulness, while some milder words became "dirty" because they
were intended to hurt, humiliate, or demean. The word dirty itself,
for instance, while not "dirty" in any sexual sense, could be negative
and insulting. It was extremely difficult to sort out all of these com-
Mg4   plex distinctions in order to explain them to children. "What is it that
makes something dirty?" the mother of a four-year-old mused, grap-
pling with this dilemma. "It is that it demeans somebody. It humili-
ates men or women. None of these things are inherently dirty. We try
to teach our daughter hygiene, for example. That's a tough one because you don't want them to think that the act of having a bowel
movement is a dirty thing by itself, and yet you definitely want her to
observe cleanliness. So we talked to her about it in terms of germs and
wanting to keep herself clean. The plumber came in and my daughter
was saying, 'You *dirty* plumber,' and I took her to task for it afterwards
because I want her to learn that it hurts when people call you names.
Therefore it's not acceptable. So *dirty* has different meanings."

        Many other parents related incidents which also illustrated this
principle; they were especially tough on sexual language when it was
Fb10   used negatively. A father said, "He's come in and said something like,
'I don't like so-and-so. He's a *faggot*.' That irks me. It's derogatory. I
would [reprimand] him in the same way about making a racist remark."
Sandy said this kind of restriction was one she applied as stringently to
Mb11   herself as she did to her children. "I do not allow him to call me a
fuckin' bitch nor would I call him a *fuckin' idiot* or a *fuckin' brat*, because
it's a very degrading way to refer to somebody. They're loaded words—
curse words are loaded words, and my feeling is that you only use them
in loaded situations." She was echoed by Vesta, whose attitude toward sexual language had grown more cautious after she had become a
Mg11   born-again Christian. "I explain it to her. 'It's a derogatory word. It's
like calling somebody that's slow a *dummy*. It's that type of thing.' "
She added that her daughter was sympathetic to such distinctions and
did not need to be further admonished. "I don't forbid her to use them.
She has enough common sense to choose what she's going to use."

        The mother of a girl approaching school age said her reactions to
Mg4   her daughter's use of certain sexual expletives "depends on the intent.
She has started using these words a lot and sometimes it's just in a
taunting way and I won't allow her to do that. I'm not sure it's hostile,
but it's taunting, it's to see if you can get a rise." She added, "In a
sense that's how children make friends at this age, unfortunately." Cynthia remarked upon the same phenomenon; children would start at a
very early age to use sexual language they knew might be hurtful, un-
Mb10   less the parents stepped in to set limits. "There was a time when Justin
was around six and all the kids ran around saying *fuck* and *motherfucker*.
And then one day a little kid came to my door and said, 'Mrs. B.,
Justin called me a *motherfucker*.' She smiled here and added, "Well, it

isn't *too* tough, if the kids still go telling the mother. But that was a whole period they went through. I think they already figured out—I mean, the kids already knew it was an insult."

Sexual language that was derogatory to women was singled out by several parents as requiring special attention. Annette, a working mother of two, who had written a doctoral thesis on a feminist topic, said of her daughter, "If every word out of her mouth was *fuck* and she's talking about women as *cunts* and *piece*, I think I would begin to say to her. 'You don't have the right attitude.'" Polly had flexible, humorous nondoctrinaire attitudes towards most sexual issues. However, she was living in a household of males and was, perhaps, sensitive to this issue for that reason. She remarked, "There are certain words I really don't want them to say in terms of being derogatory to women. I kind of object to the word *fuck* because of the fact that it has a negative connotation to it, a derogatory meaning toward women as being sort of 'done-to.' I object to the word *bitch* when men use it. I mean, I let my kids go around saying certain words, it's not going to bother me, but there are certain [other] ones I really don't want them to say." Constance preferred that her children avoid sexual language altogether, but she was especially disapproving when her son used misogynist words and phrases. "He tells jokes about women, about women's anatomy. Put-down, they are all put-down. That's what bothers me about them, the put-down part of it." Mark, the father who wanted his son to speak like a gentleman, said, "I don't want my son to be a wise-ass, I can just remember growing up with some kids who thought it was wise to dwell forever on anything that was sexual, off-color. They were always the ones who would make a remark about particular women and I found those kids obnoxious, and I don't want my kid to grow up that way, always the one with the latest dirty joke."

Mgl1

Mb7b5

Mbl1

Fb10

Cursing

Running through many parent's remarks on sexual language was a strong disapproval or distrust of "cursing" itself—that sense of "imprecation," or "affliction," or "evil-wishing," implied by the way one used certain words, investing them with a power that went far beyond their literal meaning. Penelope described how she had struggled to explain this concept to her daughter and at the same time analyze it to her own satisfaction. "I said, 'Sometimes people do not have words strong enough to show how they feel, so they just take a word and use it.' I tried to show her that the word itself is meaningless. If *tree* took on the significance of *fuck*, you wouldn't be able to say, 'You're a

Mg5

tree.' Well, . . . but *fuck* has this power. *Fuck* is derived from a sexual thing. *Fuck* is a verb, it's a noun, it's everything. It's like a negative sexual word. 'Go fuck yourself' is the worst thing you can *say* to anybody. It's not the worst thing you can *do.*" She concluded with a sigh, "Why are all 'dirty' words related to sex? The worst put-downs are sexual words, it seems." It was clear to another mother as well that her daughter understood instinctively that the word itself might be irrele-

Mb11 vant; it was the *curse* that had the power. "When I say *asshole* she smiles and gets nervous, because she knows Mommy's angry. The word has no power, it's what's behind my attitude when I say that word. It could be anything, you know, any word." Sandy had acknowledged this

Mb11 phenomenon in the restrictions she had placed on her son. "There's a distinction between using sexual language as an intense general curse, like 'Fuck it!' and using it toward *me* in a way which is unacceptable." Other parents said they would not allow their children to say *fuck* at all, precisely because in our society it has taken on more force as a curse word than as a synonym for intercourse.

One mother told a story which illustrated rather dramatically the power of the imprecation over the power of the meaning of any partic-

Mg7 ular word. "When my daughter was three, a little boy said he was going to take down her pants and laugh at her *deeny*. I don't think she had the slightest idea what *deeny* was, but the way he said it, she knew he was insulting her. He was threatening her. And she remembered that for a long time." She added, in a wry postscript on the contagious quality of such language, "And of course, she started to use it, too."

Double Standards

A number of parents admitted that they were freer with sexual language when they were interacting with friends, colleagues or strangers as opposed to their families. This was particularly true of the fathers interviewed, who, though they came from disparate backgrounds and worked at various kinds of jobs, all talked about a double standard. They used one kind of language with other men and another with their spouses and children.

For many, the workplace was the primary setting in which this double language standard operated. Jim had become an executive in a large conglomerate, after working at many non-managerial jobs. He

Fg10 said, "Because of the industries I've been involved with—you know, I've been involved with different trades and stuff like that—I have set a dual standard for myself. I have listened to and told dirty jokes away from the house, but when I come into the house, this is not the place for it. The house is almost sacrosanct from that standpoint. This is the family. These are the people I love, the people who are important to me. It's a respect. I think that really is the basis for it, a respect. You don't want to offend, you don't want to hurt, you don't want to be disapproved of." Another father who indicated that he was more casual about language at work than at home, felt that this latitude was allowed him by society. The double standard was part of the fabric of the workaday world, a "given," rather than the profound and almost spiritual choice it represented for Jim. "I don't shy away from the use Fb7 of sexually explicit language when I'm with my colleagues. I work in courthouses. It's accepted. However, in my home I don't use it. I find no need to use it in front of my children."

Several men traced the development of their attitudes towards sexual language back to experiences in the armed forces, where certain modes of speech were not only acceptable, but also served as a kind of protective masculine identity signal. For a middle-class inductee with a fresh face and a college degree, "talking dirty" helped bridge cultural gaps, allay insecurities and provide entrée into this very adult, very masculine new world. "It seemed that the minute you got into Fb7 the army it seemed to be the thing to do, express yourself in those terms," one man remarked thinking back on his army experiences in the fifties. "There are times when that type of language seemed to fit the bill much more so than some intellectual expression of concern over having caught your thumb in a rifle's breech. So I became much more comfortable with the use of sexual language." A young father of working-class background who said he had "grown up on the streets" viewed his own early dependence on bad language as a kind of survival tactic, one that had persisted through grueling wartime experiences in Southeast Asia and on up to his present worklife as a shop teacher in a tough Chicago high school. "I was brought up in Cicero and Fg5 it's a pretty tough town. It was always street talk, street language. And I grew up at a very young age. On my job, in Vietnam, both, the men used dirty language. Men, students, I hear it every day. My students are filthy."

Jerry described a very complicated set of language rules which covered many social "mixes"—casual street encounters through friendly gatherings of like-minded adults up to occasions in which children were present as well. "I have what I call street language and what I call Fg6 social language, 'social cursing,' " he said. "And some words are used just 'with the boys' and some words are used in mixed company. Some of the words that are used in mixed company can be used in front of the children. Several fathers were able to be quite specific about which words were only acceptable in "stag" situations.

Vagina's not a word I normally use, except around my daughter. If Fg6
I'm with the guys, then it becomes *cock, cunt, poontang.*

Fuck, cunt, cock is "just guys." Not in front of the kids. Fb7

A few mothers seemed to be aware that they might alter their language in various situations—talk "dirty" with some people, "clean" with others. Sometimes they were more cautious in front of their children. "I have a couple of girlfriends I talk to," one mother remarked. "If an operator were listening in I'm sure her hair would stand on end. It's just part of our relationship that we've established over the years. We use that language as a release and we do it because a lot of our humor is based on it. And it's very funny. But if my daughter were present in the room I would have to hold back, because she's not ready to use that language." But, overall, unlike men, women did not perceive themselves as having two distinct kinds of language—one vocabulary reserved for other women and another, more proper, vocabulary for men and children.

In a great many families, adults, including the parents and their friends, were permitted to use "dirty words" or tell "dirty jokes" among themselves, but sharply monitored this conduct when children were present. "My wife and I don't use any language that has any sexual connotation in front of the kids," a father said. The point was repeated by Mike, who often used sexual language when he was with his wife, "but never in front of the kids, never at all." Two fathers of older children, both boys, made similar comments. "I try not to curse around my kid, just because it's a habit he'll pick up." "I use *fuck* and *screw* and all that stuff, but not in front of the children." One mother said that her husband came from a "a very liberal family," one in which the parents "said anything," used sexual language freely in front of the children. She noted that he had drastically altered his personal language style since becoming a parent himself. "He tries not to use this language with the kids," she said. "Sometimes it slips out and he apologizes. With me he does use it."

Parents also pointed out that adult socializing often involved a richer and freer use of sexual language than any of the participants would feel comfortable with in front of children. "When company comes over, naturally once in a while street language will arise, especially when you think the children are sleeping," a father explained. "But most of my friends that come over, I don't think it's so much that they know not to do it as that they have children of their own. They realize there's a child there. We try to avoid cursing if my daughter's around." He added quickly, in order to define his attitudes toward sexual language in general, "We're not swearers, you know, where if the children weren't there we'd be cursing every other word. I mean, it comes up in conversation and nobody cares, but it's not a mode or style." He also indicated that he did not disapprove of such double standards between parents and children when these rules were designed to protect the children. Adults could not always help their bad habits, but children should be starting with a "clean slate." "I have manners when I'm with my daughter, better manners than when I'm with my friends. I'm very much more conservative when she's around. I get paranoid about it. I'm extra careful. I'm also careful about any prejudices I might have, not to display them in front of her, for the same reason."

Several other parents also described the way adults, particularly those who were parents themselves, tended to restrict themselves to more modest forms of speech when children were present or might be awake and listening elsewhere in the house. Mike said, "The couples that come over all have children of their own and we're all Catholics. When the lights go out and the kids are in the bed and everything else, it's a different story." Another father corroborated this. "Most of the friends that we have, I guess they check themselves. If the kids aren't around, they might do it. I guess if someone really insisted on telling a dirty joke and the kids are there, I'd try to usher them out of the room. Jokes that are really dirty, we wouldn't tell in front of the kids." Fb9g5 Fb7

Sometimes a "hidden agenda" existed in the way parents used language with boys as opposed to girls. Not only did they feel freer to say dirty words around their sons; they also allowed them greater leeway with sexual language than they allowed their daughters. Almost always, this attitude was expressed by fathers, and very often the "rules," such as they were, had been imposed subliminally rather than explicitly. Jerry frankly admitted that he treated his son differently from his daughter and that, without always realizing it, he conveyed subtle messages about what was "feminine" and what was "masculine" language behavior. "My immediate reaction is that I think I'm a little rougher on my son than with my daughter. I think I'm a little more open with him, less protective. And when language comes out, abusive language, he's less anxious about it. I tend to use words around him that I don't think I'd use as quickly around my daughter." He stopped speaking for a moment, thoughtful. "I don't think I'd like her to go out with a man and say, 'Oh fuck this, fuck that.' She's my baby," He laughed quietly. "I guess I'm a little chauvinistic in that way. I think it's okay for my son. It's cute. You know he's a little guy. Hopefully he'll grow up to be a strong man. I think it's part of a male-child-growing-up's personality to be a little rougher. I would want it that way. Which is interesting," he added after a pause. "I'm aware of that for the first time." Like a number of other fathers in this study, he had never examined his conduct in quite this light before and was somewhat taken aback at what he'd revealed. Fb6g6

Fred said, "I think intuitively I do have sort of a different standard for the girls and for the boys." Even so the girls in his family had disappointed his expectations, perhaps unconsciously "overcorrecting" for their father's views. "They tend to use bad language more than Fg15b11g10

the boy does," Fred remarked a moment later. "I wish they didn't,
but it turns out they do." "What would I not want my daughter to
say?" another father said. "Oh, wow! I think that any of the words
that are not considered part of polite conversation would be inappropriate. That covers a whole spectrum from *damn* to *shit* to *fuck*." But
he added, with candor, "Of course you know this is my own attitude,
being a father in his relationship with his daughter."

The issue of sexual language as it related to sex roles was clearly a
complex and elusive one, even in those homes where a sincere attempt
had been made to avoid stereotyping. Mark was able to offer this ap-
proving and nonstereotypical description of his son. "If you could see
the kid, he's not 'macho' at all. He's—I hate to use this term, it sounds
like a doting parent—but he's a very sensitive kid. He understands
people much better than I would." He added with a smile, "Listen,
my daughter is very similar to me. I mean, she looks like me. She
behaves like me. She's just as insensitive as I am. Yet my son is very
sensitive. Nobody ever referred to my son as 'macho,' believe me."
Nevertheless, Mark was aware that his son felt much easier about using sexual language than his daughter did. He described the difference that existed between his son's responses to sexual language and
those of his daughter. "My daughter doesn't swear around me, use
any kind of profanity or any kind of what are referred to as four-letter
words. She is modest. My son, on the other hand, is open, actively
curious, sexually interested." As he discussed the issue however, he
admitted that perhaps, without realizing it, he himself had set the tone.
"My daughter is different. She was always different. I don't think it's
any different message that I sent her." He paused. "Well, you know
you don't *think* you do, but you may. I don't know. I wouldn't tell a
joke that I think would embarrass her. There are some jokes that would
embarrass her but that same joke probably would not embarrass my
son. If he tells a joke which my daughter is offended by, than he is
told, 'Don't say that, it embarrasses your sister.' He recognizes that she's
shyer than he is."

Occasionally, there were unwritten rules about family behavior
in different sections of the home or for different types of activities within
the same space. Words which could be used without reprimand in one
room were not suitable to another. Fran described such a rule: "If you
want to use those words, use them in the bathroom. It's bathroom talk
and I don't want to hear it other than that." Another mother said,
"Neither of us allows that language at the table because it's not pleasant for other people. We tell her that this is not a pleasant way to talk
when we're eating." A borderline expression might slip out during
roughhouse play and not be noticed while it would have a harsher
effect at a quieter or more sociable moment. "If we're playing, if we're
being rough, playing rough, 'You little shithead' is more apt to come

Fg10

Fb10g7

Mb4

Mg5

Fg6

up than if we're just sitting around having dinner or breakfast or watching TV."

Families that were relatively easy about using sexual language had to be sensitive to the feelings of relatives whose standards might be more rigid than their own. The mother of an eleven-year-old boy said, "There is behavior appropriate to the person you happen to be dealing with. Now he may be able to say, 'This fuckin' thing won't work' in front of me, but he certainly can't say it in front of his paternal grandmother. You know, it depends on who you're with." Another mother noticed the way her daughter, also eleven, had begun to edit her language on her own when her grandparents came to visit. She knew that certain words should not be used then. "Yes, there is a double standard from my daughter's point of view. She will take into consideration that my parents are older and they may not have the same views about things, so she's careful with what she says." Mb11

Mg11

In some households a double standard was applied to visitors with more liberal language behavior, who might be made uncomfortable if immediate attention were drawn to an unsuitable word or off-color story. One mother said, "When friends say these words without the knowledge that we don't want that kind of talk in our home, the way we handle it is we laugh. We don't make the friends feel ill at ease at the time." She added, however, "We laugh, but then later let them know privately that we don't allow it." And a father who frequently entertains in his home business associates with far freer standards than his own indicated that he would not "make a big deal" out of any occasional lapses into raunchiness on the part of these visitors. "It's interesting," he said, "because of the friends we have in show business we quite regularly have parties here and my children hear other people use this language in our own house. These are not words that we use." He pointed out, however, that he was able to take this attitude because of his children's ability to set mature and acceptable standards for themselves. "I mean they have heard this language, they are aware of it, but they don't use it themselves. They have made their own choices." Mb6

Fg10

Setting the Rules: Parents Yes, Children No

In a number of families parents could say certain words but children could not. Although Annette did not have any problems around this issue with her children, she nevertheless admitted that she didn't like the idea of children using strong sexual language. "If every other word were *fuck* or *shit*, as an adult I wouldn't care, because I do it," she said. "But I think as a kid I would feel she's pushing herself too fast. Some- Mg11 how that's really all part of a grown-up's world to me. It's not part of a kid's world. I think I would tell her, 'Yes, you are too crude.' " The father of two boys expressed much the same opinion. "I may have

Fb7b4   said, 'Oh, shit!'—'Oh, shit' is just 'Oh, shit.' It was appropriate as far as I was concerned. And I said it. But I don't want my children to say it. I just don't feel it's appropriate for a seven-year-old to run around

Fg4   saying 'Oh, shit.' " The father of a small girl said, rather wryly, "*Ass* I don't think is a nice word to come out of my daughter. I can say it in front of her, yes. I can also smoke in front of her, but I don't want her to smoke." In a similar vein, two mothers spoke about words they found

Mb7   personally satisfying. "I say *bitch* myself," one said, "but I don't like to

Mb9   hear my son say it." A second mother said, "*Cunt* is one of my favorite words. It is a word unlike any other word. It feels terrific. But again I know that when I've used it I've said it in reference to someone who I really feel *is* a cunt." She added, however, in reference to her son, "I'm not crazy about him using it."

Quite often children did not need to be told what the rules were;

Mb11   they had learned. "He has heard me do it, but he knows there's a difference between what's permitted for adults and what's permitted

Mg5   for children," a mother remarked. Another added, "The words that grown-ups say, it seems only the grown-ups say and she does not repeat them."

Parents frequently admitted quite candidly that there was an ele-

Mb9b4   ment of unfairness about these policies. One mother said, "Unfortunately there is some language that I do use in front of the children but I don't want them to use it in front of me. *Shit* or *Hell*—that's about as far as it goes. But I do not like them to use it. I know that's a double standard. And I try not to, but it still does happen." A father told of experiencing two reactions when he overheard his daughter blurt out a four-letter word: private empathy and amusement, masked by the more

Fg6   "correct" parent response. "Once she used the word upon dropping some dishes in the sink. She said, 'Oh, fuck, I'm in trouble now!' She couldn't see me. My first reaction was a grin. If she's not watching my expression I'm definitely smiling, but I try to make her understand,

Mg5   'You're too young for that.' " A mother said, "If my husband or I are on the phone with one of our friends, words will come out of our mouths, jokingly, descriptively. They're used. Then if she is to use it I will have an attitude. It's not fair, but I will have an attitude. I will tell her she's rude."

Lyle, whose family used a system of monetary penalties for language offenses by all family members, finally took steps to make him-

Fg7   self exempt from those fees. "I feel for the sake of my own mental health I've got to use some terminology. I explained to the kid that I'm going to use it and I decided I'm not going to pay for these things any more." He added with a laugh, "I was slowly going broke." Another father pointed out that he, too, occasionally "fudged" on his own rules, hoping to get away with breaches he would not permit his child. "If I slip, I think she knows. If she says something, I'll apologize to her for using language I wouldn't want her to use, but if nothing is said and she continues to do what she's doing, I'll try to work my way out of it." Fg4

Because words that were considered once unacceptable in almost any situation are now spoken regularly by children among themselves, parents had to accept the fact that their children were probably using language prohibited at home out on the streets. It was necessary, therefore, to let children know that certain words which they shared with their friends still could not be said in front of parents. As one mother put it, "I'm sure that he does things with his friends that would absolutely make me want to roll over and die. But when he's with a friend, I'll never know anyway. If he says it in front of me, that's something else." She had been quite explicit in setting limits on what her son was permitted to say in her presence. "I think there have to be some limits between parents and children. I will not allow him to say 'Fuck you!' to me, because it's not nice and because I'm your mother and you don't talk to your mother that way." Mark tried to take a realistic view toward the language of the "outside world" and yet still preserve the kind of decorum he was most comfortable with in his home. "I know they are going to use it in school, the vernacular, and in front of their friends, and that is acceptable. But they will have respect for me and they will have respect for their mother and they will use proper words. What they use out on the streets I've got absolutely no control over." Stephanie's policies were much the same: "There are some things he'll hear outside that I just prefer he not use in the house. I would prefer he not use these words outside either, but I understand that sometimes the friends will use them." Mb11 / Fb10 / Mb8

A number of parents believed that the best way to maintain appropriate standards of sexual language was to set a good example "at the top." They preferred not to fall back on different standards for parent and child, which seemed to them hypocritical, and avoidable with a little self-restraint on the parent's part. As Jim put it, "My wife and I don't use that language. I mean, we are strong role models for the children and I think that's what it really boils down to. If you use dirty words or dirty language or whatever you want to, I don't think you are going to expect any less from your children. They are going to use it themselves. So you have the opportunity to set the tone in your own home." Mike set very high standards of language behavior for his children and was willing to judge himself by the same strict rules, even though it was sometimes difficult for him, a naturally hot-tempered young man with a history of using "street language" freely. "What kinds of sexual language do I permit? None at all, really," he said firmly. Fg10 / Fg5

"There shouldn't be any of it. In fact, if I slip, I'm mad at myself for slipping. Bad words do come out sometimes, but not very often. I'd rather hit the wall or take the telephone and throw it on the floor, and Mb5   I yell very loud." One mother confided that she occasionally used the word *fuck* but only "under my breath"—hoping her five-year-son wouldn't hear it. "I'd prefer him not to say it." she said. The mother Mg6   of a girl about the same age pointed out that her daughter was "picking up everything, very definitely. So I just have to be a little more cau-Mb4   tious." Lorna conceded that her son had already "picked up some of my swear word things," but she continued to try to keep her use of such language to a minimum in his presence. "I'm really trying to stay away from swearing. I'm trying to stay away from *fuck*, although I do say it occasionally. He has some dirty words and stuff, but he doesn't use them a lot."

Although so many parents were evidently concerned enough to try to change their language style for the sake of their children, one mother frankly admitted that her relaxed speaking habits were already too deeply ingrained in her personality to be adjusted. Since she did not approve of "double standards"—asking a child to do what she could not do—she therefore had ended up allowing her daughter the same Mg5   freedom of speech that she allowed herself. "I don't really think I have set enough of an example. If I wanted her not to use this language, I'd have to backtrack, erase what I've done in the past, which is let my mouth be free, and I'd have to stop using the language myself."

Another father was similarly opposed to double standards, not because he was unwilling or unable to alter his own behavior, but because of the pervasive use of sexual language in the society at large Fb11   which made such standards ridiculous, hypocritical, unenforceable. "My children tend to use a lot of bad language," Fred said frankly. "When the language really becomes bad for an extended period of time we usually crack down, which doesn't last very long." He paused here, considering carefully what he wanted to say. "Sometimes I feel uncomfortable, but thats *my* thing. I was never as open in front of my parents, so I think that probably bothers me a little bit. He's way ahead of where I was at that age," he added, echoing so many other parents in the study. "But in some ways it doesn't bother me, because I'm glad he, my son, is open about it. If I do feel uncomfortable I usually don't say anything. The kids are so exposed to sex and sexual language that for a parent to try to prevent it, I mean, it's absurd. I don't feel totally comfortable—I'm not the most liberal person in the world when it comes to that—but I think it's absurd to get mad at them for using bad language."

In a few cases children took on the responsibility for disciplining their parents when breaches of the family language code occurred. Jerry's six-year-old daughter was quick to "get on his back" about the

occasional four-letter-word he let slip out. "Unfortunately words like   Fg6
shit will come up and she'll immediately know that it's a bad word and
she'll point it out. She'll say, 'You said a bad word,' and I will rein-
force that by saying, 'You're right. It *is* a bad word. We'll try not to use
it.' " Mike reported that his children, a girl five and a boy seven, did
much the same kind of affectionate police work when they heard inappropriate language being used by him and his wife. "If my wife or I   Fb7g5
should slip and say, 'Ah, shit' now, they come back to us and they tell
us, 'Daddy, that's a bad word. You said a bad word. Mommy, Daddy
said a bad word.' They knows that we shouldn't say it either."

Annette explained that her eleven-year-old daughter was extremely sensitive to what she considered her parents' overuse of sexual language. Though both parents had rather easygoing attitudes
towards certain popular expressions, their daughter would get so upset
at hearing them that the parents had had to make contrite attempts to
weed these expressions out of their casual speech. "We have used words   Mg11
like *fuck* and *shit* and *tits*, et cetera, but it offends my daughter. She
can't stand it, so she begs me to stop using it. It's kind of the opposite—
it's the *child* restricting *us* from using the language. It's not our restricting the language. It really throws her. She'll cry about it. She
will actually cry. She will say, 'I'm ashamed. You promised me. Why
are you doing this? Why are you and Daddy using such words?' And so
it has changed. *I* had to accommodate myself to *her* needs."

Exceptions to the Rules

Often, in households that had established language codes, it was
understood in certain circumstances parents—and, sometimes children—could use forbidden words without criticism from other family
members. Such infractions were permissible during moments of extreme physical or emotional duress. Most parents who gave their children this leeway wanted to make a clear distinction between the casual
throwing off of four-letter-words—for punctuation or emphasis—and
the use of some of these terms as a healthy release of tension. "*Fuck* is   Mb11
his favorite curse. I allow it, but it has to be in the right context,"
Sandy said. "If he's furious at someone or something, then I allow it.
For anger, not for, 'Oh, look at that fucking car, isn't it nice?' No, for
real anger, when it's appropriate."

Even parents who did not generally allow sexual language to be
used freely in the home might make an exception when it came to
stressful situations. Jim suggested that such extenuating circumstances
seemed almost to change the sense of the word itself. "There are times,   Fg10

particularly in fits of anger or when someone is hurt, when a word will come out. I don't feel that it's a dirty word meant to be a dirty word. It's just an expletive of some sort." Sharon, similarly, said, "Sometimes, all right, I'll say *shit* and things when I'm mad and it comes out. I put that almost in with the [profane] curses—*goddamm it*, and all that. When my son says them and he's angry, fine. I understand it. It comes naturally. If it's legitimate expression of anger, that's okay."

Mb5

In some families these relaxed rules primarily applied to the behavior of adults; children were still more restricted than their parents, even under stress. Penelope described the way she "let herself go" in certain stressful situations: "There are times when you watch yourself, times when you're freer. Times when you're angry and different kinds of words come out. The only time I'll ever say anything bad—I'll drive the car and if somebody is really stupid I'll say 'stupid asshole!' It's the worst put-down I use lately in angry situations." But she pointed out as well that her daughter had picked up on the fact that her mother's behavior was not to be imitated. "There's some way a child knows, 'Do not use the words that Mommy might use in anger.' "

Mg5

Mg5

Another parent who permitted himself a greater range of language in physically painful or emotionally frustrating situations did not mind if his children overheard him use four-letter words. "When a situation presents itself that calls for some sort of well-placed oath—striking my thumb with a hammer or dropping a bottle of apple juice on the kitchen floor that spreads out all over the place—I have no compunction about a well-placed 'Oh, fuck!' or 'Shit!' It does a lot of good. If the kid is around and he happens to overhear it, so he overhears it. I don't feel I've marred him for life. He's just heard his father use a word that he doesn't generally approve of. I'm not going to cringe over it." But he did not believe that his sons, aged four and seven, were old enough to enjoy the same privileges. "I explained to the kid that the chances are that some day he and his brother might very well be using such words and I don't feel there should be any great prohibition against your use of these words when you are older, but at this point I feel it's important that you learn the proper use of language."

Fb7b4

Other parents also mentioned age as a determining factor in permitting "stress use" of sexual language. One mother believed very young children might be frightened to hear certain types of words exchanged between family members. As they grew older, however, they learned that such explosions were just that—temporary conditions, adults "blowing off steam." She said very firmly, "If they were two or three I would never call my mother a 'goddamned bitch' in front of them if I was fuming at her, whereas now I will. And they know that I love my mother and that I'm just angry at her at the time. I'm saying it in anger. It's an age-related issue. Absolutely." A father felt that his seven-year-old was just reaching the age at which he might be eligible

Mb11

to use more grown-up language when he was frustrated or angry. "I wouldn't like it if he used street language, but I suppose that at his age if he were provoked by somebody I could accept a reasonable expression of anger. If we overheard him getting mad at something, we'd try to understand why." Fb7

For a number of these parents, the loosening of standards during anxious or angry moments was something regrettable that happened in practice, without altering their generally more cautious attitudes towards sexual language. One mother described her own behavior in this regard: "Oh, I just resent the terms *suck* and *fuck*. I use them occasionally, only when I have a temper tantrum. When I'm in a fit of temper I use the word *fuck*, but very infrequently. I don't like it. I'd rather I wouldn't use it." Another felt much the same way about her son. "I'd hate to say I'd accept the thing *[fuck]*, but I probably almost would, considering he's really distraught." And a father who was resigned to occasional breaches of language decorum nevertheless was very leery of becoming overly dependent on such terms. "I think on occasion my daughter might use 'Oh, shit!' And whatever would provoke her to use that kind of language, while we don't condone it, it would be understood. But again, I think this is an inadequacy." Mb8 Mb4 Fg10

Lorna said she did not approve of indiscriminate use of sexual language, even under provocation. But she retained her sense of humor and seemed to be able to put into healthy perspective both her own occasional lapses and her son's affectionate and "innocent" imitation of her. "The other day the groceries spilled in the car, and he was telling somebody about it later and he said, 'The groceries spilled in the car and we said, "Shit-Damn!" ' He was telling someone that was an appropriate thing to do, in his mind." A moment later she told a similar amusing story. "I've been doing a lot of work on a typewriter and I'm not a great typist. The other day I let him peck at the typewriter and he was going, 'Click, click, click, *shit,* click, click, click, click' because that's exactly what he hears when I make a typing error. It's Click, click, click,' silence, and then 'shit,' because that's just what I do. I look at it thinking I made a mistake, so there is a moment of silence and then there is 'shit!' and so he had the timing sequence just right," Lorna concluded with a laugh. Mb4

Enforcing the Rules

Though the policies that were created in relation to sexual language were constantly being qualified, adjusted, overridden, and ignored as the contexts for the language changed, there were many clear-cut situations in which parents felt they had to check their children's use of inappropriate terms. Parents offered diverse examples of how they handled both the infractions of the rules and their children's resistance to giving up forbidden words that seemed particularly attractive or emotionally satisfying.

Often they took a constructive approach, pointing out to children that alternative forms of language were available to them and suggesting that they be more imaginative in finding "better words" to express their feelings. Sometimes the parent could help by providing the child with an acceptable alternative to the "bad" word, acknowledging rather than condemning the need to vent strong feelings in strong language.

Fg10 As this father told his daughter, "You're mad at someone. You call them a *prick*. It's just as easy to say, 'You are a real jerk!' It means the same thing." Sometimes the child himself came up with the permissible substitute. In one instance it was clear that the mother had contributed by encouraging the child to identify with the recipient of a "dirty"

Mb5 name and to "feel" its negative emotional effect: "I heard him call a neighbor's daughter a *bitch*. I told him that word is not really necessary. You don't have to use *that* word. You can get angry at people and call them names without using those words. I asked him how would he like for someone to call his sister that or call me that. He agreed it was terrible; he wouldn't like it. So I calmed him down that way and he began to call her a *witch* instead."

For other parents, getting at the real emotion behind a child's outburst and urging her to communicate it honestly was far more important than disciplining her for using a dirty word. They listened for

Mb11g8g6 the pain or the anger or the frustration behind the language. "If they are angry," Constance said, "they should express anger and not, you know, be submissive and put another label on it." One mother told

Mg11 her daughter, "If you're angry, say 'I'm angry!' If you want to say you don't like something, say 'It's ugly,' 'It's not likeable,' 'It's *something*.' Because it's just worthless to use these words." The father of an eleven-

Fb11 year-old boy used a similar tactic. "My son comes in occasionally talking that way—*fuck* this, *fuck* that, *fuck* and *fuck*.' I mean, every other word is that word. And I'll just say, 'Look, that's not a very expressive way to talk. First of all, it's just not really saying what you mean. If you are angry, say what you are angry about or say what you mean and don't just talk that way."

For Mike, getting in touch with his own submerged emotions was more of a problem than urging his children to communicate theirs. He was making a sincere effort to avoid cursing in front of his children, but nevertheless the powerful feelings that he had been used to releasing through such language in the past still cropped up from time to time. Usually he tried to do something physical to release the tension.

Fg5 "I approve of physical action over language," he said. Or else he substituted profanity for more objectionable "four-letter" sexual terms. "I'll use *hell*. I was mad at the time, and the worst that came out was 'Get the hell in here!' "

Children often resented whatever restrictions parents attempted to place on the use of sexual language, insisting that their friends and schoolmates were allowed greater freedom. Even when this was true, as it frequently was, parents needed to find ways of dealing with such social pressure without knuckling under to it or sacrificing their own standards. Several parents had found that a friendly and supportive but ultimately arbitrary approach could be quite successful in such situations. They would frankly acknowledge that other people "out there" in the world might very well be using certain kinds of sexual language frequently and casually, but emphasized that however boring or old-fashioned their own rules might seem, "In our family we don't want that." Mg7

Sharon emphasized the importance of developing personal standards along with the strength of character to disregard those standards that did not match one's own. In other words, you didn't have to swear to be popular. "My son tells me, 'Well, so-and-so says that,' and I say, 'Well, if that's what he wants to say, fine, but I don't think anybody is going to like you better for saying it. I'm not telling you you have to love everything your friends do. It's good to see there are certain things you like and certain things you don't. You don't try to imitate those bad things, words or actions.' " The father of a seven-year-old took a straightforward and realistic tack with his son, emphasizing the parents' right to set limits for the child now, while he is still under their care. "I have told him that once he's older I'll have no control over the language he uses and it will be up to him to determine what language he feels is acceptable. But for the time being, at his age, I want him to use proper language. It's as simple as that." Mb4

Each of these parents refused to be drawn into an argument over whose standards were correct, at the same time refusing to "put down" the language styles of other households or of their children's peers. The parents were simply conveying a firm, constructive point of view: Yes, I know other standards exist, but I prefer that you abide by mine.

Occasionally parents encountered potentially awkward situations when the offenders against language codes were not their own children but visitors from more permissive households. Here again, direct and matter-of-fact methods of setting limits on the visitors seemed to work best. One parent said, "If I don't like what's going on, I will say, 'Cut it out!' to the other person's kid if the other person isn't saying anything. You can't control. I don't care about controlling the other person's child. I only care what makes me comfortable and what makes me uncomfortable. If the kid is infringing upon my having a good time and my kid's having a good time then I will say something to the Mb11 kid, something appropriate, not horribly punitive—'I really wish you wouldn't say that in front of me,' or 'I don't like that,' or 'Boy, you're really not being nice to your mother.' Sometimes I say it in humor. I have heard kids from what I call 'permissive homes' saying the most horrendous things to their parents, and it makes me nuts. What I really want to say is something to the parent like, 'You schmuck, how can you let your kid talk that way to you?' But instead I will say to the kid, 'What a terrible thing to say to your mother.' "

Mg8   Constance said she had no qualms about making her own standards of language behavior absolutely clear to an offending visitor, but she also tried not to hurt the child's feelings. She mentioned one little friend of her daughter's who had "a pretty good vocabulary!" However, Constance said, firmly "She's not allowed to use it when *I'm* in there. It's me in *my* household. I just say that we really don't like that type of language in this house." She smiled and added, "And that if she feels the bad language coming, could she remember before she says it. That usually works." One father was a bit more blunt. Infractions of his family's language standards were dealt with promptly and vigorously.

Fb7   "With friends or other people's kids, I don't care who it is. I would try to discourage them from using that kind of language on the spot. I'm kind of aggressive all the time. I don't care who it is that is caught."

Handling Infractions

The majority of the parents in this study preferred to deal with breaches of family language codes through calm and rational discussion rather than punishment. Parents with children of all ages realized that language standards can be tricky and ambiguous even for adults, and understood that the rules of decorum taken for granted by adults must be fully and sympathetically spelled out for children. This mother's atti-

Mb9   tude was typical: "I don't think I would punish him because I don't think he would realize [why he was being punished]. It's not like he would be out to do it deliberately. He was just being gross with his friends." She pointed out, as well, "I really do think that society today is very confusing and what's appropriate here is not appropriate there, and you can't always expect the child to know when to change gears, so to get angry at them for simply not having the correct information just doesn't solve anything."

By far the most common approach was for the parents to tell the child, at the time of the infraction, what the word or phrase meant and that it was not language that the parent felt was appropriate. The mother of a six-year-old boy described how she would handle his use

Mb6   of the word *fuck:* "I wouldn't discipline him. I would sit down and talk to him about it. I explained to him pretty much what it meant, as much as a six-year-old could understand. I told him it was a word for making love but not in a very nice way, and I told him that it's really not a nice word to use." Jim, who has children ranging in age from ten through the middle teens and who lives in a rather sophisticated West Coast suburb, had developed a firm but friendly and reasonable approach to the inevitable lapses from his high standards. "Sure they are going to come home with words," he said with a wry smile. "You don't get overly excited about it, and you take the time to explain that these are not acceptable words. These are acceptable; these are not. Just explain in a rational way. I have not really found a problem with 'dirty words' per se because my kids know what I expect of them." But "explanation" did not work in every instance, particularly when children were more savvy about sexual language than parents expected. Paula offered this anecdote. "One day my son was saying, 'That sucks, that sucks,' and I tried to explain to him that that term wasn't a nice one. I didn't like it. And he said, 'Why not?' And I said, 'Well "that sucks" refers to something that really isn't nice constantly to say.' I tried to explain and it was very difficult because I felt very embarrassed. I said, 'Sucking is when you put the penis into the woman's mouth' and my daughter says, 'Oh, you mean a blow-job!' "

Fb15b13g10

Mg11b8

Other parents believed it helped if their children realized that certain types of language were personally upsetting to them. They told them that certain words were "not nice" or "bad" or "not correct" and should not be used. "They respect us enough to want to please us," one mother said. "So I let them know that it really makes me disappointed and angry."

Mb7b4

Once in a while situations arose in which calm, private discussion was not possible or when certain expressions had already been defined as off limits and yet the children persisted in using them. In such cases, parents could issue a calm but unequivocal cut-off order and save any further discussion until a more suitable time. Phrases such as "I really don't like to hear that," "No more," "That's too crude," or a "Knock it off!" could be quite effective in producing at least temporary silence. And that kind of direct intervention was especially important when children had become overexcited by unfamiliar social contexts or egged on to the point of frenzy in "can-you-top-this?" bad language derbies with peers or siblings. One mother said, "If he tells me something that's really disgusting and gross, I'll say, 'That's enough, Adam! Nobody wants to hear it, Nobody's interested. It's not funny. It's disgusting.' But it's always done in good humor." She added, "Sometimes we go out to dinner and they get nutty. Like he was out with a friend of his and they were getting very nutty, you know, saying naughty sexy things and telling dirty jokes, comparing milk to semen or whatever. It was really getting gross. They were getting so carried away and hysterical that we had to send them out of the restaurant. You

Mb11

know, 'Go outside and walk around. Calm yourself down because
you're annoying us and you're annoying all these people who are eating here.' They came back in and they calmed down." One father
said that in a similar situation—when his children's language got out of
hand in a public place or social gathering—he would simply "toss them
out of the room" and explain why later.

Nevertheless, sometimes nonpunitive methods of dealing with
problem language were ineffective. Children picked up bad habits from
new friends, repeated forbidden words unconsciously or compulsively
in public, or persisted in the use of prohibited expressions to tease or
provoke their parents. In such cases a number of parents believed that
punishment of some sort—anything from a chewing out to a spanking—
was both necessary and appropriate. "If he continued to use that language, I'd just have to punish him in some way," a father said. A mother
remarked, "He's used sexual language to provoke me, sure, absolutely.
He gets punished."

Two parents said they were sometimes tempted to use the traditional method of washing out children's mouths with soap (or, in an
unusual variation, putting Tabasco on their tongues) when they used
bad language, but neither had actually ever done it. A fairly small group
also said they had used corporal punishment. There were some people who believed firmly in the efficacy of good old-fashioned "spare
the rod, spoil the child" tactics. But most often such incidents were
mild and low-key, designed to get attention and act as deterrents, rather
than cause lasting pain. A little smack, sometimes more, seemed necessary if the child got carried away. "I slap him," a mother said. "I
slap his little face because he goes into a litany where he won't stop
telling me these same words over and over again. He realizes that now
it's going to hurt a little and maybe he'll stop." Generally, however,
parents shied away from any form of physical punishment, were not
convinced that it really worked.

It was more common for a parent to admonish the child in a tone
of voice or an expressive manner which clearly showed that he meant
business. "I don't like to hit my kids," Mike said. "I seldom hit them.
I'd rather raise my voice. They can see I'm talking louder, louder,
louder. 'Daddy's getting mad. Let's go to bed.' They know right away."
Jerry, who characterized himself as a "tough" father, would let his
daughter know he was angry by removing her from wherever she was
"acting up." "I never discipline my daughter in front of anyone. It's always private. I'll take her alone somewhere else, wherever we are, which
is like a death walk," he added with a smile. "She knows she's in trouble if I've decided we're going to leave the room or leave the party."

Several parents had found that a graduated scale of penalties
worked well. A warning could be issued first, then a mild form of
punishment, and on up an ascending scale of severity. This approach
had several advantages. It was fair and reasonable, since the child was

Margin labels: Fb7, Fb7, Mb11, Mb7b4, Fb9b5, Fg6

merely warned or lightly disciplined for "first offenses," and it had a kind of inexorable momentum that in itself was impressive. One father described his method: "The first infraction—'Go to your bedroom alone and when you're ready to apologize then you come back.' Then in about ten or fifteen minutes she'll come back—'I'm sorry, Daddy.' On a second occasion she gets a warning or a spanking. There's never been a third occasion." The mother of an eleven-year-old girl used a similar technique. "If I did hear her I would say to her, 'I don't want to hear it again.' And the second time I'd tell her, 'You're saying it and I'm going to have to take action.' It could be 'Go to your room and think about why you need to use that word and then come out and we'll discuss it.' "   Fg6

Mg11

Withholding privileges worked, too. One father of a seven-year-old boy said, "When he comes home with those words, I say, 'Don't do it again.' And the next time, he's grounded, not allowed out. That's it!" Another father of a boy the same age offered this approach: "There are things he likes to do. I'd have to restrict the hour and a half a day that he's allowed television, for example. I may say, every time he uses that kind of language it's going to be two days of television that he won't see, or something like that." Fines or withheld allowances could be effective deterrents to bad language according to several parents. For Sandy, withholding her son's allowance was a perfect solution because it "got at" him in a very personal way, and yet did not harm him physically or emotionally. "He's an extremely mercenary kid. He loves money and he's into antiques, so he loses money. You have to find a kid's Achilles' heel. He doesn't care about TV. He doesn't care about books. He does like food, but I would never deprive a child of food. Money is the thing that really gets to him. There goes the allowance, or part of the allowance."   Fb7

Mb11

"We have a little piggy bank for when anyone in the family curses," Lyle said. "He came home one day and he used some term and I said 'I'm going to charge you a nickel every time you swear." The system of levying this kind of penalty backfired at least once in Lyle's case, when his son caught him in a hostile exchange with a group of men in a neighboring car during a family trip to Washington. "I was alone in my car, waiting for my wife and kids—I was picking them up. I became involved in an altercation with a carload of males next to me. It was a verbal altercation and, at some point, I suggested that one who'd said something to me go fuck himself. Moments later my wife and kids reached the car. They had heard me raising my voice, and my seven-year-old had heard my constructive suggestion to the other motorist and reminded me of the fact." The son immediately demanded an enormous sum from his father. "He said, 'You owe me forty cents for that word you just used.' " Lyle paused here, with a slight smile, "I felt it was worth every penny of it."   Fb7b4

8

Where

Did

You

Hear

That?

Fb5 When I was a kid everybody was pretty naive about this stuff. I came from a small town in the South. It was a lot more strict.

Mg10 I'm thinking of a ten-year-old as being more innocent than my kids are. And that might be because I'm thinking of myself at ten.

Fb10 They are far more advanced than me. I mean, my parents were fairly liberal and I had a fairly fast upbringing, but I think they have got me far outstripped.

Children today obtain their information about sex from many sources other than their parents—siblings and peers, the media, church and school programs, books. The end product of this explosion of information is a generation far more wordly, far more sexually aware than their parents were. Over and over, parents of all backgrounds made comments like those above, wondering at what their children knew about sex, sometimes wondering as well where they had learned it all.

Some of the alternatives to parental education were more or less within the parents' control and might even aid them in the difficult task of informing children about sex. Parents could select books or television programs about sexual topics to augment what they themselves were providing. And, to some extent, they could choose whether or not their children received sex education from classes in school or through religious training in their churches and synagogues. But there were other sources of sexual information that were less subject to parental control. Many parents expressed acute feelings of helplessness about what children were learning from their friends or from the media—not the overtly "educational" material but the other, almost subliminal forms of data imparted by anything from a news story on rape to a designer jeans commercial. How could even the most vigilant parent protect a child from information he was too young to handle, or information that had been conveyed in an inappropriate tone, or out-and-out misinformation? The answer, as most parents saw it, was that control of this kind was next to impossible in the world we all live in. They believed instead that any feasible, realistic attempts at control would have to take the form of better communication and increased sensitivity on the parents' part.

In fact, the major theme that ran continuously through parents' remarks on this issue was responsibility. Parents should take pains to "listen" to what children were learning—the "hidden" messages as well as the obvious ones—and to provide reassurance and explanations when they were needed. Parents should attempt to create the kind of atmosphere in which children felt comfortable asking them to clarify the data they were receiving so steadily—from friends, from movies, from television, at church, at school, on the street. And parents should not be passive users (or abusers) of alternative sources of sexual information. Handing a child a book, no matter how well written or how cleverly illustrated, was not sufficient; it was up to the parent to make sure the material in the book had been fully understood. Similarly, even the best school sex-education class could not be looked upon as a substitute for conscientious parental treatment of sexual subject matter. "Quality control" was crucial on all levels and with all styles and forms of sex education.

On the other hand, without wishing to be complacent, yet hoping to preserve their sanity, many parents found they ultimately had to trust their children to withstand the bombardment of information they were subjected to. They hoped their children would learn to exert their own forms of control—to accept what it was suitable for them to know when it was suitable for them to know it, and to let the rest "pass over their heads" until they were ready to handle it. As one mother put it, "I can't imagine any situation where it's an advantage for a child, for anybody, not to know something. I think that if they're too young to understand, then they simply don't understand. And if they *do* understand, then it's time for them to know or to deal with the subject on some level."

It helped, too, if parents developed a clear view of what they wished their children to know, or to feel, about sex, and possessed a certain amount of confidence in these values. A child couldn't—and shouldn't—be protected from everything; but he could be given a sense Mg10 of moral identity which might help him protect himself. "I can't change the world," the mother of a ten-year-old said. "Neither do I want to change it. The one thing I can do is offer my viewpoint, which is part of me, and have it become part of my child and have it be there for her Fg3 to act on." A young father said of his three-year-old daughter, "Her sexual education will be like that. Certain things exist. She'll ask. She'll hear. But she'll have to work out a lot of it for herself as well, when the time is right, when she's old enough to want to understand."

Lorna spoke of the balance a parent has to create between two incomplete sources of sexual information—oneself and the world at large. Because her own sexual education had involved so much conflict between her parents' negative views and the more benign attitudes she had acquired from outside sources, she was wary of letting her own Mb4 son learn about sex from any single point of view. "I must say, I'm not looking forward exactly to dealing with sex education at all," she said at first, with a wry smile. "But I would much less want *not* to deal with it, because, frankly, I wouldn't trust anyone else to give the same picture I would. Neither would I want him to have *only* my ideas and never, ever, discuss it with anybody else, because my ideas are appropriate for me and may not be entirely for him. I might overlook something or give him as twisted a view as I got from my parents. So I wouldn't want *my* sex education to be the only education he gets. But I certainly want my input. I hope we can continue talking about it as he gets older, so I can have some balancing influence. I hope he feels comfortable coming to me," she concluded.

Friends and Siblings

Few parents were able to say precisely what their children were learning about sex from their friends and siblings, but nearly all of them were absolutely certain that sexual learning was taking place. They could tell from the kinds of questions children asked (or, mysteriously, did not need to ask) or from the bits of factual detail the children possessed about topics that had not been included in the parents' own discussions. They also knew that their children relished the idea of discussing such esoteric topics in secret with their friends and siblings and usually did not care to share what they had learned with adults. Elizabeth believed that her son was telling her daughter "about a woman's breasts or a man's penis" because of all the "giggling" she overheard when they were talking in secret. Some parents were almost wistful as they described the confidential nature of these exchanges. As one mother put it, speaking for many, "He's never come home and told me anything that he's discussed with his friends. He's not ready to offer any information, but just from words he comes out with I have the feeling that there is some discussion between them. I'd love to know what he's gotten from his friends, but he just doesn't talk about it. It's sort of as though that's his own little world. It's an understood thing that they don't discuss it with their parents." Mb12g8

Mb8

Other parents, particularly those who had chosen not to provide much sexual information to their children yet, were frustrated and annoyed at being able to *sense* that the children had learned from friends and siblings without being able to pinpoint exactly *what* they had learned. It was clear to Sally that her son already possessed a certain sophistication about sex, although she had not yet given him any information herself and he was just beginning a sex education course at school. "I feel *sure* that he knew before he ever had this class in sex education," she said. "They are talking with their friends and they are giggling and they are catching jokes. I think he already knows it! I don't think you have any control over that." Mb12

At least one father thought his son's reluctance to reveal the information he had gotten about sex from his friends showed a certain delicacy toward his parent. Brent is a man of forty-five who was raised in a working class Protestant family. But after a trip to India while he was in his twenties, he began to explore various types of Eastern religions and has become deeply interested in the nonmaterial, mystical aspects of these philosophies. As a result, though he does not disapprove of sex in any way, he is rather uncomfortable when it comes to discussing something so physical with his son. He was certain his child was learning a great deal from his peers but explained, with admiration, that the boy, out of respect for his father's reserve, was trying to conceal exactly how much he knew. "I would imagine he gets a lot from friends," Brent said calmly with a small proud smile. "He works things out with friends. I think it's inevitable. He hasn't come back reporting to me, no. I should say it's now got to the stage where he's being a little protective of *me*. He doesn't want us to know he knows so much!" Fb11

George's attitude toward peer learning about sex was predictably, easygoing, amused, and cheerfully resigned. He believed that his daughter was picking up more information about intercourse and reproduction from her friends at a Boston school than she was getting from his wife and him. "She's not asking a lot of questions because she's getting a lot of answers from her friends. This is probably a fringe Fg7 benefit or side effect of sending children to school," he said. "She goes to this private girls' school where I think the other kids are very much advanced. She's a precocious kid. And I think city kids generally are much more aware than their country suburban counterparts. I'm convinced that there's nothing that my daughter could not find out from one of her classmates if she wanted to know. She's not even coming home with the questions. She knows it already." Another father showed similar tolerant amusement as he described his son's unexpectedly complete knowledge of a topic he and his wife felt they had "fudged" on. "I'm not sure he made the connection of babies coming out of a vagina. He has some precocious friends. If anybody said anything it was those guys. They're in that role of teacher to him."

Sam was also convinced that a major source of his daughter's sex education was going to be her peers. This process, he felt, was out of the parents' hands. "I don't really have any information to lead me to believe that she's getting anything from her peers at this time," he said. "It's really hard for me to know because I'm not privy to her conversations with her friends and she doesn't, at this age, discuss sex at all. But I think she's going to learn a lot from peers. It's not that I prefer her to learn it [that way] but the fact of the matter is, she will." Sam also said that he himself had derived a great deal of his sexual information from his friends, and looked back on that as a positive rather than a negative experience, one he believed was far from unique. "I think virtually everyone will say that they got most of their information from their peers. A lot of us probably recall getting some misinformation, but on the other hand, I recall most of the information *I* got from peers was pretty accurate." Such recollections made it easier for Sam to accept the fact that his daughter was picking up information in the same informal, unstructured way.

Many fathers were similarly nostalgic and sympathetic about peer exchanges. Those whose own fathers had not provided adequate information often were content to allow their children to acquire all or part of their sexual education from "the streets" or "other kids." "My father never talked to me about it," Lew said. "How did I learn? Word of mouth. Literally. Yeah, you know—from peers. That's, I think, the way most kids learn." Drew, whose background was similar, had warmly tinged memories of sharing sexual information with other boys in the convivial darkness of a camp bunkroom. Though he was willing to discuss sex with his own children, he thought they might be more comfortable and open in talking about certain topics with their peers. "My father was never the kind of person that I felt I could come and ask about sex, and he never mentioned it. I picked up a great deal, you know, having been away since I was nine years old to boys' camps, where the information is rampant. We spent hours before going to sleep spreading information. My son and his friends, as far as I'm concerned, have a normal curiosity about sex. They share and trade back and forth with a kind of ease." Other fathers were equally tolerant when such information was passed among siblings. Charles described a knowledgeable exchange between his two sons in the bath. "They had some kind of sponge and some kind of other thing, and the older one was explaining to the younger, 'This is the penis and that's the vagina. That's pussy.' "

Doretta summed up the feelings of a number of parents—both mothers and fathers—in relation to this issue. "Any place you go, no matter where in the world, if you've got a group of kids together, sex education is going on. So to me it's a question of acknowledging it, and being appropriate around it. Sometimes when kids teach other kids it's far better than when adults teach kids. I don't have that thing that 'only adults know.' "

Exactly what kinds of information *did* children get from their friends and siblings? In some cases, parents were surprised at the amount of accurate intimate detail their children were learning. "I don't know who she's gotten it from. I think from her little girlfriends who are older," Sally said of her ten-year-old daughter. "I think she got some information about intercourse and how the act is performed. She came home one day and she said, 'Oh well, I know how babies are made.' And I said, 'You do? How are they made?' And she said, 'That's when the man puts his penis into, you know, what you call "down there." ' So I said, 'Yes, that's right.' It wasn't anything she had been told." Dorothy had heard her younger daughter say to the older one, "You have to hump to get pregnant." Dorothy was not certain that either child completely understood. "Melanie didn't describe what humping was, just blurted the fact out. The older one just kind of stood there and took it in. I asked her if she knew what the term *hump* meant, and she kind of showed me a little bit with her body. I don't know if she saw animals doing this or what."

Cynthia's son, Justin, had been given the scientific facts about intercourse and reproduction at various stages, starting when he was three, but he was clearly picking up the physical details in the rough-and-tumble, often rudely sophisticated atmosphere of his inner-city school. "I'm just guessing, knowing the kind of school he is in or the kids he is with," she said at first. "I don't know the quality, but I know he is getting some information. He has some friends that are older, so I'm sure he gets it from them." A moment later she was able to recall a specific instance. "One example—" she said, "recently I was driving a car pool—these are all boys aged nine through about eleven. One of the older boys started yelling something about a rubber. When I got home I asked Justin if he knew what that was. I wanted to make sure he had it right. He said, 'Don't worry, I get information.' So I said, 'Really, do you know what a rubber is? Do you know that it is a birth-control device?' And he said yes, that he has a little girl that he plays with a lot who told him what it is." Cynthia giggled as she told this story, giving an affectionate imitation of her son's wordly-wise manner. She was rather pleased that Justin's friends were able to augment his sexual education in such an ongoing, organic, and self-correcting way.

Her anecdote also illustrates the way in which parents often found themselves participating in the peer education process. They could "listen," sometimes unobtrusively, and be ready to fill in the gaps. Alex described an incident in which his nine-year-old daughter had picked up "a wonderful phrase" from her older brother and his friends. "She came dancing into the kitchen saying, 'Joey kicked me in the balls!' " When Alex asked her if she knew what she meant, she was quite confident. "Yeah, balls are the things you play with and you roll on the ground." At this point, he was able to give her some idea of what she was really saying. "I said, 'No, no, no, what they are referring to is boys' genitals. Because they're round, they're often in slang terms referred to as *balls.*' So then she thought that was hilarious. She really didn't know what she was talking about. It was just a nice, handy expression. It had a nice ring to it."

Many children were learning less from their peers than they thought. They "talked big," whispered, and giggled, and gave the impression that they were amassing large amounts of sexual information. But when their parents pressed, it turned out that this information was incomplete or had, in some way, "gone over the children's heads." "A couple of weeks ago she told me she knew what a wet dream was," the mother of a ten-year-old said. "I asked her what it was and her explanation was kind of vague. I don't think she really understood. I think she heard it in school. She didn't refer to the boy's ejaculating or anything like that. She had no report on the wetness. Just that a boy watches something during the daytime and then at night he might start thinking about it and dreaming about it. That was the only explanation she had."

Sometimes parents had to step in and correct out-and-out misinformation which their children had learned from others. Even after they knew where babies came from, many children preferred to believe the more colorful stories they got from their peers. One five-year-old who had been taught that the vagina is "a special way for a baby to come out" shocked her parents with the announcement that her friend's mother was going to have a baby, "just like a watermelon is going to grow out of her belly button." Once in a while, a child was upset by outlandish details he picked up from peers, and the parent had to "catch" the error and reassure the child by supplying her with the right information. Constance recalled how an older child had frightened her daughter with an absolutely inaccurate description of menstruation. "She was only six and the other girl was twelve and told her all about it. And I don't know what she told her, but I know that she was very horrified about blood after that. Every time she cut her fingers, it was like, what are you talking about? Until finally we had to go upstairs and ask this little girl, 'Just what did you say to her?' She had told her, and I really feel it was deliberate at that point, that women bleed because men hurt them, and that you have to wear 'Band-Aids' (meaning sanitary napkins) all the time. I said to her that the little girl was crazy, she has a problem to begin with, so you know we don't believe what she says, and I corrected the information." Millie recounted what happened when her older daughter discovered her son masturbating. "She says, 'You know, if you continue to do that you will make your penis abnormally long because you're stretching it. It will be abnormal and you'll look like a freak.' He really believed it, but he didn't want me to know that he was masturbating, because it was a couple of weeks before he even asked me. He says, 'Mommy, if I touch myself here will I, you know, look abnormal? Will it grow?' And I said, 'No, it won't.' He says, 'Oh, Tanya said it would.' She's very aware of what's going on. I think most of the things she says, she says to tease." Like Millie, most parents preferred to underreact, explain the error, without scolding or forbidding the children to share information.

Mg6

Mg11b5

But, whether the information was correct or incorrect, topics like menstruation, or penis size, which were related to sexual growth and development, were popular with children of all ages. Often, observing and discussing physical changes in this way helped prepare children for the changes that would take place in their own bodies and gave them the first inklings of adult gender differences and adult sexuality.

I'm sure she must understand. She's seeing her friends' penises because they've been at the beach together, and I'm certain she has an awareness of penis size—bigger, older; smaller, younger.

Fg3

She says Mitzi, her friend who's ten years old—that's like her model—Mitzi's beginning to wear a training bra. So she asks, "Will I grow?" and "When will I grow?" and all that. And so I tell her, "Oh, yes, but it usually takes a little more time. You're only seven, so you watch your older friends. There's a little time yet."

Mg7

He's aware of menstruation and he's aware of the changes. If my daughter is having her period, when she leaves the bathroom he knows. He'll find out exactly what she was doing and why she was doing it. He's aware that she might be using a Tampax or a napkin.

Mg11b5

With boys, especially between the ages of seven and eleven, there was also a kind of early socialization into traditional male attitudes toward female anatomy, an emphasis on the development of appropriate responses toward girls' bodies. Like their grown-up counterparts, little boys chaffed each other and compared notes about "women's" breasts and their own ability to be aroused. Many parents regarded this inculcation into the "locker-room syndrome" as harmless, charming, but only as long as older boys did not impose overly mature and competitive standards on younger ones.

Fb7   They were all comparing girls up at the birthday party. I mean just "boy talk." They all had to go into detail, the size of the girls' breasts, of their nipples. About six of them in the car.

Mb10b8   My sons will look at a pretty girl on television and make the motion that they have an erection or something. It's innuendos. They would never say anything straight out.

Fb11   There were one or two quite awkward incidents at school. I believe a group of kids surrounded him and said "Wouldn't you like to have sex?" I think they were a little bit older than him. And he didn't see what all the nonsense was about, all this business about chasing girls and stuff.

Very often, clearly, it was the tone rather than the content of these exchanges that worried parents. They were disturbed when sexual information was conveyed coarsely or insensitively. In these cases, the primary issue was not whether the facts were accurate or even whether sex itself was an appropriate topic for children to discuss. Instead, parents were concerned about intangibles—sexual self-esteem, emotional integrity, spiritual or ethical values that transcended technical knowledge of the physical act. "They have no concept of love," Jean said. "It's just all this physical thing. They know that's what you are supposed to do. They talk about sex, but they never talk about love. It's now you just 'have sex.' This is the way they talk. This is the feeling I get. I say, 'That's not the way it really is. You are not old enough to understand.' "

Maeve described what happened when her daughter brought home an overly graphic, if truthful, explanation of intercourse. Sarah was in second grade at the time. "Just the way she said it to me was very coarse," Maeve said. "Even to me it sounded awful. 'The man puts his thing into a woman.' I was, like, 'Eww, where did you hear *that?* She said, 'It was from one of my friends in school,' and then 'Is that really true? Did you really do that?' I would say it was a very, very rude awakening, and to try to smooth over that, I mean I couldn't say no, but it was like, let me try to explain it a little bit better. I don't remember exactly how I said it to her. Basically, that it was not this ugly thing, that when you were emotionally involved with somebody this was not just a physical act. I think she got over the initial shock."

Mb10b8 (margin, opposite "edge of the physical act")

Mg7 (margin, opposite "was in second grade at the time")

Brent reported that at his son's school there was a kind of "tyranny" of sophistication which militated against the more sensitive or innocent members of a group, the "children who resist." "There was one stage at school where the other children in his class talked about sex, joked about sex. Kids claimed to have had sex—at eleven—and that sort of thing. My son didn't see any point in that. Maybe because he was a little bit younger. I think at that time I tried to tell him that there was an awful lot more to sex than the physical act, and he probably knew more about it than they did, these kids who were boasting. We did manage to have one or two quite helpful discussions then." Fb11

In some cases where a child was actually better informed than the children outside the house the parent needed to help him understand that he had knowledge he might not yet be able to share with his friends. Stacey, who works as a counsellor at a family planning clinic, found that she had the reverse of a more typical parental dilemma. Because of her dedication to a theory that information about sex represents both freedom and protection, her son was unusually well informed. In fact, he often ended up teaching others. "Well, I don't know if he learns from his friends," she said. "My guess is that he is probably the fountain of information. Listen, we were discussing tampons when he was four," she added, and went on to tell a story that illustrated her son's relaxed, spontaneous, and unselfconscious approach to sexual topics compared to that of another child. "To give you some idea of his attitude—when he was about six or seven a friend of his, a neighbor who was about eleven, was here. I did some lecturing for the Cancer Society and I had breast models in a carry case. We used them to teach people to do breast self-examination. My son, Ed, had sat through many of these lectures and he took the model out with the intention of showing how one could do breast self-exam. He said, 'Hey, Frankie, let me show you this!' Frankie said, 'Put that away! Put that away! Hide that box!' and my son was at a loss to know why his friend was so upset. I felt sorry for Frankie, in the sense that it's unfortunate to have that kind of discomfort about bodies. I explained to my son that not every family talks as freely and comfortably, and we have to respect Frankie's right, too." Mb11

Media

Parents talked about the influence of media on children's sexual education at several points during the interviews. The concerns they had and the efforts they made to monitor these sources of information are presented in depth in Chapter Eleven, "Media." For this chapter, however, they were asked to limit themselves to discussing how media had contributed to their children's overall understanding of sex. In some ways, their comments were similar to those they had made about peer exchanges. They found it hard to be specific about what children had learned from television, movies, etc., but nevertheless "knew" instinctively that learning of this kind was taking place.

Sometimes when the child became interested in (or failed to be surprised by) a story, film, or TV program which contained sexually explicit material, his parents suddenly realized that he knew more about sex than they had actually told him. Often the sexual information was only implied or suggested and the parent was too embarrassed to pull it out into the open for clarification. Several fathers supplied examples from films they had seen together with their children. At Fred's daughter's tenth birthday party, he showed the movie *The Blues Brothers* to a group of her friends as well as his eleven-year-old son. "The movie starts out with John Belushi getting out of prison and they're giving him his personal effects. He takes out all this junk and he picks up and says, "One broken pencil, one prophylactic, unused," and then he takes a set of tweezers and he says, "One prophylactic, soiled." Fred was not prepared either for his daughter's reaction, "Daddy, what's *soiled?*" or his son's appreciative giggle, particularly in that setting. He decided the best way to deal with the issue was to avoid it altogether. "I left the room because the last thing I wanted to do was get into a sex education discussion with eight tenyear-old girls." When one boy heard the term "blow-job" in the movie *The Jerk*, and wanted to know what it meant, his father did not answer. But his son discovered the answer himself in still another media source, a magazine. "So, yeah, oral sex was one of the things I had ducked, but he found out anyway," this father told the interviewer, slightly nonplussed by his son's precociousness. "Probably from *Playboy.*"

A few positive media sources were cited—"educational" films or television programs which featured sensitive treatment of sexual topics. Certain television shows were mentioned very frequently and favorably: *Nova; Sesame Street; One, Two, Three Contact; Wonderama;* and a number of "after-school specials" such as "My Mom's Having a Baby." Several parents singled out *Mister Rogers' Neighborhood* with special affection as a program which dealt consistently with complex topics while maintaining a straightforward, unpatronizing yet sensitive point of view to which children could easily relate. One father, sceptical of television in general, said enthusiastically, "That's one show I don't hesitate to have her see. He [Mister Rogers] talks about things which are on children's minds." Rosaline described the way a little song about sexual anatomy her daughter had learned at a very early age from *Mister Rogers' Neighborhood* had helped give her good feelings about sexual identity as she grew older. "Mister Rogers sings a beautiful song, 'Boys are fancy on the outside/Girls are fancy on the inside/Everyone's beautiful, everyone's fine. Only boys can be Daddies/Only girls can be Moms.' This is something she's been listening to since she's about three years old and it seems very comforting, accepting and protecting."

More often, however, parents believed that children got little specific information about sex from television. What they picked up were diffuse or random smatterings of sexual lore, much of it negative in tone and shallow in approach. Here again, content was less important than style or overall emotional orientation, subliminal but forceful ideas about what was acceptable behavior, what was "good," what was "sexy," and what was "dumb," etc. As Simon put it, "The thing I Fg4 wonder about is what's being sponged up in terms of *attitudes*, that's the main thing. Not so much bits of information, but the attitudes that come across, sort of being hypnotized by the TV set." One mother of an eight-year-old boy described her son's attachment to a current female television personality. "He loves Loni Anderson. She's a very Mb8 attractive young woman and it's his girlfriend. The little boys his age just seem to love her. They're all in love with her. That's a sex object for them. Platinum hair and very bosomy and nice legs and very beautiful figure, a smart gal also. I don't know if this is giving off a positive feeling. I don't know. I'd rather have him see the *Wonderama* kind of show where a psychologist is talking to children than see the blond bombshell kind of a thing, but he likes both." Other parents complained that their children were acquiring certain attitudes from the sillier situation comedies and dramatic series, those which were filled with ambiguous dialogue, suggestive costumes and slightly smarmy "borderline" situations. Peter spoke contemptuously. "I wouldn't say that the role models that she is getting from the media Fg9 are very helpful. ABC knows how to pander to the youth market. *Dukes of Hazzard*, that's her big show, where men drive fast cars and women wear shorts."

Not all parents were totally negative about all such subliminal messages, however. Some believed that images from the media had to be accepted as part of reality, an alternative vision to that provided by the parents, informative and even healthy in its own way. Stacey said, "There are things on television that I might not have brought up. We've Mb11 seen *North Dallas Forty*, which was about a football team and was rather explicit in a lot of ways. Certainly he got that whole sense from that movie of the male kinds of sexual things that go on in the locker room, the conversations and all that. He seemed to enjoy that. I was kind of holding my breath at points, but I thought, 'Okay, this is education, too.' So I think from the media he's picked up that sort of thing. From me he gets the more technical and the more open, loving and accepting point of view, from the media some of the more rough-and-tumble kind of pieces."

Sexually Accurate Dolls

Very few parents reported that their children actually owned "anatomically correct" male dolls: dolls with realistic genitalia. Behind the
comments of many parents on this issue, however, was uneasy recognition of a certain irony: Children are aware of their own sexual anatomy
and that of siblings and peers; they have, as one mother drily pointed
out, "anatomically correct parents." And yet, traditionally, the dolls
available have been either perceptibly female or neuter. As a result, a
kind of ambiguous but pervasive emphasis on femaleness or gender-
lessness has filtered down, influencing *de facto* the play habits of children in the society. Sonia said that no matter what kind of doll her
daughter preferred, she was bound to have more female dolls than male
because that is what is offered in the stores. She felt that children were
occasionally puzzled by the discrepancy between anatomical distinctions they observed in the real world, and those which existed (or did
not exist) in the world of dolls. "My daughter's commented on the
absence of sex organs in male dolls and the presence of certain female
curves and so on in female dolls. She has giggled about that kind of
stuff. She's been definitely interested in what's included and what's
omitted." Sonia had dealt with the issue this way. "I might have explained that there is some embarrassment in society about certain parts
of the body showing up on dolls. There's a conflict going on in the
industry about what they are allowed to show and what they are not
allowed to show on male dolls. We talked about that."

One father's experiences around giving his daughter an anatomically accurate male doll underscored the irony. He described at length
with both humor and exasperation the very negative reactions he had
received from nearly everyone but the child herself. "Daddy bought
her a doll that had a penis and I don't think Daddy's ever going to
forget it," he began. "When I bought it I thought it was the greatest
gift in the world. And everybody got offended by it. They were very
upset. Not my daughter, but her mother and her aunt and her grandmother. It was a heavy. I'll never forget that. My daughter loved it.
She thought it was great. It was real. She has a cousin. He has a penis.
Therefore the doll should have one. I just felt, you have a boy doll
and you have a girl doll. There should be that difference." Interestingly enough, he also noted the rather striking contrast between these
very strongly disapproving reactions to the male doll and utterly neutral responses to another doll he had given the child: a female with
realistic sexual development. "I also got her one that grows—the hair,
the breasts. It gets taller and the breasts grow. I didn't run into any
flak on that. The girl doll was all right."

There were people who thought the "anatomically accurate" doll
was probably originally designed to appeal to parents who wanted to

make some "statement" regarding sexism or teach their children about male genitalia or put them at ease in relation to nudity. But, as one mother pointed out, it was often parents who were most comfortable with these subjects, unselfconscious about discussing them with a child in real-life situations, who would buy him or her a doll with a penis, having no particular "educational" purpose in mind. "I think most children who receive that anatomical doll are probably the very children who don't need it. The information is available to them," she said. "The kids who don't have that information really need it more. My son has the information available to him, so he was not impressed. It was there. He was interested in Martians, things he had no way of learning about." Her observations were corroborated by those parents whose children did possess anatomically correct male dolls. The children accepted the dolls without much fuss. These children and their parents shared a disinterested, objective approach. The dolls were merely realistic, after all—hardly prurient: "She has an anatomically correct doll since she's an infant," a mother remarked. "She thinks nothing of it. When she plays with the dolls there's no sexual overtones whatsoever." Another mother said, "We do have a boy doll running around the house, anatomically correct. She had it as a gift, and she liked it. It was the brother doll in her family of dolls. It was a baby boy and that was it."

Mb11

Mg5

Mg8

One father said of his daughter: "Give her a doll and it has a jumpsuit on, she's going to take it off to see if it has any organs. When she got the boy doll she played with the penis. Instantly. She was much younger and I thought it was funny. I didn't think anything of it. You know, this is reality. This is real. This is why you don't walk in on boys while they're changing. This is why boys can stand up to pee and girls have to sit down. To this day I see nothing wrong with it." Only at one point did his daughter's openly sexual response to the doll cause him any distress. "Somewhere along the line she became aware of oral sex. The way it came to me was, can she kiss the doll's penis. I said, 'What do you want to do that for?' And she told me, 'Gracie told me.' That's her stepsister, her god-like source of knowledge. I said, 'You don't want to do that. You don't do things like that.' No real explanation other than making a face. I'd be two-faced if I try to give her a lie, so I'd rather give her no answer and let her think it's wrong, and hope I get away with it. Till she's at least eighteen." he added.

Fg3

To some degree, the "Barbie" doll was also considered a sexually accurate doll because she does possess visible breasts. "They are not just baby dolls," Kathy pointed out. "They are shaped like women." Agnes reported that her children were very much aware of Barbie's obviously female anatomy. "They make comments about the breasts Barbie has. They always say, 'She has big ninnies!' " "Barbie is relatively well-endowed, breast-wise," Steve noted. "I think my daughter may have made some comments about that." He put in a wry aside

Mg7

Mg13g12g6g4

Fg5

on Barbie's male counterpart. "Ken is not anatomically correct. Not unless he had a sex change, not unless he went to Johns Hopkins." One father said admiringly of Barbie, "She looks pretty good, I'll tell you. She probably wears a 36C bra. If she were human, it wouldn't be bad at all." Jokingly he added, "I know my daughter's aware of the sexuality of the dolls. The other day she had Barbie undressed and she said, 'OHHH, Barbie's undressed!' Nudity I should not see even in a doll!" But he also made these observations on Barbie's role as a female model for little girls: "We buy Barbie because it's a way of learning how to dress. It's a way of learning femininity, I guess, in a sense what it's like being a woman. The old baby dolls, the ones that wet their pants, the ones with bottles and all that, I'm sure the function of that was to give the child an early introduction into nurturing."

Several parents had more negative feelings about the Barbie doll: A mother objected on the grounds that play with Barbie tended not to be very imaginative or creative and emphasized acquisitiveness and superficial social values. "I didn't mind my daughter playing with the Barbie doll. I found it stupid, I guess. I don't know what the big fun is to dress and undress a stupid doll. That's all they ever do to Barbie dolls. Get ten thousand clothes and dress her and undress her." Other parents believed Barbie reflected some of the skewed values and misplaced priorities of the society at large: "Barbie dolls are just like everything else," a father said. "Good looking, sure. We show our children the most attractive things there are in the world, so anything else could be a turn-off. That's one of the bad things. I disapprove of it. I think that children ought not to be exposed only to the most beautiful things in the world. I think a tendency then is to say that my mate must be beautiful, I must live in a beautiful house. Therefore, when those things do not occur there's frustration and disappointment with life. Life is not all beauty and good. And yet we buy our kids the Barbie dolls, because they ask for them, because they see them advertised or they see other children playing with them." Another father's remarks about his daughter's invidious comparisons between herself and Barbie seem to bear this out: "It was tied in with the conversation she and her older sister had together. She was telling me she isn't, you know, buxom, and I think her sister may have said something like, 'Yeah, Gee, I wish I was like Barbie.' "

Fg7

Mg10

Fg7

School

Almost all the parents in this study, regardless of their lifestyles or their orientation toward other sexual issues, shared relatively positive attitudes about sex-education courses. They did have some reservations, however. Though few rejected such programs in principle, many were concerned about how the courses were taught once they actually existed in their children's schools. They worried about the quality of the curriculum and the suitability of the teachers involved, and they did not want even good programs to become "cop-outs"—substitutes for competent parental communication on the subject. If their children were to be taught about sex in the classroom, they wanted to be aware of what was going on.

Those who favored sex education in the schools offered a number of reasons for their position. Where the parents themselves were cautious about initiating discussion with their children, they were pleased that the school could cover sexual topics in a responsible manner. Mike was "thrown" when his daughter approached him with questions about reproduction but wanted her to have the proper information. Fg5 "I believe in sex education," he said emphatically. "I'm for it one hundred percent, because I think today we really need it." And if the parent was comfortable talking to children about sex, had already introduced the subject at home, the school could still expand upon what the child already knew. "In the sixth grade in our school system, they Mb9 give them sex education and the kids look forward to it," Helen said. "They enjoy it. Even though he had gotten a rudimentary description of all these things, he came home with a great sense of pride. He said, 'Now you don't have to tell me anything—I know everything!' And he was very proud and happy. It made him feel very grown up to have had these classes in school."

A few parents even ventured the opinion that the school might do a better job than the parents could. One father felt that sexual material learned in a school atmosphere would have greater authority than that provided by the parents, and yet would not have the possibly unsavory overtones of information picked up haphazardly from peers or society at large. "Here is something that the kid will think is credible Fg3 because she's learning it in school," Randy said. "It becomes less of a hidden thing because it's not off the street." A mother agreed. "My Mb9 son enjoyed sharing this information with his peers in a way where there didn't seem to be anything 'dirty' about it. It wasn't behind the shed. I think it was a relief."

Sometimes there were topics which seemed too embarrassing for either parents or children to discuss with each other. In those cases, the school program had the advantage of being detached from the family, impersonal; information could be imparted in a scientific way, free of the revelatory quality which made discussion so very difficult at home. Polly had tried to be as open as possible in speaking of sex with her children, but she felt that a burden had been lifted as a result of the sex education course her sons were taking at school. "I'm get- Mb7b5 ting more and more pleased that the school has a sex education program. I think that many times children just don't want to come to their parents, maybe for the same reasons that I feel uncomfortable answering their questions, that kind of pressure of having the personal relationship there." Like Polly, Andrew had taken responsibility for teaching his children about sex, but he, too, commended the school program, which dealt with some topics more straightforwardly and with less anxiety than a parent could. "I tend to think the things he gets in school are done very well there—more details about the physiological, explained with the right words and the right everything else, with no problems of his being embarrassed. The school seems to do it well."

Many parents said that if a sex-education course was to be a success, it had to be well organized and well taught. "I would like it to be given, but only under certain circumstances," Stephanie said. "With a certain kind of person who would be honest and truthful and not misinform, who would have some of the attitudes I have." The same point was made by Doretta, who attributed her son's good experience in a nursery school sex-education program to the quality of the teaching. "He had a wonderful teacher. I know that discussions of babies came up. Things around touching, kissing, came up. One of the children's books on sex was read and discussed in the classroom. And the teacher handling it was a pretty okay person—a male teacher with two children of his own, with some very good attitudes, someone who really cared for and about children. I was very much pleased."

Nearly all parents stressed the importance of retaining control over the sex-education process. "It would be okay in school, if I knew how they were presenting it," Vinny said simply. Stephanie, too, wanted to "be there," to participate in program planning and "see what [the teachers] were going to do." But she was not very optimistic that the school would be open to parental involvement on a large scale. "I'm very curious about what they're doing in school, how they're going about teaching my child, but I feel that they don't want the parents in the school and they don't want them to know too much because then we'll question and we might want to change things. So I would want to be very careful about sex education in the schools."

Like Stephanie, there were parents sympathetic to the concept of sex education who were not ready to approve such a course in their children's schools. Their experiences with unresponsive administrators and indifferent or incompetent teachers had made them suspicious, even cynical, about the ability of the school system to produce the kind of program they could be comfortable with. Cheryl spoke of the difference between the ideal and the reality. "I don't feel good about his teachers. They seem very provincial and set and it's very slanted. And when I ask questions, they find it difficult understanding. They can't answer." Roger, a teacher himself, put it quite succinctly: "I believe I know the schools. I'm not very high on the schools' ability to do anything. I'm someone who knows too much about it!" Another father backed up his skeptical views with a specific example, a bad experience his six-year-old had had with a teacher who lacked sufficient patience to handle such a complex and sensitive subject. "The first-grade teacher this year couldn't be bothered with [sex education]. She goes 'one, two,' and if you don't keep up with the class, forget it! You know, 'I told you the first time—if you don't understand it, I don't want to be bothered with it.' " Fb7

Some parents also emphasized that no school sex-education program, even a satisfactory one, could replace the parents as the primary source of sexual information. Such programs were fine in themselves, but ought to be viewed only as supplements to what the child had already learned at home. Helen, for instance, who had unequivocal praise for the quality of the sex-education course in her son's school, said "I think it's good to have auxiliary explanations, a lot of back-up, Mb11 but I don't think anyone else can replace the parent's explanation." Sam said, "My daughter surely will be exposed in today's modern era Fg7 to some of the fundamentals of sexuality in school. I will confirm the school's concept and I hope that the school's standard will be confirmation of what she's heard at home."

The small number of parents who rejected the idea of sex education in school did so in fact because they believed that the task of teaching children about sex belonged solely to the family. Stacey, who passionately believed that children should be told "everything" nevertheless did not think the school should be given the role in telling them anything. "No," she said adamantly. "My opinion is that the healthy Mb11 way to establish attitudes towards sex is for it to be a comfortable piece of discussion in the home. If it's not comfortable at home, it's going to be odd coming from anywhere else. The technical stuff, sure, but that's not really the issue." Her views were echoed by a father whose daughter had taken a sex-education course. Though he did not deny that she had learned from the class, he thought the program was irrelevant and wasteful. "I'm not sure what the schools are doing devoting time, Fb8b4 money, and effort in taking over a responsibility which I think is the family's." For a third parent, the issue was her right to decide just what her children would learn. "If they didn't have a father, that would be Mb10b8 another problem and maybe the school would replace that. But by choice. A parent should have a choice whether the school teaches them about sex."

Still another parent, a first-time middle-aged father, summed up his feelings about parental responsibility versus school authority this way: "I'm not against sex education totally, unless you seem to rely on Fg7 it too much. It seems everybody knows how to bring up your kid—it bugs me. I don't really like the professional raisers of children. They tend to give a feeling of inferiority to the parents, as if there's a certain way that children should be raised. I'm a late parent. I was forty-two when my child was born, so I feel like a *mature* parent. I am concerned with a sense of values, getting across some things that I found out in life to her. I think I'm doing a good job with my daughter."

Religious Instruction

A large majority of the parents in this study said that their children had not learned anything about sex from their religion. In some of these cases, formal religious observance was not part of the family's lifestyle; in others, the family's religious orientation was cultural rather than doctrinal. But even when children were receiving regular religious instruction, most parents did not feel they were acquiring much sexual material—facts or attitudes—from this source. They noted that religion classes, at least with children under twelve, tended to avoid discussion of sex-related topics—immaculate conception, virgin birth, laws of purity—even in Bible stories that had sexually suggestive themes. And they were confident that their own morality had a far stronger influence than any church or synagogue on the way in which their children came to perceive sex and sexual matters. In fact, some parents whose children were receiving a religious education were prepared to tell them to overlook the things they learned about sex in school. When a seven-year-old brought home the story of Adam and Eve, his mother, an x-ray technician with a strong scientific background, let him know gently that creation—and procreation—was a more complex phenomenon than the story suggested. She told him, "Maybe it wasn't a completely true story but it was something that people thought up."

Mb7

Only a small group of parents spoke at all specifically of the effect of religion on their ideas about sex. In almost every instance these were people who had attended Catholic school in the Fifties and Sixties, who felt their own sex education had been inadequate or rigid and wanted to be sure that their children received a more balanced point of view. Though Doretta was brought up as a Protestant, her parents sent her to a Catholic school because it was the best in the neighborhood. She complained about the lack of physiology courses in the curriculum. "I did not discover how babies were born until my sophomore year in college and I had hysterics. I mean, I literally had hysterics. There was no opportunity for this information to penetrate." Maeve, an Irish Catholic, recalled with amusement the "old wives" tales she had heard from some of the older nuns at her Catholic academy: " 'Don't wear patent leather shoes' and 'Don't wear white, it reminds boys of bed sheets.' The patent leather shoes so they can't see your underwear," she added with a smile. "There were many of them. 'Sprinkle talcum

Mb6

Mg11

powder in the bath water so you don't see your reflection,' 'Run the shower to steam up the mirror so you don't see your reflection before you take your clothes off.' I never did it myself, but I guess it's something that stays with you. I mean, now I laugh about it. I see people who were raised in the same type atmosphere and we kind of compare notes as to the tales that the nuns told us, which sound unbelievable, I know. But it happened." Because of these experiences, Doretta and Maeve would not send their children to Catholic school, though Maeve's daughter was receiving religious instruction and expected to be confirmed at the local church.

Sean was another parent who had gone to Catholic school. Though he maintained strong ties to his faith, he nevertheless believed that "its perspective [on sexual matters] in many cases is warped." He said, "I just think they foster the improper attitude toward sex. It's something disassociated from life. There are types of sexual behavior that they would consider sinful even within the confines of marriage. It's not a natural thing the way they approach it and that is what I object to." He wanted his daughter to grow up as a Catholic, to receive values from her religion, but he too preferred that she *not* learn about sex from the teachings—and the attitudes—of the Church. "So if she is going to pick up some information from the Church, I think I would want to discuss it with her and make sure she isn't getting hung up." Fg5

Of the parents who were sending their children to Catholic school, only one was dissatisfied with the way in which sex education is being handled by the Church today. Brent is separated from his Catholic wife but has agreed to have their son raised according to her religion. "He's been brought up a Catholic—though it's not always easy," Brent said. Fb11 He gave an illustration of the kind of restricted concepts his son was getting as part of his religious education. "My son came home the other day and said, 'Abortion is murder.' So I sprang into the thing, just to try and show him that it wasn't a black-and-white issue, it couldn't be the same notion as murder: 'Supposing there was a child that you knew was going to be deformed, do you still think that child should be born?' 'Well, that would be different.' " Part of Brent's concern, however, stemmed from the fact that he was not around as often as he would like, to provide an alternative point of view. "They certainly seem to have got that into him very well. I regret like anything that he's got somebody telling him that abortion is murder. But I don't know that there's an awful lot I can do about it."

Most other parents with children in Catholic school, even those who had negative recollections of their own experiences in a similar environment, reported that the Church has "come a long distance" in the last twenty years. They were pleased with the way in which sexual subjects were handled (or postponed until children were more mature) by the current generation of nuns and lay teachers. The em-

Mg8 phasis was on "love and belonging and mommy and daddy and babies."
Loving was important because it meant "belonging," one mother
explained. "Belonging to the family of God, too." Caridad compared
her seven-year-old son's education to her own when she was a child.
Mb7 "They learn about God is good, God is everywhere, being kind to
other people. It's more a Christian learning, as opposed to a strict, you
know, Catholic-by-rote learning. So I think, as far as I know, he's never
come home with the word *Virgin Mary*." Her son's school, which is in
a suburb of Pittsburgh, was also planning to begin a program of sex
education, starting in the first grade. The parents had been shown the
textbooks—"they talked about babies and how children came from
parents"—and had asked to help plan the curriculum. There were also
conferences with the faculty and several lectures by doctors and psychologists on the subject. "They did talk more about what sex education should be, not only giving the information but giving them the
right attitude about it."

These parents also reported that their children were no longer
receiving the subliminal messages about sex that had been inherent in
many of the restrictions that had been set down in their own Catholic-
school days. Though uniforms were often required (sometimes only
on certain days), no one was measuring the length of the girls's skirts
or checking the patent leather of their shoes. And whereas a number
of parents spoke of the segregation of the sexes in their own school
days—one mother recalled that she was nearly expelled from the eighth
grade when she and her girlfriends had gone walking in the park with
some boys from their class—they noted with approval that boys and
Mb9b5 girls were now allowed to participate in all activities together. "The
children wear their gym clothes underneath their uniform and then in
the classroom the boys and girls just take off their uniforms and they
have their shorts and T-shirt underneath it," Teresa said. She was
clearly surprised that the school did not regard this kind of undressing as
provocative or wrong. Generally, in fact, she was pleased that her sons,
aged nine and five, were not being indoctrinated with rigid rules about
their bodies, about relationships, about sex and sin. But she was not
sure that would happen when they graduated to junior high and high
school. "You know, when Patrick gets older, they will be telling him
about rhythm and that's the only form of birth control and all this, and
that is actually contrary to my belief. But we haven't crossed that
bridge yet."

The most detailed description of how religion was being used to
teach a child about sex came from a Born-Again Christian. Constance
talked about her commitment to her beliefs and her desire for her
Mg8 daughter to find the same joy through faith. "She had learned that sex
is a beautiful thing, that it's something that God gave us to procreate
and that it is something very sacred. And I think at eight years old, it's

made a dramatic impact," she said. "And there was one part in the Bible where Noah was nude and he was a disgrace, and it made a very big impression upon her. We do allow nudity to a degree but now she's getting older, she should have some modesty. Just, you know, learning about modesty, that impressed her." Constance thought for a moment before she continued. "When she was learning about Jesus's mother, the Virgin Mary, she couldn't imagine what that meant. I guess they boggled her with a little bit of Scripture and I know that that surprised her at that point. Virginity is not something we fling around the room. And I know that one time she was confused with 'love one another,' and she didn't know how you could love somebody and make love. That was something she did ask her Bible teacher. The teacher handled it very well from what I understand. They told her that it was just like loving and liking and that the two concepts were different. She accepted that." For Constance, the Bible class was an excellent introduction to sexuality and morality.

Books

A number of parents found books extremely helpful in introducing their children to basic concepts about sex. Often, when a baby was expected, parents used books to explain to the child what was happening inside his mother's body. Many of these began with descriptions and depictions of mating and conception in animals, then progressed to human reproduction. When Dennis' wife was pregnant he got a book from the library for his three-year-old son. "It showed a couple of chickens Fb3 on top of each other, and on one they showed the baby inside the belly of the chicken and things like this, and that basically satisfied his curiosity at the time." Sometimes the children themselves began asking questions, and sometimes parents decided that the "time to tell" had come. "We had a book by Eric Carl, *The Tiniest Seed*," Karen Mg7 recalled. "[It] had to do with how seeds reproduce and how the little seed grows and becomes an adult seed and then does its work in the world. And I remember beginning to use that as an analogy." Once in a while the children helped choose the book or read it to a younger sibling and the mutual participation, the close contact between parent and child, child and child, became a valuable emotional component of the learning process.

Books also gave some parents the confidence to deal with sexual topics which they were too embarrassed to introduce on their own. Marilyn was generally shy about discussing sex with her sons. "I found it easier to talk about ejaculation sort of backed up by the book. I sort Mb7b5 of relied on the way they said it." Harold reported that using a book helped dispel the preliminary awkwardness he felt when he wanted to give his son some basic information about sex. "There was a book about where babies come from. I would put the book there and we would talk about it. We didn't discuss it that much, but it was moderately comfortable."

Five-year-olds, just on the verge of going to school and enthusiastic about learning to read, were particularly well suited to being approached with books; harnessing their natural curiosity and mental energy often lifted part of the burden of sex education off the parents' shoulders. Mark described how this had worked with his five-year-old son. "My wife bought a book about reproduction that started off with animals having intercourse and worked up with a little diagram, cartoon-type drawing of little stick people having intercourse. And for weeks after he read the book, every other night at the dinner table he would ask for me to explain that once more." A five-year-old girl responded with similar enthusiasm. Her mother said, "I just got the book and I read it to her one night and it very carefully categorizes every type of living species—plants mate this way and this is how bees do it—and after twenty pages it gets to people, very casually put in there. We finished the book and she said, 'Can I have that book again?' and she opened it right to the human sex part. " The father of a boy who is now ten said his son had demonstrated an eagerness to learn about sex at age five, and that much of that early excitement had stayed with him to the present day. He had pursued his own sexual education, bringing home library books on the topic, reading voraciously anything he could get his hands on. His parents had finally bought him some of his favorites. "He got his sexual knowledge from those books," his father said. "He read them at five years old. In fact, he still has them. He reads one, a great book called *T.A. for Tots*, once a week. There's one by the same author about *Who Am I and Where Did I Come From?* with a lot of, not cartoon-type pictures, but pictures. It is very comprehensive in terms of its explanation of the fetus and all that kind of stuff, so he is very knowledgable about that kind of thing."

Karen was amazed to discover how many details about menstruation (a topic which she herself found particularly difficult to introduce) her daughter at age nine had already gathered from her own reading. "I was reading *My Mother, Myself* on a train and my daughter was sitting next to me. I had just finished the chapter on menstruation and was very shaken at what I had read. I decided that I hadn't really talked to her about it at all. I asked her first of all if she knew what it was, and she did! She know from a variety of sources, but mostly from a book by Judy Blume, *Are You There God? It's Me, Margaret*, which is about a thirteen-year-old who is beginning to menstruate. So she knew quite a bit about it."

Fb5

Fg5

Mg9

Some parents discovered that books were most successful when they were simply left around the house for the child to look at if she chose. This low-key, nonchalant, take-it-or-leave-it approach was particularly useful with pre-pubescent children who were approaching the stage at which they might be curious but too embarrassed to ask questions or might resist official "discussions" of sexual topics. "My son did find *The Joy of Sex* under one of his friends's mother's beds and probably spent the better part of the night reading it . . . He was nine at the time," a mother said, "so I feel he's well informed. He saw the positions. He has some knowledge of how human beings can act." Without "pushing", Paula made two popular books about women and sexuality available to her eleven-year-old daughter. "Both books, *Our Bodies, Ourselves* and *My Mother, Myself*, have been around the house if she wishes to read, and I've let her, if she's interested." Mb9 Mg11

Not everyone had a positive experience using books, however, Often parents bought books they considered "charming," "adorable," "cute," "witty," and found the children rejected them instantly. As Helen said of her nine-year-old, "The moment I open one of those 'darling' children's sex education books, whether they're drawings, photographs, colorings—the child just turns off! They are not interested at that age." She had had similar experiences with younger children. "When they were in nursery school I tried to find the best and most charming books I could. They are still on page one: 'Shut that book! I don't want that book, I want something else.' They did not like those books." Some older children were put off by the overly factual nature of the books they had been given, perhaps associating them with school texts, and reading them with onerous homework assignments. "I bought her a book for teenagers on sex and relationships," the mother of an eleven-year-old girl said with mild exasperation. "She says there's too much information there and she doesn't wish to read it." Mb12b9 Mg11

Sometimes very young children responded deceptively well to the books parents read to them; they listened attentively, giggled appreciatively but didn't seem to take much in. "The book had funny drawings—there's one where they're in bed together and you see a heart over the bed and the sperm was made like the head was a heart shape—and it was cute. The kids were laughing. But it might have been over their heads. I think I could have waited." said one mother. Mb11b9

Tovah was very much against the use of books in educating children about sex. As she saw it, using books to explain sex was typical of a negative trend toward the acquisition of facts and away from simpler, more intuitive, ultimately healthier, forms of "knowledge." "I have the feeling that we're more and more heading into an age of technology, at the same time we're more and more heading toward alienation," Tovah said and added emphatically, "And I don't want that for my Mg10 child. I feel that at any point she can pick up a book and [learn to] label herself from head to toe. That is not what I want to give her. I want her going toward *life*, not toward a 'vaginal canal' or a 'premature ejaculation.' I can look at a pink flower and be thrilled to death. I don't need to know its name. I'm more comfortable looking her in the face and holding her hand and talking to her, offering her sensuality and sexuality as seen through my heart, rather than a book."

9

Media

In this chapter the term *media* describes a variety of forms of communication: books, periodicals, television, movies, works of art, billboards; graffiti, "adult" merchandise. For many parents these were the most insidious sources of children's sexual education because they were so ubiquitous and often worked subliminally. Most homes contained books and magazines with writing or pictures that had sexual innuendos. And one could not walk down a street or ride along a highway without passing a sign with a seductive model or a sexual tag-line. Many items which were openly displayed in shop windows, or on busses, trains, and cars—underwear, book and magazine covers, posters, bumper stickers—could also be suggestive in tone. Most parents made the same complaint about television, even though they had some control in selecting what their children watched. Not only were movies considered inappropriate for children available both on regular and cable TV but too many shows supposedly designed for family viewing touched upon sexual topics—premarital or extramarital relationships, seduction, rape, homosexuality—in order to provoke controversy or get easy laughs. Too many commercials used sex to sell products.

In a number of instances the sexual material appeared without warning. Children might be watching a movie with a PG rating or a favorite television series, and a bedroom scene would unexpectedly be included or an off-color word used. Occasionally on the way to a historical exhibit or a science display at a museum, children would pass nude statues or paintings that featured sexual subjects. What's more, the parent was not always there to give an explanation or distract a child when such situations arose. Children peeked at "dirty" books or watched television (sometimes without permission) on their own or at homes of peers whose parents were more permissive or less attentive. And they were often out in public places with their friends, with other adults, or alone.

There were other problems in monitoring the media. In the case of literature, painting, sculpture, photography, even film, parents sometimes had to distinguish both for themselves and their children what had merit and what was worthless. They might consider Judith Krantz pornographic but were less certain about D. H. Lawrence. Similarly, nudity in a famous oil painting could be acceptable, whereas nudity in a centerfold was not. Then, too, some parents enjoyed erotica, bought pornography and sexual devices for themselves but did not consider them suitable for children. Establishing standards, protecting children from what was everywhere without overprotecting them, and dealing with the inevitable moments when children sought out and discovered precisely what parents did not wish them to look at required careful and realistic evaluation of all of these circumstances, occasional ingenuity, and a sense of humor, as well.

Books

Of all the media sources of sexual information, books provoked the least controversy. Most parents did little censoring—some, none at all—of the books their children looked at and read. In a number of instances, they were guided not so much by their attitudes toward sex but their feelings about literature as an imaginative form and reading as a positive act. For many, censorship of the printed word was unpalatable, somehow a violation of both the author's and the reader's intellectual and personal liberties. "They can read books in this house Mb of any kind," Sylvia said. "Oh, sure—Norman Mailer. I feel like the way I was brought up. I would encourage them to read, you know." Parents also felt that since so much literature of value contains provocative material in one form or another—"I mean, the Bible has it," a Mb mother commented—there was no way they could determine which books (or sections of books) to censor even if they wanted to.

Lyle had two young sons in classes for the intellectually gifted. Both read at levels grades above their own and have already made forays into the family library. "We have a couple of hundred books here, I suppose," he said. "And among them are books that might have some sexual references to them, some novels, perhaps. I would not censor their reading of them." Other parents shared this point of view. If children enjoyed reading, the parents were reluctant to interfere with their enthusiasm by deeming certain materials acceptable and others off limits. Reading was also a special form of communication. Many parents believed that books were distinct from other forms of media, because the sexual images in them are less explicit than those in films, photographs, works of art. The child will take in as much as he can, but not more than he is ready for. "I don't find the printed word as threatening as the actual experience," Rachel said. Esther agreed. "I would be much less apt to censor a book or any written material than pictures. So she can use her imagination."

Wanda discussed this issue in detail. Her initial response to the question of whether she would supervise her ten-year-old daughter's reading matter was immediate and succinct. "I feel that if she is old enough to understand what she's reading, then she is old enough to read it and if she's not, any sexual references that are too much for her will just kind of go over her head." Later she said, "I really think that the best way to get information is through reading, whether it's good stuff or whether it's trash. I don't think there is anything in a book that can really hurt anybody, because they can filter it effectively for their own needs, but I'm disturbed at the amount of visual stuff that is around. I feel that it is very difficult for children because they have no defenses against it. I feel the visual has so much more impact on a mind that knows nothing else. It's a blank slate. I would rather my daughter got her impressions of love and romanticism and that kind of thing through reading first. And then later she can relate what she's learned about something that says more than just a flat-out picture and a couple of sweaty bodies."

There were parents who agreed in principle that children should read anything they wished but had in practice a "gut" reaction against allowing children books in which the sexual scenes or references were prolonged or too vivid. "There are a couple of books downstairs, in the library, I wouldn't permit my son to look at, at this point in time," Bart admitted. "I don't think my daughter could read it, at eleven." When asked when his children might be ready for these books, he was surprised by his own recoil from the idea that they might read them at

Fb7b4

Mg17b13b6
Mg6

Mg10

Fg11b6

all. "At what age would it be appropriate for them? When they're thirty-five—just kidding! Now I just blew my whole moderate thing, right? Christ, I don't know at what age." Sonia was struggling with a similar dilemma. She believed her eleven-year-old daughter should be free to look at books about sex. "I think she should feel that sex is just as good a subject to learn about as any other," she said. But she was uncomfortable when her daughter actually began reading adult material. "Well, I have some problems with that, but I'm trying to be liberal and I'm trying to keep her from having a lot of guilt feelings about learning." In the case of a number of pieces of fiction and nonfiction, it was not necessarily the depiction of the sex act which troubled parents but the implied approval of casual sex, which conflicted with their views. Like so many other parents, Linda was against censorship and was not sure there were any books she would try to keep out of her daughter's hands, especially as the child grew older. But she also wanted her daughter to understand the ways in which the family's values differed from those of the author. "I hope to teach my daughter that people can print and read whatever they want to. There's a very fine line between telling them that people have a right to do what they want, but I don't want her to think she can go out and have sex anywhere. I tell her I want her to respect her body and stuff like that. I'll tell her both the positive and the negative."

Several parents were much more strict about monitoring the books their children read. Generally, these parents relied on one of two criteria in deciding what was acceptable: the maturity of the child and the "quality" of the literature itself. When children already had a great deal of sexual information and did not seem discomfited by it, parents were not too concerned about their reactions to graphic or suggestive details. But when children were not yet sophisticated enough to cope with certain aspects of sexuality, parents believed that "getting too much too soon" could be harmful. Sonia described an argument she had with her eleven-year-old daughter. "She wanted to read something like *Wifey*—she reads Judy Blume's other stuff. We've already discussed it. I told her that she's not ready for it. She told me that she accepts that, but I don't believe she does. She has her own mind. And, of course, there are many times she has access to literature here, when we're out or doing something. She may have read it, for all I know."

Other parents objected to those books they considered "trash," not literature. Usually, "trash" meant blatantly sexual material, presented in a tasteless or exploitive manner. Mona, who censored her children's reading material quite heavily, said, "What I've always liked in books that I've read, like Zola, or literature that was written not in our time but by great writers—it was erotica but it was not explicit. Your imagination and your mind wander. I don't like Harold Robbins. I don't like visual descriptions in the book—'He put his arm around

Mg11

Mg5

Mg11

Mb11

her and grabbed her thigh.' There is no rhyme or reason for it. It is a distortion of what love is, a satire on what love is. I think there is a thing called Love and I think there is a thing called Sex. And lust or self-gratification and animalism—and I'm not trying to promote that while he's being formed. It's like reading a Zola book as opposed to reading Harold Robbins." She went on to list some of the acceptable books in the family library: *National Geographic*, Charles Dickens, all the classical books. *The Scarlet Letter* is there. I don't have any D. H. Lawerence, you know." Trude, who also believed in keeping close tabs on children's reading, offered her own list. "I adore Taylor Cald- well. She also writes descriptively but not in a sense of *diagrams*, books which are explicitly sexual. I call Harold Robbins, or somebody who wrote *The Users*, explicit. I would not keep it. I wouldn't even read it myself. I wouldn't want my daughter or my son to have a distorted view of what actually could be quite lovely."

Mg7

A few parents did admit that they secretly relished such books and kept personal hoards of "trash" hidden about the house. Most of them preferred that their children not find them, though they believed no great harm would be done if children happened to ferret them out.

> Books of all sorts. My mother finds all the filthy books she can for my husband. He loves filthy books. My daughter's never expressed much interest and if she asked I'd probably ask her not to read them. I'd just say she wouldn't be ready to understand it and that it would just not be suitable for her age. If I caught her looking at it anyway, I don't think I'd throw a big fit. I guess I'd probably talk to her at that point and still express the fact that those books don't really express the kind of love that most people know, and I would rather that she be older and have better judgment about what she's reading and its relation to reality.

Mg10

> We have a library in our bathroom up on the top shelf which I keep going through and throwing out. My husband and my older son read them, but I don't think my younger son has gotten to that yet. I don't like pornography. I'm sort of turned off by it. I don't know what my eight-year-old has seen and what he hasn't. He might come across something in the house. He's never mentioned anything to me, but it's there. If he goes searching for it, he'll find it.

Mb18b8

Parents tended to be a little more vigilant about choosing which "art" books—those with prints, photographs, or diagrams of nudes or figures in sexual positions—they would allow their children to see. Many believed that the graphic images were likely to frighten a child who still had little information or understanding about sex. One mother would not leave such books out around her house where her seven-year-old girl and ten-year-old boy might find them. "It is too early.

Mb10g7

They don't know what to do with it. I'm afraid seeing it too early will upset them, confuse them."

Parents also instinctively felt that the visual depiction—particularly in photographs—of sexual anatomy or subjects was sexier and far more stimulating to a child than the printed word. Some would not bring these publications into the house or, if they did, took steps to keep Mb6 them away from their children. "Now, I don't know about photographs, see. They're . . . ," one mother began, then trailed off, not quite able to put her negative feelings into words. "I don't think I would permit them," she finished simply. A father who had several erotic books never Fb10 showed them to his children. "I have censorship as far as what they see. I would filter what comes into the house—even though I would say that there is art pornography that I enjoy, that sexually has stimulated me, I certainly wouldn't want them to see it." In homes where children did come upon a collection of drawings or photographs they were not supposed to see, parents felt it was best to treat the incident casually, distract them, if possible, or make no comment unless the child asked a question. Trude said, "I would try to lead my child away Mb10g7 with an excuse." She did add, however, "If they happened to see it, I wouldn't say anything but would wait for the question, 'Why that funny position?' And I'd say, 'Well that's what it is.' I would be honest."

Like the parents who distinguished between "trash" and "literature" in deciding what their children might read, there were parents who restricted some art books because they seemed clearly prurient, but allowed others because they were meant to be informative or were Mg5 inspirational in tone. Linda made this point. "It depends on the reason," she said. "I let her look at pictures of the body. I don't think I would let her see a picture of an orgy or something like that. Plain bodies and the body doing regular functions, all right." Another mother Mb7 said simply, "If it's done in an artistic sense, it doesn't bother me." Elizabeth had a similar attitude toward an illustrated science volume Mg8 that belonged to her husband. "The theme was the human body. It had a picture inside, an old woman who had this gorgeous body in a bathing suit. The bathing suit was very sexual. The woman's breasts were fairly exposed. My daughter would take it out and keep looking at it. She was very interested. I never really said too much to her." Quite a few parents cited *The Joy of Sex* as one of the books in this category because it presented sex as a beautiful, loving, and natural experience, without the "leer of the sensualist." Richard's comment Fg8 was typical. "*The Joy of Sex*—I have that right out. My daughter could look at it. That would be fine." Several parents, in fact, encouraged their children to read the book because it could provoke healthy curiosity about sex and stimulate productive discussions. "*The Joy of Sex* would Mg6 be okay for my daughter to look through," Esther said. "If she asks me about it, I'll try to answer her questions."

Magazines

Most parents did not think that the articles, drawings, and photographs in magazines like *Playboy, Penthouse, Oui, Playgirl, Hustler,* et cetera, intended to be provocative or titillating, were suitable for children. But many were resigned to the fact that if they bought these periodicals for their private pleasure, their children were likely to see them. Magazines occupied a different place in the household from books. They were not shelved away neatly but were "around"—sitting in magazine racks, lying on coffee or night tables, stacked by the garbage, tossed on top of the hamper—where everyone had access to them. Even if the parents themselves did not read them, family friends and relatives sometimes brought them into the house. And children found copies on their own when they visited other homes where such materials were kept out in the open, or when they passed a newsstand, bookstore, or supermarket display:

> I wouldn't want to be forced into a discussion of sexual relationships in the middle of Shop-Rite. I would take the magazine away and say, 'We'll talk about it later.' " Fg9g5

> She goes to my father's house where there are endless *Playboys*. He collects them. And she sits there with the door closed looking through them and when I go in there she tells me she is reading the jokes. Most of which are dirty jokes. Mg11

Such circumstances all had to be taken into consideration when parents set down policies for permitting (or forbidding) their children to look at "girlie" magazines.

Some parents found it wisest not to allow these publications into their homes at all, either because they were personally offended by them or because they thought they did not belong in a home where children were growing up. Mona thought of *Playboy* as "smutty or dirty" and did not understand what gratification there was in reading it. "Because, well, in our household my husband feels that he adores his wife, therefore he doesn't need the sensation of looking at other women." Other parents expressly forbade children to buy such publications and spoke vehemently about "ripping them up" and "throwing them out" if they happened to find any around the house. Mb11

Several mothers despised the magazines because of their demeaning views of women and the shallow values they purveyed. "I don't display them around my house," Kathy said firmly. "I never liked them because of what they symbolized or what men take it as. I don't think that it should be common in your house. I can't think that my daughter has ever seen it." Sonia was equally adamant on this issue, although Mg7

her daughter had somehow gotten hold of copies of *Playboy* and "gone
through" them. "I've already taken those magazines from her, telling
her I don't want her to read it if it's *Playboy* or *Penthouse*. I don't approve very much of the way the women use their bodies. I think it's a
degrading kind of thing." *Playboy* was one of the few media sources
Esther made a point of censoring. "For my son, for my daughter too,
yes, sure. I would hate to have her look at *Playboy*. She would probably think that this was groovy. I wouldn't let her see all those girls,
mainly because I think that she would think this was a really cool thing
to do—be pretty enough to get your picture in *Playboy* and have everyone tell you how pretty you are. And I guess I see it as *using* women.
It's so superficial. I don't want her to grow up to be a centerfold. She'd
probably want breasts right away. She's expressed interest. She likes
pubic hair, too."

There were parents who did want these magazines for themselves
but remained strict about keeping them from their children. If possible,
they hid them away, like "bathroom" items of a personal nature: One
mother said, "Some newspapers someone gave my husband, *Screw* and
a few of those other joys to the world, they're in my husband's closet.
But my children have never seen them. They aren't aware that it's
here." Sometimes they simply told the children that the magazines
were not for children. In firm but moderate terms they emphasized
the difference between the sensibilities of adults and those of children,
and the rights of adults to exclude children from "adult things." According to Bart, his policies regarding most periodical reading matter
were liberal, with one notable exception. "All the papers that come
in, whatever's in there, he's free to look at. He has all kinds of magazines for his own level. I don't think I'd let him see *Playboy*. I would
just explain to him that there are some adult magazines which contain
pictures of people in the nude. Very basic, you know. And they are
considered adult magazines. I'd tell him they are things that you've
seen before. You can't look at it because it's not appropriate for you at
this time. Adults have magazines and that's an adult magazine. You
have *Sesame Street* and *Sesame Street*'s your magazine at your age." In
Betty's family, if children sought out and read the magazines, "they
would be invading my privacy because I don't think it's appropriate
for them." Privacy was also an issue in Allen's household. His son had
taken to secreting some of Allen's magazines. "My wife finds them,
hidden in certain places, so I'm sure his curiosity's getting aroused.
My wife has said, 'These are really Dad's and you ought to leave them
alone.' " Another mother took a firm stand, even though her daughter
sometimes resisted. "She might have a wisecrack or a joke or a complaint. She doesn't take it completely passively. But I still take it away.
I don't want my daughter to get the idea that I think it's funny or
cute."

According to several parents, however, such measures were not entirely effective. Children were determined, curious, alert, sure to manage a glimpse of a forbidden magazine or ferret out the parents' collections sooner or later. There were obvious conflicts for these parents. They believed it was important to "take an official stand" about publications containing lascivious centerfolds or raunchy cartoons, but believed "sneaking a peek" was only natural, not at all harmful to children growing up today. Generally, therefore, they chose not to be aware that their children were reading the magazines in secret. The feeling was that if they did not acknowledge what was occurring they did not have to do anything about it. A mother made this point. "When   Mb8
he comes to me and wants to see *Playboy*, I won't let him look at it, not with my knowledge, not to say, 'Well, it's all right to do it.' " She did think that her son "will probably sneak around [and do] it, but I would rather he not do it in front of me." "My husband has a bunch of   Mg10
old *Playboy*-type magazines that he has had for years," another mother remarked. "The kids know where they are and they know that we prefer that they don't look at them. I mean I trust them not to, but I know that they have." Olive made this wry confession: "We do have   Mg9
Playgirl and *Playboy* in the house, but I don't let the girls near them. They are upstairs and away. At one point we did leave them out and I knew that the kids had them, but I never told them that I knew they had them. Okay, I let them get away with it. Yeah, unofficially. There is a part of me that wants them to see it. I don't want to, you know, stop them at all levels. I used to sneak looks, too. But I do want to keep a little bit of control."

Even those who chose to comment when they knew their children had access to magazines they preferred them not to see tried to remain unemotional and pragmatic in expressing their disapproval. Here was yet another sexual situation in which the more low-key the reaction, the more effective it seemed to be. "The kind of censoring I do is   Mb5
very subtle," one mother pointed out. "If it's right there I'm not going to make an issue of it, but I will do my best to see that it isn't there. If there's a magazine on the table and I'm supposed to be in here making dinner, I'm not going to rush in here and say, 'Give me that!' That's silly. But, just like if you see somebody rob somebody in front of you, wouldn't you comment on that to your child? 'I certainly don't approve of it,' or 'What they're doing is not exactly right,'—you know, that's the kind of comment I would make."

Another mother took this approach when her son seemed titillated by the *Playboy* pictures his friend had shown him. "I said, 'I know   Mb8
you've seen that magazine over at Tony's house and sit and giggle or whatever you may do. But not in this house. A woman's body is a woman's body. A man's body. They are made differently. But I wouldn't laugh at you, so I don't expect you to laugh at me. It's just

Mommy. It's just skin, nothing else, just skin. It's just shaped that way.' When I say 'Mommy,' I think that hits him. It's okay. They calm down and they don't giggle as much."

Actually, a very large group of parents felt the best thing to do about *Playboy, Penthouse, Oui, Playgirl,* and all the rest was to allow children open, casual access to them. Generally, they drew the line only with magazines which emphasized violence, cruelty, or perversity in sexual situations. A few parents even felt that looking at a *Playboy*-type publication could be a positive experience, and might satisfy a natural curiosity about male/female differences (some recalled studying photographs of nudes in similar publications when they were children), and promote healthy attitudes toward sexuality. Larry talked about his four-year-old son. "I guess I want to be sure that he's heterosexual, so we have *Playboy* and he sees us reading it. He'll even look at it."

Fb4

In most cases, however, the decision not to regulate children's reading did not necessarily imply approval. Many parents thought that children were going to see the same things that appear in *Playboy* on television and in the movies. "It's just all around," Margot commented, "so I don't cut it off." Geraldine said, "If my husband is reading *Playboy* and puts it down on the table, that's usually where it will stay. If I see it, I might throw it up on the desk where she can't reach it. I might. Not always. It's there. If they don't see it at home, they are going to see it eventually, anyway."

Mg10

Mg4

Parents also believed that children who bought the magazines, hoarded them under beds and in closets, pored over them repeatedly, even subscribed to them, would eventually lose interest and move on to other things. This was Charles's experience. "A couple of years ago we went to this cottage on the beach. This place was supposed to be owned by an Episcopalian minister, but my son discovered this drawer loaded with *Hustler* and *Playboy* and worse. And he wanted to look at them. We didn't take them away from him. We weren't wild about the idea, but he kept them for a while and then he didn't pay any more attention to them. We said, 'Why do you want to look at that?' and he told us he hadn't seen quite such explicit pictures of nude women before. We don't do the things like, 'Don't look at that.' " Doretta shared Margot's view that children cannot be kept away from pornography. "Actually the pornography is really accessible. The good, sensual, erotic stuff—that's all been taken out of the libraries, but pornography is on the newsstands." She laughed ruefully and shook her head. "You just hope you did a good job and your children will be appropriate around it. They'll look at some and giggle and then find it distasteful because the real thing's better. That's my hope."

Fb9

Mg6

Sometimes parents urged their children not to be secretive, to

bring the magazines and their curiosity out into the open. "I used to   Fb8
find some *Playboy* pictures in my son's briefcase," Elias said of his eight-
year-old. "He used to hide it. He is really after girls. I told him, 'If
you want the *Playboy*, I'll just buy you it. Don't hide it.' Now he's
already much freer." Two other boys, who were permitted to have
their own subscriptions to *Playboy*, ultimately reacted quite casually to
all the nudity it contains.

> He was nine years old. He said, "I want to subscribe to *Playboy*.   Fb9
> They have a special on here." We went ahead and got him a sub-
> scription. The hell with it. He wanted it. I don't want to go around
> banning stuff from them. They're only going to fight it anyway. I
> said, "I'll talk to my leader." So we had a family discussion. We laid
> down certain rules with regard to his subscription, that he wouldn't
> leave the magazines around, that he wasn't going to haul them out
> every time his friends came over, that it wasn't going to be the cen-
> ter of his social activities, looking at *Playboy*. They are going to be
> kept out of sight. I don't think there is anything in there that he
> shouldn't know about, that he isn't going to learn about anyway. My
> daughter was offended by it, that it was sexually exploitive of women
> and all that. My wife, I guess you would characterize her as a feminist.
> She said, "I don't believe in sexual exploitation either, but there is
> nothing bad about the human body and if men want to look at it,
> that's fine." His subscription expired a couple of months ago. I told
> him I wasn't going to pay for it and he decided he didn't want it
> enough. He just lost his interest. Nude women. Not boring, but they
> are a little redundant.

> Somebody sent him a subscription to *Playboy*. Just recently. I don't   Fb11
> know who sent it. He doesn't seem to get too excited about the nude
> pictures in the magazine. I've not tried to hide the book from him.
> It's his book, anyway. It's his subscription. He likes looking, reading
> the jokes, and he'll read a story every once in a while. He'll open the
> centerfold page and look at it. When he first got the book and I was
> reading it, he didn't even go near it. I happened to see him looking
> at it after I left the room. When I came back in, we both pulled out
> the centerfold at the same time and I made a comment. "That's a
> great looking woman." He said, "Yeah, it looks pretty good."

In at least one instance, *Playboy* was an inspiration to a young
artist. Fernando, proud and somewhat bemused, told the following
story of his son's creative attempt at erotica. "My ten-year-old, who   Fb10
has a great sense of humor and is really talented in art, came from his
friend's house one weekend and asked, 'Popi, how come there isn't a
porno magazine for children?'—(who knew he even *knew* about pornography?) Anyway, he goes on and says, 'Well, I'm gonna invent one.

I'm gonna call it *Playkid.*' The next evening he hands me a drawing he did—a boy is shown, back view, with his pants down around his ankles, *clearly* masturbating—and says, 'This is for the first article in my new magazine.' "

Television

Many parents had extremely negative things to say about television. They referred quite bitterly to skewed values, insensitive programming, and the difficulty of controlling what their children were exposed to
Mb7   via the "boob tube." Valerie said, "I think that [television] distorts life. Any kind of life-style you would choose, it is distorted. It's a lot of wishful thinking, a lot of comedy plastered into where it doesn't belong. I don't think children can get an accurate picture of what life's demands are from the media at all. Children get a terribly distorted picture and in consequence have a hard, hard time adjusting to different situations, or to stressful situations, in marriage or in relationships."
Fg6   Ted complained of "the cheapening, promiscuous attitudes toward sex. It seems as if the Tits-and-Ass standards are being permeated throughout the media. I think it creates an attitude. I wouldn't want my child to see the cheapening, promiscuous stuff." Though Linda felt there
Mg5   were some good things—"like the animal specials"—shown on television, she had many reservations about television in general. "I don't think I would want her to see seductive females being very seductive. Aggressive males and submissive females. That's not the only role model available. There's enough already to show how to be seductive."

Once in a while, it's true, a production might contain sex scenes which were "too adult," too intense or overpowering, for children but which seemed artistically justified. Cynthia recalled a series on public
Mb10   television. "There was something on *Masterpiece Theater* that was pretty explicit. It was the French one, "Thérèse Raquin"—an intercourse scene. My husband sent my son out of the room. I think he just said, 'This isn't for kids to watch.' " Most parents, however, offered examples of how sex and sexual innuendos permeated every aspect of daily
Fg11b6   and weekly viewing fare. According to one father, "It happens all the time. Some of the shows get carried away, much too far. I think the regular tube implies a lot of things sexually without people even taking their clothes off. Everybody is hopping in and out of bed. Most of the time it's "in-bed-before-married." *Love Boat* pops into my head because they're always running around. *Three's Company* is another one."

Many parents cited comedies with story lines that regularly focused on singles in suggestive situations as particularly offensive. When

Betty's children watched *Three's Company*, she let them know, "I do
not in any manner or way think what [the characters] are doing is right."
Sexual themes also cropped up in dramas—"If they're watching *Hill
Street Blues*, it seems like the cop and the lawyer always end up in
bed"—in soap operas, musical extravanganzas with scantily clad cho-
rus girls, talk shows, even serious specials, and parents often found
themselves censoring programs, sometimes on the spot, in a variety of
ways. Florence's mother was "hooked" on a soap opera that contained
so many steamy bedroom scenes that she finally had to make the TV
room off limits to her daughter during that show. "I have just told my
daughter that's not a program for her to watch, that was a program for
adults. Without going into details as to why. And that was all right.
She accepted that. So far."

Documentaries and interview shows that claimed to examine sexual topics from a non-titillating, scientific, or sociological point of view,
came in for sharp criticism from parents. Charles and his wife had tried
to prevent their son from watching news features that they considered
irresponsible or overwrought, "kind of poor treatment of rape, you
know, that kind of show. We try to keep him away from them. We've
been having a real problem there. If there is going to be a show we
don't want him to see, we tell him he wouldn't like it."

Mona was surprised to discover the inappropriate ways in which
sex was exploited on supposedly respectable magazine-style programs.
When the subject matter was offensive to her, she took pains to provide her children with alternative views that more closely matched the
family's religious and philosophical standards. "I was out last week and
was not able to monitor a show he woke up with. It was either *Donahue*
or *Good Morning, America*, and it was all on homosexuality and I was
very concerned. I let him know that I was disconcerted that he watched
that when I was not home, and I discussed with him how the media
was sensationalism and thrives on depicting homosexuality as a sensa-
tional factor. And we went into what he has been taught, which is
biblical." Later, she added, "VD was on TV one night, and they were
discussing herpes. I teach my children that media pushes sensationalism and there is a portion who have herpes now for being promiscuous
and it cannot be treated, so basically we are meant to be in one-on-one
relationships for long periods, otherwise these herpes things wouldn't
crop up."

What did other parents do when children were watching television and a program or scene which seemed inappropriate came on? A
few parents said the ideal solution was to get rid of the TV set altogether, but only two had actually taken this drastic step. Joyce wanted
her children "to learn to talk to each other and not watch junk on TV."
Alex had his set disconnected when his children began sneaking down-

Mg9b5

Mb13g8

Mg8

Fb11

Mb11

Mg14b11

Fb12g9 stairs to watch TV instead of doing their homework. "We feel that reading is more important than watching TV, at this point." But he thought there was an additional benefit in living without a television. "I don't know if it's bad for them not to see TV, because the media gives them such a distorted view of sex. You know, it's all bodily oriented and the people are used as products."

No one else was willing to go as far as these parents, however, with limits placed on how much time children spent in front of the set and what they were allowed to see, television had its uses as an educator, entertainer, and babysitter. This meant parents had to confront all the problems involved in monitoring—devising and enforcing realistic standards, dealing with "gray" areas, establishing control over this all too pervasive medium.

Some parents took a direct approach. If children were found watching programs with unsuitable sexual material, the parents simply turned off the set, switched to another channel, or suggested that the children themselves select more appropriate fare. Sylvia had used this ap-
Mg4 proach successfully, leavening it with a little humor. "If I see something they are watching and I disapprove," she remarked, "well, I just walk right over and turn it off. I'll say, 'This is not for you.' I'll make a joke out of it." Lyle took a harder line, emphasizing the parents' right to
Fb7 make such decisions unilaterally. "If I didn't approve of it I would just change the channel. I would tell him that I didn't believe a seven-year-old should be watching this type of program. And I'm not going to stand there explaining what these people are doing to a seven-year-old, the reasons they are doing it and their relationship and why they are doing it on television to begin with." Parents also tried to avoid encounters with their children by letting them watch only those shows aimed at general audiences or designating certain hours for children's viewing. Usually, the cut-off time was eight or nine in the evening, when adult dramas are scheduled. This policy was fairly effective, but, as has been pointed out, parents nevertheless often found material they did not consider suitable for children aired during the "family hours."

There were instances in which the parents themselves were interested in a program but didn't think their children should watch it. Sometimes they chose to give up such shows because children were
Mb12g8 around. "[If] it's something I feel uncomfortable about having them watch with me, I just turn to another program," Elizabeth explained. But parents who were unhappy making this kind of sacrifice suggested another alternative. "Send him outside, or send him upstairs," Valerie
Mb8 said crisply. "I just make no bones about it. I would say, 'This is not for you to watch.' " Sally often employed the same tactic. "I would say, 'No, that's not for kids. Go play or do something else.' "

This approach worked well when only one child was being asked to leave the television room. In families with children in several age groups, difficulties arose, as Drew pointed out. "There are certain things on TV that I don't want the eight-year-old and the ten-year-old to watch, whereas the thirteen-or-fourteen-year-old I would accept. That's one of our problems. Sometimes I send the other two upstairs to watch TV in our room while the older ones watch with me. I'll say, 'I just don't want you watching this. It's not for you.' And of course that piques their curosity even more." Like many other parents, he admitted that setting such standards about television was ultimately futile, even though the integrity of the effort was important. "If that show's on again and I'm not home, I know damn well they are going to watch it. Then what do you do?" His answer was to trust his children's perspicacity and hope for the best: "They know what I think is right and wrong. They know my values and that's all I can do."

Some parents did not want to censor by turning off the set or sending children out of the room. This group made it a point to watch television with their children. "We all watch TV together," Geraldine said. "And if I'm not there, my husband will watch with them." The feeling was that if children were bound to be exposed to sexually oriented programs anyway in our society, parents might as well be pragmatic— exert the one kind of control that was available to them. When the family watched such programs together, the parents could insert pertinent commentary of their own, stressing sensible sexual values and answering any disturbing questions that might arise. Sonia was ready to confront any "difficult" sexual topic that came up openly and without squeamishness. "If it's rape we might discuss why people commit rapes and what you are supposed to do about it if it happens to you, how you are supposed to avoid it, or how you might feel during and after it. I'd say that some people are sick in a way that shows itself by their trying to force people to have intercourse and this can be a very upsetting experience for a female because she loses control." Bart emphasized the importance of being "tuned in" to what might be going on in children's minds as they watched sexual scenes. "I think that's part of being a parent—being a teacher and being alert. You have to make observations of these kids. And all kids don't give you verbal signs. Kids talk through body language. They show distress, discomfort, comfort, without any dialogue at all." And, like Betty, who had been so "down" on *Three's Company*, several parents felt that rather than make an issue of children watching programs that contained suggestive or inappropriate themes, they would prefer to intervene by giving children their point of view, explaining why they were offended.

Another group of parents did not feel it necessary to make any comment when sexual material occurred in the midst of regular family viewing. There parents believed that drawing disproportionate atten-

tion to a brief sexual scene could be worse than simply taking it in
stride and letting it pass off naturally. "I've never turned the channel,"
Sheila said. I've just kind of, you know, I don't like to make it seem
like it's something taboo or whatever. I guess I would just try not to
make anything special out of it. I would answer questions if they asked,
but if they didn't, I would just let it go by." Morris remarked, *"Love
Boat*—my children like that program. I'm sure there are some sexual
scenes, not real explicit, but there are some scenes. We don't call attention to sexual scenes or shut it off or do anything like that. It's just,
let it go on. If the child has not made any references to it, it would just
pass by." Another father concurred. "I can't say I approve of all the
shows on TV," he said, "but I pretty much let my children watch a
good part of them. Maybe because I don't make a big thing about it. I
just kind of let it lie. I don't get up and shut off the set. Because
that makes you crazy. And you know what else happens? That makes
them crazy."

Cassandra's bugaboo was soap operas. "Say they're in the bed and
they're talking and then when they start kissing and it really gets
emotional, I said 'Turn that TV off or turn it to another station." But
her husband felt differently. "You shouldn't react like that," he said,
"because she's going to think that's wrong and she might want to go
out and experience it at a younger age because of her anxiety. "
Ultimately, Cassandra had come around to his opinion and allowed
the children to continue watching. She also recalled her own childhood attraction to soap operas. "I had to sit back and think about when
I was that young and I'd watch soap operas. I would be saying, 'Go
further! Go further!' because I wanted to see the rest." One young
father said with a laugh, "If I'm sitting home watching television and
there's a discussion about sex or something shown of a sexual content,
I don't censor it, or turn it off. No. I live through it."

Finally, there were many parents who felt it far more important
to censor violence than sex in television programs. Mark was particularly firm on this point. "There have been programs on TV that I've
walked in and turned off," he said. "Movies with no sexual connotations whatsoever, only because all it was was people beating the hell
out of each other with chains and blood and guts. I walked in and
watched two minutes of it and said, 'Hey, I see absolutely no redeem-
ing value why you kids should be watching this kind of show.' And I
walked over and turned it off. 'Who needs this?' They get enthralled
in this and think that it is really what happens. I'm not too sure at that
age they would even tell the difference. They didn't like it, but they
accepted it." Jim agreed with these priorities: "I am more concerned
about my child seeing violence on television than I am about them
seeing sex on television," he said. "Sex, that's a natural thing. That

Mb7b6g4

Fg8b5

Fb6

Mb8g6b4g3

Fb11g10

Fb10

Fg10

doesn't bother me at all. But violence and the fact that people can become immune to violence and don't react to it any more, that's frightening!" Diane said, "There are some things on television that disturb me and that I prefer my daughter not be hearing, but they're not sexual. They're words like *killed* or *died*. We've started turning off the news when she's around because it's so violent, and at this age I think violence is more of a problem than sex is." Mg4

Movies On Television

Movies on television—cable or regular—could present special problems. Films parents would not have permitted their children to see in a theater frequently ended up on the home screen. There was quite a difference between refusing to allow a child to travel to a theater and pay money to go in and see an objectionable film and having that same film clearly accessible—right there in the middle of the living room, the den, the bedroom, the kitchen—to anyone who wanted to turn on the set. And, even in films on television that had been cut, parents were not always confident that all the offending sexual matter had been excised.

For some parents, the solution was to try to treat the movies on television the same way they would treat movies in a theater. They monitored children's viewing very carefully, perusing daily TV listings and forbidding those films they considered unsuitable. Sharon had used this method with her seven-year-old. "He'll insist on watching some of the Mb7 R-rated things. I'll tell him beforehand, 'This is something I really don't want you to watch,' even if all the [sexy] spots aren't there." The father of an older child, a girl, handled such situations this way: "I'd Fg11 say, 'I don't think it's appropriate for you to watch it.' If I caught one of them watching it, I'd yank him away if I could." He was speaking particularly of X-rated cable-television shows. Trude said firmly, "I Mb10g7 don't want them to play around with the channels. I want to always know what they are seeing. No movies for grown-ups. Only movies for children."

But other parents acknowledged that they could not always enforce such limitations. First of all, it was hard to draw a firm line between these movies and the other, more innocuous television shows that flowed so closely around them. Secondly, there were no guarantees about what happened when children were visiting other homes or when parents were out. Jean described with considerable exasperation the kinds of problems many parents faced. "My husband makes every Mb10b8 attempt to censor television," she began. "I mean, he's ready to throw the television out of the house because we've lost control. But when we didn't have the cable TV, the children were going to their friends' houses who had it. I even called the friends' mothers and said, 'Please don't let my son watch it. We don't choose to have him watch these things. And they said, "Okay, I'll respect your opinion. And then I find out that mother's not home and he's over there watching and they have video cassettes and X-rated movies, and when the parents aren't home the kids are putting them in. You just have no control!" She stopped for a minute to catch her breath, then continued. "So then I felt they are going to do it anyhow. I've told them, 'If we are going to have it, we will have certain rules here. When we say absolutely not, it's absolutely—or it is going to go. We've let them watch a few things. More than a few things. I watch it with them. But when something really horrendous is on, we say, 'Hey, this is one we don't want you to watch.' Now they might be around, across the street, watching it at a friend's house. I don't know."

Indeed, Jean's compromise was one parents often had to be content with. And a comment made by one father of a ten-year-old, was Fb10 made again and again: "Either they are going to watch it here or they are going to watch it someplace else." So if parents could not always control what children had access to, it seemed wiser to watch some of the "borderline" movies with children at home. That way parents could be present to reassure, to answer questions, to make editorial com- Mg9b5 ments. "We're *there*," Betty said. "I wouldn't let them watch if we weren't there. Therefore, they're more likely to say, 'What's going on?' and we're more likely to tell them, or point out, 'That's an awful thing that just happened right there.' " Carol made a similar observation. Mg11 "My daughter has a TV in her own room," she said, "and I'll ask her many times, 'If you're watching a film like that, you should come down and watch it with me.' I'd rather her watch it with me and then if she has any questions she should feel free to ask them, rather than think the thoughts and not verbalize them at the time." Mark described the way a parent could provide some balance, some humor, and an astringent, realistic point of view to defuse the heavy action on the screen: Fb10 "We've got the X channel and he just is totally enthralled by it, very curious. I mean, he's in a cloud. When I got home from work today, there were six or seven boys in the room watching *Fame*. I had seen the movie twice before and I knew a scene with bare breasts was coming up and so I jokingly walked over and said, 'Let's watch the news,' just before the scene came on. My son was the first to jump up and say, 'No, No, No! We want to watch this movie!' So one of the girls in the movie took off her top and I said, 'Well, what's there to watch?' You've seen breasts before. What's the big deal?' "

Commercials

A large group of parents objected to provocative commercials featuring models in suggestive poses, in skintight or scanty clothes, and to advertisements for women's sanitary products. But though they were personally offended, many did not bother to make comments to their children. Commercials were too short for the kind of censoring parents did of television programs. As one father put it, "To run around and shut the tube every time there's a commercial on would be absolutely insane." They also believed that since the sexual messages were covert, they were often lost on children, who did not listen or took in only the obvious—the tunes or dances or thirty-second story lines. Vinny described his children's reaction to a pantyhose commercial. "They just think it's funny. The fact that there's ladies running around shoving their butts into the camera." Several mothers found that though their children seemed interested in jeans commercials—"Brooke Shields sitting upside down with Calvin Klein jeans on"—they did not respond to the sexual innuendos. Valerie said, "My kids seem to think it's just some kind of weird behavior. I don't think they have understood the sexual angles to it yet. I don't particularly like them, but children are bound to see them sooner or later." Geraldine felt much the same way. "My kids can sing all the jingles. They know all the brand-name jeans. But they don't pick up on the sexual inferences, that these jeans will make you sexy or anything like that. On their level it will just make you look good and you'll be in the crowd. But you are not sexy, not yet."

Jeans commercials, in fact, came in for a great deal of criticism from parents, largely because they presented children with distorted images of what was feminine and "sexy." Rudy admitted that he enjoyed these commercials because they are provocative, but he was also aware of the strong impression they had on his five-year-old daughter. "There is one where the girls come out, the boys come out too, and they kind of stick out their rear ends and show the label. She would go through the commercial complete with sticking out the rear end. I think it was just a stage and she went through it for a period of months. We don't see that behavior any more."

Mothers were generally more deeply offended. Sonia's daughter had "noticed" the tight-jeans commercials, and "chuckled" at them. "I have conflicts," she said, "because I feel that some of those type commercials are pretty degrading to women. I might have communicated that." Wanda was particularly angry about the explicit "hands-on-the-ass type of stuff" she saw in jeans advertising. "I felt it was exploitive, particularly with children. That one I said very specifically that I felt it was highly insulting to women. I said, 'You may never have Jordache jeans.' I tell them what my feelings are." She also objected, as did other parents, to the way in which sex was used to make an ordinary article more exotic (and more expensive) than it actually was. "Not only are the commercials insulting, they are also an economic rip-off and nobody should be dumb enough to pander to that. I mean, jeans are just jeans."

Some parents feared their children were being seduced by advertising images of sex and romance. Bart's son, Gregory, would comment on the figures of the women in commercials. "One I can think of, that tanning commercial or soda commercial where a series of legs keep popping up in bathing suits. Well, he watches it and sometimes he'll say to me. 'Oh boy, that's sexy.' And I'll say, 'What do you mean by *sexy?* He'll say, 'She's pretty, Dad,' depending on how much a person is hanging out of the bathing suit, which might influence him." Sometimes Bart found it necessary to talk to his son, to see that he was not brainwashed by the media "hype" of femininity. Much depended on how taken he thought Gregory was by a particular commercial. "When he pursues it, then we'll carry it out a little further. If the kid gets turned on by a commercial and waits for it every day and I don't make that observation I'll be a damn fool. If I notice that, I'll definitely say something to him. Maybe sometimes he sees it and internalizes it. Sometimes I choose to ignore it. We just let it lay. There's a lot of factors involved. It's not cut and dried." Sylvia also tried to stop her children from taking commercials too seriously. "If I would get the vibe that they're not just listening to a little jingle then I would discuss with them that this is business and this is how people sell things, by using models—male models, female models—and they are pretty. It's public relations." Linda made a similar point. "My daughter likes commercials. I'll try to tell her if something is not realistic. 'That's ridiculous. People don't really do that.' "

When parents did discuss commercials with their children, it was in fact often to criticize the distorted values implied rather than the sexual content per se. They criticized the shallow way in which love, relationships, sex roles, and social success were depicted, and they objected to the preposterousness of the situations portrayed. Betty, for one, hoped the ire certain "unfavorite" commercials provoked would be catching. "I mean, really, some of these commercials! I'll turn around and say to my children, 'You don't really believe that commercial!' or 'Doesn't that get you angry that they would have a girl sitting like that?' or 'What does that commercial mean to you?' Sometimes I get so angry! I think it's good that they're watching it and hope it will evoke a negative response from them as well." Esther found that poking fun at commercials worked with her son, who was eleven, but was not so successful in deflecting her six-year-old daughter's fascination with them. "I discuss ads with him and everything. We laugh over

Fb6

Mb9g8

Mg5

Mg9b5

Mb11g6

them. Like, 'Oh, if you buy this stuff you're gonna end up with this beautiful girl,' and stuff. And I do the same with my daughter. She might get mad at me. I end up being a killjoy."

Commercials for sanitary products and feminine hygiene were very unpopular. In some cases, they provoked children's curiosity about menstruation before parents were ready to talk about it. When asked to describe her least favorite commercial, the mother of a five-year-old girl replied promptly, "Modess commercials, tampons, things like Mg5 that—she doesn't say anything about it. But yesterday we needed tissues and she went to get Modess instead. I told her, 'No, it's not tissues, it's sanitary napkins. Women use that.' I was in the middle of Shop-Rite, so I didn't want to get into giving her a whole explanation."

But even parents who were comfortable discussing menstruation or vaginal discharge with children disliked the commercials. They saw them as still another put-down of women and they objected to the silly ways in which much was made of natural female phenomena. "I Mg10 get awfully tired of the feminine hygiene-type of things. They are so insipid. Such as, well, the one with the gymnastics and the little girl runs up and says, 'Why didn't you *tell* me that so-and-so has a new elastic strip?' or whatever it is. 'Why didn't you *tell* me they'd improved it?' I tend to make nasty comments. I talk back to television. About that one I say just how dumb it is."

Movies

Several parents were very strict about which movies they allowed their children to see. "He can see the children's *G*, General Admittance. Mb7 He can see those," Valerie said about her seven-year-old, "otherwise, I feel a child his age has no business in the movies." Trude would not go to adult movies with her children. "They are not ready yet. They Mg7 are children. They should stay in their world." But, surprisingly, a much larger number of parents did not believe in censoring movies for their children. Sometimes their reasons were pragmatic: no sitters were available, the family was going out with relatives or friends who had their hearts set on a film, only one movie was playing in their area or one theater was more accessible than the others. Sometimes they saw no reason to keep their children away from certain movies, particularly if the children were already accustomed to viewing films or programs with sexual content on television. There were also parents who spoke the same way about film as many parents had spoken about books: children could look at whatever they chose. "He can see anything he Mb11 wants to, anytime. This has always been the case," Joyce said. In actuality, however, the majority of these parents, even the most liberal, generally did not give their children carte blanche. Relaxation of standards did not mean relinquishment of all responsibility. If a movie contained parts which might frighten, upset, or embarrass children, or if it suggested values or behavior the parents disapproved of, they would alter their policies or at least strongly advise children that this movie was not for them.

Any kind of censorship of movies of course presented special problems, since parents did not screen the material ahead of time and could not turn the picture off or pull their children away once they were inside the theater. Carol described herself as an "open" parent, who had no objection to taking her children to R-rated movies. But she was disconcerted by the scene in a "teenage" hit film in which several boys, successively, have intercourse with the same girl. "So we took them to see *Saturday Night Fever* and they were very much exposed, and I was glad I was sitting next to them. I watched their reaction—a lot of it might have gone over Maggie's head, but Will was very much aware of what was going on. Like other parents who had had similar experiences, Carol decided to handle the situation as casually as possible, not say anything unless the children raised questions. "I didn't shield them from it. I didn't cover their eyes when there was a love scene in the back of the car. I waited for her to ask me what was going on and she did. I said, 'Well, they were making love.' " Carol's comments reflect the kind of dilemma many parents faced. How did they decide beforehand that a movie had scenes which were inappropriate for their children? And how did they explain these decisions to children who were clamoring to see a movie that all their friends said was "terrific" or starred their favorite rock or TV celebrity?

For parents who had firm rules about what children could or could not see the Motion Picture Association of America's rating system was helpful not only in letting them know which films were suitable but in providing "objective" standards—hard-and-fast rules for what was permissible, from a nonparental source. Parents found it convenient to cite the ratings as consistent, unchallengeable limits on children's viewing. Allen's son, at age eight, was curious about "sexy" movies. "He asks me, 'Could I go and see an R?'—and my answer is, 'No!' " Mona was equally firm. "He doesn't see *anything* that is X-rated!"

Parents who had more flexible policies might use the rating as general guidelines, which they could augment with their own feelings about what was acceptable. Margot would take her daughter to R-rated movies if she did not think the sex scenes were overly explicit. "There are movies where you'll see people making love under the blankets. As long as it doesn't get into real heavy passion." Other parents relied on their sense of just how mature the children were, how ready to handle the material which was provocative or racy. Olive remarked, "There

Mb11g8

Fb8
Mb11

Mg10

Mg14b13g9

are a few R-rated films that if I see them first, and if the kids express an interest in seeing them, I will have then reviewed them. Then I will either say, 'No, I saw it and it's really too much for you,' or I let her see it."

For Maeve's daughter, being taken to an occasional R-rated movie represented a minor milestone on the way to adolescence and adulthood. "She saw her first R-rated movie last week. Marsha Mason, *Only When I Laugh*, which was fine. We do talk about it. It's a big thing now to see an R-rated movie. It's 'Well, I saw *three* R movies.' She was quite pleased to see *Only When I Laugh* because it was R and she could tell her friends. I saw no reason for her not to see that movie." But the process was gradual and required monitoring on Maeve's part. "There are times she doesn't get to see the movie because of sexuality or violence, and she doesn't always accept it. There are some she really would like to see—*Saturday Night Fever*. When that was R-rated she didn't see that. I told her that I felt there were some things that she was still too young to see and when she got a little bit older she would be allowed to go. She was very disappointed about that one." Mg11

Some parents found the ratings unreliable and did not refer to them at all in selecting movies for their children or used them only in conjunction with additional sources: advertisements, reviews, recommendations from other adults. Geraldine remarked, "I don't really go by PG or anything like that. Sometimes they might be rated PG but not for four-year-olds. I usually look for movies that *are* for four-year-olds, mainly Walt Disney and nature movies." Another mother took her children to see only "fairy tales and movies about animals. And love stories. I mean, nice love stories." Mona made this observation. "Some of the shows that are rated R or PG can be confusing as to what the rating is [for]. There are things that you wouldn't want him to see that are PG but you might let him see that are R. You have to know what the film is about. Generally, I'll ask people who have seen it before or try to investigate it further." She offered an illustration of her point: "I have taken him to see R-rated movies. One was *Black Sunday*. I went with [some friends]—I probably wouldn't have gone in there at all, just by looking at the ratings. They had that Woody Allen movie on one side, which had a lot of sexual scenes in it. I asked the manager and he told me that *Black Sunday* was considered a bit violent, but it really wasn't that bad, and he was absolutely right." Mg4 Mb11

Sometimes children made the job of monitoring easier through their own predilection for films with nonsexual topics. "Well, it's not so much that I censor them as that she censors them for herself," Olive said. "It really boils down to what she is interested in. She is more interested in the Muppets than something [sexy]. I mean, this is what she will censor for herself." Charles had had the same kind of experience. "There are some movies that we just try to talk him out of be- Mg9 Fb11 cause we just know he isn't going to like them. I mean things like *Blue Lagoon*. I don't think he'd like them if they were just about sex. I just tell him it's nothing you'd like and explain why, if I can—that it's a lot of talk and no action and it's a sad story. I know what he likes pretty well—action and comedy mainly. Sometimes he doesn't bug me on it," he added with a grin. And, once in a while, the children's isolated interest in nonsexual aspects of a movie with otherwise highly sexual content—cars or rock music, for instance—influenced parents.

Mg4 "She loves John Travolta," one mother said of a decision to take her daughter to see *Grease*. "The songs, that's all she knows." One father
Fb11 remarked, "It depends. I relented on *Heavy Metal*. The main reason— he wanted to see it because it had a rock-music background and he's all into rock music now."

Ultimately, therefore, most parents made decisions to restrict viewing on a movie-by-movie basis. But no matter how diligent they were, no matter how carefully they read or asked around, there were problems in figuring out exactly where to draw the line. How much sexual content was "too much"? What kinds of scenes or characters made a film seem potentially harmful to a child? As one mother observed with
Mg4 a sigh, "It depends on the movie. There's a million shades of gray. Too many different shades." And, indeed, a number of different factors could contribute.

For many parents, *comprehension* was an important consideration, though there was disagreement about the effect of sex scenes on children who were still uninformed. Several mothers feared that very young children would be upset by observing sexual activity even if they did not quite understand what was going on. More typical, however, were parents who believed that sexual material was unlikely to bother chil-
Mg11 dren who were not ready to put it all together. "So they hear it. If they understand it, fine. And if they didn't, it went over their heads, good."
Fb11 Seymour made a similar comment. "When my son was younger, and we saw a movie that dealt with sex, if he didn't understand it, there was no harm. If he understood it, it was about time he saw it!" The boy is eleven now, and is able to take in sexual information in a clear-headed and mature fashion, putting it into the context of what he has learned about sexual relationships. "I look at him and he's not embarrassed at all. He takes it as a matter of fact. He takes sex as a matter of fact. He knows his mother and father have sex and he sees it on the screen and I'm sure he's read about it in books."

Frequently, in fact, lascivious or suggestive material that might set parents to cringing was regarded by children merely as uproarious slapstick. In *Hair*, Charles's son watched a skinny-dipping scene
Fb11 with obvious sexual content. "He thought that was hilarious. He was knocked out by it. To him it wasn't sexual, it was comic." For Morris's
Fg8 eight-year-old daughter, "it was *Arthur* and he brought a prostitute back

to his apartment and she laughed at a lot of that. She really didn't know what a prostitute was. She just laughed about the bed." Cynthia had been taking her son to movies with mild sexual content from the time he was about six years old. "When he was real little we took him to an R-rated movie, *Next Stop, Greenwich Village*. One of the characters in the movie asked somebody, 'Have you had sex?' and later, when we left, he asked us, 'Was that socks?' We laughed about it. We told him, 'No, it was *sex*.' "   Mb6

For some parents, any movie that contained scenes of intercourse was a "no-no," but for others it was the *quality* or *quantity* of the scenes containing sexual activity that determined acceptability. "My daughter realizes that men and women sleep together, and if there's a scene where there's a man and a woman in bed, that's fine. I think she can deal with this," Maeve said, "I draw the line when there is a lot of nudity and a lot of sexuality because I don't think she's ready for it." Sylvia would not let her daughter see any movies with "heavy sex— *Last Tango in Paris* or whatever—those kind." Margot listed the kinds of scenes she thought unsuitable for her ten-year-old daughter: "Where you see their bodies, where it lasts for a long time, where you hear the heavy breathing and where it's a real turn-on. I guess it's if I get turned on by it—she's too young," she put in with a laugh. "She's already very interested, and I really think she's got time." She went on to provide a more specific example of the type of scene that made her uncomfortable. "There was a movie that I took her to where I felt she observed something inappropriate, which was *Private Benjamin*. I did not like her seeing it. There's an early scene where she gets married and her husband is this totally, monstrously inappropriate lover, who virtually rapes her on the bathroom floor and dies in the middle of the rape. "The rest of the movie was delightful for her," Margot laughed again, "but I really felt that was—I don't like her seeing sex in that way."   Mg11   Mg5   Mg10

The *context* of a particular sexual scene and the *attitude* with which it was presented could also affect censoring decisions. Scenes that flowed naturally out of character and incident were more acceptable than those that seemed exploitive, "stuck in" to titillate or arouse. Wanda said she would reject a movie "where the object is to show couples having intercourse," whereas "a movie like *Kramer vs. Kramer*, where it's made incidental to the plot, doesn't bother me." She remarked that she, like Margot, often used her own responses to a particular scene as a guide. "I feel like a voyeur in a sense, that you shouldn't be watching this and she shouldn't either. I tell her just that I think a particular movie is going to be too sexy and that I don't think that it's right that she should be doing it. And she handles that." For Elizabeth, the tone and intensity of the sexual material mattered considerably. She was very cautious about the kinds of movies she would allow her   Mg10

eight-year-old daughter to see. Nevertheless, certain Burt Reynolds films that featured light-hearted and humorous sexual activities—
Mg8 "Those ones he had which kind of, you know, cleaningly went over it"—were "okay."

Several parents made it clear that the *values* being transmitted by sexual material also could influence their decisions. Mona spoke at
Mg16b11 length of her strong feelings about this issue. "I don't let my children be brainwashed in any areas that are against their own values within the house. So I would not allow them to see sexual situations. A feeling of affection, yes, but every time we turn around somebody is always in bed, which is another way of saying that you can have the need for sexual pleasure but it has no meaning. I don't want either one of my children to get the idea that if they go to see ten movies on premarital relationships, where a man and a woman are living together, that I accept that. And if this is what they are constantly seeing, it means that this is what society is all about and I condone it. So, yes, I want to monitor everything!"

Other parents were concerned about scenes that involved sadism
Fg5 or acts they considered perverse. "The only thing I would consciously censor is some kind of 'Kinky sex,' or something like that," Steve said. "But just plain old kissy-kissy or get-into-bed-together or premartial sex, not that."

Several parents cited sexual scenes that, while artistically commendable in context for adults, were far too powerful, too complex, too ambiguous, or too violent for children to cope with. Betty remarked,
Mg9b5 "I guess we feel that if there's sexual intonations in a movie, it's not going to hurt them. But we would censor something that would terrify them—like a rape movie." Along the same lines, Cynthia told this story:
Mb10 "We saw a movie this summer and we worried about it. It was *Blume in Love,* and the husband was trying to get his wife back and he rapes her, and I felt uncomfortable with that. Any time you see violence with sex. It wasn't very bad and he didn't say anything about it. It wasn't nudity or anything. It was the violence of the attack that wor-
Mb12g8 ried me." Another mother said, "I didn't feel that *The Four Seasons* would be appropriate, even though it had nothing specifically sexual in it. It was just too . . . " she shrugged and shook her head. "A lot of things I do with my kids are just gut feeling. It's just in my heart I know this is right and this is wrong." She mentioned other movies she would reject on this instinct that they were, overall, simply too sophisticated for children—*Shampoo* and *Ragtime.*

A few parents mentioned certain currently popular horror films with
Mg5 psychosexual overtones as particularly reprehensible. "*Friday the Thirteenth* or *Halloween*—that kind of crap," as one mother put it, bluntly, "—sadistic violence." As with magazines and television, *violence* in the movies concerned most parents, and a substantial number considered

violent material at least as harmful to children—if not more so—than   Mg10
sexual material. "Probably the violence disturbs me more," Wanda said.   Fg9g5
"I'm just very sensitive to it. I find it frightening—very, very disturbing." Rudy also thought that since violence "is not something I would   Fb11
like for my children to be exposed to continuously," he would tend to
censor violence more heavily than sexuality. "It would depend on the
level of sexuality." Another father, who put few limitations on his son's
moviegoing, refused to take his son to "one of those karate things which   Mb11
he was dying to go to." And a mother who believed in "censoring out
violence" would not let her children see *The Godfather.* "There is a   Fb11g10
scene where it's too real. I'm equal on both sex and violence, not one
over the other."

Sexual language, on the other hand, was not a particularly important issue for most parents. Fred was resigned to a certain amount of
"raunchy" language in films he took children to see. "I consider it   Fb11
impossible to control bad language and don't really try. I don't consider it that big an issue. If you're reasonably liberal about what movies your children see, which I am, you're going to get a lot of sexual
language at home. They go to the movies, even a movie which I
thought would be very innocent—*Bad News Bears*—I thought it was a
kids' movie. Every third word was *fuck* or *ass* or something. So obviously if you're going to take kids to the movies you're implying that
you approve of the language that they're listening to, so you're going
to get more of it at home." Like Fred, Charles did not think there was
much he could do about the language his son might pick up at the
movies. "There is a lot of the vulgar language, more than they really   Mg14g9
need to have. I don't say anything. Frankly, it's pretty hopeless. My
son knows far more of those words than I ever did at his age."

Olive reported that her children themselves occasionally objected
to pervasive use of "four-letter" words in movies the family had seen
together. "I took them to see *Hooper* and the language got to all of   Fg11b6
them. I remember at one point Niki and Joellen started to count the
number of off-color words, because it was just getting to the point of
being silly." Another parent was a good deal more sanguine. "In *E.T.*
they use the word *penis* and *shit.* No problem," he remarked. "My
kids can hear those words. They've heard worse on the street. For that
sort of movie, I'm sure in its context it's just kind of a natural thing."

In spite of the care so many parents took in selecting movies for
their children to see, quite a few admitted that they had occasionally
made mistakes. On the basis of the rating, their own instincts, or
circumstances, they had taken children to films which had turned out
to be totally unsuitable. Rachel recalled feeling terribly uncomfortable
when "ostensibly PG" movies she was watching with her sons turned
out to contain explicitly sexual scenes. "I am curious myself. I wonder   Mb6
how people are coping with the fact that society now is showing much

more openly many things that you would never have shown to children ten years ago." A number of parents who had been "caught" in similar situations talked about their embarrassment and suggested some answers to Rachel's query.

Fb6   I take them to see this movie. For some reason, I don't know why, a woman came in front of the camera naked from the waist up. Her breasts were exposed and she was there for a flash of a second. Well, the only thing they remembered from the whole movie was the lady that was naked. Everything else in the movie the kids didn't really pick up on. But because there were two naked breasts on the thing for five seconds they focused on that. I couldn't understand, with all the madness going on in the movie, why. And then I wondered why I took them to see that movie. It was only because it was the best one playing and I promised I would take them to a show. I got caught on that one. Yeah, when I bomb, I usually bomb big!

Mg9   At one point he sat through a film I didn't watch first and I was a little embarrassed for a few minutes but I didn't let him know. It was an orgy scene. These bodies are swarming on the ground. I figured I can't make him get up and leave, so I figured, Okay, he could see if he could handle this. That would raise questions, I thought, but he didn't raise any. I got a little upset at the time.

Mb11   There have been several occasions where we went to see movies that were PG that turned out to have pieces that overwhelmed me. I sat there dumbfounded. We would talk about it and he took them in stride. There was one movie where there was some nude dancing and he was sitting next to me and I said, "Ed, look away, don't look at that," and I was kidding. But I think he didn't quite know how to deal with it. Afterwards I said, "I have no doubt that you know about those things. Let's be realistic about it. I was uncomfortable being there with you and I suspect you were a lot more comfortable than I was."

Museums

Art featuring nudity or sexual themes that was shown in museums presented fewer problems for parents than drawings and photographs of the same kinds of subjects in books and periodicals around the house. For many parents, the intent of the piece or the attitude toward sex that had motivated it made the difference between a work of art and a "dirty picture." I kind of distinguish between sex in art and sex as

Mb8   pornography," one mother remarked. "If you have one picture with a nude person in it or two people in it, it's one thing, but if you have a *Penthouse*-magazine picture in full-blown color, a sexually explicit picture, then it's different." Parents often had difficulty determining precisely what made some materials artistic and others prurient, but it seemed safe to say that a nude displayed in a museum had been selected for its aesthetic qualities, whereas a nude depicted in a popular magazine or book might be there just for titillation. A number of parents made the same point. "If it's in a museum, it's a thing of beauty and just treat it that way," a mother said. "And I think they'll accept it that way." Mg11

Children, of course, were not always as sophisticated about "contexts" as their parents were. They giggled when they saw the voluptuous bodies of women in a painting, smirked and pointed at the exposed genitalia on a statue. Parents then found themselves trying to explain the spiritual or historical value of this type of representation. One mother, herself a painter, expounded on "color and texture and this and that. And that people for centuries have been trying to create images of the body on canvas, in sculpture—in marble, in granite, whatever—as a piece of artwork. Masterpieces. The body is beautiful I don't say it's 'naughty, naughty' only because it shows a penis." A father put it this way: "Now if we were going to a museum and he saw this naked lady standing there, a painting, and he said to me, 'How come this lady's up there with no clothes on, Daddy?' I'd say, 'This artist wanted to paint a person's body and it became a very famous painting,' and kind of relate it to the person's works." Then he added, "If I could do that," and a moment later acknowledged, "he might not accept that." Linda told her daughter, "Oh, the body is great, Tina. God made us. We're special things, so that people like to paint pictures of the body naked." And Esther thought that observing beautiful bodies in paintings could be a healthy experience for a child. "I should take my daughter to see Rubens. She hasn't seen that yet. Then she'll ask me about bodies, yeah, but it's not like 'the Jordache look.' " Mg5 Fb6 Mg5 Mg6

Most parents applied the same criteria to pictures suggesting love-making or sexual situations: if the picture was in a museum, it was all right for their children to look at it. Lyle saw no reason to hustle his son away if he happened to catch a glimpse of "Japanese prints or something"—couples in sexual positions, for instance. "I wouldn't make a big deal of it and I wouldn't slap my hand over his eyes and drag him away. If he asked what they were doing I would answer as honestly as I could. And I can't imagine myself saying anything to the effect that, 'That's not for you, that's dirty stuff.' I would hopefully come up with some reasonable explanation, that they had dropped their marbles and were looking under the table for it," he concluded with a sly grin. Fb7

But a few parents were more uneasy about their children, particularly young ones, seeing this kind of erotica. Often, their major concern was not moral but psychological. In this area, as in many others, they wanted to protect children who were still uninformed about sex from images they might misunderstand. Usually, children who spotted a work their parents preferred them not to see could be diverted.

Mb7b6g4   Sheila said, "You don't want to get all uptight about it. I would try to steer them away, distract them." Another mother also stressed the fact that she would not want to shock or hurt her child by reacting with

Mb10   alarm. "I say, 'Oh, this is an awful picture. Let's turn around.' And I try to get his attention to something different. Sometimes he sees a picture, but not clearly enough, and then I just take him away and I don't have to talk about it. I can ignore it, but if necessary I will not ignore it. If necessary I will explain why it's not so good a picture and he will accept it."

Billboards, Posters, and Graffiti

Most parents were resigned to the fact that children were going to be exposed to blatant or tasteless sexual slogans, anecdotes, and pictures wherever they went. For that reason, they felt it was useless to make an issue over the advertising on billboards, book jackets, theater mar-

Mg11   quees, and so on. "I'm sure my mother would put her hands over my eyes," Carol said, laughing. But censorship was pretty much out of the question today, when such displays are everywhere. "You can't

Fb4   close your eyes to these things," she continued. "It's very overt." "Well, it seems inevitable," Vinny pointed out. "Kids do see these things, if only to go past the rack at the supermarket. The drug store has an incredible array of stuff. You know, it's quite out there." Morris

Fb5   maintained a realistic, moderate attitude. "The billboards—Coppertone has one which is a dog pulling down the pants of a little girl and you see her rear end. My son says, 'Oh, look at that tushy!' and we would laugh. I do nothing. Nothing."

Generally parents thought it was best not to react at all when their children saw suggestive advertising, though a few wanted children to know that they disapproved even if they weren't doing anything about

Mb11   it. One mother remarked, "We walk down 42nd Street. How can I prevent him from seeing what the titles [of the movies] are or some of the shots that are on the front. I mean, I can't keep him in a glass cage. But the thing is to explain that this is not our value. 'Mommy and Daddy don't go to see those pictures. And look at the people that come out of them!' " Other parents decided to say something if the children seemed interested or attracted by the material. One mother felt that if her daughter talked about a poster that was "dirty," she would not open up a long discussion on the subject, but she would not let it go, either. "I might mention my disapproval of it being there. I want her to feel the difference very much between reality and representations for reality." Another said that her first response if her son giggled "at a billboard with a lady with big breasts or whatever selling beer" would be to say nothing. But if the giggling continued, she would try to deal with the boy's underlying embarrassment about seeing the female body so exposed. "I would talk to him and say, 'Now, let's discuss—what's so funny, really?' Then we would get back, probably, to the fact that a man is physically different from a woman. And he would be so content with that that it wouldn't faze him again."

Parents were a little more attentive when children observed sexual graffiti. The purpose of graffiti was lost on some children—those below five often failed to notice—but others seemed to enjoy it, relish the fact that they "caught" the jokes and saw the taboo words out in the open. Sometimes they "tested" their parents, repeated an anecdote or phrase that had been on a bathroom wall, hoping to get away with using forbidden terms in this indirect fashion. Sonia said, "She's quoted things that she's read on walls. About people having intercourse or bathroom functions, or just intimate details that people scribble on walls about people they know. She thinks it's pretty funny, too." Wanda found that her daughter developed an appreciation of graffiti after she was bussed to an inner-city school from the suburb where the family lived. "The kids there are a lot more sophisticated than the ones here, and so she probably has a language rich in expletives and sexual-type words. She would come and say, 'Oh, I just saw *fuck* written.' She likes to tell me about it." Wanda chose not to say anything because she thought that "getting off on graffiti"—producing it, too— was probably a natural part of growing up. "I can remember drawing nude people and trying to draw genital drawings and that sort of thing. So I would suspect that she does some of that, too. It doesn't bother me." But she voiced a concern that was echoed by other parents. "I would hope that she wouldn't deface somebody's property."

In fact, a number of parents said that they preferred not to waste time and breath in an argument with children over the objectionable words or pictures themselves but focused instead on non-sexual issues like improper forms of self-expression and the marring of public or private spaces. Sonia deflected her daughter's interest in graffiti in a direct, no-nonsense way. "I think I've concentrated on the fact that people shouldn't be scribbling up somebody else's walls." At least one mother discovered that her son had created his own graffiti on the basement

Mg10

Mb9

Mg11

Mg10

Mg11

Mb11   wall and was more outraged by the fact that he had spoiled a room that belonged to the family than by the sexual drawings themselves. "Last Friday my son had a friend over. [They used] Mercurochrome, a spray can, and God knows what those boys were doing. I wasn't here. I was away for the weekend. You go away once a year. . . ." She laughed rather grimly. "They're gonna paint over it next Monday, as a matter of fact. They drew testicles and balls. It's quick. It's a sketchy thing. My husband went through the roof. The main thing was that they were writing on the walls!"

Mb11   When children themselves made no comment, many parents would not call attention to graffiti by criticizing or explaining it. One mother said, "Sometimes overexplaining things can be just as detrimental as not saying anything, and you just have to use your discretion. I wouldn't even say to him, 'Don't look at that. Turn your head!' There are too many things. I'd have to take his head off. I think from going into the city so much he just takes it for granted." But if the child did

Mg5   notice—"Oh, there's a dirty word!" "Oh, this neighborhood is dirty" —the parent might choose to talk about the scribblings, interpret a drawing or word, express disapproval, counteract the crude depiction

Mb11   of sex with another point of view. Mona took this approach. "I say that love and feelings are beautiful and that sex is something that is very private and very sacred and very beautiful, and to make fun of somebody's private parts is ugly."

Adult Merchandise

Several parents reported that their children had come in contact with adult novelties of an erotic nature or sexual devices such as vibrators, dildos, or "blow-up" dolls. Circumstances differed. Though most parents said they would not take their children into stores that sold these kind of things, children could stroll by shops displaying the articles in their windows. Sometimes outsiders brought the novelty items into the house as a "joke" or out of more serious interest in this aspect of sex.

Fb8   It was my wife's thirty-fifth birthday and a couple—they are old friends of ours—brought her a gag gift, something called a Venus Fly-Trap. It said Venus Fly-Trap on the outside and when you opened it, there was a zipper which you could open, and a penis popped out. My son really thought it was a plant and opened the box quite innocently. He must have turned a dozen shades of red and everybody laughed. I felt a little bad for him.

We had an exhibit, a young woman from the sexual gifts store in   Mb10
Chicago, to display all kinds of paraphernalia, sexual instruments and
stuff, and my children saw them at that time. I invited a few people
over. The kids weren't actually in the room, but they were coming
in and out, asking, "What's this? What's that?" and I told them.

In some cases, parents themselves used the devices and children
discovered them. Gail encountered several such potentially disconcerting incidents and spoke at length about how she had reacted. "A cou-   Mg4
ple of Christmases ago my husband came home with one of these
vibrators that they advertise on TV. It's got all these attachments. The
next morning the vibrator was in the box on the floor. I just forgot
about it and my daughter came down and said, 'What is this thing?' So
I said, 'Oh, it's a massage machine. Daddy was using it to exercise the
muscles because they are tight.' And she said, 'Can I use it?' I said,
'No,' and my husband said, 'It's electric and you are not allowed to
play with anything electric.' That was it." But Gail felt that she would
respond quite differently as her daughter, Emma, grew older. "Right
now—'Well, that's used for a massage.' Later, when she's older, I'll
say, 'Yes, it's for sex. It's between your father and me. That's a private matter.' I think there's a certain privacy I can request of her. I
don't think any child should feel they can ask their parents, 'Well did
you make love last night?' or 'How many times a week do you make
love?' I think there are some things that can be kept private without
being forbidden. It's just a courtesy thing. There are some things you
don't ask."

In the urban area where the family lives, Gail's daughter has had
several opportunities to see adult merchandise outside the home. When
Emma was three, the family visited an acquaintance's loft. Gail recalled,
with amusement what happened that day. "In another part of the loft
was a place that sold sexy toys, everything from dildos to the blow-up
dolls. Anyway, the door was open and she was wandering in and I
heard her say, "Mommy, Mommy, look at all these toys! Oh, all these
pink things!" And there were these huge penis-shaped vibrators and
she said, "Look at those pink mushrooms!" Everybody was laughing.
We were hysterical. Everybody was apologizing to me. I said, "Don't
you apologize. I'm sorry she walked in and that's it." It wasn't a traumatic thing. She thought it was a wonderful toy factory!" More recently,
an adult gift store had opened in the neighborhood. "She admired their
Christmas tree. They had all these sex toys hanging on it. She just
noticed them as Christmas ornaments. Each one was tied up with a
red bow or something. She didn't know what they were. I'll just tell
her, 'That's called a vibrator,' or a dildo, or whatever. She likes to know
the names of things. I think if I just say it like that, treat it as a casual,
everyday thing. . . ."

Whatever the situation, however, like Gail, most parents tried to respond sensitively to their children's curiosity. Whenever possible, they allowed children's innocent assessments of these peculiar grown-up articles—"It's like a back-scratcher," "It's a pillow!" "It's a toy"—to stand, or fudged a bit, offering relaxation as the purpose of the devices. But if such answers seemed too outlandish, they tried to be honest, though the general rule of thumb was to be brief, as well. Generally, they protected their own privacy or avoided embarrassing, overly graphic descriptions with short, truthful explanations—"Adults use them to have sex"—and left it at that.

10

. . . *Mores*

Since subjects like homosexuality, unmarried couples, single parenthood, and childlessness by choice are so openly discussed today, children heard about these subjects in various ways. Sometimes they
learned from personal experience—the family had gay or lesbian acquaintances, or relatives, a single adult they knew had a live-in lover,
a friend was being raised without a father. Sometimes they got their
information from the media—a television show or feature article on
current mores. Several of their favorite movie, television, or recording
stars moved from partner to partner; a few were known to be homosexual or bisexual.

When children had questions about these lifestyles, as well as
more "far out" ones like celibacy, or open marriage, parents were faced
with a multifaceted dilemma. In trying to explain such arrangements,
many had to come to terms with their most basic feelings in relation to
sexual preferences that existed outside the social "norm." Most parents did not want to condemn people's choices, and believed that children must learn to respect others' rights to live as they wish. But they

confessed that it was often difficult to talk objectively and tolerantly about situations which made them uneasy personally or went counter to their conceptions of morality. There was some fear, as well, that if they spoke in an accepting way of alternative lifestyles, they might be conveying the idea that it was absolutely "okay" for children to make one of these nontraditional sexual choices for themselves. At the same time, parents did not want children to feel that unless they acted as their parents expected, they would automatically be rejected. Personal freedom, self-respect, and contentment were important, too.

Parents were asked first how they would explain each lifestyle to their children, and then what their reactions would be if a child selected the lifestyle when she grew up. In answering, many parents said that they gained unexpected insights into their attitudes toward life options generally very different from their own.

Homosexuality

Homosexuality was an extraordinarily emotion-laden issue. Most parents tried to explain it to their children in a neutral or accepting fashion but occasionally had to deal with their own—or their children's—complicated reactions to this lifestyle. When children were below the age of five or so, the subject seldom came up because at that age they were unaware that men could be attracted to men and women to women. But older children accumulated a great deal of information about homosexuality on their own, from observing friends or relatives who were gay or lesbian, or simply from society at large.

Mg5   My daughter's been in the big city and she has seen people holding hands, and I have mentioned once or twice that some women live with women and that some men love men and they don't want to have girlfriends. A friend of mine had a homosexual relationship.

Mb9   I have a gay relative and I think that she indirectly or directly may have had discussions with my son. Though I haven't actually said, "Do you know Aunt So-and-so is a Lesbian?"; he can't help picking up the clues. It's not that we've discussed it openly—whether it's good or bad or indifferent. It's just that not everybody likes people in the same way.

Fb11   We have experienced it in our neighborhood. Two women living together. They were both married and now they are living together in a homosexual relationship. And it's been discussed quite openly, and he knows exactly what it is. They only live two blocks away from us. His first reaction was, "They don't look any different." Male homosexuality is a little bit different because the only occasion he has had to see male homosexuality was on two or three occasions I have brought him to the city. And he did notice homosexuals. They were walking arm in arm, two men. He wasn't disturbed by it at all. He questioned at first, because they are walking arm in arm, hand on tush. He thought that unusual and I said, "Unusual for you but not for them."

Frequently, children picked up negative attitudes toward homosexuality from the environment, as well. Sometimes they adopted slang terms for homosexual as "put-downs," assaults on peers whom they did not like or who were not in the in-crowd. One mother described how the terms were used. *"Faggot* means *queer. Queer* means *odd. Gay* Mb9 means the same thing: *odd."* Boys were especially vulnerable to this type of teasing and became very anxious or angry, even though they had little idea of what was actually meant. "He gets terribly upset," a Mb10 mother remarked about her ten-year-old son. "He will overrespond to someone tormenting him and saying, 'You queer,' and his reaction is way out of proportion to what it should be." Helen also noted the loose way in which children applied the terms. "It seems like every kid in Mb12b9 America, five and up, knows about homosexuality. They know the term *gay*. The kids just bandy it about all the time. I hear it used a lot as a kind of light-hearted insult. Usually all it means is sort of a 'dumb dodo' or 'He's not my favorite friend at the moment.' It's all over the culture." She had therefore decided to explain the real meaning in an objective manner, but discovered that it was difficult for her sons to alter the concepts they had already been taught about masculinity and share her accepting attitude. She had told her sons, "[I said] 'That's when two members of the same sex are attracted to each other and want to make love to one another.' Both my sons were really incredulous about that. That seems to them just sort of distasteful. They were just very surprised. I mean, once they heard about men and women, they just couldn't imagine why one boy would want to be with another boy."

Since children were bound to hear about "gays" sooner or later, many parents, like Helen, took it upon themselves to give straightforward explanations of homosexuality, stressing the point that it was a way of life different from but not inferior to their own. Sylvia said, "I Mg5 would try and define the thing. What homosexuality is, about their lifestyle. Homosexuals like their own sex, want to love their own sex, almost, like, marry their own sex. They could find out it's not something psychological, it's something physical, too." When Elizabeth's daughter had seen a program about lesbians on television, Elizabeth told her, "A girl likes to kiss another girl and hug a girl, likes a girl the same way Mommy and Daddy do." Some parents spoke of homosexu-

Fg7

ality in the context of personal freedom, people's *right* to do what they wish. George took this stand with his daughter. "Our friend and his friend live together and love each other. It's something that people have a right to do. She knows that her Mom and Daddy support people's rights to do what they want, privately. I think that's the lesson we want to teach her."

Mg11

Parents whose children had already talked in derisive terms about homosexuals wanted to correct these attitudes quickly and firmly. Leigh was disturbed because her daughter had called a hairdresser a *homo*. "I said to her, because she said it in a derogatory way, that each person has his or her own desires. Some people are heterosexual, they like the opposite sex; some people like their own sex, but in every other way that person is identical to anyone else. It's just that a particular need is a little different, and that's all there is to it." Paula prohibited

Mg11

"making fun of a person because he's a homosexual or 'gay' or 'a fag,' which words I don't like to use. It's like making fun of a person because he's Jewish or he's short, because he's tall or wears glasses. We don't have to make fun of people. This applies to women as well."

Mb3

Two mothers objected to their children's reactions to negative stereotypes. At three, Joyce's son was already saying, "Dancing is for girls." He had picked up impressions "from out there—from living, from being in [nursery school], from all those vibrations and assumptions that are put out there in the culture—and put [them] together in some funny way." But Joyce intended to contradict the idea that dancing (or any other activity, for that matter) was not masculine. "Certainly

Mg16b13b10g7

I think dancing is wonderful for men *and* women." Ruth's children had a French teacher who was gay. "They have heard me make nasty remarks to them when they make fun of his high-pitched voice or his fragile physique, or whatever. It annoys me because I would like them to understand that there's a minimal relationship, that you could have someone very masculine-looking, and one doesn't judge those things that way."

Like a number of parents, Stacey found it useful to demonstrate to children that hostility toward homosexuals was just another form of prejudice. When one of her son's friends began "throwing around" terms like *queer* and *fag*, she was able to give him a concrete illustra-

Mb11

tion of how unreasonable his bias was. "I said something to the boy who was using the language (who comes from a very tough kind of family), I said, 'Hey, Gino, do you like The Village People?' And he said, 'Yeah, they're really great!' And I said, 'Well, they announced they were all gay.' And he looked at me, and I made a point that it's easy to use terminology if you don't know anybody or anything else, so you can put down a whole group of people. I said, 'If you think about it, are they good entertainers?' And he said, 'Oh, yeah, I really like them.' And I said, 'Well, you're using words that would be very negative about them, too.' So we talked about that."

In one instance a parent wanted to counteract the views of a less open-minded relative. "We've talked about homosexuality because, well, for example, an aunt that we are very close to has very harsh attitudes toward homosexuality. So I've explained that to my daughter, along the lines of understanding people who are homosexual, accepting them and not thinking of them as bad or weird or anything." Polly had encountered the reverse situation. Her children were so relaxed about homosexuality that she felt she ought to warn them that not all people shared the family's tolerant views. *"The Leaping Lesbians* song— that's one of their favorite songs. I had to limit it when they had tape-recorded it and were playing it for all the neighborhood kids. I figured I would be run out of the neighborhood. But, yes, they just love that. But then they wanted to *know*, you know. Well I had to explain to them *why* I didn't think they should play it for all the neighborhood kids, though they might enjoy it. I had to explain that this is something that some people think is really, you know, bad."

Parents also expressed varying degrees of discomfort about describing homosexuality to their children. Several said they would not go into the mechanics of lovemaking between homosexual partners. Peter had introduced his son to a male couple, friends of the family. "I say they live together or could even say they're lovers but would be very reluctant to discuss how they make love." Others tried to let their children know that though homosexuals, like any minority group, should be treated with tolerance and respect, they considered homosexuality outside the "mainstream." Rosaline said, "About gay I said that a man might like to be more with another man—and the same with a woman—but that most of us like to find somebody who is from the opposite sex to make a home with." Andrew told his son that homosexuality is an "illness" but also emphasized that "all people should be treated as people." Wanda did not think that homosexuals in our society could be very happy. "I've known a lot of male homosexuals because of working for years in fashion and I have no particular problems about discussing them. We treat it rather casually. I would probably express my opinion. I feel that homosexuals are kind of a sad lot and that they are destined to live differently and it's never pleasant. And some people just love people of the same sex and they don't love people of the opposite sex, and that they have relationships and live together, and that is probably as far as I have gone into it."

A much smaller number of parents took a more distinctly negative stance against homosexuality when they talked about it to their children. The term that recurred in these discussions was "abnormal." Trude gave "just a short explanation. That it's sex between men and it's abnormal. Lesbians, the same way. Normal sex is between different sexes and not the same sexes. And they accepted that." Another mother said she would tell her son "it's abnormal and why it's abnormal. Be-

Mg11

Mb7b5

Fg9

Mg7

Fb9

Mg10

Mb10g7

Mb11

cause the female was meant to be part of the male. The union is formed to propagate. I really live by the Ten Commandments. It may sound weird in today's society. I mean, I don't go to church. But it's somewhere in there. The reason the Bible condemns homosexuality is because you are supposed to propagate." Mona spoke candidly of an experience which evoked her general repugnance to overt homosexuality. "My husband got caught in the Gay Parade one day. We saw him on TV when he was trying to cross the street. We had a few phone calls. I thought that was funny. My son thought that was funny. My husband was really pissed off. The one time he didn't want to get caught in a parade." Later she added, "My son and I talked about the Gay Parade. It's like when my son was going to nursery school and the hippie era was on then and you saw the pony tails on the guys. I would turn and say to him, 'How would like to wear your hair like that?' because that didn't look like Daddy or anybody he knew, and he said, 'Yuk.' Therefore, you start teaching your values at a very early age. We discussed the Gay Parade and I said, 'Isn't it a pity that parents have to see this, and isn't it a pity it says *Teachers*'—a bunch of teachers marching! And that people don't have to march to prove they are heterosexual—why do they have to be flamboyant about their homosexuality?"

Mb11

What If Your Child Became One?

Underlying the comments of many parents, whether they accepted or rejected homosexuality, was some anxiety about the fact that children could adopt this lifestyle for themselves. Several had already expressed this uneasiness while discussing their reactions to children playing with or deriving pleasure from same-sex peers. Haltingly, Clarice admitted that introducing the idea of homosexuality to her son was disconcerting. "A son, thinking that the words are like magic—it's going to make him one—you have to be careful that if you tell it, it's not going to happen." Fran also described conflicts she had experienced when the subject was brought up. "Probably the issue of homosexuality is difficult for any parent to discuss with a child, particularly for liberal parents, people who think they're liberal and want to be accepting of everything. And yet the emotional issue, when it comes to your own child, gets in the way of that, makes it difficult to be unemotional about it."

Mb7

Mb4

Very few parents said they would accept homosexual lifestyles for their children with equanimity. Responses to this issue varied and seemed to depend both on how parents regarded homosexuality in the abstract and how they thought their children's well-being might best be served. Some parents confessed that they just weren't sure what

they would do if their children turned out to be "gay." They wanted
to be able to accept the situation, love the child regardless, but feared
that their negative feelings about homosexuality might get in the way.
"I hope that I wouldn't have to be confronted with that situation," Mg10
Sally said. "I guess I would just have to meet it head on and see why
and try and understand her side, as well as her understanding that
maybe I'll never be able to accept the fact that she has chosen this
type of relationship. I can't guarantee her that I will accept it. I don't
know." Larry was quite concerned that his son grow up "straight,"
and allowed him to look at "macho" magazines in the hope that they
would instill heterosexual values. He admitted he would be disturbed
if his child became a homosexual. "I guess I wouldn't feel close with Fb6
him any more. He'd still be my son. But the way my mind works, I'd
try to block him out of my mind. I think my wife can accept it more
easily because she always worked in an industry where most of the
people were homosexual. I have several homosexual clients and it
doesn't bother me. But if it was close to me, part of my family, I would
imagine that I would be bothered." Ruth, mother of two boys and two Mg16b13b10g
girls, observed, "I would be most unhappy, and I think my husband
would have tremendous difficulty handling homosexuality, should my
children see it as an option and then opt for it."

Some parents' feelings were determined by the way in which they
defined homosexuality: as a sexual choice, a reaction to environmen-
tal factors, an illness, or a biological deviation. These parents' responses
differed widely, however, even when they agreed on the cause. "I Mg5
think that if she chose homosexuality because she chose it, then it
would be all right," Linda said. "If she chose it because she had a bad
relationship and she did it out of distorted feelings, then I don't think
I would like that. Again, I just hope that she'll grow up and be happy
with herself, first. I want her to like herself—and then, whichever she
chose. I don't know if this is what I would really do," she admitted.
"But I hope that I would support her in whatever she chose." Charles
saw homosexuality as an option his son could accept or reject and intended to "steer him away" if he could, "because it seems like he's Fb11
asking for trouble. Still, it's about the same thing I would have said
about mixed marriages ten years ago. If it's what you really want, but
you are going to have a lot of problems." Lyle would regard a child's
decision to be a homosexual as a violation of traditional values. "That, Fb7
I would be violently against. If my son came home and said he was
moving in with his buddy, well, I think if he was small enough to fit
into a filled bathtub, head first, I think I would—no, I would be very
upset. No matter how open a society we live in, I think it's still devi-
ant and I wouldn't want my children following that type of life."

A substantial number of parents said they would not be willing to
accept a child's homosexuality without first seeking professional help.

Mb10g7 Many hoped that through therapy their children might "recover." "Oh, I would care very much," Trude said. "I would be very much concerned. If they chose that as a lifestyle, that's terrible. We would forbid it. We wouldn't want him to continue with it. If he did it anyway, we would take him for treatment. I would definitely try to cure him from it. If it isn't possible, I would still love him. He's my son. I would

Mb9g8g5 accept it, then." Sylvia hoped she could "catch it way before it happened. I would hope that I would pick up on signs or signals. If I did, I would talk it over with the child. I would probably go through the psychiatric route and then through the medical route itself, to see if there was some kind of imbalance or whatever—genes. If I couldn't stop it, I would love my child no matter what. I don't care. But I would

Mb11 rather they be heterosexual." Cheryl said, "I'd be very concerned. I think I would check out what problems he was having. I mean, I am not completely checked out on why someone is homosexual or isn't homosexual, a zillion, thousand theories. I think I would check out what conflicts there were and try to iron them out. I would do the whole gamut, go through therapy to find out if there were any areas of discomfort. If he were comfortable, I guess I would accept it."

Some parents thought they would be concerned about their own responsibility in creating a homosexual. This was particularly true of women who were aware of the popular view that gay males had smoth-

Mb8 ering, overprotective, seductive mothers. Valerie would feel "terrible. Horrible. Terrible. I still think it is a sickness, maybe even a mental sickness, an emotional sickness. I guess it would make me feel like a failure in some ways." She acknowledged, though, that, "You have to accept it. I mean what can you do about it? Nothing." Mona felt the

Mb11 same way: "If he became a homosexual, I would certainly feel like I had failed." Betty said, "I'm not raising [my son] to be a homosexual, I hope. I'd feel terrible, sure." Like other parents, she would want him to get counseling. But she also said that in order to live with the situation and her role in relation to it, she would seek therapy herself. "I don't know if I would drop it and say, 'Okay, you are what you are and I accept you for what you are.' I think I would probably try to get him help to help him change. If I couldn't change him? I don't know. *I* would probably go get help—'What happened that I raised a homosexual?' I would have to learn to deal with it. If my daughter became a Lesbian, same thing."

The majority of parents felt they had little control over whether

Fb4 their children became homosexuals or not, "[It's] just the way things happen to people," one father remarked. "But I don't know if I could accept it." Others said they would resign themselves to the unalterable, be as supportive of their children as possible, but would be very sad-

Mg11 dened because of the emotional suffering and social rejection the children were likely to face. Annette said, "I'm a firm believer that you really can't change somebody's sexuality. I really do believe that. They are what they are. So I guess if I found out she had homosexual tendencies my feeling would be to make her feel comfortable about that. I just would never pull a guilt thing on her. I'd tell her that if this is your sexual preference you are going to have to learn to live with it, and accept it, and work with it, and be prepared for lots of problems with society, but accept yourself for what you are. Because I know I couldn't change it, there would be no point in making her be unhappy with herself." Drew shared this attitude: "I would care if my son became a homosexual," he said. "Yeah, I would. I think that intellectually I would, because I think there are a great deal of incidents of unhappiness among homosexuals, And I would dislike it simply because I was brought up to consider homosexuals undesirable. I would accept it, Oh, sure. I mean, what can you do about it? What is, is." Elizabeth had similar feelings: "I don't approve of homosexuality as a lifestyle. If my daughter were homosexual I'd feel sad for her, because I personally don't look upon it as being normal. There is something lacking. But you love your kids no matter what, just like you would love a retarded child." Fb8 Mg8

There were parents who said that their children's happiness and success as human beings were more crucial than their sexual preferences. Geraldine observed, "If my daughter did turn out to be gay, it would be a shock. But then again, it's her life. If that's what makes her happy, then I hope I'm graceful enough to accept it." Esther conceded that she could not be certain she would be as accepting as she wanted to be if one of her children actually became homosexual. "Well, things like homosexuality, I just think, from a parent's point of view, you can picture your kid being hurt a lot, being vulnerable to being hurt and stuff, and having a hard life." But she cared most of all that her children be considerate of others. "I would feel terrible if they were terrible people. That would be awful, and I'd think I'd really failed." Leigh, too, acknowledged that accepting a homosexual child would not be easy but hoped she would be strong enough to respect other qualities more. "I just let my daughter know that I don't care what a person is, that as long as he or she doesn't hurt others intentionally, that a person has every right to live the way he wants to live, and that's all there is to it. If she turned out to be homosexual I would not be happy about that. There's always a possibility. I would not be happy." Mg4 Mb11g6 Mg11

Stacey stressed good values and love first; she wished her son to have fulfilling relationships, regardless of the gender of his partners. "I would have no problem at all if my son came home with a three-foot black male and said, 'This is my love,' " she said. "What would Mb11 concern me is if my son said, 'This is the person I love, and I perceived that the person was not a loving person, not a caring person, not someone who was going to nourish him and enrich his life, but was someone who was going to drain him or hurt him, be a negative piece of his life. That would worry me," she said, shaking her head, "[even if] it turned out to be a very conventional, very rich, beautiful female with the best education in the world, in every way fit to the standard cultural pattern. That's going to be pain, a negative thing in his life. I've tried to say to him that if you care about someone, that's the key. It's very hard to find someone that you can love, and if you do, congratulations. That's how I see it."

A few parents who clearly preferred that their children not become homosexuals confessed that there were, nevertheless, other lifestyles they considered far more objectionable. Wanda admitted that she would feel "very sad," if her daughter became "gay." Then she qualified her remark, "That wouldn't be the worst of all the alternative styles," she added, "because I have known some very nice and well-adjusted homosexuals who have been able to lead a happy life. I can't say that I've known anybody living in a ménage, or even an open marriage, but I have the feeling that you can't live that happy a life." Unhappy as he might be if his son chose male sexual partners, Seymour said he preferred that for him to a life with no sexual partners at all. Sylvia remarked, rather wryly, that if her children picked same-sex lovers, "I would take them to the psychiatrist. But on the scale of open marriage, unmarried couples, ménages, I don't think homosexuality is as bad."

Mg10

Fg18g15b11

Mb9g8g5

Living Together

Children who still knew little about sex or did not come in contact with unmarried couples took it for granted when a man and a woman were together they were married. Some parents, therefore, did not need to discuss this lifestyle, so much less "visible" than homosexuality unless they chose to: "So far as I know he just assumes people go out together and then they get married," Morris said, then added, "We are mostly in a circle of married people." An unmarried couple had rented a home in Elizabeth's neighborhood. When her daughter automatically began to call the woman "Mrs. So-and-so," Elizabeth had to correct her. "I said, 'It's *not* Mrs. So-and-so. They have different last names. They are not married.' And she really didn't question it much, probably because she doesn't know anything about sex. To her it's

Fb5

Mg8

probably very normal for a man and woman to live together. She doesn't know that they go to bed or anything."

But given the fact that "living together" is not at all unusual today, free of the taboos that once put it outside of the social pale, children were more likely to become aware of unmarried couples, or to imagine themselves in such arrangements. For that reason, even parents who did not entirely approve of current mores felt they had to accept them— "I've too many other important things to worry about," Carol said. But they wanted to convey their own values, as well, when they discussed these relationships with children. Betty had arrived at this compromise. "I don't want to be so rigid as to say, 'I disapprove of it wholeheartedly,' and I don't want to be so liberal as to say, 'There's nothing wrong with it.' So I want to come to what I would feel comfortable with. I do know couples, naturally, who have done that, later going on to get married, and sometimes not. How it affects them I could care less. How I would tell my children, of course, is different. I can tell them how I feel."

Sometimes, children knew adults who were living with lovers and discussion flowed easily. A mother said, "One of our cousins lives with someone and my daughter knows they aren't married but they are living together. So she thinks it's quite normal for them to do all the actions that she sees us doing. We said, 'They aren't married because they chose not to get married for some reason. They feel they have a relationship together and they are not ready to make that final commitment.' And so she's aware that it's out there." Sonia made this comment: "One of our cousins off and on lives with her boyfriend and in fact our next-door neighbor lived with a boyfriend before they got married. I mean she has seen it all over the place. It's just very commonplace. I told her just that it's their business. They have the right to choose to live together or not as they choose. It's their business." In one case, it was the children who adopted the traditional view and pressured a family friend and his girlfriend to "make it legal." Carol said, "My daughter knows that this particular couple are living as husband and wife. Oh, yes, she knows. In fact, the children have said, 'Why don't you marry her already? What are you waiting so long for?' In other words, they would like to see the ring on her finger. They really do feel that way."

Many parents emphasized that in so liberal a climate it was especially important for children to learn that intimacy involved mutual obligations and responsibility as well as sex. A minority, in fact, objected to couples living together precisely because they thought these arrangements tended to be more casual than marriage and one partner, generally the man, was likely to be "using" the other. One mother spoke heatedly about the issue. "I told my daughter she'd have to be a fool to live with a man. That in any relationship you have to have total com-

Mb15g11

Mg9b5

Mg10

Mg11

Mb15g11

Mg16b11

mitment, and if you can't give a total commitment and get married you have no relationship to start with. And it's just as heartbreaking to break up after living with somebody for five years as to go through a divorce. It is still your emotions and your feelings are involved just as deeply, especially being a woman."

But most parents were less disapproving if the couple was mature, and serious about the relationship—not just "shacking up." Sylvia had

Mg8   told her eight-year-old that the man and woman in question "fell in love. They love each other. They're older people and this is the way they choose to live. It doesn't mean it's right and it doesn't mean it's wrong. It's what's right for those individual people. That doesn't mean it's right for everybody. It's not right for me. It's not the way I believe, and I hope that you will believe this way, but I'm not going to con-

Mg10   demn anybody." Wanda took a similar approach. "Basically, unmarried couples, if they are young, probably would be better off not having the relationships. Sex involves more than just enjoyment. There's always the responsibility that you might be creating an unwanted life. It's important not to do that. If you are old enough to take care not to have a child, then you are probably old enough to handle a whole relationship and everything it implies. But casual sex is destructive. I make the distinction between young people and grown-ups because grown-ups can generally handle their lives. We would hope that these people that are in these relationships will decide that they love each other enough to have a happy marriage, because that is what the whole thing is supposed to lead to."

Then, too, there were parents who felt that being happy with someone was all-important, whether the union was official or not. Though she laughed a lot at her own cynicism, one mother offered

Mb11g6   this unromantic view of marriage. "We know more people who aren't married—who are either divorced, or never been married, or, you know. I've just told my children that I don't think marriage is necessary, or that everyone has to get married, or that it's so marvelous and wonderful." A second mother, who was herself involved in a living-together arrangement, was willing to speak quite frankly of her lifestyle—and the way she had explained it to her daughter by an earlier marriage.

Mg5   "Obviously she knows we're not married," she began. "We are going to get married. My daughter has this idea that you have to be married. The first time she asked my sister how you have babies, my sister said, 'You get married!' A little uptight. But I would like my daughter to think that you should have a partner to have a child. But she knows that I am not married and that I have a child. She doesn't question that at all. I told her very frankly that I use the word *marriage* simply to describe a man and a woman living together and sleeping together. I told her that before, 'I lived with a man and we made a baby and you were born. And the man wasn't a good man, and so I moved and then

I just lived by myself. He was your daddy but he didn't do anything good for you, so I left him. Now I have a boyfriend. I like him a whole lot, he loves you, I love him, and so he can be your new daddy.' And she thinks that's all right. You can tell she's confused." This mother admitted, "Maybe it's too young to tell her but I try to tell her, you know."

Parents were asked what sleeping arrangements they would make for unmarried couples who were staying over in their homes. By far the most common solution to this problem was to allow the couple to sleep together. And most parents didn't feel children need be told anything special about such couples, except that they were "together." "It's no big deal," Lyle said. "They would share the same room and the same bed. If my son asked if they were married—I can't imagine that question coming up—I'd say 'They are not married. They are just close friends. They live together and they are just not married. It's as simple as that. Some people feel they want to live that way and some people don't.' "   Fb7

Indeed, many children were too sophisticated to be startled or shocked or disillusioned by these relationships. Sonia expressed this point of view: "Whatever would be comfortable for the couple—assuming that we have enough furniture to go around. I wouldn't feel any need to explain to my daughter, not at this point. If it had happened several years ago she might have asked why they were sleeping together since they are not married. I would have explained that it's their business. At this point I don't think I'd have to explain, because I think she accepts different types of couples, a variety. I think that comes to her through the media or friends—to a good extent from us, too." Geraldine had unmarried friends who regularly shared a bed in her home. She reported that her children took the relationships in stride and were not at all curious about the adults' private arrangements. "They see them as a couple and they are similar to Mommy and Daddy. They never really asked who's married and who's not. It doesn't seem very important to them." Olive was about to face this situation and was prepared to take a down-to-earth, practical approach. "My sister is coming to visit and she is going to be coming with her boyfriend, and there would be no issue raised. I have no qualms at all about them staying together. They are there to stay, and that's that. I would explain that Aunt Wendy is not married to him, but that they are living together and it's okay."   Mg11   Mg7g4   Mg9

Some parents had different policies for different circumstances. If the couple was very young, they might be more reluctant to put them in the same room. Valerie made a distinction between mature couples who had an ongoing involvement and those who were just spending a night with each other here and there. "If I know they live together, they can sleep together. They could stay in the same   Mg6 room. If you ask me about some late teenager or something, I should say, 'No.' "

Other parents feared that children were likely to see teenage couples, home from college for the weekend, for instance, as models Mb8 they might want to imitate. "If my son knew they were not married, well, then I guess I wouldn't allow it. I would not have them sleep together." Seymour was more concerned that in permitting his eigh-teen-year-old daughter's friends to sleep together at his house he might Fg18g15b11 be acting against their parents' wishes. "If a parent knew that a boy and girl were sleeping together I don't think there would be anything wrong in that. It would be okay if my daughter slept with her boy-friend in our house. I wouldn't keep them apart after the occasion arose." With an older couple, "more in my age range," there was no problem whatsoever. "If they came to my house and they were going to stay over, I would have them share the bedroom if they wished."

Once in a while parents relied on the emotional context of a par-ticular situation to determine the kinds of overnight accommodations they offered an unmarried couple. If the couple themselves were em-barrassed about being perceived as lovers, parents would do whatever made them comfortable—arrange separate rooms or place them in a part of the house, like the basement, away from the family's sleeping areas. Sometimes, instead of reserve, a couple displayed just the op-Fb11 posite. Charles thought he would make a decision on the basis of "who [the couple] were, in terms of how they behave." His children had friends whose parents had "live-in lovers," so they were accustomed to the idea. But he was not certain he would allow two people "who were flamboyant about it" to sleep together in his home. Wanda described Mg15g10 an instance in which she had asked a couple to sleep separately. "We had dear friends who were divorced and the girls were very fond of both of them and we were all very close. After the divorce the hus-band brought his girlfriend down, and it was so soon after, and the girls were just so [upset]. So I said, 'I'm going to put you up in sepa-rate rooms because I think it would hurt the girls to think that you replaced your former wife. They feel very threatened by the divorce.' And he said, 'Fine.' His girlfriend didn't understand." But she did not expect to apply the same rules to another couple—also friends—who decided not to get married but had been together a long time. "Time has passed, and now they are a couple just as if they were married. The girls know they are not, but feel that this couple are grown-ups and they had both had unsuccessful marriages and they really want to be sure before they ever get married again. So if they came here I would allow them to sleep in the same room. I would tell my girls that grown-ups who are adult, responsible people will have relationships and that's their business."

A very small number of parents said that they would not want unmarried couples to sleep in the same room under any circumstances. For some of them, sex outside of marriage violated moral standards, and though they did not want to impose these codes on outsiders, they did not want to be parties to something they disapproved of. One mother was adamant. "Oh, no, no, I wouldn't want that," she said firmly. "I would just offer them single rooms. What they do is none of my business, but for my children's sake. My children believe only married couples sleep together, married couples make love to each other. We teach them that and I wouldn't want to disturb that. They understand that's right. I shouldn't invite unmarried couples in our house because it is the opposite of what I am telling them." Another mother said bluntly, "It's not something I condone. Therefore, I don't want it under my roof."

Mb10g7

Mb11

There were also those who had no vehement moral objections. But they did prefer that their children remain unaware of this alternative lifestyle as long as possible and continue to see sex as an activity that occurs only in the context of marriage. Elizabeth said she wouldn't allow unmarried couples to sleep in the same room. "Not necessarily because I don't approve of it, I just guess I don't approve of it for my children. I don't want them to see that, right now, as an accepted way of life. They are going to come to that real soon." Sylvia observed wryly, "I would explain to them either they're going to have to lie through their teeth that they're married or they're going to have to sleep in separate rooms. Because my children are under the impression hopefully that when you fall in love, you get married, and that's when you sleep together. At this age in their lives, that's all they can handle. It's hard enough for me at my age to understand it."

Mb12g8

Mb9b0g5

When asked how they would feel if their child chose to live with someone rather than marry him or her, most parents would prefer marriage but could honor their child's decision. Those who were least comfortable with the idea objected not to the illicit nature of the arrangement but to the lack of emotional commitment they felt it represented. "Unmarried? I would hope not." That was Valerie's response to the question. "I would tell my son the consequences of such a lifestyle. I would [describe] all the unhappy ones. I see in my own marriage how important and often how difficult it is to work on a relationship. Unless you have a commitment to each other there is no way a marriage can work out, definitely."

Mb8

Others felt that this lifestyle precluded having children—"It's not the way you love your partner. Get married and have a family"—or put too much burden on both people to share everything equally instead of one accepting responsibility for the other. One father said he would expect his son to marry a woman after he was earning enough to support her. "Once they're married, it's the husband's responsibility

Mg7

Fb11

to provide." His remark reflects the traditional views a few parents brought to the issue. To these parents, "living together" on a permanent basis was less desirable for a woman than for a man. They feared that their daughters would somehow be "used," taken for granted, unless they were married. The old adage, "If the milk is free, why buy the cow?" still applied. According to one mother, "There is a dual standard, no matter what they tell you. If my son and a woman lived together and were not married, it would depend on the circumstances. If it was my daughter, I would feel another way, because of the dual standards."

Almost everyone else agreed that they would accept their children's choice of this lifestyle, provided it was made responsibly and the relationship was serious. Sylvia could understand the reluctance to rush into marriage but did not approve of casual sexual liaisons. "Well, my husband would kill me if he heard this, but it's true. I'd say, 'If you were really in love and he was really in love, if you were committed to one another, and if it wasn't something you practiced every month of the year, I would probably say, "Okay." But you can't give it to me, "because other people are doing it." It has to be what you want as an individual.' " For Seymour, too, the quality of the relationship was an important consideration. "My daughter can sleep with a fellow if she's in love with him. I don't say crawl into bed with a guy just to go to bed with him. But if my daughter was seeing somebody and she had a good feeling about him, I wouldn't object." He thought that if for some reason one of his children would not (or could not) marry, an unmarried arrangement was the second best option. "I think it would be a wonderful choice." Sonia felt this was "a lifestyle I could be comfortable with, unless she decided to have children, and then I would urge her to have the legal protection of marriage or something—I'd want her to sit down with a lawyer. We'd have to work out the legal aspects."

For some parents the age of the child would matter. They believed they would be very unhappy if a child still in high school or college announced he was moving in with his girlfriend. But older children were grown up enough to determine what was best for themselves. Olive made this point. "When they are in their twenties and thirties and wherever on, whatever they want to do—and if they want to live together, then that's no problem with me on that. I don't like to see kids that really don't know what they are doing. I would like to see a little more maturity in the decisions. I think the only alternative lifestyle that I would come close to accepting would be if she chose to live with somebody, and then again at an older time." Sheila expressed some of the same reservations. "I don't think I would have a right to become angry with him or tell him to change his lifestyle, if he was old enough to make that decision—twenty-one or twenty-two, in that range

Mb9g8g5

Fg18g15b11

Mg11

Mg9

Mb7

or older. As a teenager or a college student, I would feel he's too young to know exactly what this is all about. If he felt that it was a lifestyle that he wanted to adopt, I would have to let him do it. But I would still let him know that I wasn't really in favor of that lifestyle."

No matter what the feelings, however, most parents assumed they would have little control over this area of their children's lives once they grew up and left home. Children were bound to be influenced by the climate of their surroundings and times. The more tolerant society became of unmarried couples, the more likely children were to give at least some consideration to this alternative lifestyle as a possibility for themselves. Also, parents were not sure they had the right to interfere in so personal a choice. Children had to do what felt right and made them happy, as long as they did not hurt themselves or anyone else. "Who am I to pass judgment?" Carol asked. "Who am I to make her decisions?"   Mb15g11

Single Parenthood

Given the widespread availability of birth-control methods and abortion, as well as the possibility of single adoption, children in the eighties are seeing single parenthood as a choice rather than an accident. In part, this perception has been fostered by the media—soap operas whose characters decide to have babies out of wedlock—or just by the ideas which seem to be "free-floating" in society. A number of parents mentioned that their children had asked them whether unmarried women can have babies, though they had no idea where the question came from. When families lived in cities where alternative lifestyles were neither uncommon nor frowned upon, children sometimes knew an adult who had chosen this option. Henry said of his daughter, "She   Fb6
knows an unmarried mother. Her teacher had decided she was getting old, in her late thirties, wants a child and doesn't have a mate, so she has had artificial insemination. I'm pretty sure my daughter has had that described to her. She knows that the woman doesn't have a husband, that she doesn't have a regular mate, and she's having babies. She's aware that there's a lot of single-parent families around." Another urban parent also reported that his daughter "knows that there   Fg7
are a lot of children growing up in one-person families."

When children were curious about single parenthood, many parents thought it best to give them as honest a picture as they could of the circumstances under which someone might raise a child alone. One mother told her son, " 'Some people may want a baby but they haven't   Mb9
found someone who is right for them. Or they might have wanted to

get married but something happened to the relationship with the man—
he didn't want to make a commitment to her—and that's why she has
a baby. It could be for a number of reasons that she and the baby are
together without a father living there.' I usually explain these things as
'people are different.' " Ellen's son, Carl, attended school with sev-

Mb5 eral children who had only one parent. "They never got married or
they're divorced or something." When Carl was concerned about why
his friend's father "never wanted to live with them," she gave a simple reply. "So I told him that people, they make a baby and they don't
want to live together." Bart preferred not to go into detail, but let his

Fb6 son know that everyone has a right to his or her own lifestyle. "I'd try
to make him understand that it's really their choice and that it's neither right nor wrong, and it's not his decision and that he's too little to
be concerned about it. So I would just tell him to be friends with the
little boy and mind his business."

A number of parents chose to respond to what they sensed were
children's fears of abandonment when they asked about single parents.
Sometimes, like Carl, the children identified with the children in these
situations; sometimes they identified with the woman (it was almost
never the man) who was "left." George was the godfather of the child
of "a woman who chose to have a baby without marrying the father."
Though the woman knew who the father was, she did not intend to
tell. When George's daughter saw the baby's picture, she wanted to

Fg7 know, " 'Well, does he know who his father is? Does his mommy love
his father?' I think I rationalized by saying that Ann is going to have to
be a mommy and daddy to little Wally. I think my daughter understands the concept." When Morris's housekeeper became pregnant,

Fg8b5 "the kids brought up the question, you know, how could she have a
baby when she wasn't married," Morris said. "We explained to him
that she was very lonely and she had no family and thought she would
be happier with a baby. And that was the extent of it, and they accepted that." Sonia hoped her daughter would regard a family friend's
decision to raise two children without a husband as a positive choice.

Mg11 "I told my daughter that she was doing something very admirable and
very strong. Wonderful parent, just a wonderful parent. Just that it
was a different choice, and very admirable, in her case."

Some parents used children's queries about single mothers as a
springboard for discussion of how babies are made. Children who
thought that somehow marriage led to pregnancy were filled in on details about lovemaking. Rosaline thought the idea of an unmarried
woman bearing a child would have been difficult for her daughter be-

Mg7 fore she understood the physiology of intercourse. "Now I think it's a
little more clarified that you can be close to somebody and have relations." In most families where the subject of opting for single parenthood arose, there was no discussion at all of sexual morality. When

parents were srongly disapproving, they talked about the lack of con- Mb5
cern for the welfare of the child. "I just don't think it's fair to the child,"
Betty said. "I think a child needs a mother and a child needs a father.
If something happens to the mother or father, that can't be controlled.
But while it can be controlled, it should be." A second mother was
even more adamantly opposed to this lifestyle. "It's very selfish!" she Mb11
exclaimed. "If God deprives you of your father or your mother, that is
something out of your hands. But I think it's very important for a child
to know a father's as well as a mother's love. It's a very selfish relationship even if there's a father and a mother but they are just not married
because those parents don't want to make a commitment—even a commitment to the child."

Other parents were more accepting but tried to be realistic with
their children, as well. They would tell them that having a child alone
was not necessarily wrong but nevertheless could be grueling and stressful for the parent and difficult for the child. Karen had told her daughter, " 'No, you don't have to be married, but it makes it much easier if Mg11
you are,' and I kind of ended it there. I've told her often that it's hard
to raise a child by yourself, that the child is better off with a mother
and a father, that's all. And I told her to imagine herself with only one
parent." Ezra had responded in much the same way to his son: "I didn't Fb8
say you've got to be married to do it. But I do say to him, for a couple
of years now, it's best to do it when you're married. When you come
into this world it's nice to have a mother and a father who are married,
in a house, stable, taking care of you." Esther had a friend who was
raising three children alone and then got married, "but not because Mg6
she wanted to be married." In explaining the situation to her daughter,
she expressed the same thought that Karen had: "It's hard to raise a
kid by yourself."

This theme was sounded over and over when parents talked about
how they might react if their children chose single parenthood as a
lifestyle. A mother of a four-year-old said, "It's not only better for the Mg4
child [but] better for the parent to have another parent. Children are
very difficult to raise with two people, let alone one." Parents said
they would try to warn their children that life is tough, particularly
when one "goes it alone," and a child would be still one more burden.
They also wanted children to understand how emotionally and physically taxing the responsibility of caring for another human being could
be. One mother said she would talk in terms of the expense involved, Mb5
the difficulties parents experience "if they have to work and worry
about money at the same time as raising a child." Nevertheless, though
parents described a wide range of personal emotional responses to the
possibility that a child of theirs might want to raise a baby alone—some
would be "madder than hell"; some saw "no problem"—almost everyone agreed that, ultimately, they would accept the decision and sup- Mb9g8g5

port their child. Sylvia said, "Well, I wouldn't be overjoyed with the   Mb9g
fact that my daughters or son had a child without a spouse. But if they
were doing it for reasons other than not being hip—if let's say they
became pregnant and they really wanted the child (in 1999, of course)
and they weren't in love at that point, or were in love and love stopped,
or whatever—if they really wanted it, I would say 'All right.' I would
deal with it."

Childlessness

There were children who were curious when couples in their parents'
circle did not have any children. In fact, a number of parents said they
would discuss childlessness out of concern that a well-meaning child
might offend people—especially those who had fertility problems—by
Fb11   demanding to know "Why . . .?" "Well, he does ask," Charles said of
his son. "I mean, 'Why don't so-and-so have any children?' and 'Is it
that they don't want to or they can't?' I say, 'It's none of our business
so we're not going to ask them!' " When Geraldine's daughter raised
Mg4   the same question about friends of the family, Geraldine told her, "I
really don't know, because it's between them." Some children just
assumed that anyone who did not have children could not have them.
Mb7b6   This was the case with Sheila's two sons. "My husband had an aunt
and uncle that could not have children, and they know. One of their
friends, they know that she is adopted and her brother is adopted, and
they wanted to know why. They were told it was because her mother
and father could not have children and they adopted a child."

Many parents thought that if children had not already grasped from
exposure to the media that couples could *decide* not to have children—
several popular dramatic and comedy series centered on husband-wife
teams who were childless—it was up to the parent to let them know
that this was an option. Parents pointed out that different people had
different priorities—jobs, recreation, education—and children did not
always suit their lifestyle. Trude had described this kind of situation
Mb10g7 to her children. "Well, we have friends who just decided not to have
children, and they have more time for each other. We talked about it.
I said, 'Some grownups just don't want to have children, they just want
to stay with each other. Others like it and some don't. Maybe they
want to work and have their career and business, maybe they want to
travel a lot. If they have children they cannot travel so much—you
want to care about your children.' "

Several parents feared that children who understood that some people found a family burdensome or intrusive on their lives might assume they were unwanted. These parents were careful to stress their own happiness and the rewards of not being childless themselves. One mother addressed herself to this problem. "I've told my children that some people decide not to have children today. That's their own style or they want their careers and everything. I have felt that it has given me great pleasure in having children and hope that some day it will them. To have children you have to have a sense of selflessness, and it's hard work, but it's very rewarding if your children turn out to be all right. It's not to be judged any more than anything else. You must do what is right for you." Mb11

One adoptive mother told this rather poignant story: "My daughter said, 'What would your life be like without children? Empty. You would have nobody to worry about.' I said, 'Well, plenty of people have decided not to have children.' She knows. And she feels sorry for them, that they don't have children." Mg11

Most parents expressed sadness at the prospect of their children perhaps choosing childlessness as a lifestyle. Even some in their twenties and thirties felt they would be sorry to miss out on the joy of being grandparents. The father of an eleven-year-old said, "I think I would still like to have grandchildren. I'd like to spoil them rotten." And they regretted that their offspring would be deprived of the rewards they themselves had found through being parents. Lyle thought he would have a talk with his son, tell him, " 'You do what you feel is best for you, but the pleasure that we've had out of you and your brother, I would hope that you would have the same thing.' " One mother said rather resignedly, "All right. If she chose not to have children, there's nothing wrong with it. It would be sad, too, yeah. But maybe she changes her mind. Maybe she would be without children for the first ten years and then have children. It's still early enough." Fb11 Fb7b4 Mg7

But, overall, most parents believed they had no right to exert pressure on children in this area. Children had to decide for themselves what would make them happy. Mothers in particular were aware of the compromises involved in having children. Wanda acknowledged that "It would be wonderful to have grandchildren, but that's a selfish thing. Because again of being a feminist and encouraging my children to have careers, if they decided that they wanted to do that or if they just didn't want to have children, I could accept that." Joyce discussed quite frankly her own mixed feelings about having children. She was aware that becoming a mother—"I guess I made that life decision carelessly, immaturely"—delayed her beginning a career as a marketing consultant, which has given her success and an enormous sense of self-worth. But now that her son is eleven and her daughter is fifteen, she is "really glad it happened when it did. As I get older, I get more Mg15g10 Mg15b11 and more glad. Probably as I get older I'd get into this whole continuity thing. I think I'll really enjoy the role of being a grandparent." But recalling her own history, she was sympathetic to the possibility that her children might not want children of their own. "I can see childlessness as being an appropriate life decision. I think you deprive yourself of some things—there's a richness. I think there's other ways to get it." Sonia said she would find a decision by her daughter not to have children "fairly easy to accept because I think that you should have a real good reason to *have* children, not a real good reason not to. So unless she felt ready to have them, she should be childless."

Mg11

Celibacy

In general, celibacy was never discussed with children. Not all parents were even aware that some people chose this as a lifestyle for other than religious reasons. "People *want* to live that way?" one mother exclaimed with astonishment. When the subject was talked about, in fact, it was usually in relation to priests, nuns, monks, and others who chose to live without sexual partners in order to dedicate themselves more perfectly to spiritual life. "I've said that the priests are celibate. That when you are devoted to God, you are celibate, if you are from the Catholic church. I don't know anyone else who's celibate." In a few cases children had seen television interviews with individuals or groups that advocated non-religious celibacy and had asked questions. Parents found the most useful response was, "It's their own business," and left it at that.

Mb10

Mb11

Many parents were appalled by the idea of their children choosing celibacy. "I think that I would be more upset with a celibate life than I would be if he was a homosexual," Seymour said. "Really. Because there would be no joy at all." Several parents indicated that if a child chose not to have sexual partners, they would definitely think something was wrong. To them, celibacy outside of the church seemed an unnatural way to live. Mona observed, "If he was a businessman and he were celibate I would wonder what his problem was, and I probably would wonder if he was a doctor. If he was a priest, I would consider that a part of the total picture. I'd feel I'd failed. Yes, it's abnormal to be celibate. Not if he were a priest, but I think that would be a little unique—being a Jewish boy being a priest."

Fb11

Mb11

Though they were not sure they had the right to interfere, some felt they would want to "talk it out" with children, try to understand what traumas or personal difficulties were causing them to behave so strangely. One mother of a four-year-old girl put it this way: "Celibacy! I would be curious to know why she chose that! Maybe she's sexually turned off. I would want to know what her reasons were for her choice. I would want her to explain to me why she has made the decision she has made. Celibacy seems a very difficult way to live." Another mother, with three children, said, "There'd definitely be something wrong. Just the same, I'd have to see what's going on with them. I wouldn't get angry. I would ask them why. I'd say, 'Let's discuss this.' I'd say, 'Well, do you have any interest in anything else? Have you had any bad sexual experiences?' To me, it always sounds as if there's something behind it, like there might have been some kind of rejection along the way. I would still feel it was psychological."

Others said they would react in much the same way to celibacy as to homosexuality, and urge their children to seek therapy. "I would be alarmed that there is something physically, mentally wrong with them, and I would look to see a doctor," one mother said. Another said, "If my daughter decided to be celibate, I'd probably want to have a long conversation. I'd want to find out why she chose it and I might even urge her to get counseling before I would say it's fine with me, go ahead. I think anything that would be away from the norm, I'd urge a lot of conversation about it, a lot of study, and maybe some counseling too."

Quite a few parents simply couldn't think of celibacy as a serious option for their children. "I really can't envision that happening to my children," Betty said. "I mean, we're not a religious family. I can't imagine my son would want to become a monk or her a nun, or anything like that." She also thought that the family's intimate and affectionate style mitigated against the possibility of her children choosing so solitary a situation. "I mean, we are a family-oriented group, maybe too much so. Very dependent on other people." Some parents believed that their children already showed too many signs of natural sensuality to be attracted to a nonsexual lifestyle. Steve said of his five-year-old girl, "I just don't see it as being possible for my daughter." Charles's son is eleven. "Somehow I don't think that's going to be a problem," he said with a smile.

The Ideal

Clearly, parents hoped children would choose the "usual," most orthodox lifestyle: a legal and emotional commitment to one person of the opposite sex; children. The ideal was stated by a number of parents in a variety of ways:

Fb7b4   Basically I'm very traditional. Maybe more traditional than I would possibly admit. But I would have no control beyond hoping my son would select a more traditional lifestyle, only in terms of perhaps a greater sense of security and love.

Mg11   I hope she will be a normal, happy kid and live a fruitful life. That means—get married, have a family, have a career, have whatever she wants, whatever her choice is. I think her mind is set toward someday having the normal kinds of lifestyle.

Fb11   My child, he would, I'm sure, do well in school, become a professional, and get married. I really believe that. I think he would follow the age-old pattern.

Mg14b13g9   In my visions, I see the kids grown up, married, and with kids.

But more than that, parents wanted their children to be "good," "happy," fulfilled human beings, regardless of how or with whom they Fg9g5 chose to live. "I would accept anything my children would do as long as it makes them happy," Rudy said. "I can't think of anything that would be excluded from that category. I don't see the girls as harming anybody. I mean, they're nice kids, and I assume they will continue to be that way. So those things in terms of sexuality, those are their values. And whatever they come up with, that's okay." Esther had Mb11g6 similar feelings about her children. "I tend to think that it's not the lifestyle. It's who you are inside," she said. "That's the way I am and I would want them to be honest with what they're doing and with me. I also want them to be good citizens." This was a recurring theme: Parents could only "lay the foundation." The children themselves had Fb6 to find a way of life that was best for them. As one father put it, "No one has a perfect lifestyle. There are no perfect 'matches in heaven.' Let them choose their own lifestyle."

About the Authors

The Study Group of New York is an interdisciplinary group of educators and researchers concerned with issues confronting contemporary society. Its members have wide experience in popular culture and language, media, psychology, and education; thus, this book pools the skills of specialists in a variety of areas.

Emily Trafford Berges is an Assistant Professor of English at Jersey City State College. She teaches courses in British literature, creative and remedial writing, women's studies, and media. She holds a B.A. from Smith College, an M.A. from New York University, and has also studied at The New School and at City College. Ms. Berges has written three novels with contemporary themes and is presently engaged in research for a historical novel.

Shelley Neiderbach's career encompasses teaching, teacher training, communications, counseling, and psychotherapy. She received her doctorate in psychology from Union Graduate School. The author of *Lovestalk*, a book of poetry, she is currently working for Counseling and Psychological Services at Jersey City State College, where she holds the rank of Associate Professor. She is the recipient of a grant by the National Endowment for the Humanities, and is President of Crime Victims' Counseling Services, Inc.

Barbara Rubin, teacher of young children for many years, is currently an Associate Professor of women's studies at Jersey City State College. Cofounder of its Women's Center and director of its Women's Studies program, she has lectured widely on human liberation topics in this country and abroad. Her articles and poetry have appeared in such publications as *The New York Times, Response*, and *New Directions for Women*. She is co-creator of the nationally and internationally acclaimed photohistory exhibition, "Generations of Women." Near completion, her Ph.D. dissertation examines mother-daughter relationships in the 1980's.

Elaine First Sharpe, graduate of the University of Pennsylvania, holds the rank of Associate Professor at Jersey City State College. She is a specialist in family studies and has written two books for children. As founder and director in the 1970's of the highly acclaimed Womanschool Adult Education Center, she spearheaded the movement in this country toward skill-oriented, career-directed education for women. Dr. Sharpe has appeared as a guest on numerous television and radio programs and has been a consultant to corporations. She is the mother of two children, Alison 14, and Richard, 6.

Rita Weinberg Tesler holds an M.A. from Cornell and a Ph.D. with distinction in English from New York University. She has worked in junior high school, high school and college and is currently an Assistant Professor of English at Jersey City State College. In addition to literature, she teaches a variety of subjects, including research, popular culture and ethnic studies. Dr. Tesler has published a number of book reviews and articles, and has given presentations in her fields of expertise, literature, communications, and writing, for professional organizations around the country.

Index

DATE DUE

NOV 1 1988			
NOV 2 8 1988			